HEART TANTRUMS AND BRAIN TUMOURS

D0584481

Heart Tantrums and Brain Tumours

A Tale of Marriage, Misogyny and Muslim Feminism

Aisha Sarwari

HURST & COMPANY, LONDON

First published by Penguin Random House India.

This edition published in the United Kingdom in 2023 by
C. Hurst & Co. (Publishers) Ltd.,
New Wing, Somerset House, Strand, London, WC2R 1LA

Copyright © Aisha Sarwari, 2023

All rights reserved.

The right of Aisha Sarwari to be identified as the author
of this publication is asserted by her in accordance with the
Copyright, Designs and Patents Act, 1988.

Distributed in the United States, Canada and Latin America by
Oxford University Press, 198 Madison Avenue, New York, NY
10016, United States of America.

A Cataloguing-in-Publication data record for this book
is available from the British Library.

ISBN: 9781787388932

www.hurstpublishers.com

Typeset in Adobe Garamond Pro by Manipal Technologies Limited, Manipal
Printed and bound in Great Britain by Bell and Bain Ltd, Glasgow

*For my ami and for her fear that what
I write will be used against me*

CONTENTS

Contents

PART THREE
WORK–LIFE UNBALANCED

FOREWORD

It was a hot summer day in Lahore in 2000. I was visiting home from Rutgers. The green phone in my room rang and a female voice boomed: 'I am in Pakistan.' 'Who are you?' I asked. 'I am Aisha Sarwari, remember we spoke in the US about meeting in Pakistan. Well I am coming to Lahore.' With this phone call Aisha Sarwari waltzed into my life. I found her idealism about Pakistan somewhat naïve but awe-inspiring. In our first meeting she dropped a bomb: 'I want to make a true Islamic state.' We still laugh about it. Exuberance was the one word to describe her. As I drove her around in Lahore, blasting *Junoon* songs, I began to fall in love both with her naïve idealism and her exuberance.

Over the next two years we would meet in Karachi, San Jose and Newark. By 2002 I was back in Pakistan after graduating, and she followed the next year after her graduation, burying the idea of grad school, which she regrets to this day. How different things would have turned out had she gone to grad school. We got married in December 2003. It was something out of Elvis Presley's 'Can't Help Falling in Love'. In retrospect, Aisha should have done her due diligence. Her brother warned her not to marry into a dysfunctional broken home but she wouldn't listen.

What follows is a lame excuse for my own behaviour. My family was the definition of dysfunction, part of which Aisha talks about in the book. A large part of it had to do with my parents' own strange and complicated relationship that was a taboo given the religious differences and family backgrounds. There was a lot of trauma there, especially for my mother, which made her particularly incapable of forging healthy relationships. My late father also faced great challenges, both personal and financial. He also couldn't reconcile himself to the fact that my mother was an independent working woman, or at least she appeared to be. For all his qualities, my father could be extremely misogynistic. The earliest memory I have of conflict between my parents is of a fight where my father was terribly upset that my mother had ridden shotgun with a co-worker. That was the kind of possessive control freakery I saw all my life. I grew up in a home that was not quite sure of what it was, religiously and financially. The work that I did years later with my therapist showed that growing up as I did, an only child in chaos, I lost all bearings that instil in us a confident persona. I have been unsure of who I am all my life. Given that my parents were neither poor nor rich, my very existence was a bundle of contradictions, going to expensive private schools where I was bullied for being too poor. I also ended up going to a military-run boarding school where I was bullied for being too rich. My parents sent me to the US to study but I lived there like a complete pauper, often dressing up like a hobo. When Aisha asked me what my parents did, I told her that my father was a pilot (he had flown planes in his younger days at the Lahore Flying Club before he got unfit) and my mother was a bureaucrat, i.e. she was employed as a medical doctor with the government. My return to Pakistan had not been better. Despite a US degree, I was unemployed for a while and I didn't hear the end of it from my father. I gave Aisha the exact opposite impression of my childhood. I told her that I had a very happy childhood filled of fun and joy. Tragically for her, she believed me.

Unknown to me at the time we got married were two further complications. My brain tumour was already in its earliest stages and I was a long-term undiagnosed sufferer of obsessive-compulsive disorder as well as generalized anxiety and depression. Had I known the sum total of these challenges, I like to think that I would have distanced myself from Aisha. As I look back on the twenty years of our often-rocky marriage, I hope that the many mistakes, and there were many, had to do with my own medical challenges because otherwise my behaviour is inexcusable bordering on criminal. Other than the violence in the early years of our marriage, there was the infidelity which almost broke us apart. Consequently, I see Aisha's suffering as a personal failure to live up to the ideals that I have always held dear. Aisha mentions my obsession with Jinnah. I admire Jinnah for the qualities that are synonymous with him: honesty, integrity and fairness. I have always wanted to be a just and fair person and those are the precise virtues that have been lacking in my conduct.

Aisha has stood with me through thick and thin. She was there when I collapsed on the gym floor in 2017 and almost died. She was there with me when I woke up. Not only did she bear with me often at great cost to herself and her reputation, she saved my life through the two life threatening brain surgeries I had to go through during the last four years. Anyone else would have quit a long time ago. Aisha, however, withstood the dysfunction and my self-destruction. Years rolled by. We had two beautiful daughters but I have been an ungrateful lout for all that Aisha has given me. Reading through her memoir is painful because it is also a mirror and one doesn't always like what one sees in the mirror. One finds solace in the thought, as I said above, that it was not me but my disease. Whatever it was, I broke Aisha's heart again and again and caused unbounded pain to an idealistic girl who had come to Pakistan searching for love and belonging. I do not know how much time I have to make it up to her.

As Aisha says in the book, our youthful idealistic patriotism, born as a result of constant bullying by Indians in the US, brought us together. Aisha has lived up to her patriotism by making it a positive force for change, be it women's rights or helping the poorest and most marginalized sections of Pakistani society. As a career professional, she has carved out a path for herself out of adversity. In the last four years she has held the fort all on her own, as a supermom working ten to thirteen hours a day to put bread on the table. As a writer, activist and a career professional she has lit up a path for other Pakistani women in a country where gender parity remains a distant dream. Aisha has also raised two amazing young ladies who are about to enter the real world, confident and strong like their mother. She has truly lived up to what I once dismissed as naïve idealism. What was once exuberance has now become fortitude. Though, thankfully, Aisha is no longer as committed to making a 'true Islamic state' as she was then.

Truth be told I was thoroughly undeserving of a partner like Aisha. I plucked a beautiful flower and then trod on it. That is what makes our love story a tragedy. That we have stayed together in spite of me is what makes it beautiful. There was something there that made us stick together despite everything. It is not like Aisha was trapped. As a strong-willed woman she could have got rid of me at any time she wanted. Some dreams, however, endure and so did ours, dreamt so long ago.

Yasser Latif Hamdani

PART 1

YASSER IS MY LITTLE PIECE OF PAKISTAN IN AMERICA

Our first meeting was online. It had to be.

I was a media student in college in California, writing an article on the human-rights abuses in Kashmir. Yasser was majoring in economics, all the way across on the other side of America, in New Jersey. We met on a website called Chowk, on the cusp of the twentieth century. In Urdu, *chowk* means a roundabout. Prophetic, but I didn't know then what I know now, as is often the case with stories.

Chowk's membership comprised prominent thinkers, activists and intellectuals from South Asia, but somehow, Yasser and I connected because of the intensity of our personalities as well as our love for Pakistan. His first reaction to my article was to ask me out: 'Ms Sarwari, are you available?'

I was raised conservatively. A vastly liberal and open college life was a culture shock that I coped with by being even more Pakistani. I gravitated closer to those who articulated a confidence in their Pakistani identity, something that described itself other than the Muslim part carved out of Hindu India. Yasser embodied that confidence for me.

No one had called me Ms Sarwari, and no one had asked me anything of consequence, let alone permission to court me. I immediately wrapped up my sophomore homework and stalked Yasser over the next few days using painful dial-up internet connections. Who was this boy?

I found myself drawn by his clarity and his deterministic point of view. There was one right answer for Yasser, and he would go to any lengths to prove it. I found myself skipping class to read up on his realpolitik views, article after article, at the student computer lab, sometimes missing essay submission deadlines. I was moved. It was 1999 and, even in modern California, I felt that there was no such thing as the American melting pot.

There were hundreds of articles and discussions to read through. Yasser had written on how Pakistan should adopt Turkey's governance model and '*fundocide* the *mullahs*', Atatürk style. He wrote on hundreds of now obsolete message boards. He wrote letters to the editor of his college newspaper, the Rutgers University's *Daily Targum*, which gave compelling reasons for why Pakistanis deserve a place on the table. He may as well have spoken directly to my repressed fears.

He wrote that Jinnah had had no choice except to create Pakistan, that Partition was to be blamed on Mahatma Gandhi for dragging religion into politics in the first place. That was new. He wrote that the West Pakistan-East Pakistan split had been inevitable and that everything would be much better if we had stayed secular as Jinnah had always wanted it.

My days in San Jose were about catching buses to campus, where I would struggle through Statistics 101. Yasser showed me the world with his words. His abruptness was fresh. I was tired of propriety and of being stereotyped as a person who belonged to a rogue country. Even before 9/11, there was a nexus of Pakistan haters in the United States. I felt unsafe in the US—almost alien, and certainly temporary. The hate was unmistakably visceral— without Pakistan, it seemed, there would be no terror. These haters thought that our nuclear arsenal would soon be taken over by the Taliban. It was a lucky day if anyone knew where Pakistan was; luckier if they didn't.

We have a name for it now, and it is Islamophobia, but then, being Pakistani was being Muslim and it was just something you felt apologetic for. I found myself over-explaining that I am indeed opposed to the felling of the twin towers in the name of a 'just war' in Islam called *jihad*.

While George W. Bush had called Iraq, Iran and North Korea the 'axis of evil', he may as well have replaced North Korea with Pakistan in his declaration. The front pages of the US newspapers that stared back at me from bus-stop newsstands felt like a direct condemnation of Pakistan. I felt that what I heard was hate and that it was hard for Americans to tell us immigrants apart with the with-us or against-us narrative. We were terrorists, or at least we felt that way looking at the headlines. It took several years for *Newsweek* to call Pakistan the most dangerous country in the world in a cover story, but the work to get there started when I was in college.

How I was made to feel, by the professors, the people on the bus, Fox News and the books at Barnes & Noble, felt personal.

No wonder then, that for me, Yasser didn't only make sense, he was the only truth-teller there was. He was unapologetic and Pakistani. He was defiant in the onslaught of the shame that I internalized, which he rejected outright.

He was so sure that not only did we have a right to belong in the US 100 per cent, but that we should also be ones that were heard first.

A few days after his very public show of interest, I realized that apart from being crazy enough to ask me out on a Reddit-like discussion board, Yasser was also obsessed with Pakistan like I was.

He had the same burning passion, almost to an existential level, to be Pakistani. He was often up all night arguing with strangers on the Internet, trying to right wrongs. His username on Chowk.com was Greywolf, and he excavated the big question of the subcontinent: was Jinnah right or wrong in the creation of Pakistan?

Yasser wrote like his life belonged to the truth of that question—referencing books and journals for hours in the library, resorting to Punjabi expletives if his arguments were rejected.

Yasser may have proposed to me in jest, but I had already made my mind up about saying yes.

He wasn't the only crazy one here.

Like the website, Yasser and I have been committed to the insanity of going round and round the Chowk for twenty years since my article on human rights abuses was first published. We met, we fell in love and we parted. Repeat.

We have, since then, fallen apart. Yasser defined the coming together. Yasser defined the falling apart. I get to retell the story of how things fell apart.

The doctors later told me that Yasser's brain tumour had begun to grow slowly, dating back to around 1999—about the same time we met on Chowk.

I found out about Yasser's grade-one oligodendroglioma in 2017. Until then, I had only been able to second-guess the Yasser who courted me. Often, I've wondered which of the two really asked me out that day: Yasser, or his golf ball-sized tumour?

As we loved, married and had two kids, his tumour did the same. Located in his right temporal lobe, the very part that drives personality, charm, obsessions and tics, the tumour and I were in a love triangle with @therealYLH, his combative Twitter persona. Over the last twenty years, I have loved the tumour back. I have stayed married to it and had babies with it.

Here is a big question: does one believe in unseeable things like the idea that someone would love you if they could, or does one only believe in what someone does in practice?

It matters to me that Yasser cared for me. It is what tames me and calms my fears that I've never truly belonged to Pakistan. If your passport is first world, my fears will make little sense. For me, home had to be in Pakistan because my father didn't have any other nationality and he also decided to die on me, so perhaps I felt the way to retain him was to stay grounded in his identity. Everything I lost with Abu, Yasser returned to me.

My husband is a three-piece suit addict. He can out-talk you in almost any area of history, politics and religion. He gels his hair back, Al Pacino style. In soft lighting, he can pass for a Bollywood star. He insists on putting on his shoes with a shoehorn. He loves good cars and regrets dropping out of the Pakistan Air Force School. His wit is a blend: half Seinfeld, half dark British humour. He eats his vegetables as grudgingly as a spoilt, smothered Lahori boy. He whines a lot.

When he is not himself, Yasser is not Yasser in the most absolute way possible. When he is not doing things that normal people do, he's extreme. He's a jerk, he's pathetic, he's impossible. In loving him, I've experienced loss that is both futile and dumb, one that serves no purpose and leaves you considerably worse off. The man I chose to love wholly has a shadow man inside him who is utterly unlovable. The three of us—me, Yasser and Yasser's shadow self—go round and round and take turns at winning. We never get to play for the same team.

I've been ashamed of what I have had to endure.

Of course, a man with a brain tumour will be violent. Any medical journal will tell you that. Serotonin levels fluctuate in a brain tumour patient, crashing destructively against emotional defences, altering behaviour significantly. I have spent the last few years utterly confused, torn between wanting to leave and wanting to stay—only because science tells me that Yasser is not the one who is the jerk here. So, I've stayed, but staying has meant putting myself in harm's way.

Yes, I've been struck by Yasser.

Somewhere in the first couple of years of our marriage, Yasser hurt me so hard that my molar rolled down the stairs. This was humiliating enough, but the fact that there was an audience made it harder, somehow, to register that I had been hit. His mother was there. Our daughter was in my arms at the time.

I instantly checked if my jaw was intact, because it felt like it had been yanked out of my body. My strongest wisdom tooth had torn loose from its mooring. It rolled gently down the stairs, bumping from step to step, entirely gravity-owned and utterly dramatic. I watched it, but not through my own eyes. I, too, seemed to have come loose from by body. My shame felt slightly second-hand.

To be properly understood, this moment had to be broken down into tiny little pieces first.

Think of it this way. There is an elephant in the room. Now, you must eat it. Bit by bit is the only way.

Tusks. Trunk. Feet.

The nails, too. Cuticles are easier.

The liver.

Spleen.

And so forth.

That's the thing about atrocities; even the worst of them are bearable when they are bite sized.

Every insane moment of violence can be endured if it doesn't happen all at once.

Pain shape-shifts, so you can revisit it and measure it for what it was worth. In the aftermath of what had happened, I found it very hard to tell whether I should go to the police or the neurologist.

I couldn't go to my family; I felt the family—mine and his— would condemn me.

Even with a US college education and a well-grounded head on my shoulders, I couldn't figure out whether I should report Yasser or admit him to a mental institution. It took many years and an epileptic fit for the final big reveal to the question I had been asking myself all this time. Should I stay or should I go?

Yasser was checking out of the world. I didn't expect the universe to throw that at me.

If I trusted Yasser's love, I trusted his hate too. Before the tumour was discovered on the computed tomography (CT) scan, I never knew that his strange behaviour and bouts of anger stemmed from neurological and chemical irregularities. All I knew intuitively was that he was just as shocked at his rages as I was.

Over time, I grew to expect violence, both mental and physical, sporadically.

Yet, like death, when it happened it shocked me.

There was nothing I could do to prepare for his immense anger. Denial helped sometimes.

My shock dovetailed with his violence like smoke and fire.

His repentance would follow. Then there would be the guilt and the overt efforts to earnestly tell me that I didn't deserve his insanity. Yasser asked me to leave him many times. In an honest bid to protect me, he would say there was something wrong, I needed to go and save myself.

I know the drill of domestic violence and the WhyIStayed hashtags. No need to lick my wounds. For the most part, the violence is now a distant memory that only surfaces during road rage or extreme ill health. Yasser hurt me, big deal. He stopped soon enough, didn't he? And we caught the tumour that was doing all the bad things.

So, move on, Aisha.

The doctors cut the tumour into small pieces with scalpels. Twice. But you know as well as I do that no ghost story ever ends. The bad spirit is always caught, but the victim stays eternally spooked.

I'm afraid you judge me for staying, but it's not like you can't relate. You've done this before too, haven't you? You've believed your tormentor; you've dined with him and you've invited him into your dreams.

But there were times when I didn't take it lying down. I gave my own share of sorry-assed sucker punches, hurling them at Yasser's jaw. I called him appropriate names, like son-of-a-bitch, but I think I am willing that upon my faded memory. The shame is so rusty, and so deep . . . as rusty and as deep as the sunken *Titanic*. I can still feel the metallic taste of blood in my mouth. This is me, with a phrase running on loop in my head:

What a shame. What a shame. What a shame.

Shame that I was hurt so hard that my tooth slipped out between my lips and to the floor, like a sigh. Shame that someone saw this happening and did not stop it.

This is many years after I responded to Yasser's Chowk proposal and said, 'Yes, I'm available.' Perhaps he hadn't really meant it as an offer of marriage. But I was all in.

This is me. This is later.

This is me feeling my tongue walk its way to the front of my mouth like it's about to jump off a tall building. This is me feeling disgusted for just standing there and taking abuse, when my knees were strong and my spirit too. This is me at the peak of my youth, in the middle of a semi-decent future, hiding a secret—that right from the start, I was deeply unsafe in my own home, away from my family and very coercively controlled in my day-to-day life.

When her father struck me, I felt my baby daughter's confusion in the stiffening of her tiny body, in the cradle of my left arm. I'd rather not have had his mom watch, because it tends to feel like someone will come save you if they know. When no one saves you, it becomes rather anti-climactic. You go ahead and make evening tea, sleep early for work the next day and feed the children. Even if I couldn't look away, they should have—out of respect for my indignity in that moment. But no, they continued to watch. They continued to not save me.

I was unwell enough to lie next to my baby daughter while she slept and ask her to save me. What, pray tell, is this cruelty towards my child?

This was not my house, even though I was married into it with much fanfare. That much was clear. I was the intruder. These were not my green-carpeted stairs and this was not the flaky wall of my home.

But that over there was certainly my tooth.

To the world, my husband is the author of a celebrated biography of Mohammad Ali Jinnah. To me, his wife, Yasser is the author of my life. I'm not being delusional. I feel that I lived the years before I met Yasser, only to let him hold the pen to the pages of my story, like none of my life before I met Yasser had been my own.

I am resentful that Yasser gets to tell two stories. He is the author of his own life as well as mine. I get nothing. He gets the power.

Yasser's brain tumour was not a patch on his male privilege. The tumour sits in him, while he sits on most of my many lives. Yasser was a husband, a dad, a lawyer and a friend. But soon, he also became his tumour.

In losing my Yasser to that shadow Yasser, our love became impaired and twisted. The fact that I stuck around to allow it, want it and even cherish it leaves me a bit twisted too. I feel sorry for my lost years. I feel for my lost opportunities. I feel for the person I could have been, without the self-doubt and self-disgust that inevitably accompanies victims of domestic violence.

Thankfully, I have the tumour to blame. I'm not Yasser's victim. I'm the victim of the wretched disease, of indifferent neurochemistry. I found cause outside myself, outside Yasser even. You'd think blaming the tumour for his hate towards me would make it easier, right?

No.

It is just as hard to live with a man who hurt you because he couldn't help it. The algebra of blue-black bruises is just as difficult as it would have been if the striker were a narcissistic, vicious and evil man.

Of course, Yasser was only sick, not hateful, but my body refuses to accept the idea that I deserved those hurts and damning emotional put-downs. Above all, I feel like I deserved the days he forgot me, as most sick people do. Nothing hurts like this person looking through me in a room where it's just the two of us.

In the early years in the US, right after the Chowk days, I did pick up on something being off with the boy I grew to revere intellectually. Evolution makes us uneasy around dark people. My body felt the uneasiness but did not act upon it. I acted instead upon a deep sense of intuition that he was someone with a refined sense of justice. I knew danger is danger, threat is threat and harm is harm, but I refused to listen to anything else but his unamiability.

Typically, I know you would say that there is no coming back from grave transgression like cruelty, but Yasser always comes back to me as the young twenty-something boy he once was—pure and mine. I always rebuild with the help of this strange feeling we could call love. Yasser is acceptable to me in his scraps, and even those tiny bits of the loveable him are of great service to my broken heart.

I walked off a cliff for Yasser when I married him. Since I took that Herculean leap of faith for a stranger, I will walk, even if not leap, off another one, and yet another. This man redeemed himself. This son-of-a-bitch gathered his sins and walked to the river of apology to cleanse them. But even as he washed them clean, new sins were being committed.

I can't really tell you *why* Yasser gets to keep my heart, but I can tell you how he wins every single time.

YASSER MADE ME RETURN THINGS

'What is grooming?' Yasser asked.

I was changing into my pyjamas after a long day of work. He was not really looking at me. His computer screen had all his attention. He was lying down with the dark-green, raw-cotton duvet drawn all the way up to his chin with his laptop on the duvet. I had tossed my jacket and pants aside for the maid to arrange in the morning. I was too tired to do it now, but not too tired to take down Yasser.

'What's grooming?'

I smirked. 'Grooming, my love, is what your father did to your mom.'

Yasser took twenty seconds to process what I said and looked up at me, standing there in my pink pyjamas.

I explained. 'Street-smart, punk, city boy charms a nubile, impressionable village girl. Immediately retreats when she falls for him. She ends up being more into him than he is into her. Score. Checkmate.'

'You mean what I did to you.' It was Yasser's turn to smirk.

It was actually a pretty good comeback for a two-time brain-tumour surgery survivor, especially one who had just undergone gruelling radiotherapy. Yasser was currently on month two of a six-month-long regimen of chemo. Credit where credit is due. If I were undergoing chemo, I'd also be undergoing fuck-the-universe. Twice.

But Yasser did groom me. We were eighties kids who had graduated during the dot-com surge in Silicon Valley (me), and the post-apocalyptic world that America became following 9/11. Yasser was way ahead of the dating game when I met him. He had had one girlfriend and one breakup, while my attempt to have a first boyfriend had failed.

Yasser 1. Aisha 0.

He was wearing his red Rutgers University hoodie even now.

It helps with the chemo blues, he said.

With his hair loss and the bloating brought on by the anti-seizure medications, he looked like a cream puff experiment gone wrong. But I don't really look-look at him. Our forties have not been kind to us, even though we can pass for twenty-nine-year-olds if we try.

I wore my San Jose State University grey hoodie and got into bed.

'You should change your hoodie,' Yasser said.

Maybe he was getting even with me for the comment about his mom.

'No,' I said.

'It'll get ruined,' he said.

'This is my university hoodie, not yours,' I retorted. He sat up, his sigh giving away his frustration. 'This is how you ruin my things too,' he said.

'You are the one who's ruined,' I said.

'Just wear anything else.' He ignored my personal comment.

'I'm sick of you controlling me. I'm tired and I love this hoodie.'

'You shouldn't wear this to bed,' he said.

Just last week he had made me take off his red Rutgers T-shirt which I had worn to bed.

Red and soft, it was a hundred per cent cotton that felt like candy floss and lived next to my skin like a grandchild would. I loved it because of how Yasser loved it—like it was an animate object. You see, I wanted what he loved, so I could feel a little loved too. But I also knew that Yasser had strict rules about wearing anything but pyjamas to bed. I still tried my luck. After all, things were things; it was people who gave things meaning. To me, Yasser was choosing the T-shirt over me when he asked me not to wear it to bed.

If I could, I would sleep in my office clothes, snapping open the bra hooks, undoing their clawy straps and pulling them out from both armholes.

We were cuddling when Yasser smelled his own Calvin Klein cologne on the shirt I was wearing.

'Are you wearing my Rutgers T-shirt?' he said into the dark. I said nothing, half hoping he would let it go. I loved him.

I loved the shirt. He loved me. He loved the shirt. We were hugging. The world was in perfect equilibrium as far as I could tell. He should have let it go. He really should have.

He unwrapped his arms from around me. 'Take it off.'

He switched on the light and I blinked, rubbing my eyes in the harshness of the light.

I stripped off his red T-shirt. I folded it and put it back in the cupboard. I wore something else, something terribly cheap and crinkly.

He jumped back into bed after making sure that it—the T-shirt—was safely in the cupboard. Turning his back to me,

Yasser slipped soundlessly into a deep sleep. Soon, there was snoring.

After staring into the dark for a few hours, angry with Yasser's attachments that trump me and trump our loving moments, I gave up on my loneliness. I fell asleep.

Once upon a time, Yasser's sleep was soundless. I don't remember when he started snoring like a diesel tractor in a sugar mill. His snoring is a lot like his love for his things, especially his clothes—unapologetic, ruthless and loud. If you insult any of Yasser's things, you insult him. They are like his causes.

He will fight for things he loves—old plane models, hats people gave him as gifts, coffee mugs, books, conference tags, backpacks, shoes, shirts, ties and cufflinks. He would fight me for not saving them from the sun, or the air or some element of nature, as if it were a real person. As if giving up on the thing meant giving up on him.

There have been enough fights about things he gets attached to, things he projects identities and feelings on to—earphones, ear pods, figurines, pens and shoes I've been accused of giving away.

If I had slept in his favourite tee, I may as well have disrespected it like it were the judge of a high court and I had showed up and spat in his lordship's face. Yasser may as well have been the judge wearing the shirt.

It was so exhausting to wait to see what his next attachment would be and when he would call for some obscure item to be produced right there and then.

'Where are my black polo shoes from 2010?'

I love things that people give value to, so things acquire a life of their own. So, a red, soft, Yasser-smelling cotton tee is valuable to me because he loves it.

I toss out anything that doesn't represent life. Not in a Marie Kondo way, but in the sense that we accumulate things and those things burden us needlessly with memories. I'm a migrant. My people were migrants. I can't help but be proud of the people who left everything behind, taking only what was in their hands, on their hips and upon their heads. I am proud of how quickly they recognized that things end up possessing you if you cling too hard to them— they can blind you to danger and eat away at your sense of adventure.

Everything out there, including the stars and the cosmos, will seem too vast and meaningless if you keep focusing on the shackles on your feet.

I love the idea of minimalism. It gives me control over what I do have. He behaves as if saving everything he ever owns will bring him great fortune.

So, here is how our equation has played out over the years: I would throw things out and Yasser would throw Aisha out for throwing things out.

One day, when the kids were little more than toddlers and Yasser was at work, I decided to empty the house of old, useless things. I'd donate the extra baggage that had accumulated over the years. Yasser came home unexpectedly and was incensed by what he saw—boxes upon boxes of the kids' clothes, newborn stuff they never used because they grew up too soon, old cardboard boxes, broken toasters bought half a decade ago, warranty cards of long-dead UPS batteries, remote controls of devices that probably belong in museums and my own old clothes that were terribly unfashionable.

The maid had summoned a taxi to take some of the boxes to the charity shop and the remaining to the city dumpster.

Yasser lost his temper at the sight of the taxi, half filled with boxes.

I would imagine this is what happens to cheating wives when their husband walks in.

I was so embarrassed, and he was so angry at being lied to. It wasn't just a life-design issue, it was a life problem.

We just weren't a team. I was his adversary as far as he was concerned because I hated his things and was trying to rid him of them; when in reality, I was just a normal, US-educated girl who had to make room to grow.

Eventually there were outright bans—I didn't get to touch his things.

Maybe a cheating wife would be more forgivable than one trying to cheat a hoarder of his stuff. He had trusted me to understand that his things were his universe, one in which those items imbued him with a unique identity. Instead, I had violated that trust when he wasn't looking.

I, on the other hand, interpreted this as yet another thing to control me with.

He brought the neighbourhood down with his screaming, accusing me of betrayal and lies, of disloyalty and deceit. He was living with a thief and a con artist. Who was I, really? If I could do this, I could do anything.

We almost got divorced that day.

The kids asked me what would happen. I said to them, Mama and Baba are over. My hands were shaking from all the yelling. My ears were ringing, and my neck constricted like a python digesting prey.

'This is it, girls,' I said. 'There is no coming back from this.'

The maid, her husband and the taxi driver fled so fast on foot that they forgot the taxi, their wallets and their own toddlers at my place. That was how horrific Yasser's wrath was to anyone who got to witness it first-hand.

For days afterwards, those boxes, crammed with stuff to be given away, were left limply stacked in the corner. It was understood that it was strictly forbidden to touch them.

So perhaps you can understand when I tell you that the day that I actually got to tear that very special Rutgers T-shirt of Yasser's into tiny bits, I got my revenge.

The Rutgers T-shirt tearing day went like this:

It was around 2018 and I was in Karachi for a work trip, for a job where I felt I had certainly punched above my weight. The thirteen-hour workdays were a drain as were the office politics.

Life was hectic and deadline-driven, and I was often frazzled enough to forget to breathe. Yasser had accompanied me because he needed one of his routine magnetic resonance imaging (MRI) scans after his first surgery. The Aga Khan Hospital in Karachi was his tumour treatment centre. During his second surgery, the Covid-19 pandemic was just kicking off and no company knew if their workforce would be wiped out or if their kids would die. People were more on edge and most were forbidden to leave their homes.

While in charge of Yasser's medical regimen, there were times when I had failed in carrying out my good nurse duties—I am guilty of delaying his biannual MRI by nine months because I was scared that the tumour might have returned and avoidance was a sensible choice amongst paralysing fear. Yasser would relegate so much of his treatment plans and follow-ups to me, often because he was clinically depressed and uninterested, that I sometimes folded from the sheer responsibility of it. Sometimes I would be unable to give him his medication on time because of online meetings that would run over, and there were other times I'd be rude to him for being so high-maintenance.

He was a patient who was dependent on me, partly because it was impossible to inculcate independence after I had seen him so far gone in the weeks post-surgery. Yasser needed a lot of genuine, tender care, but he was either just immobile with dread, or angry at the world and blaming someone—with both rather useless phases, I got nothing to hold on to, and I slowly started wearing down like an old woman, my hairline receding, my lips grey and my hunchback ribs caving into where my heart once was.

I was afraid that, as always, Yasser would be bad news.

These were times when it was hard to separate the person from what had happened to the person. Not just when it came to Yasser, but when it came to me too. If my husband had a tumour in his brain, you see, I was the one who was then doomed. At any moment, the sky wouldn't just fall on his head, it would fall on mine too.

Everything was a mess and would continue to remain an epic mess.

We had just arrived at Marriott Hotel in Karachi. I was tipping the concierge who had brought in our luggage and trying to get to the loo before I peed my pants.

Meanwhile, Yasser decided to be a problem.

He got into a flaming war with an online friend on Twitter.

This was a mutual friend.

Then Yasser roared: 'I want you to unfriend Irfan now.' 'Why would I do that?' I shot back.

We were finally in the room and by then I had reached a point where I wanted to be done with him, put him to sleep like a dog. I was really that exhausted, although I didn't vocalize it.

Yasser was like a bull in Pamplona, running amidst humans who did not understand that they shouldn't be running with bulls.

'Just do it,' he said.

'I want no part in this insanity. Why would you even fight with someone like Irfan?' I snapped.

'He's a *chay*,' Yasser said.

'Why would you pick fights on Twitter when we have other things to worry about? Like the brain-tumour recurrence?'

Yasser was not listening to me. In his trance, he would be with himself. Only himself.

'I need you to call him and tell him that he's a *chutiya*,' he said.

'The only chutiya here is you, Yasser. You're obviously having a focal seizure,' I replied.

During a focal seizure, Yasser would experience electrical currents in his brain that would present themselves as emotional seizures—paranoia, aggression, inability to reason or have any perspective on a fixation that develops. Airplane rides, lack of sleep, stress, too much light, LED flickers—anything, almost anything, could trigger it. On the other hand, during an emotional seizure, his pupils would dilate, his eyes would look feral like those of a frightened animal and he would be hyper alert.

Strong. He would become very strong. I would absorb his energy so intensely that my body hurt even before any assault happened. As if it had already happened. Yasser hadn't hurt me in over a decade, but I couldn't tell.

When he had such a seizure—something that took me years to figure out with inputs from his neurologists and neurosurgeons—I would go into an episode of my own. I would panic loud enough for it to sound like a highway pile-up. I think I would have probably been able to take on an army of three hundred. My heart would pump many more gallons per second than it needed to, culminating in a huge build-up of unexpended energy.

'Some people are chutiyas even when I'm not having a focal seizure!' Yasser yelled into my face.

'Shut up! This is a work trip!' I yelled back, grabbing his arm. His bicep was hard against my manicured nails. I dug in, my teeth grinding.

My boss was in the room adjacent to ours. All this chutiya-chutiya talk was not going to go down well, especially because I had been specifically hired to manage my company's reputation. Just the thought of a public scene made me want to kill myself.

Suddenly, Yasser made a beeline for the door. Since he had to go past me for it, I instantly blocked him. A man with a focal seizure is like a kamikaze warrior on a rampage. My blocking had to be a bit more charged—I took on Yasser like I was a veritable force of nature.

In a flash, I was on the bed, on top of Yasser, pinning him down like the animal I was inside. My arms were superhuman strong, clawing his thin wrists, at odds with the hard biceps into which one had to dig nails after great effort.

When reality returned, as if it had run off into the woods, the Rutgers T-shirt he had been wearing was ripped, its soft, much-adored fabric in tatters. Yasser's face was a deep purple. He was looking at me like a salmon would look at a brown bear as it leapt upwards out of the water and into the bear's mouth—a sort of morbid eye-contact.

How did Yasser's favourite Rutgers T-shirt turn into a few dozen shreds of fabric?

I'm not sure.

The soft, expensive cotton rested on his body, as if pleading with me to stop. There was desperation, the moment pregnant with victory. A brown feminist atop her tormentor, scavenging the rot of his mental illness, eating away at his momentary weakness with her unforgiving canines.

This was a borderline human-rights violation. By me, not by him.

You cannot hurt someone who is mentally ill. You just cannot.

It's also a bit strange. His nipples looked askance at me from beneath what was left of his ragged T-shirt. Yasser's nipples are tiny. They seemed to be pleading with me to jump back into the present. But part of me, you see, was squarely anchored in that bygone moment when Yasser had hurt me hard enough to uproot my molar and have it bounce down the stairs. The other part was frozen in time when he had humiliated me for wanting to be done with the clutter in those boxes.

There were about fifteen or more years between those two moments, but it may as well have been the length of a song. Not a long song, like Nusrat Fateh Ali Khan's *qawwali*, but a short song, like 'Happy Birthday'. Does time have no regard for sunrises, for hummingbirds, for sunflowers born between Molar-gate and Tee-gate—the two moments of mental violence Yasser perpetrated against me and I against him?

I guess it hurts. I guess it hurts me, this person here, now typing away, to realize that no one remembers or cares about my pathetic molar. No one cares enough to save me. I went to the dentist and patched it up sometime halfway between the two incidents—my loss of dignity at Yasser's hands, and Yasser's loss of dignity at my hands. The dentist said it was the oddest tooth break she had ever seen. It was diagonal. Guess how I tore his T-shirt?

Diagonally.

I feel it adds a bit more distinction to this story when I add details. Otherwise, it is all too shameful. I have to answer questions like, does a mentally ill person have a soul?

What about the person taking care of that ill person?

Do their souls merge like the frothy ocean foam, nose-diving into the sand because they held on despite all odds?

If I had known that Yasser punched me because he was ill, would I have ripped his beloved shirt to shreds?

If there was a trial in court, would I be indicted for hurting a brain tumour patient at a moment in time—after a gruelling, eight-hour awake craniotomy and before yet another gruelling, eight-hour awake craniotomy?

You answer those questions for me.

YASSER IS THE NEW MASTER

I wore green on my *mayoon-mehndi*, one of the five days of a *desi* wedding. I wore green and felt green. My wrists had *gajras* made of yellow marigolds, bright as the sun. The previous night, I had my entire body smeared with *ubtan*—a mixture of chickpea flour and olive oil. It was daubed on to my freshly waxed skin to lighten my complexion to the greatest extent possible. The wedding was to take place in Karachi, since that was my abu's city. Even though Abu wasn't there himself, his brothers and my brothers would still perform the bridal honour of giving me away on my wedding day. Friends and family had travelled from Africa, Australia, the US and the UK to give me a joyful send-off as I embarked on my new life with Yasser. This was a transfer of power that many were keen to watch and others obliged to do so.

As the bride, I would be the cynosure of all eyes, so I had to be pretty; it also entailed that I heeded all the advice and pearls of wisdom rained down on my bowed head, and obediently did as I was told. Yasser said I was fat, so I aimed to be a slim bride. I put myself on a self-regulated diet, which included a couple of days of not eating at all. Starving wasn't too much of a problem. I remember fasting for days at a time as a teenager and never craving food. I was only a couple of years away from nineteen, so going without food was still quite easy.

On the night before our mehndi, Yasser summoned me, his tone on the telephone very peremptory. He told me that he was upset that I was not going to sit with him on the stage. This was his first notable tantrum. Many would follow.

I sighed. I had to go out on to the balcony to talk to him.

Ami was a bit cross because I was on the telephone with him all the time. She grumbled that over-exposure to the groom before the wedding reduces the glow on the bride's face. With Yasser throwing tantrums, I understood this on so many different levels.

There was a lot of traffic on the road below the balcony. My *chacha's* flat was in a brown apartment complex which was separated from the adjacent building by the narrowest of alleyways, so you could see into your neighbour's living rooms and figure out their menu for the day. All too closely packed, it deprived people of their privacy.

I never really liked cramped spaces. I also didn't like the idea of not being in a hotel. I was thinking like an American brat, constantly cribbing about the living conditions and the innumerable rickshaw rides back and forth from the tailor's and the jeweller's. My main grouse was the toilet, which was literally on the floor, which meant I had to squat to pee. The flush was a pail of water. There were three people per room and the adult-to-toddler ratio was way off—everywhere you looked there were kids running around even though most were from the general neighbourhood. I was grateful that my chacha's family had generously put up Ami and me during this time. In retrospect, I think some of my angst could've been attributable to the gnawing hunger pangs.

I closed the balcony door behind me.

'I'm not allowed to sit with you, Yasser. Weddings, as you know, are fraught with tradition and as the bride, I'm the person with the least say in any matter; so, you see, I'm in no position to fly in the face of convention on the eve of my wedding.'

'Am I marrying a child bride against her will? If you must quote tradition to me, then I'll have you know that Punjabis have the bride and groom sit together before the wedding to dine and dance at the mehndi reception. I had better see you next to me tomorrow.'

I didn't like his tone. 'Or else what?'

Perhaps the balcony was not the best of places to seek privacy to have a tiff with your husband-to-be. The twinkling fairy lights around me seemed to be mocking me. It was abundantly clear to every person in the neighbourhood that I was the bride from America. Young men, old women and even the maids had come out on to their balconies to enjoy the free entertainment. Although it made me deeply uncomfortable, I didn't react. My rising anger had a target—Yasser, who was being out of line. Despite the December breeze that fluttered my green *dupatta*, my jangling nerves wouldn't calm down.

Yasser went on.

'You had better be on the stage tomorrow and I had better be holding your hand.'

'Until the wedding ceremony is over, I don't officially get to be your bitch, okay?' My voice had obviously reverberated downstairs because Ami was soon knocking at the balcony door which I had shut behind me.

'Can you please keep it down? Everyone for miles can hear you.' Ami's voice was polite, but her embarrassment was patent. We were not being gracious guests. Not enough imposing on our hosts' hospitality, we were now disrupting the delicate balance between tradition and hierarchy that passed for culture here. I chose to ignore her.

'Why are you ordering me around? Can't you just focus on the fact that we're getting married rather than on the minutiae of the ceremony itself?'

'No. You will be there tomorrow, and I WILL see you,' Yasser insisted.

When Yasser insisted, Yasser spoke with an authoritative force almost like he had some God-given right to do so.

'My family WILL not allow it. This is the last thing I'll be doing for them as a daughter of this household, so you had better back off. I thought we were going to marry to fix these backward and conservative rituals.'

'Day one and one can't even ask the bride to obey me, when it's literally tradition to allow the groom's side to have their way,' he said.

Suddenly, I didn't give a damn that the world and his wife could hear me. I shouted at Yasser from the rooftop. The rickshaw-wallahs in the narrow street looked up at me, shell-shocked. Even the *salwars* on the clotheslines seemed to shudder. This was high drama indeed and it seemed as though the good people of old Karachi, behind Radio Pakistan, had never seen a young woman screaming into a cell phone before.

My American education came back to me as did my obstinacy and recalcitrance during my childhood in Uganda. I didn't survive everything only to be tossed around by the entitlement of my husband to-be.

Nonetheless, I was acutely aware of my insignificance and the fact that I seemed to be leaping from the frying pan into the fire. I just wanted to jump off a ledge and call it quits. I felt trapped between two worlds. In a week's time, I would be his. I felt a bleak premonition.

'You're doing this to me because I am a woman,' I said, my voice vibrating with emotion.

Ami barged out—no longer worried about incurring my wrath. She snatched the tiny, grey Nokia phone from my hand and disappeared back into the nether regions of the apartment soon enough, but only after delivering a stern lecture about the good manners which all gently born girls should have.

'Is this what I've taught you and how I've reared you?' she seethed. 'What is this *batameezi*?'

I've learnt to dread that word all my life. Batameezi simply means badly behaved, but it is almost always used in the context of girls that are out of hand.

'Brides are expected to enter into a union with the blessings of Allah. You have to conduct yourself with patience, decorum and acceptance during these days leading up to your nuptials. But here you are, roundly cursing your future husband.'

The journey hadn't even begun.

I sat in the corner of the balcony, the traffic starting to flow again in the streets far below. I wept into my green, *gota-wala* dupatta. I drenched the sunshine of the marigolds with my tears and snot. I thought of the person I was to marry and wondered why he would choose to pull rank on me today of all days. He wasn't really like that. He wasn't the sort to do something like that. Maybe it was a case of wedding nerves?

Someone else came to fetch me. I headed downstairs to join the party where my cousins were singing. There was a *dholki*. A spoon. A Musarrat Nazir *tappa-song*. There was mehndi and sugar water to ensure that the mehndi stayed on my hands until my skin had leached all its colour. According to the old superstitions, the deeper the colour of the henna that stained my hands, the more would I be loved by my husband. There were prayers that he did, indeed, love me. Prayers that I had a kismet in working condition. Nothing too outlandish, just the plain kismet that doesn't leave you dead while you're still young. There was a couch arrayed in roses and more marigolds. Everything smelled of saffron and milk. There was laughter. There was teasing.

Don't come back to Karachi looking like that fat cow, Anjuman. Don't come back with that horrid accent.

Don't forget us. Remember to call.

Give your mother-in-law the red-chilli chutney. Fatten up the in-laws.

Keep them happy.

Make sure you don't shame us by only cooking daal for them. Nihari all the way.

The very first day following my wedding, I desperately wanted some peace and quiet to make sense of everything.

I felt like I had started the race already defeated by the life I had consciously chosen. The very fact that things had happened so fast had been my cue to run. Something was drastically wrong. However, I still waited for a respite from the breakneck pace so I could figure out what it was.

Days turned to months and months to familiarity. I now had another family.

I wasn't entirely sure whether my family back home would welcome me back with open arms or summarily disown me if I tried to return to them.

YASSER IS LAHORE, AND LAHORE IS HARD TO LOVE

I was a married woman now. Things sank in. I was married with children and Lahore was my home.

I had inherited everything that was my husband's—his seven dogs, his weird pheasants and his senseless chickens, all crammed into the backyard. I had inherited his mother along with her possessions—the tea sieve and the dresser. His father, too, had been bequeathed to me and became my own. This part was rather nice.

Nonetheless, there were issues there as well. I called Yasser's dad Abu just as I did my own father. However, this Abu smoked and drove expensive cars and he didn't handle evenings well. I had also come into possession of Yasser's books, but I wasn't allowed to touch them. I ended up also falling heir to the way Yasser fitted into his family—except Yasser was the only child.

This was a mother like no mother I knew. This was a father like no father I knew. Yasser had no siblings. There was this concentrated syrup of attention, intense, sharp and pungent, that was only offered to Yasser. Yasser's room. Yasser's TV. Yasser's books. Yasser's published articles in newspaper cuttings. The fact was everything Yasser loved was tended to by his mom and, to some extent, his dad. And now, here I was, the latest of Yasser's acquisitions.

I felt like I had stepped into an open prison, armed only with goodwill and the hope that if I ignored everything long enough, maybe, just maybe, I wouldn't feel like I was part of a strange new cult. Probably anybody in my shoes would have felt as I did. I felt alien because, during the first year of wedded bliss, marriages are meant to make one feel a bit alien. The more the alienness the better, in fact. The more ambushed I felt and the further I was from my own family, the better my chances of survival. I was taught that clinging on to your past family was going to squander your chances of winning over the new family.

The how-to-be-married manual had the word 'survival' stamped on every page.

Everything in my new house felt removed. Yasser's mottled brown pheasant looked really odd. It was invariably placed on the kitchen counter before the house was locked up for the evening. I found their lockdown routine so dumb because of how utterly ceremonial it was. At the end of the day, the doors were padlocked. I found it weird that the house keys didn't have a keychain. A chunk of keys, naked and on their own was ugly and disrespectful to the ceremony of safety.

'Why are there padlocks on everything? Locks on the kitchen doors, both the outer and the inner ones, not to mention the locks on the front gate leading to the porch, the front door and even the doors to the rooms?' I asked.

'I've heard that thieves lurk everywhere.'

'Robbers have been known to jump over low gates, break padlocks and take whatever they want.' When I said this, I was ridiculed.

'This is not America,' they scoffed.

The dogs, Tommy and his family of Russian pups, were adorable, albeit rather highly strung. But what I found really strange was that when the dogs barked in unison, the people inside the house barked back in Punjabi slurs. This would go on for a while until one party relented. It was usually the dogs who were the bigger people.

Over time, I started to dread Tommy and Co.'s barking. I grew paranoid about intruders breaking into our home and taking away something precious.

Desi weddings come with gold. My mother-in-law had decided to take over as the custodian of my gold jewellery and had packed all my valuables in a small suitcase, burying them in a metal *tijori* which also served as a linen closet and was, therefore, full of cotton duvets. The tijori was secured with two large padlocks. I had never seen so many padlocks in all my life.

Was I the one who had brought the potential danger of burglary into this household?

Not having had the opportunity to see what life had been like in Yasser's home before our wedding, everything bad was personalized and me-centric.

Cups, plates and spoons were washed twice, thrice even, because there was a possibility that an animal may have licked it.

Animals? What kind of animals? Lizards, silly.

Lahore had a thriving gecko population that terrorized everyone. These house lizards could poison food by sneaking into the fridge in the night, like cheeky monsters, to lick the refrigerated food which could culminate in your dying a painful death.

I was aware that the world was different in this part of the universe, and I also knew that I was the one meant to do the adapting into this environment. I hated the idea of my being a brat, disdaining

the 'natives'. I suppressed my feeling of alienation, my need for a
sense of belonging and did my best to absorb the new shocks in my
integration adventures. This was me doing my part to save the world
from division with one broad stroke called a marriage.

We settled into a routine soon enough. I headed off to work at
a Silicon Valley start-up almost instantly. In the evenings, I helped
my mother-in-law with the cooking. Although Yasser taught
economics at a high school, his rage tantrums were exclusive to
the Chowk website and he vented his spleen on the Internet. No,
of course I had no time for Chowk, so naturally I felt resentful
that Yasser spent endless hours online, publishing articles and
being livid with Indians who dared to challenge him.

He didn't give a damn about my resentment. Yasser was
nervous about our new life. He wanted me to like his pheasant
and his mom's tea sieve, but he wanted me to keep in mind that
it was my duty to like them. Sometimes he was indifferent to me,
and at others, eager to show me Lahore, to take me places and
prove to me that Pakistan was modern and up-and-coming; that
the economic future of Pakistan was bright; that our history is
extraordinary; that the Mughals and British left us with something
to build upon. He took me on road trips around the *neher*, the
irrigation canals built in the colonial era.

He took me to Sheesh Mehal palace in Lahore where the
famous film *Mughal-e-Azam* had been shot. He sent me old
Bollywood songs from a bygone era like *Chalte-Chalte*. He took
me to Jinnah's mausoleum in Karachi. With Yasser, I got to see
Mayo Hospital's historic, red-brick building in Lahore and take
the bus to Punjab University, passing by Charing Cross and Kim's
Gun—local attractions I had only read about and now was seeing
in real life. But I was unmoved. I felt as I had done in Karachi,
standing on my chacha's balcony. I didn't want to impose. I

wanted to be a good guest. I would politely go along with all the fanfare because I could feel the excitement with which it was brought to me.

I would almost always come home from these trips and throw up in the loo. Thank you, heat exhaustion. Lahore was hot and humid, harsh and unforgiving.

When Yasser was alone with me, I got to see the same youthful boy from San Jose, the boy from a year ago. Things may have been strange, but they weren't straight from hell either.

I called my ami using really pricey calling cards and the newly acquired Blackberry Pearl that Yasser gave me for our first wedding anniversary, which he paid for in long instalments. She unfailingly reminded me to cooperate and be good towards my new family. I could read between the lines in the words of her caution—I had to complete year one without getting divorced. You see, according to the common desi adage, if you survive the first year of your marriage, your odds of making it in the long run quadruple.

The question of surviving the first year became a no-brainer when I discovered that I was pregnant.

Twice.

Three years and two beautiful daughters later, I was still trying to adjust to life in Pakistan.

Yasser and I never really managed to break even because the cost of milk formula and diapers burned holes through our salaries. We accumulated a massive credit-card debt. Both of us worked multiple jobs to keep the ground from swallowing us whole. The moment our heads touched the pillows, sleep would abduct us and pitch us into deep comas.

As was to be expected, there were squabbles and arguments during the first five years or so. I still felt like I was a new bride, like my skills were being weighed and tested. I may have used the wrong oil. I may have thrown things that undoubtedly deserved to be trashed. I may have been in a mood. I may have been unhappy, but that was unacceptable as a reason for my carelessness. I may have even spoken harshly to Yasser's mom. I may have slept in at times. I may have made eggs in gravy, which was a strict no-no. I may have added coconut to every dish, also taboo. I hadn't a clue about how to cook. Three strikes right there in one go.

Maybe *I* found *them* dysfunctional.

No one discussed outstanding issues like adults. That was the domestic backdrop against which I found myself. My strengths were strongest when I shut up and scrubbed harder. The American dream had taught me that, if you worked diligently, the system would reward you. All right, this wasn't America, but I could just keep my nose to the grindstone both at work and at home and see if something gave. It had to.

Then there was the political world where Yasser and I had met, but which had quickly become exclusive to Yasser.

All my time went into appeasement and learning to cook, while Yasser took on the Internet. Things only escalated—they never de-escalated. I learned that the only outcome of daring to disagree with Yasser was to leave feeling stupid or emotionally wounded.

When the people on Chowk or other websites were upset by Yasser's irascibility, I became the person they called. After a few hundred online squabbles, someone or the other would call and ask me to take Yasser to a good psychiatrist—not because they were concerned about his mental health, but as an insult to him. Calling him mad was such a common slur, it took away from it being a clinical possibility.

I felt slightly justified. I had enjoyed watching Yasser going off the beaten path. For me, the fact that he was considered disruptive to the classist, Pakistani, intellectual guard was a good thing.

Slowly, I began building my own network of friends and family, via Yasser. It was embarrassing for me, but I didn't really have any friends. I had to use Yasser's undoubtedly wide range of networks to build one of my own—to survive.

On weekends, I would look forward to getting out of the house, to visit someone's home. Sometimes Yasser would get free passes to concerts or Basant (Spring) festivals because he was an alumnus of an elite high school. We enjoyed the full bloom of President Pervez Musharraf's reign—from *mujras* to *mushairas*, to meet-ups at Pak Tea House to plot and plan to subvert the right wing with banner campaigns.

If there was anything political, anything even remotely revolutionary, Yasser was at the centre of it all—his law, his history and his early childhood roots in an elite school permitted it, and I rode along, saying a few words here and there. Sometimes I followed the politics and got immersed in it, like the time when Punjab's Governor Salman Taseer was murdered by his own guard for alleged blasphemy. At other times, Pakistani politics felt like an episode of a Spanish soap opera that had the same actors after six seasons—stilted and not as large as they had once seemed.

It was his steadfastness to his convictions, or even senseless whims, that made me both admire him and find fault with him. I assimilated it and built a B-brand version of it in my own dabbling in human-rights—rights for women especially, to allow them to ask, is this all there is? Daring to want more—even though my enhanced needs required Yasser to be a bit less.

A see-saw. We strived to be a modern couple with equitable rights and responsibilities, but it was more like there could only be one taker. Soon enough, when I was done playing feminism-feminism, I had to go back to taming my man. Somehow coming to Pakistan had transformed my obsession with fixing the country into an actionable one. Yasser was a mere citizen, but to see the fearlessness with which he fought the State for more gave me so much courage. The source was unknown to me at the time, but almost through osmosis, Yasser's rage, his idealism and his hammer on the sculpture of a better Pakistan won me over and I wanted to be him.

However, I was stuck with the operational stuff. Within its confines, I worked hard and honestly, paid my taxes, hired people from under-represented communities as managers, worked on teams that built good tech products and ensured that the household's utility bills were paid on time. I no longer cared if the Indians on Chowk considered us scum and an illegitimate country, born of mayhem and bloodshed. The fact was that, when the sun rose in Lahore, it felt pretty damn real. Yes, the summers were insanely oppressive, but besides that, there was enough commerce for human life to thrive and survive. That was a B-plus in my book.

B-plus was good enough.

The frequency of calls asking me to tell Yasser to watch what he was saying in print, or on TV, or at dinner parties continued unabated. This, of course, would lead to confrontations with Yasser. I'd tell him that he was alienating a large number of people who formed the circle of his influence. I warned him that if he was not careful, his reputation would be one of a combative and confrontational guy who was obsessed with Jinnah; that Jinnah was all he could talk about.

It never occurred to me to ask his friends to talk to him directly. Why were they shaming me for his behaviour? Then, I thought, it was perhaps because Yasser did take things too far.

He personalized arguments, attacking people for their weight or their weak, 'sell out' forefathers, degrading their debates as based on propaganda pamphlets.

At one time, he cuttingly remarked, 'I wouldn't hire Imran Khan as my chauffeur!' On another occasion, he accused the powerful head of the council of Islamic ideology of taking money from the European Union to combat radical extremism, even as the cleric continued to spew sectarian hatred.

The interventions kept pouring in, but they were almost always directed at me:

> *Teach him some manners.*
> *Control your husband.*
> *You're not doing a good enough job of distracting him now, are you?*
> *Have a kid and soon. Maybe kids will fix his angst.*
> *Does he really think we don't care about Pakistan?*
> *Tell him to chill.*

'I'll work on it,' I'd always promise.

In the first couple of years of the marriage, I would come home from work in the evenings in a rickshaw. It was noisy and I hated the rickshaw-man's habit of staring lewdly at my boobs for the entire ride. At work, I had checked an online board where someone was calling Yasser's mom a *gashti*, a whore, because he had had a heated political debate online.

The online hatred that Yasser generated is now called 'cyber harassment', but, at the time, it was just plain hate. Hate affected him adversely. It affected his behaviour towards me. Anyone who trolled him eventually ended up disrupting my well- being because Yasser was unable to block it out.

Sometimes by confrontation, sometimes lovingly, I'd tell Yasser that what he was writing was far too intense for the community in which we lived, for the people who had gotten here first. It was upsetting for them that Yasser was so relentless.

'Is this your interpretation of a marriage, Aisha? That I am attacked for no fault of mine and because I feel too strongly?

Instead of sticking by me, you take the side of these spineless, pinko liberals? I thought this was about us versus the world, huh?'

I felt like I was failing—failing at being a good wife. He did have a point. Good wives are proud of their husbands. Good wives stand by their husbands through thick and thin. Good wives convince their husbands to see the world their way. Now that I was Yasser's wife, I realized that I was doing nothing of the sort. I was a windsock, cowed by the low opinion of a mix of socialites and genuine well-wishers. I was also really out of touch with what Yasser was fighting for exactly.

And so, the rift between us began to widen.

And despite that chasm, the grown-up conversations continued. They had to. As his wife, I had to now reform him and fix him. It was what was expected of me. People were particularly cruel when they discovered that Yasser was not as protective of me as someone who co-walked my life's path should be. They came to me—the men were importuning the women with their pity. If the women were older, they praised me for my fortitude. If the women were younger, they told me that they would rather die than hand over the reins of their lives to a raging lunatic like Yasser. They said Yasser only cared about Jinnah, Pakistan and the ramifications of the 1946 Cabinet Mission Plan, which had proposed a multi-tiered administrative structure for British India.

Then there were the crass jokes.

Aisha and Yasser are in a threesome, but who is the third person?

There were inquiries about him: the crazy *phaddaybaz*, the fighter cock.

Is he still the same unbalanced guy?

Is he still an emotionally absent husband?

I wonder about the things he does to you in person considering he is so terrible online.

What is it that he gives you that has kept you with him all these years?

How are you coping? Is he better?

When we knew him in college, he used to crush Coke cans. The guy had a temper.

Good luck to you making a family man out of him.

The derogatory commentary was unending.

There was only one person with the humaneness to see what I was experiencing. He made me recognize that Yasser's behaviour may be problematic because of a psychiatric issue. Raza, an author, a family friend and a peacenik, called me and asked me to seriously consider getting medical treatment for Yasser.

Raza was the kindest towards me by offering an alternative possibility—that Yasser wasn't a mean person who routinely messed up his family with his instability or the last man standing in a just revolution, and that he was, in fact, a little unwell.

Raza said, 'I know this is too much of a struggle for you.' I felt seen. I felt seen by Yasser's tribe.

This was the first time that Yasser's important world had bled into mine and I leeched on it for dear life. I belonged. I was cared for. I wasn't alone.

Maybe, just maybe, I wasn't trash as a wife. Maybe Yasser was not utterly crazy; there could be some bad cells somewhere in his head, making life impossible for him.

Raza allowed the humanity of the man I had married to shine through by deliberately obliterating his darker parts.

Raza's suggestion was like the antidote I had been seeking and I desperately hoped that treatment would fix at least some of this mess.

He gave me proverbial maggots to put on the rot in our marriage. The happier the maggots, the happier would we be and most certainly the happier would Raza be. After Yasser started selective serotonin reuptake inhibitors (SSRI) medication, he immediately cut down on calling Raza a paid agent or accusing him of stealing the Shakespeare books from the side table. Yasser doesn't have a brother, but Raza comes closest to being one.

I felt safe in Yasser's arms again after a very long time. Things began to make sense.

There were all sorts of pills that could solve this problem.

The sweetheart Yasser from San Jose was not the angry Yasser in Lahore because somewhere in between he had fallen sick. Bad brain chemistry is what took my Yasser from me. I just had to find the old Yasser in there somewhere.

The first time Yasser agreed to see a psychiatrist in Lahore, my imagination ran riot and I saw myself finally coping with my Lahore life. I sang again. I planned on going to the movies without worrying about punches being thrown. I planned on vacations in Europe. I thought of book tours. Of children in Crocs, playing in puddles in the rain.

I could focus on feeling empathy for Yasser rather than my usual low opinion of him.

I could imagine just how hard it was to be him.

Have you ever had your acupuncture needle plunge too deep? Have you ever stepped on a six-inch nail wearing foam slippers? Have you ever run into your school bully and felt the visceral flight-fight-freeze reaction? Have you ever fled war? Do loud noises frighten you?

Maybe Yasser feels all this when you get South Asian history wrong. If you were to tell Yasser that Jinnah was a bad man, Yasser would melt like salt on frozen nails. Sizzling. Life and death. I knew Yasser had some form of Pure O, different from obsessive-compulsive disorder (OCD), that did not allow him to exhale as he solved moral question after moral question on history and politics and religion.

The mind is a wild place and neurons can misfire, can't they? It is forgivable.

I saw Yasser as a victim, and my protective instincts kicked in. I felt bad for misunderstanding him.

I took Yasser to a psychiatrist in Lahore and then later, when we moved to Islamabad, he was seen by Dr Alma. Soon enough, he was on a cocktail of drugs. Yasser cooperated, openly talking about his mental-health struggles. He wore his obsessions like a badge of honour. His Twitter bio was Sipa-e-Jinnah—Jinnah's soldier.

Although Yasser took his medication, sometimes I had to put them into his mouth if I wanted an uneventful day. Sometimes I had to coach him to develop independence—he was a partner in his health regime, it wasn't just me. Sometimes, I told him that his over-reliance on antidepressants, serotonin-norepinephrine reuptake inhibitors (SNRIs), SSRIs—drugs that modulate the critical aggression hormone, serotonin—and antipsychotics were making him lose his resolve to be kind.

Yasser on medication was a much better Yasser. Fewer tantrums. Fewer fights. Measured words. More productivity at the job. More published journals, blogs and books. Improved relationships. He also became a better dad. His eye contact improved and with that his social skills. He could hold longer conversations.

This version of the man I married is mean and violent without his medication. Prior to his treatment, he was unfit to have a family, to hold a job or travel long distances or enrol in an educational programme.

This version of the man I married needed my permission for everything. Yasser took so much from me in order to outrun his demons of rage and sporadic anger. He sucked out my kindness to become someone with an independent sense of purpose. He clawed me all over to be able to live long enough so that his insane fists in the air started looking like meaningful motions of purpose. Yasser engulfed and ingested me like an amoeba just so he could be an author, a barrister, a lawyer, a human-rights advocate, a researcher and a journalist.

What remains of me are the parts that Yasser didn't take. I became my own shadow, growing in the moist darkness like fluorescent algae. I adopted my own life purpose and meaning, drawn deeply from the well of Yasser. His rage became my shield.

Now, I am armoured. No one can get in, except this man who was born the day he married me. I am not his mom, but I did hatch him. A trauma bonding of sorts. Our neurons fed off each other's fears, envy and lust. Then they travelled into the void and created magic of their own.

'Yasser has a problem.' I began to say to people when they called to caution me about his insanity.

Yes, he is taking something for it. Yes, keep us in your prayers.
Thanks for your concern.

I would plead with him to stop fighting with trolls online. Sometimes, I would fight with him for doing so, as I did on the evening that I discovered I was pregnant.

'Can you please stop offending people?' I said, tossing my dupatta aside and switching on the noisy, split air-conditioner. It took a minute to start and it took longer for Yasser to look up from his Blackberry. I still had the same Nokia cell phone. No Internet.

'People can go to the pits of hell,' he said.

'What good is it to tell them to go to hell??' I asked. 'I don't have time for your nagging lectures,' he said.

I had one foot on the gas pedal and the other on a hamster wheel. Paying bills and keeping up with inflation on the one hand and on the other, keeping my husband on the same page as I was.

Here's what I really wanted to tell Yasser's detractors:

Go fix your own messed-up lives.

You won't let the young woman who holds your child in her womb sit beside you because you are afraid your wife will find out.

Go scrub the self-harm cuts on your inner thigh clean because you have daddy issues.

Learn to cry into your pillow because your cousin molested you and your parents think you're an idiot for bringing it up.

I know you feel bad because you dumped the person you loved, and now you will die alone. I know. I can hear it in your voice when you tell me my life is a mess.

Go unfuck yourself.

In these years, the violence and vulgarity of words had seeped into my lexicon, and I couldn't see the pretty stuff anymore.

Yes, the split between us had happened long before this, but it was at that very moment that it crystallized. Yasser now considered me permanently domesticated, like a washing machine or a toaster, while he was the one saving the world, negotiating peace pacts and speaking for the downtrodden.

There was a betrayal here.

Where was the freedom and equality he had promised me? Where was the dignity?

It was all very convenient for him to allow me to settle into the gender role, to diminish me and toss me aside. I had no power. He had no empathy for my lack of power.

It was in my powerlessness that I felt most corrupted and corruptible.

If I had power, in some form, social or legal, Yasser would have caught a whiff of it and what I was asking for would have resulted in some change in behaviour on his part. Instead, he called me out on it and said I was the one who was not acing my wifely duties. I had graduated, but into a role that is revered in letter and puréed in spirit.

I didn't want this life.

I went to the bathroom and remembered to take a self-test pregnancy kit with me. I had been late for a while now and had thrown up enough times to suggest I was pregnant.

I silently sat on the pot and thought about Yasser's words. *People can go to the pits of hell.* It seemed to be empty bravado, without any empathy for how I felt. An attack on me, or on the world via me. There was no question of meeting me halfway.

I got off the pot, washed up and asked my mum-in-law to let me off the cooking that day because I was tired. I wasn't tired, I was disappointed, but that emotion was not permitted.

People, dear Yasser, destroy the wife of the person who gives zero damns about others. You should give a damn about people because otherwise you are the one impacted by their ostracization.

The man's social equity account balance is worth zero damns, after all. The man who struggles with human connection because of his Asperger's syndrome is the man who will have the woman in his life shamed for choosing him.

What I would love instead, is for these people to ask me how I am doing today.

THERE WAS AN IMPRISONMENT
BEFORE MINE

Bhai had applied for US chain migration for me while I was studying there, and now, fifteen years later, we were hoping I would be eligible for a green card. That would mean Yasser, our teenaged daughters and I would also be eligible to be residents in the US for five years, then perhaps even become US nationals. We got an email from the American embassy in Islamabad to appear for an interview.

We dutifully showed up. There was something about the lure of a superpower which you witnessed as an outsider, and then there was something about the lure of the superpower when you were on its inside, meshed with its working in some legal way. The latter was something we were not dumb enough to refuse, although it brought up all sorts of mixed feelings of alienation. All it took, it seemed, was capitalism for Yasser and me to drop our 'Make Pakistan Great Again' dream. But that was a different story.

Currently, I wanted to thwack Yasser on the head with my leather-soled *khussa* because he had picked a needless fight with the embassy guards outside for not letting him park in a high-security zone. Whenever he feels the pressure to behave himself, he doesn't. Despite my own annoyance, I kept repeating that everyone needed to calm down.

We were body searched. Set your belongings in a safe at the entrance of the grey monstrosity of a building. Shoes off. Pass through security gates. Me. Then Yasser. The girls. Shoes on. Here are your security badges. Do not take them off at any time. This way. Wait here. Do not cross the red line. Wait. Follow me. Wait here. Sit.

The waiting room was sterile. Breathe. Just breathe. You have a home here. There is no need to be nervous.

Finally, the four of us stood awkwardly staring at our own reflections in the bomb-proof, double-glazed window with a microphone that allowed us to hear the officer who would ask us questions and then snap—we were either in or out. If you pressed your face against the window, you could see the humdrum of an office on the other side. There was a chair with a high back-support waiting for someone to sit on it.

A US federal immigration officer has power. We had seen them drunk on it during visa applications and we were shit scared. Half-wanting to quit, and half-wanting to stay and not be pegged as immigrants.

A Bradley Cooper look-alike appeared before me and I found myself smiling back at him gently, trying to look genuine. Yasser cannot smile. It's an Asperger's thing. He says it makes his face look too toothy. I'm not sure what the girls were up to. They were behind me.

Zoe and Zainy wore fashionable jeans and T-shirts with the latest fads emblazoned on them. Born in modern Lahore, very Pakistani and rather well globe-trotted, they found the whole exercise rather amusing. I could imagine that the immigration interviews were meh for them. They refused to hold the file with our original documents in it—properties, degrees, affidavits and the rest. They wanted as little to do with this as possible.

The Cooper doppelgänger tested his mic by tapping it with his index finger.

'Who is the primary applicant?' he asked.

'I am.' I stepped closer to the window, Yasser close behind me, clutching the file of documents so tightly that I could feel the tension in his forearms in mine.

'And what do you do?' he asked.

'I am the corporate affairs director of a Dutch-based telecom company. I also worked for the United States Agency for International Development (USAID) for about six years,' I replied. He nodded at that detail. Sifted through some papers on his desk. Clicked on his computer trackpad and squinted though his glasses at a large, liquid-crystal-display (LCD) screen that only he could see.

He looked at us.

'That's a bold haircut,' he said to Zainy.

She smiled shyly and tucked a strand behind her ear. She had a pixie cut at the time, very Audrey Hepburn. It suited her. Although I did wish she had brushed her hair better.

'Thanks, but no one in school cares,' she said.

'That's too bad. What do you want to do in the United States?' he asked.

'I'm not sure, but I'm guessing design school, because I like digital sketching,' she said.

He looked behind Zainy at Zoe.

'How about you? What do you want to study in the United States?' he asked.

'My uncle wants me to be a computer engineer. So, I guess that's settled. I'm also kind of good at that stuff. Maybe from

Massachusetts Institute of Technology (MIT) or even CalTech,' she said.

Good job, I thought to myself.

'Isn't that three-piece suit too hot for this weather?' he asked Yasser with a slight smirk.

'Yeah, it makes me feel confident,' Yasser said, using the pompous voice he used when he was in court. Formal and very unnecessary. I winced. I had told him to take it easy and here he was, playing the grand duke.

'Sir, when was the last time you entered the United States?'

'About six months ago, for my human rights fellowship at Harvard Law School. I was on a J1 visa,' Yasser said.

'That's interesting. You don't get many people like that around here. So, pardon me for asking since this isn't about your case, but, um what was the fellowship about?' he asked.

'I don't mind your asking. It was about researching the ways in which the Ahmedi community can find a way to secure their Constitutional rights in Pakistan as it becomes increasingly theocratic,' Yasser replied.

'Okay. Not a popular topic?'

'Not at all. I like to answer questions that no one is asking,' Yasser said.

'That's impressive. Anyway, your case is straightforward, but I have to ask you some boring questions, if you don't mind.'

We nodded.

Bradley Cooper went over some terms. Speed-read though some questions Yasser answered. Clicked on the computer. Question. Click. Question. Click. And then . . .

'Have you found yourself breaking any laws during your various stays in the United States?' he asked Yasser.

'Yes,' Yasser said.

Silence.

No click.

Bradley Cooper rotated his entire self along with his high-backed chair to look at Yasser. He looked almost disappointed.

'I'll repeat that. Have you found yourself breaking any laws during your various stays in the United States?'

'Yes.'

An uncomfortably long pause. The kids looked at their shoes.

I looked straight at the glass.

'All right then. In that case, I'm going to have to ask you to fill out this new form. I'll need you to answer these questions: was there more than one incident?'

'No.'

'What year was this incident?' '1997.'

'What was the charge?'

'I violated a restraining order.' 'What were the circumstances?'

'This happened when I was at college in New Jersey. At the time, a love interest had rejected me. After being unceremoniously dumped by her, I decided that she had made a mistake and went over to her place to convince her otherwise. She filed for a restraining order. At seventeen, I was terribly heartbroken that she would refuse to see me. Unaware that you cannot go convincing people to take you back if they have broken up with you, I kept crying out for her at her door. She called the police on me.'

'Were you restrained or in custody?' 'In custody . . . for about eight hours.' 'Where were you held?'

'New Brunswick county jail.' 'Was there a hearing?'

'Yes, there was.'

'What happened there?'

'I was let go, of course, after some hours of community service. There was some anger-management training too.'

I thought I heard the girls mutter 'thug life' under their breath and giggle.

'Would you say the broken heart healed well?' Yasser looked back at us. His eyes softened. 'Yes, I'd say it healed well.'

More typing. More clicks.

Bradley Cooper had the all-in-a-day's-work look on his face. 'Understandably, the process is no longer straightforward, thanks to the broken-heart situation. Now several US departments will be notified to carry out further investigations to corroborate your husband's story—this may take months, years, decades. However, if you so choose, you can separate your paperwork from his, and you and the girls have a better chance of getting through earlier. Would you like to separate your application from his?'

'No, thank you, I'd like to apply together as a family. I don't mind the delay,' I replied.

'Good luck to you as the primary applicant, ma'am.' 'Thank you.'

We were ushered back to our car. We returned our badges and retrieved our cell phones. It was a five-minute walk to our car parked in the high-security zone. Yasser had been relentless with the guards and in the end, they had let him park where he wanted to park.

I sighed and rested my head on the headrest. The girls were imitating Yasser's exaggerated British accent—*Yes, my lord I have indeed broken the supreme law; therefore, I must now offer you my fanny.*

All I wanted was a nap.

YASSER KILLED ME SOFTLY
WITH HIS SONG

Yamini Pramanik waltzed into my life by way of a middle finger that I first saw in one of Yasser's photos. It was a picture I gazed at for hours because the longer I looked, the more my nausea grew. Something was wrong. While I was all the way here, my husband, with a fresh traumatic brain injury (TBI), was hanging out with someone who nauseated me. This was bad.

Yasser went to Harvard for his law fellowship, that I paid for. The fact that he had made his way to Yamini by way of the funding provided by me was a betrayal I took personally. It almost felt like I had led my husband to adultery by being brave, courageous and self-sacrificing, by putting his dreams and needs before mine.

After Yasser's first surgery in 2017, all I wanted to do was to curl into him. The world was frightening from within, and Yasser's beating heart was the only thing that helped me feel secure. So, when the fellowship he had applied for before the surgery came in, it made sense to opt for the show-must-go-on approach.

He didn't want to go, but I thought giving him the will to live was more important than my notions of romance. I read on the brain tumour-society page that recovery is aided by pursuits of meaning. So, I put everything in. I hand-delivered him to the woman I loathe.

My therapist says it is easier for me to hate her than him. Yamini dominates my therapy sessions. She became the metaphor for my stupidity, loss and self-pity. She helped me crash teeth-first on to a granite floor off a cliff in a canyon.

I was colossally metaphored by her finger, which, as the universe would have it, was for me, my idea of love and my love of love. That was the beginning of the end. The end of romance. One would think I was a big girl, but it turned out that I was a little girl after all, with outdated notions of long-term relationships. I thought my nationalism-fortified relationship would protect my marriage, but the fact that an Indian tore down those walls was, let's admit it, slightly dramatic, albeit historically accurate.

Yamini also went by the sobriquet YamYam, and had the gall to sermonize me on how to be a woman when I finally confronted her.

Both tell me that there was no sex involved in Bill-Clinton-esque confessions, but how two adults are supposed to have a platonic affair is a bit incredible. Maybe I would make a better homewrecker than her. To wreck a home and get bad sex out of it, or even no sex, seems pathetic. This was the realm of my ego-wreck because I always felt that if anyone had the licence to cheat in this marriage, it was most definitely me.

While I made my way to discovering the truth, I was taken through a rollercoaster of lies and conspiracies. It was no longer Yasser and me against the world, it was Yasser and YamYam against me. I felt mugged.

Together, they got off on small things like my promising to send her Lahore's best *khussas* because she had admired mine on Instagram. I knew this because I hacked Yasser's phone and found their chats about almost everything under the sun—their cigarette breaks at Harvard, their thoughts about a mutual colleague, the sky, Nargis from Bollywood and her songs and, most upsetting, my girls.

Sixty days after Yasser's first surgery in 2017, he had to make up his mind about going to Boston for a fellowship in law and human rights at the Harvard Law School. Despite the trauma, I insisted he go because I knew it meant a lot to him. If he delayed it, I didn't know whether he would live long enough to realize his dream. He had survived the surgery, and even if this would be a struggle logistically and cognitively, he would come out the other end a Harvard Fellow.

I funded the trip and even left my £450-a-day consulting job to drop him in Boston, pay his rent and settle him in. It was a cute trip to Cambridge, Massachusetts—a kind of a mini honeymoon. Yasser was hesitant, confused and excited, but his steroids and high doses of anti-epileptics kept him glued together. When we reached Cambridge, we slept for a solid fourteen hours, ate at an Italian pizza joint where the owner took a liking to me and promised to take care of Yasser when I left. Quick to make friends, I told him our saga and he shed a tear for our love, devotion and ultimate sacrifice for family and education. 'I'll take care of him and fatten him up, don't you worry,' he said to me. I left him good tips and, in exchange, he gave me nothing but endless joy and the feel of a family Christmas.

I wonder to this day if Yasser ever took Ms Pramanik to this pizza joint, and if he slept with her like he slept with me that first day in Cambridge—for fourteen hours, intertwined. No sex, of course, for either of us. How can a man, barely keeping it together after brain surgery and convalescence, think of anything but the essential functions, right?

I found out that Yasser was in love with her when he was back in my arms in Islamabad—safe and sound and with a wonderful thesis on how to give constitutional rights to victims of religious persecution in Pakistan. I broke into his email where he had sent her a song on YouTube the night before. The song was: '*Dum bharr jo idher mu phere, oh Chanda, mai tumsay pyar kar lungi, batain hazar kar lungi*'.

The song was about the joy of stealing love by the light of the moon.

That email was accompanied by a one-liner: Don't say anything, just understand.

The Lata Mangeshkar song was sung in the film by the iconic heroine Nargis. My mind is a blank on the title of the song or how it went, but there was a moon in it. The moon had to hide its face in the clouds so that the lovers could unite. There was also a boat, as there are in so many love songs. Waves and water, of course.

There was a lot of water.

While I was asleep, Ms Pramanik had responded to that email, rather lyrically. 'I understand,' she wrote, 'there is a secret language.'

I knew that secret languages evolve only after much declaration of love, trust and self-respect.

I don't understand how the body doesn't declare loyalty. I would think we become more committed to those who have given us nursing care in times of crisis. But no, the body is disloyal. It betrays you with sex. It betrays you even without sex—by seeking a connection outside of those who stood by you when you couldn't help but pee outside the toilet during post-operation care.

This is my jealousy speaking.

If I could, I would make chutney of Ms Pramanik. Then I'd sprinkle her remains on Yasser, like confetti. All the while, I would be chanting, 'Walrus, walrus, walrus.'

That is my rage speaking.

Instead, when I actually found out about it, I wrote her an email. Rather, I forwarded her an email I sent Yasser after I felt betrayed by him. I forwarded her a chain of emails between Yasser and myself. The email to Yasser began with '*Dear Chutiya . . .*'

It went on to number a few choice bullet points to insult his mom, to tell him that I was finally free of this marriage and that there would be a lawyer involved. I forwarded her the email. I also added more bullet points to make it clear that my fight was not with her, it was with Yasser.

As an aspiring feminist, I was not going to make her the target of my rage—Yasser was, as were his choices. I told her that I looked forward to meeting both her and her husband, and that we should remain cordial. Having written that, I added that she should be aware that she had callously destroyed my painstaking efforts.

She wrote back instantly to say that she was grocery shopping and that no 'self-respecting woman' would put up with what Yasser had put me through.

Even as I wept, parked in the parking lot of the Islamabad Marriott, I found her remark strange. Why would you condemn the very person who had just tanked his own marriage, complete with two young daughters, for you? I replied that Yasser had had only good things to say about her. He was, I said, even willing to fight with me and gaslight me every time I suggested that she had any ill intentions.

I'm done buying groceries, she wrote back, but now that I have read the whole conversation beneath your email to me, I can only reiterate what I said before, that you should not be with a man this horrific. That is, of course, only if you are 'a woman in possession of her self-respect'. She then added, 'I've been embarrassed by

Yasser's self-centred behaviour, where he plagiarized my ideas and published them in a newspaper's opinion editorial.'

'I'm sorry you feel plagiarized,' I replied. 'I know what it is like to have something you love, like a precious thing that you made and loved and nurtured, be snatched away from you.'

'Anyone with self-respect would understand,' she replied.

You see, I was understandably distressed. It was true, everything that I felt at the time about Yasser. I had stood in the operation theatre, in charge of all the questions of life, all the calls to make on medication, travel and aftercare. It takes a toll when you have a life in your hands, regardless of whether the decisions go your way or not. That is the toll I was referring to when I told Ms Pramanik about loving someone. It wasn't about respect at all. It was about doing the hardest thing in the world, taking a call on saying yes to surgery, despite a 13 per cent risk of death, coma, paralysis, stroke or being left in a vegetative state. When you are dealing with a 13 per cent chance of your children's father dying and you still give your assent to something, that person has the emotional onus to be the warmth of a fire in a cold cave, or a baby's toes in the arms of a barren woman.

I was talking about living through some of life's hardest and most unimaginable things. She was talking about the kind of things I could find in the white people's self-help section: self-respect.

Listen, I don't have the bandwidth to deal with your marital issues and whatnot. I have my own marriage to deal with.

I have all your messages and texts to my husband downloaded, I slammed back. Man, I smirked, that was a shitload of bandwidth with which you came on to Yasser, engaged in a romantic affair (no sex, of course) and then, having alerted my suspicion, you proceeded to advise him to delete the bandwidth along with everything else.

She did not address that observation. I guess no self-respecting woman would.

What was I doing? What was the point of winning this self-respect contest now?

What mattered was that Yasser, who had been so overwhelming smitten once upon a time by me, had lied to me like a weasel. I was shattered. I was humiliated. In fact, I was annihilated.

Yasser had broken me down many times and often. Once the scuffle ended up with a black eye. I went to the doctor. *An elbow accidentally rammed into my eye.* The doctor had looked at my blue-brown eye, swollen to the extent that the eyelids was a mere slit, generously engorged with blood, looking like an overripe eggplant.

'I see,' he had said sarcastically, 'An elbow accidentally entered your eye and left you almost blind.'

'Yes,' I had retorted defiantly.

Yasser had already broken my tooth, but you know that. But did you know that he had also broken my hip and my jaw, not to mention the neck-hinges. But he had never lied to me.

Until now.

Yasser had acquired a whole new skill and I hadn't even known. The Ms Pramanik episode happened right after his surgery. He became hers and I felt rather badly about being replaced. I imagine working mothers feel this way when their child walks for the first time and they aren't home. In healing Yasser, I re-parented him. The child was thriving, no sex yet, of course, but like any over-protective parent, I was upset to realize that I was no longer needed.

You see, until now, Yasser had needed me so much that I secretly wished that he would die. He needed me for his meds. After his seizure, he needed me to go take a piss. He needed me to tell him he could publish his article without something bad happening to our daughters. He needed me when his intrusive thoughts had to be slain with the sword of my reason. I would explain to him that there was a connection between his thoughts and his deeds, and that if he thought something was wrong, the deed mustn't happen. Yasser needed me to help him fall asleep. Please play with my hair so I can stop overthinking, he would tell me. When you touch me, the world stops expanding and I can rest.

He even needed me to help him set up shop in Boston during the fellowship. I created a comfortable situation for him in an apartment in Somerville, where a windmill would spin when it started snowing. His roommate was a Jewish guy who hugged me and promised to take care of him while I went back to our lives without him. We named a skirted lamp in his room after me so he would miss me less and I'd be a godlike presence watching over him. I did joke about his not being able to bring a girl to the room while I was away, thanks to lamp-Aisha. He had joked back, 'When did a lamp ever stop a man?'

They say the best caregivers are those who have struggled with their needs being met as young kids. Here I was, making sure Yasser had enough white oats in the pantry so he would not need to go to Wal-Mart, that his meds were in a pill dispenser and his socks were arranged by colour, so laundry could be done once a week. I left him enough money to hire a maid.

Where can I find a mop?

That was Yasser's first Twitter update from Boston.

I think of YamYam's middle finger as a premonition of things to come. Maya Angelou said that when someone shows you who they are, believe them. No friend would do that. Friends don't waltz into friends' lives and look at them as defragmented, two-dimensional beings, independent of their familial structure.

That is how I first learned she existed—she was just a middle finger.

But soon, my curiosity grew. The last time Yasser was this excited about someone was one mild, office affair and before that, it was me.

Everything reeked of a deep, propane-heady danger—an explosion waiting to happen. My hyper-clairvoyance was on turbo, crunching away but without necessarily understanding the direction from which the bad thing would come. I had no Aisha Sarwari of my own to call, to tell me that my worst fears had come true, to hand me a sword to slay my anxiety. Women like me, we have no one. We don't even have ourselves, because we're already giving so much to others, like our tormentors, our lovers, our children and our bosses. But I have never had anyone to say to me: Aisha, it'll be okay.

There was never anyone to look me in the eye and say: *Yasser is yours. He will not betray you. He will always need you.*

He will squeeze the toothpaste tube from the bottom just as you like it. He will post playful pictures of you. He is full of mischief and joy now because he is in the US and it reminds him of his younger, carefree, college self. He is simply recreating coping strategies so he can miss you less.

Remember when he told you that you had poisoned everything in Boston. Your presence there with him made him miss you achingly, and now he avoids those places. It wasn't a mini honeymoon for him as it was for you. Let him self-soothe, Aisha. He will come back to you, sans a tumour. A brand-new Yasser 2.0. Your home and your life will be complete. Everything will be okay, Aisha.

I would have listened to this voice—a creepy, Woody Allen kind of voice. There may have been lingering doubts, but I would've been able to use that age-old tool of the South Asian woman: ignore the threat of danger.

But I was an evolved brown woman. Instead all I heard were relationship sirens.

Ms Pramanik got Yasser cigarettes and a maid to clean the house and his room. Probably there were oats involved, but I am made to believe that there was no sex. What do I think she is? A brown woman with self-respect.

When he was back from the airport, Yasser told me that he was sorry for constraining me. I should feel more liberated, he said.

I think she had got him Quaker oats too.

I reacted like a wife would: I befriended her. She pretended to befriend me. Later, I discovered that everything I ever said to her was passed on to Yasser and notes were exchanged. She was patronizing me. Here were scholars and elite lawyers, and here was this third-rate phony they were all tolerating for the sake of the kids. I tell you this, this was one of the most traumatic out-of-body experiences I ever had. I watched myself being referred to as someone with deductive reasoning, who apparently needed to have more self-respect. As if I were floating in and out of a life they had built, I was on the outside looking in.

I hadn't known this until now, but I was very afraid of being abandoned by Yasser. Yes, I wanted out. But I also wanted to be honoured for staying put. It was all very paradoxical and confusing for someone who hadn't had their arse handed to them every day for a few decades.

YamYam attacked me on Twitter. 'I want her off your Twitter now,' I said to Yasser.

'I agree with her point,' he said.

I paused to moisten my mouth, which felt as dry as sand.

Words hurt.

'I didn't have an opinion to go with the article I posted, an article written by another author. It was a link for discussion,' I said, defensive and teary-eyed.

'Well then, she is discussing it and she disagrees with the author, as do I.'

'She called my reasoning "deductive and embarrassing"; how could you be a silent bystander?' I demanded.

'Because, as I said, I agree with her point,' he replied.

'I don't care about the point of the article. Why would she feel compelled to get into a preaching argument with me on my wall without invitation while you just sit and watch?' I asked.

'You don't know her like I do. She is argumentative and gets real specific about facts. She did the same thing to me in Harvard.'

'I don't care. I don't care about the points you are making. I care about how I feel about her, and she should not have done that to a "friend's wife",' I retorted.

He was distressed by now, the same distress he has on his face when I argue with his mom. I know this about his romantic disposition—it is inclined toward motherly, nurturing and care-giving women.

He telephoned YamYam and told her that I was upset and that she should delete her comments on my Twitter. But she dug her heels in and said I should suck it up . . . or something like that.

I knew then that whatever I was afraid of had happened.

That Woody Allen voice in my head was a first-rate liar. Yasser didn't come back to me. He came back with her. He left himself in Boston. Whichever way it was, he wasn't mine any longer. It was the first time I experienced a loss of self in such a permanent way. I was stripped bare by autumn. It was a long, cold winter, made colder by the realization that Yasser had left me before I could leave him.

No matter how you spun it, I was always the other woman.

There was no home to go to any more. A roof is a roof. It protects you from the cosmic expanse of voices in your head. I've never told Yasser this, but when I touched his hair, my world dropped dead.

There was only ever him.

Of course, the day I found out about Yasser's affair with Yamini was a momentous one, no doubt, but even more definitive was the day Yasser shut down my song.

Somewhere in the third year of the pandemic, between my third Covid-19 recovery and a work deadline, the girls, Yasser and I decided to make a trip down to the grocery store. As is tradition, we all get a song each. I played a Reshma je song called 'Mainu Tu'. Yasser wanted it shut down, saying that it was weepy and pathetic. I protested that it was not. He insisted that it really triggered him. Zoe said it was arse cancer. Zainy agreed.

He explained that Reshma je's grating voice was a disgrace. I stopped playing the song.

My heart felt constricted and the tears, cold but warming me inside, surged out like waves. Maybe I was PMS-ing. Maybe it was because I could never get over the metaphor of asking me to stop playing my song. Maybe it was because I always measured Yasser's love for me by the speed with which he discarded me for that other woman. Maybe it was because I listened to Reshma's songs only because it buoyed me enough to stop choking on a very sad and lonely existence. That evening, the three loves of my life played their songs: Zoe played Punjabi MC, Zainy played a song from *Hamilton* the musical and Yasser played Linkin Park's 'In the End'.

I dropped Yasser off to the home I rented for him and his mom. He chose to stay on for her. I went home to the other apartment that I rented.

Yamini helped me learn the fact that Yasser would not chase me one block away to the apartment where I lived with the girls.

Yamini helped me learn that I was the other.

Yamini helped me give up on other people's songs and look for my own.

YASSER, THE TUMOUR AND
I SHARED A BED

When a transgender woman called Alesha was left to bleed out in the ward of Lady Reading Hospital in Peshawar, her death became enmeshed with my life—exactly at the point where a crack in my universe had appeared. She belonged to so many places at once and to none at all, like me. She had many births and many deaths, just like me.

Alesha's successful resurrections and failed resurrections defined everything that is wrong with a society that doles out power based on gender roles.

In an ideal world, I would be married to Yasser, but not compelled to live with him. We would have separate bathrooms and then slowly graduate to having separate rooms. I have one of my own upstairs. I've already started working towards a me that has no Yasser in it.

My mom taught me to never separate the marital bed, to always sleep together. Never take quarrels to bed, she warned. 'Sort things out while you're cuddling in bed, before falling asleep.'

In what used to be dominant Punjabi culture, men made their wives sleep on the floor. At best, the women were given a bed in a separate room. In fact, an elder in a friend's family once bragged about his riches and blessings, precisely because the wife was kept away from the man's bed.

Conversely, I was horrified at the thought of a married couple sleeping in separate beds, unless of course, their marriage had been annulled. I believe I was only four when someone suggested my chacha and *chachi* use my room during a visit. My room had two single beds and my chachi was a bit overweight, so I gave my counsel by screaming, 'But they are married and need one bed!'

So, it was unthinkable that Yasser and I slept separately for even one night, but it was necessary after the tumour came to live with us. Yasser's behaviour was erratic, yes, but something else had broken: a fissure right through the centre of my universe.

I hope you die.

You have punished me all my life for something I stopped doing thirteen years ago.

You are a nasty woman.

Everyone has left you because of who you are. Everyone cannot be wrong in hating you.

I regret marrying you.

And so, after Yasser's tumour was diagnosed, I found myself a bogeyman. The tumour was a way to debunk the myth that I was a bad woman corrupted by Western influence. A woman with too much freedom. A maverick.

So, by those standards, I ought not to have taken his words to heart, however, every word that Yasser uttered after the diagnosis was a poison-tipped spear. When it lodged in my chest, it hurt. As I heal after yanking it out, I almost miss its ache.

The first day that I slept away from Yasser while we were in the same room was when the babies were little. He said it made no sense for two people to stay awake when both had to work the next day. As wise as that was, I stayed awake all night, even when the kids were asleep. I knew what sleeping away from one's husband meant. It meant that I was on my own in a hostile country and a hostile home, where everyone saw me as an attention whore. I was less powerful.

Alesha died. Fine. But she took with her a version of me: an Aisha. She defined for me how people who don't belong eventually end up, after a very long road of trying to belong. She took me with her into that crevice in the universe. They didn't just fail to save Alesha. They killed her on the sword points of their archaic values.

In seeing how things turned out for her, I was staring into the soul of my bleak future.

Power came from the man and the man had bought into the philosophy that the *zanana* or women-only chambers, must fulfil its desired role away from the *mardana* male-only chambers. So rigid are these bifurcations that Alesha bled to death in hospital corridors, because no one could figure out which ward to treat her in. She died because patients from both wards complained about her presence being a breach of their privacy. These patients—some on their own death beds— expelled her from their wards because she broke a code which they considered sacred. The natural order must prevail. It gave them a sense of control. Control trumps everything, even the saving of a life.

This is Pakistan. This is the place I call home. This is the place where I live. This is where I belong. I call these people mine. This is how parts of me are split like pieces of paper in a shredder—in order to belong, I, too, have to be sliced.

But as a woman, I graze at the bottom of the food chain. This is who I am. Yasser allows me to move from the zanana ward to the mardana ward. Yasser gives me status. With him, I am tagged. I belong. There is a place for me in the universe of things.

Why is the marital bed so Yamini-ized? What negotiations take place in the white linen and feather pillows that cannot take place elsewhere?

In every household, there is deep permeability. Everything echoes, from whispered voices to the flush of the toilet. You cannot conspire or keep secrets without being exposed in the harsh light of day. The seductress has full access to the ears of the man of the house in the bedroom, over or under the sheets. There is something she has that he needs. So, anyone in her in-laws' house can spite the wife during the day, but she can retaliate by turning the man of the house—your son—against you. If the wife has the smarts, she gets what she wants. In the end, the boy can be lured by sex, and turn against blood. If that's the case, you're the one who's who needs to worry.

The bedroom is the only place where the zanana and the mardana merge. The only place where power is transferred from a man's manliness to a woman's womanliness. Women get a taste of patriarchy. Some never recover from it. The power of mundane secrets, petty squabbles and defiance is intoxicating because they are accompanied by character judgements. However, women die. Death is the natural order of things.

I may have been unaware of this power I wielded but when I was put in my place often enough by my new family, I recognized that they wanted to clip something I might have.

No one knows whether you have power over your man in the bedroom. I may have been pregnant soon after, and then again soon after that, but it still says nothing about a woman's ability— my ability—to trade sex for social equity.

Did Yasser really desire me? Had he always desired me? How did I remain relevant to his desire? What could I do to win his attention back? I was not trained in this art. The home and the bedroom were places that I went to when I wanted to feel like I mattered, to be caressed after a bad day—not to broker power.

I felt that I was competing for my space in Yasser's headspace, where there was a permanent bedroom. Where he was in charge of his own thoughts and could curate his own desires. There was no playbook for that either.

My jealous rage against Yasser's interest in modern pin-ups like white porn, was born of my deepest insecurity: I wanted to be the white woman any desi boy wanted. My brown sexuality was designed by the male gaze in all its perversions—the breach of consent, the presence of exploitation, the thrill of escalating violence and a manicured perfection that looked nothing like what is portrayed in the porn industry.

The further a representation of sexuality was from me, the closer it was to my idea of ideal sex. Therefore the more elusive it remained, the sadder I was. They say the opposite of sadness is vitality. A brown woman's lack of sexual empowerment is far from life-affirming. It is sick and cyanosed.

As a near middle-aged woman, the earlier perfection is no longer exciting to me. The lack of representation in sexual content is a political foe. I am no longer insecure—at least, not completely. Yasser's desire for me no longer defines me. I've lost his interest, regained it and again lost it out of my own accord; there now it rests, latent for the taking, if life permits.

When I was young and beautiful, people thought Yasser's desire powered me. They were wrong. Young people know nothing about good sex. Now that I am older, fewer heads turn.

Now people think that the desire Yasser once had powers me. Wrong again.

As the wife of the cancer patient who isn't getting a dirty look from her husband, I am now suspect for being on the prowl. Alternatively, I am seen as a strong woman of faith who has circumvented the need to be wanted sexually by a man. They say I hang on and that is somehow noble. It's not.

I'm absolutely sexually frustrated and very bad company and yes, I've been known to even ogle trees. There is nothing wrong with the raw truth of wanting intimacy and sex, especially when the person you want it from is fighting for his life, sanity and status.

Something outside the bedroom keeps Yasser and me together. I never would have imagined that what desi culture defines as the epitome of female seduction was, in reality, so pathetic and ephemeral. One small dent and it's splintered.

A big part of the way I now see myself is as a survivor of that horrific notion—it consumed me and shattered me. I rejected the idea that a happy marriage rests in the bed where bodies combine.

I pieced myself back together by recognizing that it's okay if the bed is not where I am to find my identity. I did not belong in the seductress's club, but neither was I taken in by the virtue of a celibate woman's dead sexual desire. I am a woman with a voracious appetite for sexual intimacy and no, I have no idea how to convert it to social currency by manipulating a man's needs. I have failed grandly and with absolute finality on both counts. Like Alesha, the binaries have rejected me. Like Alesha, I have bled out. It hurts like hell when a man doesn't desire you back enough or entirely or always. I learnt that it meant that I wasn't doing enough. I had to amend myself.

Being evicted from the marital bed threatened me. Yasser desiring me less, or not at all, was that eviction?

More frightening than that was the fear that this tiny piece of information would be revealed to the world and his neighbour.

If people knew that Yasser's love is not constant, would I even be worthy of love?

I really haven't grown up to think of a woman as respect worthy if her husband thinks she isn't.

Yasser's marriage to me, symbolized by the marital bed, gave me not just status but oxygen. How does a Muslim girl like me, now a woman, go back into the world without that status?

Going by the gold standard of societal perception, I hate that there have been two phases of my married life: my husband's raw desire for me, and his complete lack of desire for me.

This is where patriarchy colossally gets things wrong. In its control freakery, it forgets that, just as Yasser has his own brain where thoughts are free to roam, I have one too. In fact, mine is more secluded—behind the shadowy canopy that divides the happily married woman from the unhappily married woman.

The mind of a married woman is nothing like that of a married man. Her mind is fresh. It has everything a salad has—air and salt, crunch and perishability. Her head is free of sexual inhibitions in the real sense so the objects of her desire are poetically imperfect. They are there because they want to be there, not because they are being paid, filmed or have no alternative escape. It is an honest place. If I were patriarchy, I too would be shit-scared. There is no way of controlling absolute freedom, it is absolutely incorruptible.

This world in my head turns me on, but it's a world where I am safe from being called a *randi*.

I've taken everything that culture has permitted to men, and I have permitted it to myself in this world that no one can reach.

In this dream space, I am as I am in real life: perishable. This is a home, not a house. There is a lime-green roof, a huge, tree-filled yard which opens out into the forest and these men's wives are tending to our communal kids, making sure that they are safe, that their meals are on time, that no little kid sticks his fingers in electrical sockets and no teenage kid smokes pot behind the kitchen. I'm grateful to these women. They are my friends. Some of them know that I'm with their men but they play along because they blindly trust their husbands.

I would do the same for them, so withhold your judgement. If someone came up with such a beautiful escape plan from patriarchy, I would support them too. Where is the solidarity? Where is the ultimate goal we all fight for—the right to pleasure, often and much.

There is no patriarchy in this green-roofed utopia. Men ogle me lasciviously at times and at other times with a pure cuddle hormone drive, just tenderness. My head doesn't have the registrar's office, so there are many people who inhabit its deep desires, all of whom are free to come and go as they please. Often these men choose to stay. Yasser is only a part of that harem—one of many. He can also choose to come and go as he pleases but here, in my head, he's eternally blissful with my happiness.

When these fictitious but real boys are not tending to my fantasies, they are fixing their shoelaces before they head out to office, playing the grand piano, researching law or practising quantum math in the common library. Yasser lives in this joint-family system (go along with it) in my mind's eye, often smoking a cigar, seated on a sofa, looking on half-approvingly at this world of mine.

Are they jealous of my shared time and shared affections, or of each other? No, because I desire them differently but I am affectionate the exact same amount towards each of them. I don't play favourites.

I escape to this place when I am in my actual marital bed and my anti-depressants don't allow me to play with fireworks. Yasser's on his side of the bed, Netflixing.

To have a fantasy, you must first have a home to dream it from. Yasser is, and always will be, in every version of mine.

OUR TINY VACATION HOME

You can only sleep with someone you trust enough not to kill you when your guard is down. This means especially when you're awake and your guard is up.

Yasser trusted me with his life when he was convalescing.

On my thirty-ninth birthday, we stood looking out of the window of our friend's apartment, blinking in the bright sun. Our friends, Kiran and George, had been kind enough to lend us this wonderfully cosy place on Karsaz Road in Karachi where almost no one was poor, not even the passers-by. In Karachi, the city of 21 million crazy souls, wealth matters.

Kiran's father had recently passed away with multiple sclerosis. His hospital bed and his intravenous-therapy (IV) pole were still there. This was before the awake craniotomy could even take place. As we entered the apartment, the pall of Uncle's death loomed over us, sometimes with the smell of iodine and angry antiseptic and at other times, with the chart that allowed him to blink at what he wanted Kiran to do. This chart was rather interesting. The bottom right corner read, 'Go away! And leave me alone.'

Yasser did not feel that about me. During his first surgery, he accused me of trying to kill him by giving him the wrong meds.

This time, however, he let me in all the way. For some reason, this broke me into a few billion pieces of sand.

This home on Karsaz Road was Uncle's home, and although he had died there, I felt he was with us, telling us that all would be well. A dead man can be a consoling force. When I would do my yoga, cry in the bathroom, shower, help myself to a binge eating session at 2 a.m. or when I'd be gazing out through the window, smoking with Yasser, he seemed to say to us, 'All is well.' Yasser took a drag on the cigarette which I had broken into four quarters because cancer kills, and puffed on it like he was orgasming. From his right ear to the anterior fontanelle somewhere near the middle of his head, a gash had been sawn open, and stitched up again for the second time. It was covered with plain gauze—the same kind I would put on my daughters when they scraped their knees. Staples held everything in place. I couldn't help but stare at this marvel of science.

'What are you looking at?' His lips quivered involuntarily as he asked me the question.

'Nothing. Just at you coming back to me. Again.'

The other three-quarters of the cigarette had to be utilized so I puffed away too. Yasser had the side with the filter. He was the one dying so he had priority.

'Do you want to give me your last puff?' His lips quivered even more.

I shook my head. 'No way. Without the cigarette butt, it's like smoking fire. Not worth it.'

'You said, "butt."'

'Very mature.' We smiled, everything forgotten.

We threw the last of our cigarette butts on top of the air conditioner's outdoor unit. A few hundred butts rested there like a butt graveyard. Cigarette butts and pigeon poop.

Later, Yasser waltzed into our bedroom.

We had taken the room without any bed because I was afraid Yasser would fall and hurt his head. The first thing they tell you after a brain tumour operation is, don't hurt your head. Seventy per cent of brain tumour patients end up dead because they become stupid or careless or self-harm-y. It's amazing how much the most obvious advice is ignored. So, Yasser was to sleep on the floor.

Yasser's face looked like it did when I caught him cheating with Ms Pramanik.

'What have you done?' I asked.

'Shut up.' He was abrupt, awkward. Desperately trying to be authoritative.

'Why is your mouth white?' 'Pigeon poop.' Pause.

I was really disappointed. 'We had a deal.'

'Well, consider revising upwards to half a cigarette. A quarter feels like eating arse.' He disappeared into the toilet.

I could see Uncle watching us from the sofa, newspaper in hand. He wasn't the reassuring old man this time. He seemed to asking with his eyes, 'Why did you let him?'

Three days later, I dragged Yasser back into the Intensive Care Unit (ICU) for severe dehydration. In a bid to get him back to health, I had asked my aunt to cook some minced meat for him. When Yasser had eaten that, nothing stayed down, not even the oral rehydration salts in his favourite flavour. He puked on almost all the floors in the house, apologizing endlessly between vomiting bouts. Eventually, he felt so bad for making me clean up after him that he moved Uncle's reading chair to the bathroom sink. He was wearing a yellow T-shirt, against which his skin was a teal green. It was like a sad painting that should have been in the Louvre.

As I watched him, I had a random thought.

Why don't people frame loss?

Loss is so much like fear. Palpable, like sitting for a hard exam and being sure the results will suck no matter what you do; time is linear, and you will find out that you failed. There is no possibility of mercy. Someone should frame that moment. That year, in May 2020, the novel coronavirus had overtaken the world. A global pandemic was raging but my love had relocated down the sinkhole, while I watched along with Uncle's silent spectre.

Still, never for a moment did Yasser react to my insane nagging to have a sip of water by snapping go away and leave me alone.

He just kept saying *Aishi. Aishee. Aaaishii.*

I wanted something potent to drown my own sorrows, my constantly aching head and my stomach which felt like pebbles in a riverbed. The first time Yasser underwent surgery, a friend baked me marijuana brownies. I would have two at one go, even though he had prescribed only half for a day. If I had had them this time around, I'd stuff some in my eyes and ears too. But I didn't have anyone to bake me brownies this time. I didn't have anything to quiet the rumbling sense of wanting to run far away—to the Cayman Islands, never to return again.

So instead of pot brownies, I worked on my faith. I kept massaging Yasser's feet and praying. The *Surah Fateha* and the *Chaar Kulls*, over and over again, more than all the cigarette butts in the universe. I knew the fear of loss was upon me, but I prayed for mercy.

Mercy. Mercy. Mercy.

Day three from the day of the second surgery was the worst. I called my friend: 'Shall I take him to Aga Khan Hospital? Yasser hasn't had any water or food in three days, and he is very nauseous. He will die here if he doesn't get a drip. He's badly dehydrated.'

'What do the doctors say?' he asked.

'They aren't telling me anything clearly.'

'They have to make the call, Aisha. Not me or you. There's a pandemic out there.'

I was sobbing. 'I can't figure this out. He's too delicate. I think he may become comatose if I don't do something soon. I need someone to help me decide.'

'Only a doctor can decide. I cannot,' he said.

'I don't care if you take the wrong call but please help me decide, that's all I'm asking for. I called the hospital, but they say they can't say for sure whether he needs to be admitted,' I said.

'I can't make that call for you,' he said.

'You said call me if you need anything. This is me calling you!'

'I can't make that call for you,' he repeated.

'Well then, don't offer to help next time. Just say you're on your own,' I screamed into the phone. I was shaking.

My words felt like acid burning my mouth.

May there be a special kind of hell for people who don't help desperate people. I just needed someone to walk me though the right choice, but no one is ever there when you need them.

No one. It's just you and Yasser and a global pandemic. No one is coming to save you, Aisha. No one wants to save you. You are bad news.

The sobbing became a background noise in my life, like the hum of a water pump. Even Yasser began to ignore it.

With tears running down my cheeks, I walked back to Yasser's mattress.

'Hey, boo,' I said, brushing his matted hair gently away from his forehead.

Yasser opened his eyes. They were like a dead goat's eyes. 'The car is here. We need to go back to the hospital,' I said. He shook his head.

'I know you said no. This is a dangerous situation. You have low electrolytes.'

I spoke very slowly, enunciating every word clearly, even though I was still crying.

Yasser turned his back to me, lying on the side of his head where the surgery had taken place. 'Leave me alone,' he mumbled.

I tried again.

'I need to take you at least for an IV to Aga Khan. Let's go, Yassu.'

I tried lifting him. He was rigid under my touch, braced and ready, almost as though he was prepared for a fight. My voice, my tears, nothing would soften him. He had already decided that he wasn't going anywhere. But I had decided that Uncle wasn't going to call him to the other side. Not on my watch. I cupped his shoulders and lifted him against his will. Grounding myself like I used to do before deadlift weights in the gym.

Yasser resisted.

I now needed reinforcement.

I called for the person hired to assist me during emergencies. Gerard was 6 feet tall and although he was in his twenties, he could pass for a fifty-year-old. Poverty ages people. This was an emergency. I made Gerard sanitize his hands, wear gloves and two K95 masks.

It took a scuffle, but between the two of us, we made Yasser stand up.

'Just drag him if you must,' I told Gerard.

Gerard looked at me questioningly. Like I was the insane one. 'Take him against his will,' I said again, sobbing but firm.

We dragged a fighting Yasser to the elevator. His punches wouldn't land but even if they had, they wouldn't have hurt. I handled Yasser's head. Gerard and the driver, who had by now joined in the tussle, handled everything else. I locked the door to the apartment.

I made a mental checklist. Water bottle, check. Money, check. Phone, check. Medicine box, check. Head on the shoulders, check. Tissues for blowing snot, check. K95 mask on Yasser, check. K95 mask on me, check. K95 mask on the driver, check. Hand sanitizer, check. My own meds, check.

Why didn't I call an ambulance? you ask. Because I couldn't think straight.

Yasser was crammed into a tiny three-by-three Suzuki Mehran and wheeled into the private ward of Aga Khan Hospital. He cursed, protested and screamed the whole time. It was 41°C in Karachi that day and the unrelenting sun beat down on us. Yasser alternated between pleading piteously and issuing furious ultimatums. He flitted between consciousness and unconsciousness—it was the same drill.

I kept repeating, we have to. 'We have to. We have to. Yasser, we have to go to the hospital.'

He kept saying, leave me alone. 'Leave me alone. Leave me alone.' Then he would say, 'I have needle trauma. For god's sake, Aisha, why would you do this to me?'

'I'm sorry, Yassu, I have to.'

'I have to,' he mimicked mockingly, sounding bitter and very, very loud.

His head bumped against the roof of the tiny car as the driver tried to navigate the midday traffic. He even jumped a red light and fled from the traffic cops so that we could be rushed to safety. No one wants someone dying in their car. Remember I told you I was bad news?

All at once, as if in a time jump, the next thing I knew was that I was screaming at the top of my lungs at the hospital staff.

Yasser was in a wheelchair, weaving in and out of consciousness. All alone.

'Please! Just take him to a room. He needs help now. Please ask Dr Adnan to come and see him,' I screamed.

'Ma'am, this is not the place to take him, admissions is on the first floor,' a nurse in a white lab coat said.

Everyone looked strange in their identical, pale-blue masks. I felt confused and disoriented. My heart was in my throat. I expected everyone to stand by in a hospital's private ward, ready to rush in and help, but no one received us. There was a mix-up.

No one was listening to me and I was shouting in a private ward with critical patients—some of whom had emerged from their rooms, IV drips in tow, to see what the commotion was all about.

'I can't have him wheeled down again. Please just give him a room. This is a re-admission case, and I was asked to come straight here as a special case by Dr Adnan.'

The attendant at the reception desk looked visibly upset. 'I don't have any such instructions,' she said to me sternly.

From behind me Yasser started yelling, 'She's brought me here against my will.'

He looked like something straight from hell. His Ray-Ban sunglasses tipped drunkenly to cover only one eye. His face droopy and his speech slurred. His eyeballs travelling to the back of his head.

'My mom is a doctor. This woman is trying to kill me. She is lying about everything. She's a liar. She is trying to kill me,' he announced.

Even when we were finally in a private room and my panic attack had subsided, he kept looking at me suspiciously and fearfully, like I was trying to kill him. He did not recognize me.

'Why would you bring me here when you know what they will do to me with the needles?' he demanded.

Finally, a male nurse walked in. 'Would you like some water?' 'No, I will not have anything. No water. No needles. No needles!' Yasser screamed.

I was sobbing.

'What do you want us to do if he is uncooperative?' the male nurse said.

'I want you to first try giving him some water. Then call in the psych ward. I don't want him to get more agitated,' I said.

'Fuck the water. I was going to have water at home. You didn't *have* to bring me to this place for a sip of water!' Yasser's mouth was already foaming.

The nursing staff were standing by, waiting for him to calm down enough to take a blood ceruloplasmin (CP) test.

But first, I needed to stop sobbing. Then I needed to take charge. I needed to sign paperwork and make payments. I needed to calm Yasser down and persuade him to cooperate. Take a sip of water, so gradually his veins would expand and become penetrable with IV. They had collapsed flat because his dehydration was extreme.

The nurses needed to draw blood. The tests needed to be run. The IV needed to be administered after a review of the lab results. At the very end of it all, Yasser needed a sedative—the right dose, so that he wouldn't suffer heart failure.

So much needed to be done, but I wasn't yet ready to jump into being in charge. I was still adjusting to this new, unkind Yasser. During his post-surgery days, he had mellowed into a lotus flower. His mania, this attitude of blame towards me and the intensity of his personally directed rage was too much and all too soon. I was collapsing.

I called his psychiatrist, Dr Alma.

'Aisha, do you understand that Yasser is not Yasser now?' Dr Alma asked.

'Yes,' I said.

'Do you understand why this is important for you to know?' she asked.

'No,' I said.

'He cannot enter into any contract. You see, the hospital will not take any decision until, as his caregiver, you tell them and show them that you are in charge. Any delay in your taking charge can harm him. Nothing he's saying to you now is relevant as it's not from a place of Yasser. Disregard it,' she said.

'It is him. He's talking about my dragging him here now. His insults are about right now and very much about me,' I wept.

'Think of this as a child throwing a tantrum. Think of him as someone you must protect from themselves.'

I did exactly as Dr Alma suggested. I took charge. I asked the doctors to formulate a plan to have him sip a few millilitres of water. We would introduce a new nurse towards whom he was not hostile. He would pretend to be on Yasser's side and bring his paranoia down. I would sit in the room, but I would be calm. I would not respond to Yasser's threats and insults. Slowly, the friendly nurse would convince Yasser to take a few sips of water so he could go home soon. Soon Yasser's veins would be penetrable for a blood test, followed by the doctor's review and some intravenous fluids.

The nurse tapped for the vein. Gently, in went the butterfly needle meant for kids. Nothing came out at first. Then, at glacial speed, thick, pomegranate-coloured jelly emerged. It stuck to the tip of the needle. The nurse retracted the needle.

'I'm so sorry, sir, but your blood is too thick.'

'It's her fault. She brought me here,' Yasser whined plaintively. 'It is absolutely her fault. Will you drink this glass of water for me?' the nurse said.

'No, first tell her to apologize. She's just sitting there,' he said. 'We aren't even going to talk to her, sir. I'm going to get you out of here.'

Yasser managed to down half of the water in the glass. Then a quarter of the half.

They were going to go in again. Try to draw blood for the lab tests. Hopefully, this time, it wouldn't be quite so viscous.

Again. In went the needle. The blood was too thick. Out again. Yasser shoved the tray table with the glass of water to the floor. The needles hurt him. They hurt me too.

I had hiccups from crying now, but I kept instructing the nurses to keep trying. Our neurosurgeon was here by now. He dimmed the room's lights to reduce all stimulation. He asked only the nurse to be present with Yasser, with me standing out of Yasser's line of sight.

They went in again. Needle in. Blood drawn. Still very thick, but manageable. One test tube of blood. Then another test tube. This would have to do for the lab tests now.

Yasser's tongue was white. His mouth frothy. His manic eyes as fierce as ever.

In about forty minutes, Yasser ended up permitting more needles. His hate-filled glares at me and his mumbling of abusive words continued unabated. The IV was next and as soon as we managed that, Yasser grew less vocal and more placid.

Two hours after we had walked into the hospital, Yasser drifted into an exhausted sleep.

The doctors confirmed that if I hadn't brought him back when I did, he almost certainly wouldn't have made it.

I didn't think to myself, Wow! I'm such a genius, thank god I saved his life by making the right decision. Instead, I shoved my face into a pillow and bawled like a baby. This was a lot of responsibility. It was a lot of dependence. It was a lot of neediness for someone to come save us.

The nurses and the doctors came to save us. We didn't need to call in psych, we didn't need to restrain Yasser and we didn't need to have any more of a ruckus than we had already had.

When he woke up the next day, he didn't remember what had happened the previous day.

I was at his bedside, sponging his hair. 'Hey, Aishi,' he said. 'Hey.'

'Where were you?' he asked. 'I'm right here.'

'Thank god,' he said.

Yasser was not fully recovered.

Over the course of the next few days, he accused the hospital of trying to steal money from us by re-admitting him for a fake reason.

The medical team was kind enough to hand me some Lexotanil as a sleeping aid. I took lots of crying selfies of my own puff-adder face, for posterity's sake.

On day four, we went back to Uncle's home. Gerard helped us bring our things back to the apartment.

'You look well, Yasser *bhai*,' said Gerard. 'When wasn't I well?' Yasser said with a smile.

Day six and Yasser was asking me to stroke his forehead. Asking me whether I was mad at him about something. He didn't believe me when I told him nothing had happened. Asking me to come back soon if I left the room.

He sat on the sofa and hugged Uncle's pillow with the legend, *The World's Favourite Nanajan.*

'I'll never be one,' Yasser said to me. 'You don't know that,' I said.

Yasser nodded with his eyes closed. I didn't let Uncle take my Yasser.

Someday. Maybe someday, if the girls so choose, Yasser can be a nanajan.

YASSER MADE ME GO CRAZY

The fight with Yasser has always been on the spectrum. He was the aggressor at one extreme end and at the other end, I was the one brutalizing him.

One day, when his defences were down and my medication was not sufficiently effective, I lunged at him, choking him with my elbow because he wouldn't stop wailing—he was begging me to stop beating him up even before I attacked him.

All I wanted to do was to shut him up with a vehemence I didn't realize I had in me.

When I turned violent, the downward spiral was like falling a thousand meters mid-air in an aircraft. We would have fights about the silliest things.

He would want Domino's Italian thin-crust pizza for lunch and I would order a large serving of Pizza Hut pan-crust, instead. Invariably it would culminate in his throwing a tantrum.

He bombastically declared, 'I hate Pizza Hut! I told you to order thin-crust. Not Italian crust. Not pan-crust. THIN-CRUST. Not from Pizza Hut. Domino's!'

My interactions with Yasser fluctuated through all the gradients between the opprobrious and the mundane. I desperately wanted Yasser to be my buddy, somebody with whom I could let my hair down at the end of the day; I simultaneously wished that he would just drop dead.

During my domestic-violence-recovery therapy, I had to keep a journal. I wept through two dozen boxes of tissue as I told my therapist how I really felt when I was being beaten, how I felt that no one cared enough to check on me, to protect me and to pull me out of a dangerous situation, a medically dangerous situation, an emergency, and how I felt when I realized that I had to make my peace with a potentially dangerous situation. I had to tell her how I coped with it.

What were my great coping strategies and what were my destructive coping strategies? I told her how I grew from the experience and what parts of me atrophied for good. We did years and years of this. An audit of my heart and soul.

I learnt that sometimes the victims of domestic violence become complicit to the violence—either by looking away or even craving it at times in an inexplicable way, even sometimes nudging perpetrators to strike them. Provoking a beating because they are addicted to the pain and the anticipation anxiety that gets too much to bear. If you keep waiting for something bad to happen all the time, it gets so exhausting that you end up evoking the bad things.

I've done this. Created enough psychological hell to provoke an extremely violent backlash. I've done it many times both before and after Yasser was diagnosed with a medical condition.

It was three years after his brain tumour surgery and only a few months after his second surgery when Pizza-gate happened.

When he asked for the pizza to be thin-crust, I paused my life and watched the recap with loathing, distaste and a very personal sense of failure. What had I done to deserve to be the custodian of meeting Yasser's precise pizza-crust needs? It symbolized a life gone horribly wrong, and it had gone wrong because I had messed up. I wanted to stop messing up. I wanted to say, sorry, I got the crust wrong, let me fix it, but that was what I would typically do. This time I wanted out. I no longer wanted to fix things. I wanted things to break and stay broken.

I screamed my protests about this not being the life I wanted, that I wanted an escape from the pettiness and senselessness of his entitled and selfish needs. I threw things and staged a walkout to convey that my life was meant to be elsewhere, anywhere but here where the demands on me to order the perfect thin-crust were not met. I want to be penalized for bigger things in life rather than for getting pizza crust wrong. I think I threw my phone. I think I wept. I think I hurled shoes at a wall. I think I wanted so badly to escape who I was because who I was had become unrecognizable. I was a stranger to myself. Nothing felt familiar. Yasser was not the one being violent at the time; it was me bringing the roof down, upsetting the kids and terrifying the neighbours about how I wanted this life to be anything but this moment of negotiating pizza crust.

I was sabotaging my life because the damn thing just wouldn't let me go. It just wouldn't break so I could be set free.

No matter how terrible things got, I turned around afterwards, and Yasser was there, always there, refusing to go and leave me be. Always there, like a shadow, tormenting me.

Yasser and I have had our married life divided into four quarters. The first and the last sections are chaos: the first being upheavals by Yasser and the final disruptions created by me. The second quarter was recovery and the third quarter was waiting for all hell to break loose again.

You know that feeling in your bones that something shitty will happen soon, but you can't quite put your finger on what or when? They have meshed with my fearful nerve endings, always screaming fire. I don't know who will hurt me next; my remaining brain cells are working overtime, trying to figure out when and how a feral Yasser might jump out from behind a metaphorical bush and sink his fangs into my neck.

These fears poison everything. They poison our Netflix binges of *Doc Martin*, *The Discovery* and our YouTube playlists. They poison breakfast, when he reaches for the toast and I duck, and when I reach out to brush a lock of hair off his forehead and he ducks. We both look into each other's eyes with the question, why would I hurt you?

Then the next minute, apologetically, we lower our gaze in mindful remorse.

The brain tumour did this to us. It turned our love into a curse. It turned him into a mean person and me into a bundle of nerves. Strangers live in us, commanding us to love and hate in extremes.

We love the strangers within ourselves because we understand why they live inside us like a foreign body, but it is hard to understand why that stranger would live in the other person. Our own transgressions have made the other a suspicious beast.

In my audits with my therapist, I confess that I am worse off than Yasser. My rage has no basis. I didn't start off broken and yet here I am being a savagely self-destructive woman. I have had to swallow my self-righteousness for being on the receiving end of narcissistic abuse. I no longer hold the mean stranger who lives inside Yasser in contempt. I am his worst form of meanness.

I no longer demand 'How dare you?' I know exactly how.

As his victim, I had developed a deep-seated hatred for him. When he fell ill and became my victim, I found my hatred turned into a deep knowledge, even awe. I learnt first-hand how one's mid-brain takes over, hijacking one's thinking and inhibitions, and to strike like a mortally wounded animal.

Yasser's attacks on me shocked us both.

Whereas mine on him was premeditated and vengeful.

We were driving to the gym one evening. On an incredibly long traffic light on Jinnah Avenue, I felt particularly regretful about my behaviour towards Yasser whilst he was in remission. I glanced at him and saw the scars left by my fingernails on his throat.

'I'm sorry about the scratches on your neck,' I said. He looked at me for a moment.

'Just the scratches?' he said. 'No, not just the scratches.'

'You are freakishly strong,' he said with a side smile. 'Do I sense admiration?'

He smiled.

'No, but I feel equal enough to look into your eyes now,' he said. 'Equal?'

'You know, my score versus your score.'

'No one is keeping count but if we were, then the ratio of my pinning you down versus your pinning me down is 3:6. There is a long way to go for even,' I said.

'Well, as long as we are getting there,' Yasser said. 'I am really very sorry.'

The light had turned green and we were on our way. I turned my head to the window on my side and hid a tear.

'I know. I'm truly sorry for what I have done too. It haunts me every day,' he said.

I nuzzled in his left armpit which smelled of walnut and firewood on a winter night. Islamabad looked beautiful and we were at a truce.

YASSER WAS LOVE SOMETIMES

When I was pregnant with my firstborn, before the madness set in, Yasser would kiss my tummy for the length of a few songs. He would get on his knees and talk to my belly button, press it gently as if it were a diamond, illuminating everything. He would coo, coddle and be unmistakably mine. We built something together and the fascinating curiosity of it made us fall in love with life.

'You are going to make life make sense for me, Zoe, okay?' Yasser said to my belly button.

'But Baba, I don't even know my butt from my elbow now,' I chirruped in a tiny voice from the belly button.

'I don't care, Zoe, you just have to, because we are going to put extra performance pressure on you like crazy desi parents, and you had better come top of your class in making us figure out life,' Yasser replied.

'But . . . but . . . but . . . Baba, I'm a twenty-first-century baby and I don't care what you think. In fact, I'm eating my own shit right now and later you will eat my shit too, okay Baba?' I squeaked.

Yasser pointed authoritatively at the button, 'Now that is precisely the attitude that helps me make sense of life,' he said.

Then he melted into a million gentle kisses all over my tummy, making cooing sounds.

When I went into labour, I had tiny, Pakistani-flag stickers all over my humongous belly, marker-pen drawings of F16s and lots of smiley face sketches.

Yasser's love language is kisses. If he loves something, he kisses it. I figured this out when we were hanging out in college and my bobby pin came loose and he reached out and brought the bobby pin to his lips and then made love to it with his mouth.

It was hilarious. I used to take Yasser rather seriously even when we were both in our twenties. He was insanely well read about almost every aspect of history, law, politics and religion, and I was a beginner at these. So, seeing him seduce the bobby pin was such a nosedive of dignity. How could someone who knew all about the architectural interior of Cesar's palace and the Roman army's formation styles, snog my bobby pin like a Romeo?

My love language is love. It was how someone made me feel. Mostly the words they used to make me feel safe and secure. But Yasser was Punjabi, and if you know anything about being raised Punjabi, you know that everything is intense. From buttering the toast to funeral rites. There is a lot of self-flagellation, a lot of pointless and vociferous exhortations, expletives and exclamations you don't mean. Also borderline manipulation because the ends unfailingly justify the means. Also, pain is not something to shy away from. In fact, you embrace it, let it destroy you, then you get over it like a fresh change of clothes on a Friday night.

No. I neither understood nor agreed to live this way. Parenting was lovely, however, because kids are kind of like this—on a stubborn spree of want after want, need after need that must be fulfilled.

Having kids with Yasser was a recreation of childhood. Most people say Yasser and I look young for forty-year-olds. We haven't really done much but we've more or less been perpetually stuck in a childhood loop along with our kids.

It's not like things were always childlike. Sometimes shit got real.

Zainy was born jaundiced. She was literally yellow. I was bone- tired after giving birth and we were all sleeping in the same room at the hospital because the doctors wouldn't let us go home for a week. Yasser, his mom and I were taking turns baking Zainy in the fierce lights of the incubator, in which she bawled like a tiny, tormented creature. I'd fish her out and put her to my aching breasts for a feed. She would calm down instantly. Despite the doctor's instructions, I would let her sleep on me rather than toss her back into the incubator for more phototherapy.

Yasser wouldn't eat or sleep; he would sit there by the incubator and weep like we were on the verge of some impending doom. In times of crisis, Yasser cried or raged. Both unhelpful states. But also deeply intense.

Zoe, small and peachy, would shuttle between her new sister, *Dado*, Baba and me asking questions about her new status. I was mean to Zoe and told her rudely to be quiet; I felt maternally ambivalent. At that moment in time, from rejoicing in the joy of having kids, I became an exhausted and overwhelmed mom, who was a resounding failure at almost all of her basic parenting tasks. At this time, however, Yasser and Ami were there to fulfil the kids' needs. Love, kisses, hygiene, adequate nutrition, safety and overprotection from all the unknown unknowns out there in this wild world. I mostly stared blankly into space and missed my old life.

Zainy was going to have a blood transfusion if I didn't toss her back into the incubator with the eye patch, which she loathed, firmly over her eyes. Yasser stayed up with her night after night, holding her tiny hands through the incubator to calm her cries, his own eyes wet.

He saved her. His calming kisses and incredibly crucial, physical love language saved her. We went back home after a few days with baby Zainy, still looking rather yellow and tanned, but alive and well. Every time I turned over in bed to adjust the locus of the pain caused by my stitches from Zainy's birth, there he would be, hunched over like a bow, gently playing with her hands, talking to her in whispers and asking her to live so life could make sense for him again.

Punjabis 1. Others 0.

YASSER WAS GONE ONE DAY,
BACK THE OTHER

Is it possible to forgive someone who has cancer? To permit yourself anger against a brain tumour cancer patient in the first place.

It is ghastly the way ugly and messy parts of life happened to us when we should have still been in the rainbows-and-butterflies phase of our youth.

Then again, why should we be exempt from the games nature and fate play by interchanging wrath and gifts?

It was a winter's day and we were on our way home from a dinner at a journalist friend's place where an ex-PM and three former ministers were also present. We had been sitting around the fire, talking about how messed up their political party is.

It was almost midnight and the moon was missing.

This was Yasser's chemo week and his anti-seizure meds were three hours late. I noticed he started behaving oddly. On our car window, the flower sellers' roses and jasmine bracelets were wilted. They were imploring us to buy the last of their stock for the night, in exchange for a prayer, of course. They said, May your marriage last a million years. We didn't buy anything from them, but they stood there pressing their faces against our car window, beseechingly.

Distracted, I stopped the car a bit too close to the one ahead of me at the traffic light.

Yasser looked like he was trying to not say something. Then he said it: 'There should be a distance of one car between us and the car ahead of ours,' said Yasser, looking apprehensive and also half-ready for my mood. I hate that he still doesn't trust me behind the wheel. Just the other day, we had had another fight about teaching Zoe to drive an old car rather than a new car. He obviously wanted her to learn in an older car and I felt she should have an automatic gear car with power steering.

'I've been driving for twenty-five years, I think I'm okay,' I rolled my eyes.

'But look, it's dangerously close to that car's bumper,' Yasser replied.

'That's because neither car is moving,' I countered. 'Can you please just drive carefully?'

'Is the car all you care about?' I snapped, my heart already heavy with dread and anger.

'The car is at risk this way,' he said.

'The car is at risk. You are such an amazing husband, to the car!' I half-accused, half-vindicated.

'You can do whatever you want to the car when I'm gone,' he said flatly.

'Can you not?' I pleaded. (Pause)

I wanted to kick myself for always fighting about the car.

Things got real very fast. I wanted to retract my anger.

The lights turned green and I drove on, slower than usual, a wide berth between our vehicle and the car ahead.

'You have to be prepared, Aishi,' he said quietly.

I wanted to say so much, but instead I held his hand. There was cold sweat on it. Yasser has cold sweat on his hands when he's unwell or when he has an emotional seizure.

His hand got colder and he refused to open it for mine.

'Can you please drive with both hands, thank you?' he said finally.

I felt a cocktail of anger and fear shooting up inside me again—almost grief. Yet I held my peace.

He moved his hand away from mine—clammy fingers peeling away from my soft, warm ones, trying to convey a meaning.

My hand lay unreciprocated on his lap, like a damp squib—a letter in a bottle smashed against the cliffs. I put my hand where it belonged, gripping the steering wheel with both hands.

'I forgive you, Yasser, and I hope you forgive me too. I really thought love would be enough,' I said to the road ahead of me.

* * *

We were in Karachi for a case fighting for the right of Pakistani Hindus to opt out of affirming that they are not Muslim. Yasser was arguing that saying you are Hindu should be enough. Being Muslim is not a baseline. Having to explicitly make the second statement on religion while filling in official documentation was clearly discrimination. Obviously, he was not going to win it. This life we have here is no place for wet dreams of progress and emancipation. We were in the hotel bed. I had just had a cold shower in the middle of winter because the hotel was shit and I had already had a go at the manager for the mishap.

I was in bed under the covers, nasal and stiff, and he was on his phone, watching the news about the Biden inauguration that night.

I was on the brain tumour support group on Facebook. I was reading out examples of people who had a longer prognosis than five years.

'Take, for instance, this person, Hope Johnson. Her husband had a glioblastoma and he made it to fifteen years. The doctors gave him only two years,' I said.

'I'm going to miss doom-scrolling about Trump,' Yasser said. 'Are you ignoring me deliberately?' I asked.

He kept scrolling.

'Hey?' I nudged him in his ribs with my phone. 'I heard you,' he said.

'Well?'

'Well, what?'

'People don't just die when they're told they'll die. Oligodendrogliomas have an eight-year median prognosis but that doesn't mean that you'll die five years from now.'

I was excited to find this Facebook support group where patients had defied the odds. Yasser almost always met my joy with distracted indifference. It was beginning to get to me. So, I poked him with my phone visor this time.

'Ouch! What?' he said, louder than he intended to.

'I only want to know why you keep saying five years is all you've got when there is evidence that worse-off people do better?'

'I know,' he said, even louder. '"I know" what?'

'I know that people live longer,' he said.

'Then?' I knew I was pushing him, but I wanted him to relent. 'I don't. I don't want to live longer than five years, Aishi,' he said.

'What! Why?'

'I don't have it in me,' he said. He looked at me straight, his eyes sad.

His lip trembled, so he bit it. 'I know you don't want to hear this, and you're trying so hard to keep me alive for as long as possible. But Aishi, it is not easy to be in my head.'

'But it was always like that in your head with OCD, why now?' I pleaded.

'Every moment, my mind tries to tie me in knots, get me down, wind me up about words, pronunciations, history, being on its right side and being deficient. You see, as soon as I give it what it wants—becoming a barrister, getting a Harvard law fellowship, having kids, getting some book published, travel—the next thing I know it is trying to tell me my family is in danger because I did it. It tells me to roll over and die and when I do that, it tells me that if I were to roll over something bad will happen to Mom, you or the kids. I want it to end.'

'Yasser?'

'I need rest,' he said.

Two quick tears fell on to the bed from his nose, eyes and chin, like cars on a racetrack. I wanted to reach out and catch them before they fell, as I usually do, but I let these ones go. They were fast and furious.

'Okay,' I said.

There were some tears of my own.

His eyelashes were beautiful. Even chemo couldn't do a number on them.

'The obsessions don't let me be. The voices won't let me breathe. I've never been happy, except that fleeting moment when Zoe or Zainy walk into the room, or maybe in San Jose in our early days or some moments in court, but that's it. They come and go, and I can only feel them as if in a distant memory before some obsessive thought paralyses me again. It's a relentless loop. I answer the voice, but it comes back again with something harder to hit me with. This life is too much for me. I can't do it anymore. I don't have what it takes.'

'Okay,' I said.

'I'm sorry. I know you are happy when you see a longer prognosis, but for my sake, I beg for mercy. I pray for fewer years. Less treatments. Fewer days of recovery. I so want to call it a day,' he said, holding my shaking hand. 'I tried not to tell you. Today was a very bad day and now I've blurted it out. Now you'll be so sad.'

'Can I ask you for something?' I asked.

Yasser looked at me with sincerity shining in his eyes. He nodded.

I burst into tears. He held me.

'Don't go. Please stay. I need you. I need you to stay even if it hurts you. Please choose me. Stay for me,' I whispered, from inside his embrace. 'Stay. Please stay for me. I can't bear to see the world without your seeing it with me. I'm afraid of waking one morning and your not seeing that morning with me.'

I kept repeating it over and over again. Stay.

Stay.

Please stay.

Yasser held me until my nose was so blocked, I had to go into the bathroom to blow it. I looked at myself in the bathroom mirror, foggy from the hot water I had splashed on my face.

There is no metric system for pain, no unit with which to measure it. Maybe my fear was worse than his; maybe his lifetime of dread was worse than my fear. There was no winner here. Only love. I could only hope that he loved me enough to choose to honour my fear over his.

I went back into bed and lay in his arms again. A few moments of silence had passed.

'Okay,' Yasser said quietly. He pushed my hair away from my wet eyes. Kissed the top of my head.

'Okay?' I held on to his hand, looking at him like my very life depended on his answer.

'I'll stay.'

PART 2

AMI IS HOME

Home is a large green field with clovers and unruly daffodils. In its arm rests an L-shaped cottage. The roof is sloping, red-tiled, stained by moss, the front porch lined with old, cylindrical oil tins from which now bloom dahlias in every colour of the rainbow.

Home is large because I am small. There's a cement bench on the porch. Sometimes I climb on to the bench to see what the neighbours are up to. I can just about see over the wall that divides us. The wall is tall because I am tiny.

Even so, the walls are the same to me as they would be for a grown-up—worn out from love and crusty from neglect. *If you grow up seeing walls every day, at some point, you stop really seeing them.*

A jamun tree—tall and spreading—has lived behind the cottage's wild backyard for as long as I can remember. It was there on the day I was brought home from the hospital in a bassinet, I am told. I was photographed in its shade, so we could all remember the days when I was little. The shadow of its branches covers the tiled roof. The jamuns turn the green grass lavender with all the stomping I do, just to hear the squishy sound under my bare feet. This means that I must scrub my feet longer and harder before bedtime.

Around this big jamun tree, there are many soft-bark banana trees that bend like old men carrying sacks of fruit on their backs.

The paint on the walls of home was once white. Never mind the paint. It is the rose bushes one must look for. I smell the roses. Sometimes I get too excited and end up cutting myself on the thorns. There are so many of them—white, pink and even black—in rows that look like the pretty pictures in my book of nursery rhymes. However, where there are roses, there are also millipedes and centipedes, hairy and many-legged. With time, I have learned to not scream for help when one of them comes barrelling towards my little toes. There's no gate, of course—there have never been any gates to our home. The shrubs are plentiful enough to provide a boundary wall and a gate.

The sun shines yellow and feels like the warmth inside my soft Kiki blanket. No breeze. No trembling leaves, except when it rains. I forget what rain feels like because when it does rain, it's over in a flash, and the friendly sun is out again within half a song. The soil, if the grass permits you to see it, is the colour of the people here. Black. Black, like Uncle Jerome and his family. Black like everyone I see, except for us.

There is an outhouse. Sometimes they call it the servants' quarter, but I'm not allowed to use this term. It is nestled in the front yard like a bit of misplaced jewellery from Ami's jewellery box. The outhouse is not quiet. It is not home.

The many offspring of Uncle and Aunty Jerome live in this outhouse—crawling, sitting, walking and running everywhere. Aunty Jerome wears colourful clothes with puffed sleeves and a different-coloured headband each day to match her sleeves. She walks with a baby on her back in a cloth sling. The baby cries all the time; she ignores it until it falls asleep, exhausted. Ami says I am not to go near the outhouse.

There is the clothesline. The line is made of orange nylon with knots in places where it has snapped from the weight of too many heavy bedsheets. Ami washes and re-washes the bedsheets with homemade soap.

It is the clothesline that separates us from the outhouse, cutting across the front garden diagonally, like a fence, cleaving the yard in two. On one side of this line, we have all good things like the big cottage and the big tree. Ami also has a big sewing machine that is called Singer—like a person who sings. It does seem to sing when she uses it. We also have a very big TV, but it is big only from behind. There is nothing good on TV—only news and football for Abu to watch. I am not allowed to tell anyone we have a TV because it will get stolen if I do, but I do want to tell someone these things. For this, however, I need a friend whom I can trust.

Joshua is my friend. He is Uncle Jerome's son. He put his forearm beside mine to show me how I am not Black. He is slow, always hungry and never utters a word except 'bread'. He always tells me I am different with his eyes. I get head lice and ringworm if I play with him too long, but I trust him, so we sit on the steps of the outhouse and I put my arm around him, even though he has yellow mucus running down to his lip from his nose. I cup one hand to his ear and whisper the secret to him—*Joshua, you are my friend. This is a secret. We have a big, big TV.*

He takes it in, breathing slowly, heavily. Then he cups his hand to my ear. I listen eagerly. He whispers—*I am hungry for bread.* I go into the house and get some bread. Ami says taking food without asking is stealing, but this is not stealing.

I hide the bread anyway. Just in case.

There are five chickens that cross the clothesline because they do not obey their mother like I obey Ami. The woman who is casting the clothes over the clothesline is not Aunty Jerome. That is my ami. She's very fair; her skin is like the skin of a white person. But she is not white. She's not Pakistani, like Abu. She is Indian.

No one has told me that you can stop being an Indian or stop being a Pakistani. Ami and Abu are both Muslim, that's all I know. That's why they were allowed to marry each other.

The hens cross the clothesline, here and there and everywhere, running between Ami's feet as she moves down the clothesline, hanging her laundered sheets. They are our chickens. I think they are there for me because little girls need to grow. Some are white and fluffy, others scrawny and puckered. The rooster is a bad rooster. He is very big and very red and very noisy in the mornings. I do not like how he is rough with the fluffy hens and how he bosses them around. I have touched his comb. Someone holds the rooster and muzzles his beak while I examine his red feathers, neck and comb. The holding of the rooster is provided to me. I can ask for such things from any grown-up I want.

His comb is like a tongue, but much dryer and colder than it looks. *Sometimes, you have to touch things to really see them.*

This rooster is destined to end up in a biryani for one of Ami and Abu's home-cookout parties; I look forward to the day. These are big parties and there are more brown people who attend these galas than there are chickens in Uganda.

Uncle Jerome and his family are not in the yard when there is a party because the party is for brown people. I think the Jeromes were not invited. I want to play with Joshua when my brown friends play hide-and-seek with me, but he doesn't come out when I knock, although I know he is behind the door. I tell the door that I have lots of bread today. But Joshua still doesn't come out of the servants' quarters. Instead, I hear babies crying.

That morning the rooster escapes, mid-slaughter. It runs blindly around the yard, into Ami's rosebushes, into the jamun tree, up the steps of the porch and crashes through the flower-filled, tin flowerpots. Its neck, half-cut, his head dangling at a crazy angle to one side as it runs. I am looking out of the window and I see him, running wildly, looking up at the blue sky with upside-down eyes.

I know the words *upside-down*. I read the Ladybird books with the white girl, Jane, and the white boy, Peter. I know how to read and write *upside-down*.

The rooster runs in an infinity sign around the field before it falls to the ground, very dead. I notice that when he is running, nobody comes to catch him. They let him run until he drops dead. That evening, the members of the Pakistan Society of Uganda love the rooster that they find in the biryani. There must have been more roosters than I remember to have made biryani for so many people.

All the Pakistani aunties and uncles gobble up Pakistani food at these events which Abu makes Ami host. Ami must obey Abu. She is his wife. He is also the president of the Pakistan Society in Uganda—a big deal. Hundreds of brown people turn up at our home when there is a party. They come in their best saris and *salwar-kameez*. They ignore our ugly walls, just as we ignore them. Everyone talks in Urdu. The wives praise Ami's cooking. The husbands praise Ami. The young boys praise the centipedes. The young girls ask me why I am not wearing shoes. I reply, *Joshua doesn't wear shoes.*

Is Joshua a girl? No.
Is he Pakistani? No.
Can he read?
No.

Then how come you are his friend?

They will know the answer as soon as they see him and touch him.

The garden always transforms magically when there is a party. Chairs appear from nowhere, sourced from the high-school classrooms. You see, we live in the campus of a high school. My home—this L-shaped cottage in a green garden—is a teacher's house. Abu is a teacher.

This isn't his house, of course. Teachers don't own houses. But I don't know this yet. I will find out this secret about homes much later. There is no home that is ours. I don't have a friend who will tell me this, whispering the secret into my ear through cupped palms.

There is no one who can tell me that homes can be stolen.

AMI IS TIRED

I watch Ami from behind the rosebushes. They are tall and offer many hiding spaces for a child. Ami has just wrung out the light-pink, double bedsheet. She makes a whip-lash sound by whipping it hard through the air and in one big fisherman's swoop, she spreads it over the clothesline. Next come the clothes pegs at either end. One snaps and breaks. She gets another from the pail and reminds herself to fix the broken one with superglue. Whenever something in the house breaks, it reappears, magically fixed.

The fluttering of the bedsheet is very inviting. The clean smell of homemade laundry soap gets the better of me and I decide to make tiny handprints on Ami's washed bedsheet. My muddy, three-year-old paws look nice. I go back and sit in the bushes to admire my handiwork.

Ami comes back after fixing the broken clothes peg, just as I knew she would. She has not noticed my artwork on the sheet. She is bending over the pail and squeezing out the last bit of water from the white uniforms of Bhaijan, Bhai and Baji. She has other children like me, but they are much taller and speak in whole sentences.

One end of the clothesline is tied to the trunk of a banana tree and the other to the lamp above the door of Uncle Jerome's house. That is our door and that outhouse is our outhouse, but the Jeromes have occupied it like the White people had once done to Uganda.

Although Ami is a very nice person, she has always wanted to kick the Jeromes out. That way, she can use the outhouse as a sewing station for her own solitude. Sometimes she wants to buy more chickens by selling the clothes she makes. But Ami always looks after the many children that Jerome insists on having year after year—until one year, his wife eventually dies. Ami says that they had to keep having children every year because Jesus was their lord and saviour. Sometimes the Jeromes take me to church, but I am always bored. The priest wears a funny collar. He puts treats in my mouth, if I kneel like the rest of the congregation and clasp my hands politely.

The Jeromes watch Ami hang out her washing to dry. They eat the sweet potatoes, cassava and yams that Ami gave them yesterday. They look at her like she's sport. She doesn't let them see what she doesn't want them to see. But she has seen my handprints—two tiny handprints, five fingers spread wide. Her mouth turns downwards. She adjusts her glasses on her nose and sighs.

Later, much later, I decide to never buy light-coloured bedsheets in a country of loamy soil and centipedes.

She pushes up her very thick eyeglasses from her nose's tip to the bridge of her nose with her hand that is always raw and pink. Her nose is sweaty, so her glasses invariably slip down to the tip of her nose however many times she adjusts their position. Sometimes they break because she sleeps on them. Then she tapes them up with Scotch tape until someone buys her a new pair from

Kenya. Kenya is nicer than Uganda. Ami's sisters and brothers are in Kenya and she is here with her real family.

Ami's nose is from India—straight and long. She lets me pull at it when she is asleep and perhaps I'm the one who broke her glasses last time.

She looks at the mud prints, the size of a kitten's paw, again to make sure she isn't seeing things.

She undoes the wooden clothes pegs securing the sheet on the line and tosses them into the pail with tiny thuds. She draws the sheet off the line slowly and folds it. It's wet and heavy. Although her back hurts, it's okay. She's okay.

The sheet is back in the metal bucket. Ami walks back into the veranda with the pail over which she will now bend for another hour or so, eradicating the stain I have inflicted on her morning, for no apparent reason, except maybe a curiosity to see what she might do. But I should know better. She will put the sheet up again as soon as it's washed and spotless. She will be annoyed, but she will not show it. Ami is a nice person. She will put her annoyance in an airtight tin, just as she hides everything else. Ami never shows what she feels.

Sometimes, I think that her heart is a Quality Street chocolate-tin with a royal carriage on it and white people who wear gloves and have perfectly brushed teeth and hair. I wish Ami had gloves too, for her raw, pink hands and all the places her skin is annoyed with her.

She does not call my name as she does when she calls me for milk and I'm playing with Joshua—*Aashi!* She wants to, but she does not.

I watch her next move, like a thief from behind the rose bushes. She has chosen to let me hide behind the bushes. She does not hurt me. Maybe it is because so many Black people are watching.

Maybe it is because she is nice. Maybe it is her tin heart.

ABU COMES AFTER AMI

The architecture of a home depends on the hierarchy of the people in it.

Ami used to sing in the kitchen but only after Bhaijan, Bhai and Baji had gone to school and she was alone at home with only me, still half-asleep trailing her with my soft, blue safety blanket, Kiki. She never sang *ghazals* when Abu was home. When Abu was home Ami marched to his drum, often hurriedly and very unsure of herself. Maybe she had always been diffident and Abu just happened to be in her life, but three-year-old me discerned a pattern I couldn't quite understand between the independent Ami and the bonded-labour Ami. Ami was uninhibited and exuberant when people weren't watching. When she noticed that I had woken up, she would carry on singing to herself and say with a musical lilt, *I wonder whether there's a cat in the room, I sure can smell one.* I would invariably giggle, and that was home—just Ami and me, free to be ourselves.

Ami was like milk and Abu was like *karak* chai. Ami was pure and Abu incorruptible because he was rigid. Ami was musical and Abu never sang, which in itself is a dead giveaway of people who know how to deal with pain as opposed to people who don't.

Ami flowed. Abu stood. Although I liked Ami so much more than Abu, he fascinated me.

Ami made things—pancakes, biscuits, origami, dresses and slippers shaped from clay. Abu just wrote and read and held forth. Sometimes his orations were excessive. Ami was quieter than she needed to be. As the youngest of four children, I think I got the best qualities of Ami and Abu. I'm told they were worse as parents before I was born. Which meant Ami was even milkier and Abu was far more over-brewed than he was now. They did look a bit like milk and stewed tea because Ami, although forty years old at the time, looked thirty and Abu, fifty, looked like an old man of seventy.

Long ago, when Ami was busy drawing pictures of daisies in her Kenyan school notebook, Abu was almost killed by a militant Hindu's sword swiping at his back. He was only fourteen when his home in Indian Ajmer was set ablaze during the riots. He was separated from his family. He was finally reunited with them as he escaped into a refugee camp in 1945.

It stands to reason that Ami sang and Abu didn't.

Uganda chose my family a few decades later. Abu was shipped off to Uganda by the Pakistan education department under a commonwealth programme to teach Ugandans history and geography. Ami's family was already in Kenya in the pre-Partition years to build the East African railroad project, a British conspiracy to get richer on the backs of Black and brown people. An unmistakable hierarchy of Whites, browns and Blacks—milk, tea and black coffee.

People think they choose their places, but I think the places call to you. Kampala had been a colonial town and was coming apart at the seams as post-colonial cities were wont to do. There was neglect in the unpaved roads and the flooded gutters, and almost all my classmates had diseases caused by the unsanitary conditions and malnutrition. I didn't have a single Ugandan friend who didn't have lice, a body rash, a gastro ailment or an acute protein deficiency like Kwashiorkor, which presented itself as distended bellies, making children look like they were pregnant with twins.

Others had Beriberi which is a Vitamin B1 deficiency and if you had it, you would basically look like you had been hit by a truck and then reversed over by the same truck.

We read about these in the science textbooks. The teacher always told us to eat a balanced diet and not just rely on the millions of banana varieties that Uganda produced or on yams or maize for our nutritional needs. Eat more protein. No one told us how to source more protein. Ami knew how to feed me protein in beans and chicken yakhni, which she force-fed me sometimes, but these kids didn't have Ami.

My substitute teacher had elephantiasis—he had the gall to show up in class with his legs swollen to the size of, yes, an elephant's. Nothing is more entertaining to bored and starving kids than massive-legged teachers walking into class after the break. We just couldn't stop laughing, even though we were aware that there would be dire consequences for our amusement, but madness was our friend that day and we had chuckle after chuckle. The teacher, frothing with rage, plodded around the classroom, hitting all of us with the blackboard eraser, books and his strangely agile hands, but we only laughed all the more. That day, we refused to curb our mirth.

Soon after, we were lined up in the playground, a dusty land where play rarely happened, and we were dealt corporal punishment with a bamboo stick—three to four canings on each child's butt and thigh. There was hysterical weeping now.

It was on days like these that I momentarily found connection in the human condition, even if mine was comparatively better than that of my classmates. Communal laughing and crying does that.

I would not blend in in Uganda. I stuck out no matter how hard I tried. Ami and Abu had no idea how much more inhospitable the Ugandans were to me than they were to them. At some point I stopped trying to convince them that Uganda was not home.

I was a *muindi*, someone who is brown in Africa. As far as the architecture of Ugandan society went, the Africans were living in their country—Africa for Africans—and we were the subcontinent Asians, B-grade invaders subjugating the Africans through economic slavery and refusing to let them have sick days when their children died and having them work our factories until they themselves dropped dead. Abu was a high-school teacher in Kampala making a schoolteacher's salary and giving his family high-school groceries with zero appliances like a fridge and a blender. His attitude was suck it up and read a book about progress instead. He owned a motorbike and sometimes, when he wasn't up to doing too many trips, we would all ride on it together—me straddling the engine, which sometimes got searingly hot, Ami and Baji sitting sideways in the pillion seat like the prim-and-proper ladies that they were. Ami wore saris so straddling was not even an option, even if it were the safer alternative.

Kampala, Uganda was once the jewel in the crown of Africa.

However, for my family, who chose to stay on for thirty-five years and not budge even during the Idi Amin dictatorship's Asian exodus, it continued to be glorious. It was perhaps because people like Abu, who had already seen migration carnage during Partition, just wanted to stay put. Migration fatigue was the culprit. They lived in the yesterdays of their lives. They would rather risk death than leave what they now considered their home.

Idi Amin had started off as a benevolent guy but, like all tyrants, he ran out of ideas and resorted to terror to extend his rule. Indians and Pakistanis, like Ami and Abu, had no home to return to but were, nevertheless, evicted overnight and ordered to leave via Entebbe Airport or be shot on sight. He used fear and rage, the two companions of benevolent dictators gone rogue, to tell Ugandans that all their pain and suffering stemmed from the racism of the muindis.

Those were us, brown folks.

NOT-THE-AMI IS ABU

Ami was short, a little less than 5 feet. She slouched, so that reduced her height by another inch. Her shoulders lived close together as if her ribs weren't sufficient to protect her heart. She was always in a rush.

I was Ami's lastborn. She had three healthy children before the sickly me was born, so we were two boys and two girls— she said she had a complete family but, like most women of that generation, she had lost children as well. A grief which she bore in her stride; it was Allah's will, she would say, almost nonchalantly. She lost twins. That too was Allah's will.

Abu wrote a cute poem about us called *Achay Bache*, good children. Abu was an aspiring poet. Thankfully for us, that wasn't his day job. Being a schoolteacher paid marginally better than the livelihood of a failed poet.

I saw Abu and I saw strength, some of which was fuelled by his ire and some of it by his words. Like most men of intellect, he wore glasses which came of reading too long and in dim lighting.

He taught history, geography and politics, and led the drama club.

Abu never just sat—he sat with a book. When I woke up in the middle of the night to pee, he would be reading. He would look up from his book and say something endearing and return to the book. He always seemed troubled while reading. The two deeply entrenched grooves between his eyebrows failed to separate him from his worries. When I came home from school, he would be reading; when I woke up in the morning, he would be reading. He read books in Urdu, mostly. Although his library was large and extensive, I wasn't allowed to touch the books, which was precisely why I did touch them.

The *Encyclopedia Britannica* was all I was allowed to borrow and I never ever picked up that monstrosity, although I'm told it was bought when we couldn't afford money for food.

Abu would light up when he saw me. There was no doubt about the fact that he liked me almost as much as he did his books and would rather have me close to him than anyone else. I'd play with the hair on his arm as he read. Sometimes I'd play with his thick eyebrows and we would both fall asleep. He was an eyebrow-tickle fiend and asked for it like a puppy, almost begging me to do my magic with my little hands. His eyebrows were so thick, made of twisty steel, the individual hairs longer than they needed to be, crawling over his forehead and under his glasses. When Abu began to snore, I'd nudge him awake and he would start reading again; then he would snore, and I would wake him up. I would say, 'Abu!' and he would jerk wide-awake, deeply apologetic for resting when he should have been reading. That was our thing. Those were our moments.

At this age, when I'd seen so little, time felt stretchy like the bubblegum I had secretly stuck under Abu's reading desk to mark my presence.

Abu taught me to draw Uganda's map using colour pencils. He showed me how to shade in the map with a scrap of paper which was darkly coloured in with a block of colour. He taught me about contours and he taught me about topography. History and geography were his pet subjects. I was his pet.

I grew up on university campuses. Although Abu was a only in a high-school teacher, most of his friends were university lecturers.

Life was very gated. Within the gates were brown people, mostly, and their helpers. Outside the gates were Black people. All of Ami and Abu's friends were brown like barley.

The problem with Abu was that he was not always Abu. Every evening, Ami and Abu promenaded on the veranda, sometimes on a moonlit night, with me perched on Abu's shoulders, clutching at his hair every time I thought I would fall.

I was never old enough to make Abu a sandwich, but I wanted so much to make him something which he would relish. I just didn't know enough about death or about making sandwiches for Abu. All I wanted was more Abu and if I ever incurred his wrath, I learnt to wait until he returned to giving me love. While I waited, I tried very hard to forget the days of his wrath.

Abu wasn't always nice to me. Therefore to me he was strange and unfathomable. And no, sometimes his face wouldn't light up when he saw me.

He even pinched my cheek, one day, in rebuke for a very minor offence—I had inadvertently spilled ink on one of his student's final-exam papers. He was so furious about my messing up this kid's paper I feared that he would personally hand me over to the state penitentiary.

I never forgave him for pinching my very soft, pink, cotton-candy cheeks with his huge, calloused fingers, fingers more suited to masonry and manual labour. I felt that he ought not to have forgiven himself for such barbarism either. *Savage man.*

I didn't talk to him for days after he pinched me.

He was repentant enough and would chase after me as soon as he came home from work. Looking for me was his first parental duty the moment he arrived home. I often waited for him, delighted by the fact that he would seek me out right away if I wasn't there to greet him.

Mere Aisha beti ko kaun tang karta hai? Who dare upset my Aisha? he would sing.

Abu was like a Bollywood hopeful, humming tunelessly, sometimes even flamboyantly; home was his stage.

You, Abu, you. You're the one who upset me. There was no jury to appeal to if Abu was the offender. Abu was the highest authority there was and like his favourite word mankind he, God and the prophets were fused into one big entity. Therefore I couldn't be mad at him either because then I would be mad at all of mankind. If anything, I should be penitent.

I would refuse to emerge from my hiding places for days. I think I rebelled against the notion of not having a space of my own whenever I felt that Abu's anger towards me was unwarranted. So, I found myself nooks and crannies to sequester myself— under beds and behind bookshelves and in the garden and on the spreading branches of tall trees. If Abu was mad at me, I was bad.

Sometimes Abu wasn't Abu, sometimes he was not even the greatest Abu.

When you loved someone as I loved Abu, it's so easy to forget that he had parts of him I never liked at all. Waking up the following morning, I would rush into his arms, forgetting he was mean—not just sometimes, but often and much.

Forgetting. Forgetting. Forgetting.

Time duped me and confiscated my memories to help erase my pain.

AMI IS ABU'S

Ami was Konkani and Abu, Muhajir. Although their parents originally belonged to India, they were no longer from the same country. Ami's parents moved to East Africa, but Abu's parents were kicked out of India into Pakistan. I didn't know or quite understand the ramifications of these different things. I thought that these were just words that people tagged on to their last names. I didn't know that these were things that could hurt you.

Through the eyes of a child I saw things as they were, but I was socialized into thinking of Ami as a delicate princess and her family, a pure, racially superior clan, belonging to the morally righteous, close-knit community called the Konkani Muslims from India. The Konkanis upheld their traditional values, even in savage Africa where they made a success of themselves against all odds.

The Konkanis, some fifty-odd families, controlled the community in Nairobi by establishing annual sports galas, Quran-recitation competitions and potlucks along with an elder called Sheikh Saab who would moderate the events like a mumbling grandpa everyone respectfully endured because he had built

125

a community's legacy. From funerals to graduation parties to weddings, nothing was official until Sheikh Saab Uncle declared it was. He was always the designated priest of sorts, petite, mic in hand but at an ineffective distance from his mouth and his faint voice. He declared people man and wife. He matchmade for Konkanis. Konkanis married Konkanis and would actually refer to people as *one of ours versus not one of ours, good people versus bad people and good girls versus bad girls.*

Is she among us? No. How terrible.

He is among us.

How wonderful.

So, I was a Pakistani living in Uganda with a Pakistani father who was the president of the Pakistan Society Association. My abu was the Sheikh Saab of all of Uganda's Pakistanis. I already had all the alpha-male dad a little girl would ever need.

Konkanis were very Indian, and sometimes that meant they were anti-Pakistani. When I carried Abu into the lives of the Konkanis, I found myself alone. My father's legacy had no place in their lives, besides some mild reverence, but he certainly was part of my personhood. I jumped from a very secure, born-into-a-sovereign-Pakistan identity into a to-hell-with-Jinnah identity.

No one warned me that my life was going to be entrusted to people who would be opposed to all the ideological beliefs of my father. In that way, Abu died twice. One with a burial, which I didn't attend, and the other, sans burial.

Indian Muslims defined themselves in the most extreme way when they lived in self-exile in an eighties' Africa. They defined themselves as Muslim first and Indian next, and insisted that Pakistan only created trouble for nothing.

My teens, immediately after losing Abu, were all about self-justification. I grieved him by way of history.

The first racial slur of my life came when I was four in Uganda and was called a muindi.

The second was when I was twelve in Kenya, and I was called a *kuku-paka*. Kuku-paka is a concocted name to define the uniqueness of my background. In truth, kuku-paka is a Kenyan food but as a malicious epithet, the kuku stood for Konkani and the paka for Pakistani. Simply put, a sort of a confused half-caste—a no-man's-land; a person whom no one wants to claim; an outcast.

The Konkanis from Ami's side of the family did lots of marrying into Konkanis. Abu's side of the Sarwaris did lots of marrying into Sarwaris. There was a lot of familial pride and reservations on both sides of the family when Abu was asked to marry Ami.

Abu was a teacher and his best friend recommended his sister, Mehrun-nissa, saying she would make a decent wife to the thirty-year-old.

Konkanis belonged to a fishing village, but their descendants went bougie when they came to Africa and held my father in contempt. He had completed his master's, was an avid reader and spoke in ideas. To the Konkanis, Abu was old, uncouth, loud and lacked propriety.

Yey kya! Hum bahar nahi dete hain. Our women have been taken by outsiders.

It was the same with Abu's family. They had forgotten how to stay above the poverty line after Partition, but they sneered at Ami.

Bahar ki hai. Udher ka hi hokayrah gaya hai. She is from among the outsiders and we have now lost him to them.

Historically, too, there was a problem. It was said that, once upon a time, the Sarwaris too had been driven out of their homes in Ajmer. As migrants, they clung to their own yesterdays.

So, Ami wasn't considered an ideal match for Abu by the Sarwaris, at least initially. Ami couldn't really be expected to show devoted obedience to Abu's family—she would need to jump through the hoops of loyalty tests to the tribe in order for her to be ideal.

In spite of this, Ami and Abu got married. Women find a way to become ideal, somehow.

So, it was thanks to providence and a lack of choice that Ami and Abu became my ami and abu. Here they were. Brown people in a Black nation, making a home, washing and cooking and making babies. But Uganda was never their true country. They both liked Islam more than they liked Pakistan or India. For both of them, Allah was number one. Pakistan and India were numbers two and three on the list of goodness. I grew up singing to Allah *subhana-wa-taalah* and to Quaid-e-Azam Mohammad Ali Jinnah.

Before I was born in 1981, white people and brown people were mean to Black people in the Blacks' own country. In the year that I was born, Black people were very angry. They wanted to kill the nasty, non-Black people. Idi Amin had publicly declared that if Africa was for Africans, then Africa must be returned to Africans, only then would all be well.

Idi Amin was a scary man. Even Abu was afraid of him. But not Uncle Jerome. He loved Idi Amin. He told me once that he would tell this Idi Amin to come and get me, when I wouldn't listen to him and refused to go to school.

All the white people had a home to return to, so they swiftly vacated Uganda. Even the nuns left.

Brown people—the ones who worshipped *Bhagwan* and who owned businesses in Kampala—also left. They could return to India to set up their shops there. White Christians went to Entebbe Airport and never returned. The Hindus headed to the Kenya–Uganda border towards Mombasa from where they boarded ships to Bombay. They abandoned their cars with the keys still in the ignition and left their shops unlocked to make it easy for looters.

Ami once told me that she had travelled in a convoy of cars that had been negotiated safe passage by the United Nations High Commissioner for Refugees (UNHCR). I was a baby then, she told me. I was on her lap. Ami and Abu had cooked and cleaned in Uganda for too long to have a home to return to, so Ami came back home to Uganda. Here, Ami and Abu both hoped for the best. But hoping for the best is as ludicrous as simultaneously believing in our lord and saviour, Jesus Christ, in Bhagwan and in Allah and his Prophet Mohammad (PBUH) and in the Quaid-e-Azam, all at once.

AMI ALSO HAD AN AMI

Ami's Ami didn't have children, she had litters. The first batch had three sons followed by a batch of five—three girls and two sons.

For me to have happened, Rashid *Mamujan* had to have happened first. He was the brother who mediated the alliance of Ami and Abu in marriage. Rashid Mamujan was Abu's best friend. He got his sister married to his best friend. Eventually, because he was an engineer, he qualified to migrate to Australia.

Rashid Mamujan was his ami's third son—batch one.

Ami always spoke about Rashid Mamujan with respect and reverence, but it was clear that the bond between the two men, Abu and Rashid Mamujan, was pivotal to the story.

Ami's ami came to Kenya from Konkan, India when she was fifteen and Ami's abu was seventeen.

Ami's ami was called *Bua*. Ami's abu was called *Nanajan*.

Bua had seven children that lived, and a few that didn't. Bua wore white cotton saris all her life, with white blouses and white petticoats with white drawstrings. Bua was the colour of milk and had freckles like White people. I have her freckles although I'm the colour of caramel.

Bua had a mouth that turned downwards like Ami's. I've seen Ami giggle and laugh, but I never saw Bua doing either. Maybe it was because too many of her children lived.

Of Bua's sons, one was a judge in the Kenyan Supreme Court; another, a businessman who migrated to the UK; yet another, a failed, serial entrepreneur in Kenya; and yet another, a businessman in Kenya; and then an engineer who migrated to Australia. Then there were three girls. The girls were homemakers: Ami was a grade-A seamstress and cook; older *Khalajan* was a grade-A knitter; and younger Khalajan was a grade-A car driver. Younger Khalajan's husband was a doctor. Older Khalajan's husband was a mechanic and Ami's husband was a schoolteacher. The husbands' economic statuses were commensurate with the wives' skills and looks.

Ami's siblings who didn't migrate lived in Nairobi.

Her brother, older Mamujan, the economist and the man with a good head on his shoulders, worked in the family's oil-and-gas business with younger Mamujan. Think of younger Mamujan as a grumpy Tasmanian devil, for whom everything sucked and someone else was always responsible for its sucking as much as it did. Younger Mamujan was the embodiment of toxic masculinity, entitlement and poor coping strategies that the desi communities, including his three sisters, idealized, enabled and overtly compensated for. He was always proclaiming decrees or throwing tantrums or losing money or womanizing. He was plain bad news.

Older Khalajan and younger Khalajan both lived in Nairobi in a place called South C, well-heeled and with a beautiful temple and mosque and a cute corner shop. It was a good place for a family with children. There was endless food and we had clean and timely meals, warm beds and showers. South C soon became a concept, the ideal bootcamp that could have raised a hundred other kids to become wonderful professionals. The boys especially got a lot of care and preference. After local cricket matches the boys were served food first.

You had to believe that family was sacrosanct in exchange for all the services you got. For all the clockwork-study times rolling into meal-prep time, milk-buying time, chores time and family time, there were even moments when the family would gather to watch Haseena Moin's *Dhoop Kinaray*, a soap opera which the children would also be allowed to watch.

I told younger Khalajan when I was five that it was hard for me to differentiate between her and older Khalajan. She gently and firmly held me by the shoulders like a headmistress and said, 'I am the good one because if you had said to older Khalajan what you just said to me, you would be slapped for not knowing your own family.'

I nodded with a gulp when she released me.

I detested the bond between these siblings because it felt terribly lopsided. The three sisters, Ami and my two Khalajans, deified younger Mamujan almost as if they existed only because of him; because he had graciously given them their heartbeat. It was bizarre. Meanwhile, older Mamujan was loved in a more natural way. Just loved. No major status bestowed on him. Strange.

I hated it because all my siblings had gone away to settle in other cities at about the same time that Abu died.

Sometime during my teens, I stumbled upon a trunk full of economics books that I was told belonged to older Mamujan. I saw the demand–supply graphs and the complexities of calculating inflation in the books and couldn't help wondering why older Mamujan wasn't quite as revered as younger Mamujan. I didn't dare ask Ami because I knew enough to know that, while she wouldn't slap me or reprimand me, she wouldn't know the answer herself and would transfer her discomfort at that lack of knowledge to me in some form.

Why do some people take up more space than others?

Her sisters and brothers were Ami's refuge and sanctuary. She always compared her life to their lives. Ami was devout, so yes, she was grateful for what we had, but you could sense her lighting up when we went to Kenya to my uncles' and aunts' homes. There were grand pianos there. There were keys on furry key chains; there were mealtimes and routines like mandatory *maghrib* prayers. There were rigid rules like not spending more than five minutes in the loo, even if you were constipated or needed a relaxed shower. They had cars.

They had money. They had.

We didn't have.

So, sometimes my questions were embarrassing to Ami.

AMI HELPED ME BE A GIRL

Ami taught me a lot of things. She helped me learn to belong to the world, but as a girl.

Polite and demure is what she wanted from me.

Time was like the tinkling sound of Ami's bangles when she brushed her palms over my hair. Time replaced one thing with another.

One person with another. One mother with another.

Don't pee loudly. I learned to clench my sphincter so my pee would trickle, not spray—no loud noise. If someone heard me pee, I would be disgraced. The word I heard all the time to get me to be a good girl was batameez. The worst thing you can be, besides being a girl, is being a batameez girl.

I watched Madonna twirl tassels on her nipples on TV at her concert, and the TV remained switched off for a week. A crocheted cover shrouded the TV's blank face as if to obliterate the memory of what it had seen and showed me. Madonna was batameez. I had memorized the lyrics to *Like a Virgin*—it must have played on the tape recorder one too many times. But I never dared sing it out loud.

I was to not do anything batameezi, else I could very well be on my way to becoming another Madonna. I was taught to walk noiselessly and without dragging my feet lest someone should hear loud and clumsy footsteps to herald my presence. I was not to gulp loudly when drinking. Small, ladylike sips were appropriate. Farts were wholly taboo. Even in the toilet, they were not to be heard.

But I was a forgetful child. I would sing in the loo. Ami would knock and remind me that no sounds were allowed to come out of the loo. I would blush on the pot. Not bad enough that I had the misfortune to have a gut, I had the gall to sing during the act of expulsion. That was batameezi.

Ditto for sneezing. Just a muffled sound was allowed. Blowing into hankies was allowed but, again, silently.

Hair shouldn't be found in the hairbrush. Girls should dispose of their hair by coiling it neatly, placing it in a tissue, wrapping it in plastic and then placing it in the dustbin.

In time, I learnt to be quieter. I ensured that no one would see me walk into the loo. I would slip in and quietly do my business. However, the noise of the flush deeply embarrassed me. You see, sometimes, I would need to flush several times. Then wash my hands. Ami would call me over and over—*Aashi, Aashi, Aashi!* But I wouldn't answer. I knew rules were rules. She would get mad when I wouldn't answer, but I would remind her that her pupil was now her devotee.

When I was in pain, there was to be no crying, definitely no bawling. This was the hardest, because I invariably wailed, my mouth wide open. I changed how I wept too. I buried my face in the crook of my elbow and muffled my sobs.

Hiccups were allowed.

I had to say a lot of pleases and thank yous and sorrys.

If Uganda meant Catholic school, where the classes were at a beginner level, Kenya was boot-camp with a drill sergeant striking you at every turn. Ami's sisters and brothers mattered a lot to her. They all grew up together in East Africa in a time of great uncertainty and cultural-identity challenges, so it made sense that they would bond. But it was after Ami got married that her hunger to seek their approval intensified. As I grew older, I realized that they had to have withheld their approval in some way in order to have created this hankering in her. No one ever craves what they have in abundance.

That's why, I think, Ami taught me that everyone liked me better when I constantly apologized for existing. That I had to be a good girl because I had to actively undo being a bad girl.

But I digress.

Half an hour into the Nairobi South C house, I had already committed about four violations. I began by walking in mopey. Then I compounded that by wanting to hide behind Ami's dupatta, refusing the foul-smelling milk masked with strawberry-flavoured syrup. Our milk in Uganda tasted like arse, smelled like arse and looked like fungus, but I had ways of not drinking it. In Kenya, you had to gulp it down and if you threw up, you had to drink that as well. According to family legend, older Khalajan asked Bhai to re-eat the cabbage which he had vomited. That legend made me visualize the horror of drinking puked strawberry milk. By the time it was maghrib, I would be crying from the overwhelming rejection handed out by the unfiltered labels—*nakhra, chui-mui, na-shukri, rondu.* They said I had a diva attitude; I was being too precious and princess-like; too ungrateful for the bounty of God; too weepy. I was just a bad girl.

When I told Ami I was upset, she became a drill sergeant herself, pinching me in punishment. She would grip the flesh of my arm, or my side, or my thigh between her thumb and index finger and give it a firm twist. Those hands had washed enough dishes, made enough suit jackets and lacy skirts, and wrung out enough bedsheets to give any sea crab a run for its money. By pinching me, Ami hurt me both physically and mentally.

To make up for whatever she didn't want to experience, she took to pinching. Ami hated travelling and her nausea was destabilizing. That was bad enough, but on top of that, her little daughter was being a pain in the arse. When we reached Kenya, both of us left the classroom and entered the exam room. But nothing we learnt in theory would ever work in a warzone.

In Kenya, South C was the hangout for all Konkanis. South C was different from home. Ami must have felt it was a good kind of different because she took us there for almost every holiday, almost every wedding and almost every Eid. We went there more than we went to Pakistan to visit Abu's family. Yes, Kenya was closer to Uganda than Pakistan was, but I suspect it gave Ami relief from the chaos in her own home in Uganda. In Kenya, instead of doing two and a half jobs, maybe she did one job that ended with *Isha* prayers. For me, however, Kenya was where I learned to make myself inconspicuous in bigger ways.

For instance, I was dirty. This was a fact. There was so much emphasis on cleanliness in Kenya that it interfered with my plans to observe prayer, to eat or to even talk. Before I entered any room, I was asked if I had washed my hands. I usually hadn't. I was dark, so I was often asked if I had washed my face. Scrub harder, they would say.

There was great emphasis on skin and beauty. I asked what a conditioner was.

It is hair food, younger Khalajan explained. I nodded obediently.

I was being civilized.

In Uganda, we washed our hair with yellow soap that got grimy in our hands. In Kenya, younger Khalajan taught me that hair can be soft.

In Uganda, we didn't have pretty cups with flowers on them. In Kenya, there were biscuits from flowered tins. Even the biscuits had flowers on them. In Uganda, Ami made biscuits from scratch with custard powder. They were yellow, and I got to put an orange, food-colouring dot on them with a toothpick.

Uganda had no pencil sharpeners, pencils that bent for the sake of bending, key chains or hooks behind bathroom doors instead of nails, theme calendars or cars that had automatic windows. In Uganda, we didn't have hot water for showers. In fact, there were no showers. We had taps and buckets. We had no dining table, no newspapers and no grandparents. In Uganda, I was always schooled on who I should not be, things I should not know, people I should not look up to. I felt a bit like a fleabag.

In Kenya, I was told that I was off my rocker, crazy and ghastly without God's fortune. I think it all started when they discovered I didn't know how to read Arabic or Urdu—two essential characteristics of Muslims like us living in non-native lands. Not knowing the languages meant you were a barbarian and indistinguishable from the host country's savages.

There were gasps. *You mean she hasn't read the Quran thrice? Then she is not a Muslim. By this age, she should have fasted for one Ramzan and prayed five times and memorized the Surah Fateha, the four Kulls, the Ayatul Kursi and the Surah Rehman.*

It is true, though, that Ami did do her best to teach me the things I should know. She would sit me down at the coffee table at home and tell me to read the Quran verses, one after the other, as she had taught me to. Then she would run off to make a roti or scrub a pan and return to catch me daydreaming with a vacuous smile on my face.

Aashi! Did you read?

Pause. *Yes.*

How can you lie with your hand on the Quran?

I'd snatch my finger off the Quran.

Then she would give up and say *just go.* I would kiss the Quran gratefully and with overwhelming reverence and run off to play with the butterflies.

Where mothers failed, older Khalajan would prevail. She would not spare the rod and spoil the potential of a good Muslim girl. There were no butterflies in Kenya, only malls and Khalajan's will. Other wild kids had been tamed.

Older Khalajan started her first lesson by telling me that shame and I were literally synonymous.

Never tell anyone that you haven't read the Quran in Arabic the prescribed three times.

Just because you're bad doesn't mean it is your Ami's fault . . . entirely.

You're all grown up now. And although you haven't got your period yet, you're still a woman. Your bad deeds are being counted. Your sins are all yours now. They've been all yours for a while now. The angel has been watching and recording all your bad deeds. You're personally responsible for what you don't know.

You'll go to hell. You can redeem yourself by finishing reading the Quran faster than the speed of light.

Ami would give excuses, saying that I struggled with reading, unlike her other kids, and with all the housework devolving upon her, it was hard to give undivided attention to religion. Ami would apologize on my behalf. Sometimes she would pinch me with her eyes. But only in Kenya was she really mean.

When the pinch happened, I always felt that all my hard work until now counted for nothing. All that sphincter-muscle control, all the quiet sneezing followed by *Alhumdulilah*, the ladylike crossing of legs when sitting on a chair, the greetings and smiles when I didn't want to greet or smile, and the constant self-effacement was all in vain. In truth, I did it all for Ami, and Ami failed me by hurting my feelings.

The sting. The sting. The sting.

Mothers hurt us in irreparable ways.

AMI AND I WERE INSEPARABLE

Shame is an evolutionary gift to keep people from doing harmful things to others. In Uganda in the eighties, being a muindi meant that you were ashamed of being born in need of political help.

I remember the first time I felt the sting of shame, of feeling inferior because I was rich and everyone else was too poor to afford a bike. Then, feeling the shame of belonging to a privileged family who thought I must be dropped at school while in my peer group, everyone walked to school independently. Then feeling the shame of having an old dad in a suit, who rode a motorbike. The first time I verbalized shame was when Abu dropped me at school on his motorbike and I asked him to stop a few yards before the school gate. When he asked me why, I didn't answer. He understood. He turned the bike away from the school gate and I hopped off.

My classmates made fun of me. Bullying is common everywhere; but in Uganda, what differentiated me from them was that *nothing* was common—colour, class, creed. My schoolmates were Black and I was a muindi.

I was neither Muslim nor Christian. Imagine a tiny, post-toddler me, with two pigtails in red ribbons, light-skinned enough to be White, with a language barrier, trying to get by with Urdu. My schoolmates had a field day. Even my hair was different.

Imagine me, fearfully trying to integrate, trying hard not to be rich but feeling very poor nonetheless, asking Abu to drop me far away from the gate. Sometimes I had to duck under desks when there was gunfire—by the army men, of course. Others would not duck under the tables, I always hid first with my hands on my ears.

Sometimes there were mandatory naps called head-on-the-desk. I liked that because it felt safer and also because I could hide my tears. Uganda was deeply Christian, and many were saved by Christ. I had no Christ by my side, no matter how many times I recited *Our Father who art in Heaven* at the morning assembly. They knew I was from that other faith. When I was asked whether Christ had saved me, I said that I didn't know whether He had, but that I would get back to them on that query.

This was an unsatisfactory answer. Someone would have to make it okay for me to be a muindi. Someone else out there somewhere would have to change the xenophobia that Idi Amin had instilled to establish his reign of tyranny on his Black constituency. Someone else would have to like my hair, my nose, my skin, my brownness, my economic status, my parents, my language and my personal Christ. Someone would have to be accepting of my fears, but first they would have to see me.

So, I ate lunch alone, I walked to classes alone and I spent all my break time alone. Everyone walked home with friends. I walked home alone.

Now imagine what Abu might have felt. His lastborn munchkin was ashamed of him. He mentioned it to Ami. Ami asked me about it later. I said, 'I wish you would drop me off instead.'

I hated being away from Ami because she was the only one in the whole wide world who saw me. And yet there were times when I felt that she didn't see me either.

I remember that I was dressed for school. But I don't recall finding any joy in it. Uncle Jerome had been summoned to take me to school. Jerome uncle was not a kind guy.

On my way to school with Uncle Jerome, I ended up getting bruises because of his hard grip on my tiny arm, so hard that I almost felt battered. It was only natural that I kicked up an enormous fuss. My tears made nice brown droplets in the crooks of my elbows, mixing with the morning dust from my ride with Uncle Jerome. I vaguely remember his resorting to slaps if I tried to escape, but it is a distant memory, like I had watched it happening to me, rather than *felt* it happening to me. Everyone on the streets could see it.

Just another day in Uganda. A Black man dragging a recalcitrant, muindi kindergartener across the road to the tiny school, a stone's throw away from home.

No one intervened. Uncle Jerome should not have been allowed near children, let alone distressed ones with an identity crisis and separation anxiety. I felt somehow that Ami knew this but didn't care.

I didn't like school. The toilets were so dirty that the kids did their business outside the latrine instead. To make your way to the latrines, you had to step on human defecation, which was a bigger fear for me than the Ugandan rebel army that had been ordered by Idi Amin to shoot muindis on sight.*

There was the ominous terminology that the regime would use, for example, 'go to where they sleep,' to deal with people who

* https://www.nytimes.com/2003/08/17/world/idi-amin-murderous-and-erratic-ruler-of-uganda-in-the-70-s-dies-in-exile.html

took the Ugandans' economic wealth from them, but Ami always recounts those days with the words, 'shoot on sight'.

Uganda was something of a beautiful hellhole. I felt very brown, very alone and very shitty from smelling latrines all the way into the classroom. I didn't know how to say all of this to Ami, but I believed that if I kept running away from Uncle Jerome's painful grasp often enough and repeatedly returning home bruised and with muddied, knee-high, white socks, someone would be able to piece together the authenticity of the problem.

Ami didn't.

One day, when I came back home, she was still in her nightdress.

Ami: Where's Uncle Jerome? Me: *Sniffling.*

Ami: Did you come back on all your own? Me: *Nod. Tears streaming down my dusty face.* Ami: Did you cross the road on your own?

Me: *Hiccups from the uncontrolled crying.*

Ami: *Sigh. Anger. Muttering under her breath.*

She turns away to change into her going-out clothes. They are tight on her. Maybe she is sweaty from the housework and the kameez was stuck in her armpits.

Me: Please don't take me back to school, Ami. Ami: You HAVE to go to school.

And so, Ami dropped me back to the dreadful school near our house. She hated venturing out of doors. I could tell. It was over very quickly. There was a handover to a teacher who was in the middle of a class, trying to draw a C for a cat and fitting the letter between three horizontal reference lines.

That was that. The transfer of power.

I hated being away from Ami. Ami was a safe feeling. Ami was home. Ami smelled of jasmine. Ami was soft. Ami was kind.

Ami sent me to school in the middle of a civil war with a strange man who wasn't Abu. But Ami wasn't responsible for the horrific latrine or the shootings or the iron grip of Jerome, the child abuser. Ami knew that Jerome could be an arsehole, but she really wished that he did not hurt me and that is how she coped with being a woman in the middle of several wars.

For instance, about this time, she heard that Bua, her mother, had a breast tumour that could be malignant and Ami grew homesick. She felt guilty about her homesickness because her pricking conscience said that she ought to consider Uganda as her home and maybe devote more time to me and my needs.

I didn't know Bua was sick. I wanted Ami with me—proximity matters because people are safer if you're watching them all the time. Ami left me for her mother, which made little sense to me.

Separating from Ami felt like the universe was Uncle Jerome dragging me away from her. It felt that the only way to survive was to escape my predicament of being at the mercy of Uncle Jerome and having to face the torment of my schoolmates and run back to Ami.

I run back to Ami, hoping that Ami will be there, that she listens to me and doesn't send me back to hell even after hearing of my piteous plight.

AMI'S HANDS WERE POOR

Even as a child, I deeply empathized with Ami's aches and pains. Maybe it was because Reagan was in power, and the world was not good to poor folks in the Dark Continent.

When her skin was rubbed raw, my compassion for her relayed her physical pain to me. I didn't quite understand why she always had wounds. Now, of course, I know.

This was Uganda. We were poor, but Ami's hands were the poorest of all.

She had repetitive injuries on her burns and blisters from careless moments on the cooking stove or the oven door, even before the scars could heal from a previous mishap. I watched her wince in pain and make a hissing sound, but always with a rueful smile, which made it all the more heartbreaking.

She had nicks and cuts all the way up to her elbows. Her forearms were covered with the scars of myriad scratches from the thorns of the rosebushes that she pruned. Sometimes I wondered whether she was merely masochistic or if someone or something was punishing her. She took it all in her stride, but her body was so frail that it protested in rainbow colours—blue, black, indigo and red, radiant as the setting sun.

I would gaze wide-eyed at the gaping wounds and cuts, unable to look away. Sometimes I would offer tiny bits of solace with the meagre skills and resources at my command, but there was no point in anointing her burns, cuts and scrapes with salves when she would promptly plunge her hands into water almost instantly. Work. She always had to get back to work. All of Ami's waking hours were spent working.

When I saw Ami get hurt, something would physically convulse in my heart like a contraction, nausea and a hiccup, all at once. This never happened with anyone else's pain. I felt the same contraction like pain when my own daughters hurt. It was a uniquely mother's wound that recreated itself in me. Our nerves may well have been connected at an subliminal level.

I imagine that I figured out, early on, that in order to escape this pain, I had to escape Ami. She was a pain magnet, often attracting it to herself like a powerful forcefield. She wore a plain gold ring on her finger which she eventually had to relinquish because her knuckles had swollen alarmingly. She would respond to that reality by hunching over a sink, soaping her fingers so she could get the ring off forcibly, sometimes using the help of her sons, or her daughters, or even her teeth.

I hated seeing all this with such ferocity that I think my child-self believed that it was I who had inflicted this pain on her.

Ami's greatest nightmare was hurting others. To me, she seemed to find a way to harm herself by overworking. I know people who have less than perfect amis, and I envy them. It's a direct mother-child relationship. I was a fan of my ami because there was social pressure to adore her—her love, her fortitude and her patience. I am not sure whether that is a parenting bond.

By the time I was in middle school, however, I was on to her. You see, Ami was deliberately submissive as some sort of a deep con game. By now, I had realized that she wasn't all that powerless but was choosing to do this to herself—a series of atrocities on her body and spirit. Maybe this was the point when the convulsions in my heart turned from pure pain and empathy to shame. *My ami is a poor sod* soon turned to *my ami is a disgrace.*

She wore her meekness as her strength but by middle school, I hated her docility more than I hated the way she buttered toast—tearing the bread carelessly as she clumsily spread lumps of frozen butter across the slice unsystematically and hurriedly. She was beat, so why was she rushing to butter my toast like that? Where was she going to end up? Who was she ever going to be? No one. It wasn't like she was inept, far from it; she would draw the most life-like rabbit in my kindergarten-class homework. It was just that she was careless with my toast and my heart. She knew I hated toast being buttered with callous disregard for evenness and symmetry, but she still did it like a rebellious child. Morning after morning, it was ripped toast and my tears that I had for breakfast. Something had failed me in such a fundamental way and Ami was very much present during that part of my life—she got caught in the crossfire, maybe, or maybe she was undeserving of my reverence. That something which failed me was Ami. She was once wonderful and conscientious and, after Abu, she was the only choice of a parent I had, which in and of itself was unfair, but I also felt that I had inadvertently gotten stuck with the pathetic one.

Ami was once not pathetic at all but after Abu, she was like a leper, losing limb after limb of power to the family structure around her.

So, you see, somewhere in Ami, there *was* the power to refuse service.

When I was a teenager, Ami did the worst thing ever.

She let Abu die. She couldn't save him. I saw her try. I saw her feed him a softer diet, take him to Kenya for better treatment and be on the phone with relatives so she could find the best diagnosis, from piles to colon cancer. I saw her take him for walks, insist on his resting and I saw her muffle her cries in a cringe-worthy optimism—*everything will be okay.*

But Ami's burned, scarred and soft hands couldn't put Abu together again. She watched him go, taking it all in her stride like a stove burn, hissing her way into a good-for-nothing existence. I came of age at the same time as Ami and Abu becoming empty-nesters. I came of age just as Ami became a single mom. My teens were the worst teens of the universe. I wanted to turn to Ami but Ami was busy, stove-burning her heart into a million pieces. The man she had been loyal to was no more. All that cleaning and washing—for nothing. She lost all her power and diminished right before my eyes, and hate was all I could feel. Everything else was too much—too intense to be felt or permitted into my soul. I detested her with every molecule in my fifteen-year-old being.

Imagine if I didn't hate her. Imagine all those innumerable convulsions in my heart that I would suffer. If I permitted myself to love Ami, I would die because her pain was so extensive—a billion burns and cuts.

To my teenage self, all the pain that came my way was because Ami didn't protect me.

Ami was supposed to instinctively know that I hated it when people died on me unexpectedly—as Abu did. He just rode off into the sunset when I needed him the most. She should've saved him. She should've become a larger-than-life force. Yet she did the next best thing to dying—she existed as if she were invisible; unassuming and mute. She blended into the background like a good woman should, with her gratingly sweet voice, her medium-paced gait and her enormous heart which had the capacity to give endlessly to the world. Everyone thought I had the best Ami ever, but I knew I only had a make-believe Ami.

I think Ami didn't expect Abu to die. When he did, she was shell-shocked, like she had been struck by lightning. The clarity of the morning revealed that, even as Abu was buried under a mango tree, Ami went with him.

She was family before Abu, and after his death, she became a mother to my brothers before she was a mother to me. Ami practically parented me via her sons. My every request to her elicited the reply: 'Ask your brothers nicely.'

She was grieving, but to me, she wasn't there.

There had never been any fight in her to begin with, but after Abu, any remaining gumption dissipated almost entirely before my very eyes. She would pray on the mat, her dupatta tucked behind her big ears, her thick glasses cast aside, all the better because they weighed a ton. Ami was practically blind anyway. I rarely saw her eyes or what was in them.

She would perform her ablutions before praying, carefully washing her elbows, the back of her ears, her hair and her feet. I would watch her carefully and notice that, in the months after Abu's passing, her scars healed, and the new ones formed slower. She was fair-skinned—a virtue in desi cultures—and she was innocently plain. But to me, she was pretty and smelled like jasmine all the time. When she would be done praying, she would read *durood* and then blow gently at my face for blessings. I would ungraciously respond each time by turning my face away and saying callously, 'I don't want to catch a cold.'

After tending to Abu for two years and then having him die anyway, she finally found time for me. But, by then, I was resentful and made it a point to tell her—*thank you but no thank you for your too-little too-late affections. I became a priority to you only after all your other loved ones were gone. Bhaijan was married, Bhai was married, Baji was married and here I am—headed to a similar fate—no, thank you!*

To this day, I fault her for sobbing, for sniffling into handkerchiefs with bordered patterns and cross-stitched roses in pink and green, sometimes pale yellow. To this day, I feel that she should have mourned his death differently. I am not sure how that would've played out. Did I want her to have made a scene in public in proportion to the devastation we experienced? Or did I want her to have taken it in her stride?

To this day, I am confused.

I've no idea what Ami could've done to have shielded me from what I felt after Abu's death. I felt that everything changed so violently and suddenly that it had to be of Ami's doing. There was no one else around but her, so she had to be held accountable. I felt like she had burned me and then had lied to the world that I had burned myself, and that I had only myself to blame.

Abu, who cherished me, just upped and left me. So, now it was just Ami and me.

Imagine being stranded on an island with a music cassette but no Walkman to play it on. That was how I felt about Ami and my life after Abu's death. I still had a parent; only one parent was dead, but I was saddled with the one without any power.

Ami was only good as a sidekick for Abu and without him, she was of no use to me.

After all, there is so much wrong with being obsequious when your husband has just died. There was so much wrong with Ami that I choked just at the very thought of her.

Looking back, I think my own instincts answered my unanswered questions. The way I was seeing things then, with my siblings serially married off into respectable Konkani families, there were three distinct stages to a woman's life: when she is of marriageable age, when she is married and when she is dead. Unless they are in one of these three stages, women are irrelevant. If I could not escape any of these stages, I would sally forth and make myself a fourth stage: my own song.

My own permission slip, from a liberal, progressive husband who would love me enough to encourage me to do something more individualistic than needlepoint, or doing dishes, or getting our kids through college. For instance, I wanted to figure skate. I could write, too, if I couldn't figure skate. In actual fact, I didn't have a clue what I wanted to do in life, but I sure as hell did know that I wasn't going to do what Ami had done all her life. I wanted to do what the men did. I didn't see them cooking or cleaning. I didn't see their backs bent, rounded and hunched over the sink or a hot stove, their voices mellowed down to a whisper and I never saw scars on their hands. I wanted to be men. Men had more than four stages to their lives, hundreds.

Take Abu, for instance. He got to come home from his teaching job, change into his comfortable *lungi*, an attire he borrowed from Bangladeshi culture. He'd nap in his white vest while Ami took a break from housework to read him to sleep.

Imagine that. The privilege!

Actually, I wanted that—I wanted precisely that. To be given a priority as soon as I returned from work. I wanted to be read to while I drifted in and out of my afternoon siesta. I wanted someone waiting on me hand and foot when I came home, and I wanted to demand silence from the children when I was not to be disturbed. I know everyone around me would remind me of my place if I told them I wanted to be Abu, so I secretly harboured this dream and waited for its time to come to fruition. I wanted power. I wanted it for myself, and I wanted it for Ami.

Born in the same era as the tassel-bra-wearing Madonna, I felt that a unique boon had been granted to me. She seemed to be a kind of a symbol—that I could inch forward in what I was allowed to do. My female cousins were not allowed to thread their upper lip, or cut their hip-length braids, or even go on field trips. I could perhaps marry into my own people. Get away—go from marriageable to married, to being a writer and then dying. That would be victorious on so many counts. Meanwhile, Ami was the epitome of everything I was never ever going to become.

AMI'S BODY IS A USEFUL THING

Ami used her body well. She used it to transport souls, to make bread and to provide for Abu and us.

She had an old-fashioned laundry iron to press the clothes; thick and black, almost like it had been hewn from volcanic rock. It had a latched lid that could be raised. She would first light the coal with a combination of matchsticks and newspapers. If the coal was dry the matches would be wet—something would invariably be off. She somehow managed to put the hot coals into the belly of that damn iron. She did that not with the tongs but with something dumb like a wooden spatula, or her own bare hands, or a puffy newspaper. After a few burns on her hands, the iron would finally be ready for use—on Abu's *kaunda* suits or safari suits or our school uniforms. She couldn't take her own sweet time with this task because the iron would go cold.

She had a banana palm-leaf winnowing tray, curved along one edge and flat on the other side. Ami used this for separating grit and husk from the rice and wheat. She would toss the grain into the air and deftly catch it in her tray. Magically, the grain separated from the chaff, as the saying goes. Men have long immortalized the various tasks women do by making sayings about them.

However, men have also humiliated women for getting things wrong. Many a time, Abu would stop chewing his food and glare at Ami through his too-big-for-his-face glasses. Everybody at the table simultaneously stopped chewing at that instant because it was a moment of deafening silence, like someone or something had died.

I don't recall the exact words, but I remember the sting. Ami would be told off in no uncertain terms for attempting to break Abu's jaw with sand particles or grit in his food. Abu was a paranoid man who rarely, if ever, gave Ami the benefit of the doubt.

The sting that Ami felt during those sinister moments still resonates in my bones.

It was sinister because I would always be amazed at how many times Ami would toss the rice into the sky, like a skilful air- bender, without allowing any grains to fall to the ground. Ami was an expert at cleaning the rice. She didn't deserve this.

She painstakingly picked over the wheat with her fingers, bit by bit, bent over, straining her half-blind eyes and Scotch-tapped glasses to make sure that no contamination ever passed into our food.

It was sinister because I'd always tell her how amazing she was. I was only as tall as her knees, but I knew how to tell her what I thought of her. It was the decent thing to do. You see a goddess, you bow down to her; I told her, in my own broken words, that I considered her imbued with magical powers.

The world hadn't yet taught me how little sorcery she really knew and how utterly craft-dependent her sleight of hand was. Whenever Abu found gravel in the bite he took or spat out husk, he flew into a rage and gave Ami a sharp putdown. In those moments, I felt Ami's magic ebbing away in silence. Abu found ways to shake Ami's faith, our daytime Ami-Aashi moments, with sand particles. Abu had never touched hot coals in his life. He had never hunched over a tray to separate the food from what it grew in. He had a lot of power all the time. I was enamoured by Ami, but did she like me as much?

Sometimes, albeit rarely, Abu seemed to me like a freeloader. Ami and I had an unspoken code language.

It went by way of our eyes meeting, and when I saw the code in her eyes which translated into—Abu is being a pain—we both immediately shrank. We didn't do any more magic tricks. We apologized, we admitted blame, we were happy to have been made an example of, we knew we deserved it and we were grateful to have been taught that we had forgotten our limits.

But you know the thing about magic: for it to work, you must believe in it.

After all, if we could handle fire with our fingers, we knew how to tame it or, at the least, relegate it to its grave.

AMI HAD SOME OTHER CHILDREN

Baji was always a sourpuss. Especially when Bhai gave me his attention and not her. I think she secretly wished I hadn't been born or, at the very least, that I hadn't made it—like the twins. Imagine that—having a body to get a soul into, but then missing the station. Baji sometimes looked at me like she wished that my soul had not entered my body. Her eyes would puncture my psyche, try to travel me back in time to end me. I didn't care. I was very cute. Baji was seven years older and at a very awkward age.

Bhai was fourteen years older, and his smile lit up my life. He used to make go-karts for Baji and lightbulbs by manufacturing his own electric circuits and give her day-long rides on it. But the music stopped for her when I came along. I don't feel bad at all because to have lived and gotten Bhai's love is worth throwing someone else in front of a bullet train.

I did hear though that Bhai, too, had wanted me dead. Apparently, Bhai loved Ami as well and he had just about had it with Abu always getting Ami to have babies and jeopardizing her life. Bhai did not like Abu. I hear that, despite Ami's promise to come back alive with a healthy baby (me), Bhai hadn't believed her.

Bhai had grabbed Abu by his shirt collar and had pinned him to a wall, 'If anything happens to my mother, I'll kill the child.'

You see, between all the housework and childbearing, Bhai was convinced Ami would die.

Life had other plans.

Ami came home with me. We both lived, contradicting Bhai's pessimism.

Bhai was smitten by my tiny, intelligent eyes, and I do think that he saw circuit mechanisms in me—a way to light me up. Toss tiny me up in the air, feed me honey, rock me, wrap me, croon to me and eventually tell me to climb trees and get myself enmeshed with the stars up there where he always wanted me to fly.

All Baji got was the few years of general play and doting.

When Ami walked in with me wrapped in neon-blue velvet from Nasambia Hospital, Bhai made me more than merely an object to dote upon. He made me slightly more girl, but always treated me like a boy.

Go, get that yourself, I'll prop you up. You touch the roof.

You look at the nestlings in the oak tree in the backyard. You won't fall, I'm right here.

If I had a sensitivity to something, he exposure-therapied it out of me.

Beat that!

Bhaijan was all of that but without the extra turbo energy that Bhai had. His modus operandi was to dote and love and support whilst studying for his exams. But while Bhai called me Mimi, it was Bhaijan who called me Boy.

I was an eighties child reparented by the boomer brothers, who vowed to do things differently for me. Yes, yes, you can go with your friends on the field trip, to the temple, to the church;

yes, I can throw you a few feet high in the sky and you can find yourself safely on the ground.

Bhaijan was the silent type. He would always frown over problems and give them life and longevity. When he was learning what was in *Gray's Anatomy*, or some such thing, I was at his feet, massaging his soles with my tiny fingertips, a chore I didn't mind at all. Apparently, it soothed him enough to study. It soothed me that it soothed him.

Bhaijan introduced me to cocoa powder mixed in with bits of sugar served in a saucer and told me to lick it directly from the saucer like a cat.

Bhaijan had status, like the pope or someone, but a pope of smarts. Legend has it that Bhaijan never used an eraser while working. Today, that would be akin to saying an author never used the backspace tab on the keypad. That was an ode to his conscientious and mindful research into anything. He folded napkins precisely in the way they needed to be folded. He was eighteen, for god's sake! He was a model kid, and his name was spoken in awed whispers to slow kids, as they were known then, to be ashamed of themselves because just look at what he had achieved with nothing but a public library in godforsaken Uganda during the wars. His name would reverberate in the house like a prayer.

Bhaijan outperformed all standards by always topping his class, whatever that class was and whatever that top position was. I heard the word 'position' more times than I heard my own name. Be like Bhaijan. What would Bhaijan do? Bhaijan this, Bhaijan that.

Thankfully, because Bhaijan was paying attention in his biology class, he did save my life.

While Bhai was threatening Abu to kill me if Ami was brought home in a body bag after birthing me, Bhaijan was supportive— helping with the dishes, helping Ami put together a hospital bag.

He also lovingly joked with Ami that had he been a girl, they technically could've been having babies at the same time. When I was a newborn, Ami starved me of breast milk because she wasn't lactating. One of the perils of a woman bearing a child at an advanced age, I guess, but why wouldn't she just supplement this with goat's milk?

I would bawl all night and Ami would be distraught but unable to figure out why. It was Bhaijan who pointed out to Ami that I was just hungry and that they should try feeding me two bottles instead of one.

She told Bhaijan he didn't know what he was talking about, after which there were three more days of crying and starving. Then Bhaijan took matters into his own hands and fed me an adequate amount of goat's milk that a human baby must have. When I had downed the seventh ounce of goat's milk, Ami conceded: 'Yes, I have forgotten how to be a mom.'

Bhaijan loved order and his books. Bhai would not respect the fact that chaos is not the norm and Bhaijan was said to be more or less tolerant of Bhai's messing up his study desk. Until one day, Bhaijan was not more or less tolerant and delivered a jab into Bhai's lungs. After that, Bhai just had to take his disorder and creative chaos elsewhere.

Bhai would physically push Baji's face on to the floor if she tried to play with some plastic shopping bag that floated its way into our poor house as a playground entertainment for the week. That was their relationship.

The three of them don't say much about how they were with Abu. But Abu did apologize to Bhaijan for his physical violence before he died. Abu couldn't work up the courage to apologize in person, so he wrote it in a letter, which is how I know it is of significance.

Bhai—well . . . we all know how he saw Abu—adversarial, especially in the context of Ami. Baji was respectful of Abu, fearful even. I know there was an incident where Baji took Abu's file divider and gave it to some friend—it backfired, and Baji got some sort of punishment. When the file divider was mentioned, the stink of death and silence filled the air.

When it came to me, however, everyone was there in service. In love. In admiration. In wonder. In joy. In service.

Abu permitted everything for me, everything except toys and snacks—so that was no good, really. I was aware that I was lucky to be born to a man whose hands had tired. I was lucky my father appeared more loving because his bones and anger had been eroded by time.

Ami may have starved me, but she really did have her limitations, arthritis being one of them. Yet she did whatever I asked, no matter how painful her knobby knees were.

We were a family that didn't ever say things to ourselves in a self-congratulatory way, but we were a unit that produced the finest humans without any favours or a single dime being spent that belonged to anyone but Abu's schoolteacher salary.

I am the greatest beneficiary of those fine humans.

I've never forgotten that I belonged among the stars. Even when I was eating shit.

AMI MISPLACED MY ABU

I was eight.

I saw blood in the toilet and called for Ami. I was alarmed and panic-stricken.

She didn't flinch. She calmly said Abu may have used it and forgotten to flush twice (Ugandan plumbing).

It's nothing. It's just piles.

It was colon cancer.

And so, when I was a pre-teen, Ami started disappearing. It reminded me of the way my teachers disappeared, wiped away—I would learn later—in the Ugandan acquired immunodeficiency syndrome (AIDS) epidemic of the 1980s. Except with Ami, she was just not there in her own head. She was maternally ambivalent, confused and stricken by loss and grief.

That's the adult me talking, but the way I saw it as a child, it was betrayal. I was newer than Abu and I needed more of her than he did. He had already got her. He had already had her. It was my turn.

As she cared for Abu, giving him more and more chunks of my time, she no longer smelled like jasmine. She began to age, with rickety, calcifying legs that hobbled obediently to fulfil Abu's whims. I had made my mom a goddess. Now, I made her a witch. The truth is somewhere in between, but we must not speak of the in-between.

The in-betweens resolve nothing.

I saw Ami on a prayer mat. I saw Ami cooking. I saw Ami cleaning. I saw Ami entertaining guests. I rarely saw her sleeping and when she did sleep, she made sounds to ward off some spirit, asking it to leave because she had a right to peace. She had a right to sleep.

I also saw Ami fighting with Abu. She would demand he lower his voice. He would respond to that by raising his voice. I noticed that Ami pushed back, but only sometimes, and even then it was only to protect the family's reputation from eavesdropping neighbours.

Ami took care of Abu. She did all the chores for him and his children. She read to him almost every day when he came home from work. But other than those two things, I often saw him upset and Ami deeply uncomfortable because he had no qualms about making his annoyance abundantly clear to her. The doer of all upsetting things was Abu, and the receiver of his upsetting conduct was Ami.

Still, there was a bond between them, whatever that was worth.

She rushed to meet his nap time by completing all her work before he summoned her. I think she rather looked forward to the reading of *Kawateen Times,* Pakistan's women's digests with romance and love and in-law squabbles. There was the reading of Razia Butt, who was the Danielle Steel of Pakistani romance. Razia Butt wrote stories about love and courtship, and love that makes sense of relationship chaos. There invariably was a damsel in distress in these stories and good deal of rolling in the hay.

I got to stay for the racy content of Razia Butt, unlike when they watched Indian art films where I would be asked to leave the room but watched anyway through the pea-pod-sized peephole.

Abu called Ami *Mehra*. When he was particularly affectionate, he called her *moto*. I asked him why he would call her a word that meant fatso, and he said, *pyar say*.

They would walk hand in hand in the moonlight. When I was on Abu's shoulders, he had to let go of Ami's hand to hold my legs. I would clutch Abu's hair. His hair was plentiful, jet-black and combed to perfection. He loved it when I tilted my head back and pretended to fall, grabbing on to his hair to save myself.

Ami seemed frail to me—I wanted to save her from fading away, but little me didn't know how to do so. It wasn't the drudgery of the endless housework that faded Ami. It wasn't the civil war in Uganda against Asians that melted Ami. It was the constant state of exile. The uncertainty it brought with regard to food supply and the perpetual worrying whether the kids would return home safely from school.

Can one recover from six months of that? Thirty-five years?

After that incident of seeing blood in the loo and the discovery that this was merely Abu dying, I didn't know what it meant for Ami and Abu's relationship.

But without Ami interacting with Abu through house fire arguments and fights and acts of service, I didn't understand how the world would work.

I didn't know what safety blanket to take from the Ami-Abu era to the Abu-less era. But I sure did need that Kiki blanket of mine one more time, the one the army people made me outgrow all too soon.

AMI HAS TO TELL LIES

I must have been about three or four years old, all dressed up for Eid. Bangles, glitter and gold clothes with *gota* on it, delighted to be perched on the kitchen counter, as I waited for the custard biscuits to be done. Ami was pouring boiling milk into my mug. The large saucepan slipped and there I was, right there, to receive its entire scalding, white contents just below my pee hole. The custard biscuits burned with me. Charred, hard and useless enough to be tossed directly into the bin.

When he heard the screams, Abu rushed into the kitchen.

'I didn't do it,' Ami denied hurriedly. 'Aisha herself was shaking the table and the milk spilled on her.'

Ami lied. She lied because she was terrified of Abu's wrath. Imagine how much I belonged to Abu. I think of that all the time. I liked belonging that much to him. Even now. There was a time when I belonged to someone so much that the woman who birthed me hid from him because she had harmed me, albeit inadvertently.

I liked the concept—a lot. I almost want to recreate it.

I remember the milk-scalding incident in flashes. Me, high up on the counter, my legs swinging way above the kitchen floor, something happening, panic, Abu rushing into the kitchen, then I was by the door, someone was holding me aloft by my armpits, someone else removed my silk pyjamas and then, along with my pyjamas, this yellowing thing peeled off, a cross between wax and pale, chicken skin.

Chunks of me falling to the floor like melted wax. More panic. More screams.

I think I slipped into a coma from the shock.

Later, I lay spreadeagled on my cot my legs apart to make sure they weren't touching each other. I looked down. No underwear.

There were so many visitors in my room. Home felt like a funeral wake and I was the one being mourned.

Thank god, they said, she is saved; a few inches higher and she would have to remain unmarried. I had tincture of iodine and butter-yellow Burnol smeared all over me. Waist down, I was almost a rainbow. The parts that were not anointed with medicine were salmon-pink.

Nothing hurt; it was just a sweet, fever-like feeling. I asked for Ami and she was promptly summoned.

Ami. *Guria*. Ami. Guria.

She started crying. I can't be sure. Maybe I cried first. Everyone gave us a moment and left.

'Don't tell Abu,' she whispered. I nodded and dropped back into my fever-sleep.

It never occurred to Ami that she could say, sorry, I burned *my* child, it was *my* mistake. Let *us* take her to the doctor. She had to fib a lot. I believe it was a survival tactic when people around you were unreasonable.

Abu was unreasonable.

I couldn't walk for months.

ABU MADE AMI INVISIBLE

Not only was Abu dark, but just like the Africans, he was poor. The man would just not spend money. Everything about money was a no.

Can I get a pudding?

No.

Can I buy a petticoat, so my developing breasts are no longer an embarrassment?

No.

Can Baji get sanitary pads?

No.

So, here was this man, who was going to give my ami a real taste of African poverty in a new country she knew nothing about.

The Konkanis whom I knew had a manufactured identity— they sought to establish their inner sense of belonging by insisting that Pakistan was not to be. That it served no purpose. That Jinnah was a selfish politician and by creating Pakistan, Indian Muslims were now worse off, not better off. They also said that Islam had no room for nationalism. So, the two meccas of Konkanis are anti-Pakistanism and Arabization.

Konkanis are from the Konkan region. This is a region along the western coast of India, including a part of Goa, Maharashtra and Karnataka. Hence the obsessive coconuts and the Marathi-Gujarati feel to the Konkani language. I am yet to meet a Konkani who is okay with being Indian and okay with having Pakistan exist. I am told my nanajan was one such man. Nanajan, an avid supporter of Jinnah, had this revolutionary leader's picture in his home. He watched the politics of the subcontinent unfold from the home he had built in Nairobi.

There was a Konkani Muslim hierarchy in Nairobi, with a club called the Konkani Muslim Club. No points for creativity but full marks for the cultish emblems like the sports team, the community centre and the group leader. Sheikh Saab was the master of ceremonies for all events because he knew how to write and speak in English. He was diminutive and unassuming.

There was a mad woman who would go around kicking people. The rest of the women usually steered clear of her, but she inevitably met her target head on and furiously. Every Eid or wedding or funeral required personal visits to people's homes where I saw more mentally unwell people. Konkanis are big on marrying Konkanis, but drew the line at marrying their own siblings. That was it as far as standards went.

I would invariably burst into fits of laughter during these visits. I think it was the absurdity of my life and things like being served ZamZam water in a thimble-sized brass cup that triggered this unbecoming mirth. But it flew in the face of all propriety to sneer at people's culture in their over-the-top drawing rooms with the doilies and the Ayat-ul-Qursi's framed in the exact same way in every home. It was very bad. I wasn't just being a bad kid; I was being a bad person.

That's the other thing about Konkanis in Kenya. Perhaps because they watched Doordarshan TV and Star Plus dramas as a staple for political astuteness, they really were stuck in the era when Nanajan migrated. It was like a time freeze. I think I did take liberties because these people took themselves too seriously and it all appeared ridiculous in the backdrop of my repressed trauma.

I was always filled with a deep aversion whenever I entered a room full of Konkanis, a vacuum just waiting to be filled with some loyalty test to bring in some sense of belonging.

Perhaps Abu felt it as well; however, he never showed his resentment even if he did feel alienated by the Konkanis. He just sat there with the confidence of a king, and why wouldn't he? Abu, after all, had a master's degree. He knew a lot about history and politics and geography—too much to care about what these simpletons thought of him.

As far as Abu was concerned, he was going to liberate and civilize the middle-school dropout he'd married in Ami, by making her read stories to him every day during his siesta until he died of colon cancer.

Of all the truths out there, the absolute truth of cancer cells prevails eventually.

Abu could school Ami's entire family on literally how pathetic and disenfranchised their lot was. Also, and more importantly, Abu was Pakistani, a migrant Pakistani. So, Abu knew what anyone who had lost a home had experienced—in all fairness, *they* were the ones who should have really been washing his feet and drinking that water.

Inferiority complexes are terrible things. They are infectious and are passed on from generation to generation into posterity.

ABU FRIGHTENS AMI

Ami struggled with being believed. Even for stories she was the only witness for. She was deprived, it seemed to me, of basic social standing.

Some of my earliest memories are of Ami trying to get Abu to not yell at her or insult her near the windows. People would hear. That was her biggest fear.

Ami's fear, that someone would hear Abu's acrimony towards her, became my fear. It settled in my milk teeth and then into my permanent teeth. It set my teeth on edge whenever he yelled at her, but I would be incapable of helping reduce her shame.

She would start drawing the green, leaf-print curtains whenever Abu began his rant. Abu hated being discommoded, but drawing the curtains was easier than trying to mute Abu by retaliating. So, she negotiated her self-respect by asking for private humiliation.

Please don't scream near the windows.

I bet Ami liked to be liked. I bet it was hard for her to have the world know your husband doesn't like you.

I watched. I watched. I watched.

From under the table once. Another time from behind the sofa. These people who brought me joy were unrecognizable to me.

What were they doing? Why were they wrecking what felt like home?

Why wouldn't Ami fight back?

It's really not nice to admonish someone who reads you romance novels while you nap.

ABU SAID UGANDA IS HOME FOREVER

Abu was ill even before he was ill.

Love makes you ill and do stupid things like wishfully thinking your way out of a war by repeating to yourself: all will be well. I wondered what made them love Uganda so much.

I remember Abu's saying we wouldn't be shot on sight by the army despite their orders to do so. He said: *We are not them. We haven't oppressed anyone and we have no need to leave.*

My parents suffered from a case of facts, just as my teacher suffered from a case of denial that his legs were way past their use-by date, weighed a ton each and ought not to be dragged to school every day.

Ami and Abu should have evacuated Uganda like everybody else had done.

Kampala had very little going for it. Sure, it was green and quiet. There were lots of pedestrians and cyclists, which perhaps gave the illusion of calm. Beyond the walls of the educational campuses in which we lived, a guerrilla warfare raged with rape, plunder and people being attacked with machetes just for belonging to a different tribe. I was born in 1981, the year of the AIDS epidemic; it was also the year after Milton Obote came to power for the second time, but the Idi Amin loyalists didn't just leave. In 1985, Obote was overthrown by military leaders Bazilio Olara-Okello and Tito Okello, before Yoweri Museveni took power in 1986. Museveni is still president today—almost four decades of rule by one man. One of his classmates is his chief of staff, another a minister. Uganda is tribal to the core. People grow cassava and bananas and corn, but not every hoe and machete is used for nurturing crops.

Ami liked Museveni because after his coming into power, she got milk and fish and wheat in time, and the children and Abu returned home safely.

The nightly news was read by a smiling, middle-aged newscaster with a neatly trimmed beard who reported the most horrendous chaos and death tolls with a smile.

Abu and Ami were wholly obsessed with all things Pakistani: Pakistani literature, Urdu poetry, Pakistani society, Pakistanis, Pakistani food and, on the side, some Indian food, Bollywood and our community of Hindu and Christian friends. It was a state within a state—which really helped with the delusion of not knowing your terrain.

There was always death and violence around us. People died of AIDS, of disease and of murder. Lots of Ugandans murdered rich, brown people. Lots of Ugandans murdered Ugandans. Sometimes, Baji saw them dead on the sidewalks when Abu would insist school should not be missed just because there was a war going on. Sometimes the war hit home, and Ami got shot at.

Another time, our neighbour, Varughese uncle, didn't return home and Annie aunty cried into the curtains, lamenting like she instinctively knew he was already dead. But he wasn't dead. He had gone to buy milk for my friend Angela, and had gotten caught in a crossfire between the Obote forces and the anti-Obote rebels, so he hid in an abandoned shack for two weeks until the firing stopped.

He didn't emerge until it was safe to mount his motorbike and head back to the high-school campus where he too was a teacher. I don't exactly know how Annie aunty felt as she received him home when he rode into their driveway, but I can imagine it was easier to assume he was dead rather than alive. Our home was always a sanctuary. Everyone left their stuff in our house when they left on overnight trips. All the lonely women, whose husbands were not home, came to Ami and Abu.

I would have been five-ish when Museveni was in power.

If Abu hadn't died of cancer, maybe I would've still been tied to the rural campus life in Uganda. I would've inherited his disease of refusing to be rooted and stagnant.

In any case, I inherited the Pakistan bug as well; its own kind of identity-insanity, where you overvalue things and undervalue them outside of the reality before you.

Our Kampala home was a cottage with a red-tiled roof and a garden that was filled with more of Ami's favourite bluebells and dahlias and roses of all colours. There was a gigantic oak in the backyard. A swing was slung on its branch for me. However, as the swing's nylon rope was too tough on the skin of my thighs, Bhai taught me to climb the tree instead. There are tons of pictures of me in the lacy dresses which Ami made, smeared and ruined by tree gum and gunk. There are loads of pictures of these gardens that could as well belong to a glossy magazine.

Indoors, there was the desi orderliness arranged by Ami: the *ajrak* (or block-printed) bedsheets from Karachi, the table and chair and Abu's ceiling-high, room-wide bookshelf that had books both in the back and the front—thousands. In the front were the important ones. Geography, *Britannica*, compilations of the best of *Reader's Digest* and the Holy Quran wedged between the atlas and the Pakistan history textbooks. The Quran was the only scripture we were told was ours to read and believe in. The notion was that it was a complete text that didn't need any further reading on religion and that the *sunnat* of the Prophet, published in the *hadith*, was not the word of Allah, the benevolent creator, and therefore less central.

Ami's side of the family felt that that was irreverent, which is why when we went to visit Ami's family in Kenya, there was trouble. I wouldn't know how to recite the Ayatul Kursi, and Abu used to lead the congregation prayers in misspoken Arabic. They also felt that Abu's prayers were embarrassingly rushed and short and followed up too often with the announcement that the food was getting cold, when in fact the food hadn't even been served.

Ami was different in Kenya. Uganda was home. Kenya felt like old money. But Uganda felt new money, accompanied with a sense of scarcity.

There were issues with the architecture of homes in Kenya, but who cared? We had our own home in Uganda.

The hierarchical flowchart of my favourite places and people in Kampala home was something like this: Ami at the top; Bhai was next because he was always choosing me over Baji; Abu, because he always let me sit on the engine of the motorbike; Abu again because he was much more interesting than Ami when he sat on his reading chair reading or writing in his diary with his fountain pen; Abu again because he tended to take up a lot of space in a room; then Bhai again because he would always be dismantling and re-assembling things; Bhai again because he was causing trouble and was sometimes up to no good, but he was always showing off to me that this was the way to be; Baji because sometimes she made me Ovaltine and sugar and let me lick it like a cat; getting to sleep between Ami and Abu when I was sick, or when I accidentally sliced my head open; then, there was the reading nook behind the space between Abu's bookshelf at the back and the window that opened out into the backyard.

This is where I hid and looked at the drawing-book guide in which there were nude sketches of men and women. I think Ami knew that I was there, but she never barged in. It was tiny enough to only accommodate a fat cat or a small child. Then Abu's shoulders when he and Ami walked in the moonlight. Then Bhaijan because he was so smart and introverted that I never quite got him. Maybe sometimes when he would ask me to massage his clean, soft soles while he read *Gray's Anatomy* textbooks for his A-level exams and ended up topping the country. The smiling newscaster spoke his name over and over again in the news. Lastly, my least favourite place was the spot on the cement floor that Bhai had refilled with cement after the rebel, in his camouflage uniform, had fired at Ami with his rifle and the bullet, which missed hitting her feet, ploughed into the cement floor. The new cement patch was a lighter colour. Every time I entered the living room, I'd do my best to avoid looking at that filled-up crater on the floor but end up staring at it, mortified.

I didn't want anything to hurt my ami. She was number one in the hierarchy of a home. The crater was a metaphor for the way I was powerless over the things that hurt her.

NO LAST WORD FOR AMI

To this day, Ami has never retaliated—neither on my behalf nor hers.

She never had the last word. She may have believed that I was being bullied by her siblings, who were my uncles and aunts as a teenager, but she never said, *Leave my daughter alone, she's mine and she's fine just as she is.*

Each time there was a family intervention to fix me somehow by the khalas and mamus, she would be quiet and unobtrusive. She would let the others berate me by being a loyal audience.

Their verdict that I was broken prevailed.

Hers never existed because she didn't ever speak up.

Is it not surprising then that I wanted to draw the curtain between myself and the world? The first thing to do was to not let anyone know that a bad thing was happening to me.

Two bad things—one, that my being a bad girl had been discovered by Ami's beloved family and two, that they were hurting her by hurting me.

Ami's family was somehow oblivious to the fact that, time and again, Ami had been severely tongue-lashed by Abu. Now that

Abu was dead and that chapter was permanently closed, she could use some peace.

I was sad for her more than I was sad for me.

I wanted to ask her, Ami, do you think I'm a bad girl? But I never did so because I was afraid of what her answer would be.

If she thought I was unfairly and undeservingly being labelled a bad girl when I was, in fact, a good girl, that would be sad in its own way. If she agreed with her brothers and sisters that I was a blot on their stellar standards of godliness, then my heart would break irreparably.

Some things are just not worth knowing.

I would rather live not knowing than find out that she had so much self-loathing that it automatically transmitted itself to me as if I were a conductor. She didn't insulate me from the ugliness of what the world did to women who belonged to men who were either absent or not powerful.

She was a victim of Abu and I, a victim of her family. Ami and I shared trauma.

The only way to leave the pain was to leave Ami.

Abu's death loomed over our heads—Ami's and mine—like we were somehow responsible for it. Like we had been caught red-handed being bad, that for a while we had tried to be cool but the gods of uncool had finally found us and had descended upon us like it was judgement day. Why else would Ami droop her shoulders and just stand by as her siblings cut me down to size when I was a mere teenager? Why else would my own family perceive me as a threat?

At least they were whispering, unlike Abu who would condemn Ami within earshot of the neighbours. Yet, in their whispers lived some nuclear power that made me feel like I was responsible for genocide, the Great Plague or some spectacular evil, and these good people were doing their utmost to name the evil in order to distance themselves from it. From me.

They say insult and shame light up the same pain receptors in the brain that a physical thrashing does. Man, are they spot on!

After my relatives left, I would be exhausted. It was like my body was asking me to shut down a million times over. It was in these days that I developed the habit of staying inside the duvet when crumbling.

That was a very special kind of shame I felt, to see her break down like that. I may have had a sense of causing Abu enough pain to leave me, and now perhaps my ami's pain was also my fault somehow. In both pains, I was unable to distinguish that they were both already gone. All I had was myself.

ABU WAS A COIN TOSS ANYWAY

Ami didn't like anyone knowing that she was poor and had never owned a fridge for most of her life. Abu thought Ami asked for too much. Who needed a fridge anyway when there was so little food in the first place?

Although I'd never witnessed any domestic violence, I suppose my siblings had. It was never anything so major as to send her to the emergency room, but it was enough for them to intervene to protect Ami.

Ami's first week of marriage ended up being a week in the life of Scheherazade—and her only coping strategy was storytelling. Ami was ostracized for marrying late. She married at the same age as I did, twenty-two, long past her sell-by date because her peers had married at sixteen. She had received only two proposals for marriage, which was 100 per cent more than my number of proposals, but they were considered too few a number—her peers had half a dozen each. One proposal was from her cousin (of course it was, because which Indian Muslim family doesn't marry cousins?) and the other was Abu. Her cousin was a nice, vanilla guy; Abu was an educated man, much older than her, and lived in Uganda, not in Kenya. Abu also wasn't as good-looking—he had a rugged side to him. Meanwhile, Ami's peers had pretty men.

Talk about peer pressure. Ami and older Khalajan married on the same day. So, Ami was stood next to her weird-looking husband and older Khalajan was beside a guy who looked like Richard Gere. That sucked for Ami as she sat there in a white sari and red dupatta, feeling old and already filled with a crushing suspicion that she had got this strange dude because she wasn't good enough as bride material.

Ami was practically blind. If she didn't have on her really thick spectacles, you could walk into the room butt-naked and she wouldn't bat an eyelid. Her schoolmates bullied her, saying she wore the bottoms of Coca-Cola glass bottles on her eyes. Despite being a gifted artist, she could barely see what the teacher wrote on the blackboard and eventually flunked out of middle school— so, more shame. Anyway, there she was on her wedding day. Was she kneeling on a mat, her legs tucked beneath her and bent double with her head on her knees? As if being a virgin wasn't subjugation enough for this culture, they had draped a dupatta over her bent head and shoulders which hung over her face and neck. Not enough, she also had on a *ghunghat* obscuring the lower half of her face like a *naqaba* bravo-for-war-booty moment.

Now this school dropout, who had waited so patiently all her life for a suitor, was sitting beside someone she had chosen by way of a coin toss. I understand fate plays a big part in life, but my mom was smart enough to understand this and opt for a game of probability. I do salute her choice. I mean, what if she had chosen to marry her cousin—you do not need to go to school to understand that inbreeding is a very bad thing. So kudos, Ami!

If two sisters are sitting side by side with their respective husbands, don't you think it is only natural to compare the couples to see who won the lottery of great looks and more gold? Everyone at the wedding, looking at these two couples, would cast slurs about Abu within Ami's earshot because who gave a shit about women's feelings anyway?

Ami had been told that Abu was ugly, old and uncouth. They also called him *kaala*—colourism abounded in that Konkani community. Abu looked like an African beside the three extremely fair-skinned people who shared the wedding ceremony with him. Abu was kaala for sure. When on his shoulders, I'd notice how evenly roasted he was. He was not tanned; he was dark, just like the continent.

Being kaala was akin to being poor because Africa was poor and Black. Indian Muslims came to East Africa to build the railroad during British imperialism and stayed on for at least three generations because it was fun to be light-skinned and richer. It's great to feel superior about something, even though the empires you've built are on the backs of Black people. Ami's family had a merchant streak and so they had set up large supermarket chains before it was even a thing. There was a layered classism that made it all the more fun to stay on in a place where you were no longer the scum of the earth—which is what the Konkanis were back in Konkan, feasting on their prawns like God's offerings and trying to spin their own self-worth story. Yet, along come the railroad construction call and off they went like migrating birds into a place that was marked lethal—the Dark Continent.

I would not share my wedding with anyone. But then, Ami and I ended up doing very similar things after our weddings—we plunged into hostile countries we didn't know.

Had both Ami and I felt betrayed by our families?

People jump into the fire only if they're already in the frying pan.

ABU WAS THE BOSS OF AMI

Ami's body was a dead giveaway of the calamities that had befallen her. Before Abu, she could flow into all sorts of yoga positions: the plough, the shoulder stand and even the headstand. After Abu, she would face the wall and weep, trying not to throw up the blood borne of her stomach ulcer. She succeeded; nonetheless, it stained her teeth crimson. Ami's life ran the entire gamut from being a force and then, not; her existence shocked, humbled and enraged me.

Ami's hands spoke volumes of how bruised she was on the inside. I was a child, what did I know about pain, except that the most precious thing in my little universe always had the hands of a mineworker? Her knuckles were knobbly from early onset arthritis. They reminded me of something that wasn't supposed to be there growing inside of her. I would massage her hands in a futile attempt to make her feel better, and she would say something tender and loving like—*now that you have touched them, they will heal.*

She was very diligent and active, and even made her own soap at home. It was alarming to see her listlessness after she became a widow. But after Abu's death, she could barely eat. Ami always had gut issues, but after Abu's death, she was ruled by them.

When Ami watched TV, she simultaneously shelled peas or did cross-stitch for our faded sofa's antimacassar. She was a glutton for multitasking and I never saw her do one thing and one thing alone, except maybe pray on the *musalla* prayer mat. But when I think about it, she even interrupted her conversations with God because the milk could boil over—and the damn milk was always boiling over. She was ruled by milk.

We didn't have a fridge and so the milk had to be boiled from time to time to keep it from curdling. So, you see, even milk was high stakes for Ami.

After Abu's death, we bought a real refrigerator. And Ami's hands improved—now, she no longer needed to boil milk thrice a day.

It was the uncertainty of Abu's illness and the two-year lead-up to his death that finally destroyed her life as I knew it.

She was like powder I'd feel on my fingertips when I'd go butterfly catching. She was like that butterfly's last moments—fluttering around so it could divert, deflect or dilute death that was in the air right beneath her wings.

She is my only living parent but after Abu's demise, her status plummeted lower than mine. I was a mere child yet she was deemed incapable of looking after me. I was transferred to my uncles and then my brothers, but never to my ami. This was not decreed, as in a will or testament, but I noticed how nothing pertaining to me was decided by her. Instead, I was communal property for which there had to be collective deliberations.

I wanted Ami and me to have a moment at Abu's grave, to weep. I wanted time to simultaneously grapple with the fear of death by doing normal teenage things, like kick rocks until my toes bled. I wanted the universe to shatter so I could contain mine. Although everything went on as normal, Ami didn't . . . which is why I should've been locked in with her and her alone, so I could deal with my grief.

Instead, it was decided that we should immediately move to Kenya to be close to family.

Soon, I retreated from Ami. Whatever separation anxiety that I suffered as a child, to the point that I cried when she went into the loo, had to be reined in now. There was no more Ami. As a result of Ami's grief, she was stripped of the motherhood that came so naturally to her. This made no sense to me even as an eleven-year-old. After all, she raised four children in a war-torn African country in abject poverty and still managed to read respected literature every day. She practised and perfected being Ami all her life.

Yet, it was not enough. Ami was somehow not enough and just because the man she was with had checked out, she had to check out too.

It was almost like there had been a permanent role change. *That's not Ami, that's your Abu's widow. Say hello to her. Hello, Abu's widow. Now go to hell!*

Who was going to care for me if not Ami?

Someone else decided that Ami's ephemeral lifespan ended when Abu died.

No one asked her if perhaps, after the sadness was over, she felt relieved on some level that Abu was no more. No one asks the real questions because the real answers make for bad women. Ami was always a good woman. She baked. She even knew how to make fresh sesame-seed oil, for god's sake—the woman was epic. But now she wasn't even worthy of the title of a good woman.

Now she was just a poor woman.

THINGS FALL APART IN AFRICA

After Abu died, life as I knew it was suddenly thrust into an action movie where I had only a perfunctory role to play.

Wake up and go to school. Come back and watch cartoons. Force-feed myself and pretend to do homework, and then go to bed.

Then I was told it was time to go.

I came home to packed boxes. It was the 1990s, and no one had talked to me about what they were planning to do. They just did it and I found out about it along the way.

I was yanked out of school in the middle of my final year of high school in Uganda. Someone thought it was a good idea. I was put in a car with all my life and moved into a green house in Nairobi, Kenya. Think Idaho to New York Bronx.

I guess it was inevitable. The Islamic University of Uganda, where Abu had worked after his job at the high school, was done with him. They were so done with him that they buried him in their football field. They were so done with him that they even withheld his last six months of pay, the last six months during which he would lean on me, his arm around my thin shoulders, just to walk to work. The rector claimed that there was a shortage of funds. They hadn't told Abu that they were strapped for cash for fear that Abu would have stayed home and not come in for work.

Someone else was going to replace Abu as the registrar now. Someone else would move their family into my home. Someone else's kid would get my room. Someone else would be in Abu's office, using Abu's stapler and Abu's chair and Abu's files and file covers. Someone else would eat the fruit of Abu's Pakistani mango tree which we had reared from a seed and someone else would cut Ami's long-stemmed roses for their vases.

This was what eviction felt like. It felt like death being experienced from the outer corners—creating shadows of the home you once knew.

Ami was there in the shadows too, but in no position of authority because she wasn't much more than a shadow herself.

Bhaijan, Bhai and Baji were away, heading back into their new lives soon after Abu's death.

Bhaijan was married off in a rush because some genius had come up with the brilliant notion that Abu's living skeleton had to be present in the wedding photos. Baji was passed on to Mamujan's son, the same Mamujan who initially introduced Ami to Abu, so that marriage had come a full circle. Bhai was doing his master's and dealing with big feelings.

Bhai's feelings were so big that he got me an electric keyboard, an electronic typewriter and a list of things so precious that my guilt-trauma has blocked the memory. I was overwhelmed by it all since Abu never got me anything. It really felt great somehow— Abu was gone and being under a new, liberal management was superbly lucrative for my worldly lusts. I daydreamed about having a grand piano while I absentmindedly sucked on the plugged-in cord of the keyboard and proceeded to give my face an electric shock.

We all deal with grief differently, but I absolutely loved the way Bhai dealt with Bhaijan's credit card to save me from the loss of Abu and Ami and school and home.

AMI DRAGS ME AWAY FROM UGANDA

Soon the gifts were packed and Ami and I set off for Kenya. It was Ami's home before Abu came into her life.

It was, however, not my home.

There were too many big-city people who were nothing like the small-town Uganda people.

My room in the big, green house overlooked a loud Black family whose kids kicked up a ruckus all day and all night.

We lived upstairs in the green house. My elder uncle and aunt, Mamujan and Mumani, lived downstairs.

Bhai got Ami a blue car so she could drop me to school. God knows what kind of grandiose delusions those were. Ami gave up driving after she almost killed a fruit seller who sold pineapples. That car was relegated to younger Mamujan.

I tried to play 'Silent Night' on the keyboard at 3 a.m. to channel my insomnia and nightmares, but the keyboard was swiftly discarded like my feelings.

Ami became my nightmare. Every time I saw her, I'd want to slam her across the door. Her weeping nauseated me. Her existence gave me vertigo. She wore her sadness on her sleeve. I wanted her to take it elsewhere and leave me alone.

She couldn't make sense of the world, and it was her job to make sense of it for me.

Life as I knew it was over and she hadn't even asked for my permission to take it from me.

My biggest grievance about Ami was that she was meek even after Abu died.

A doe-eyed faun just waiting to be game. Everything that came at her was absorbed stoically, like a sponge—offence, rain, children, disrespect, joy and other people's expectations.

Nairobi was noisy at a time when I desperately needed peaceful and pastoral surroundings.

I was furious with Ami for not understanding this. I was filled with angst as I waited for her to acknowledge my mood. I wanted her love, but I was demanding it in the most terrible ways—lashing out at her, slamming doors and calling her ugly.

I tumbled headlong into a world of more cousins than all the fingers and toes on my hands and feet. Why had so many Konkanis gatecrashed into my life suddenly?

No one asked me whether I wanted to follow their weird etiquettes and routines—milk in the morning and milk at night. I was lactose intolerant even before that was a thing. That ritual of nurturing was pure torture for me.

They expected me to pay my respects to every elder with whom I inadvertently made eye contact, when all I wanted was to gouge their eyes out. All of them wore spectacles with lenses as thick as the bottoms of Coca-Cola bottles—a whole lot of bad genes, if you asked me. I too developed myopia, but over my dead body was I going to look anything like the Konkanis. *Nako-nako*, I would say in my head, mimicking their Marathi-esque words for no-no.

They also insisted that I prayed five times a day and that I was 'proper' for a girl, whatever that meant, and warned me that there were certain uncles and aunts that one had to be wary of—I only found out the hard way that they were live wires. Sanctimonious prison wardens. Their charity was unwelcome.

I didn't ask to be there, but somehow, I was their burden. I was called names by the lot of them. I was told I was moody and not at all a nice girl. Before Kenya, I never realized I was a girl; I was a kid. I knew all about being a bad kid but being a 'bad girl' was as heavy as lead.

Just look at so-and-so, what a lovely disposition she has, I was told, while the tailors measured me for my new clothes—clothes which were charity to me from an aunt. I was told I didn't eat enough which was why my breasts were underdeveloped for my age. Mealtimes were disgraceful because I never quite understood why coconut had to be infused into every bite. Food was heaped on my plate for good measure. As I wasn't used to three meals a day, I often struggled to finish their milky food and my livid aunts told me off in no uncertain terms for being an ingrate and undisciplined to boot.

Bad girl. Bad girl. Bad girl.

To make things worse, there wasn't a single relative or cousin who had just lost a dad and could sympathize with my plight. I thought: *How come you, who are so appallingly pathetic, have all been spared death's scythe? How come your fathers are still alive? Well, it's not going to be for long, you bastard. It's coming for you too. Disparage me to your heart's content, but this much I can assure you: it's coming.*

I was shamed for having longer baths than the designated time. There was no water. What they meant was: there was no hot water. *Be specific, arseholes!*

They were many cousins, but soon enough I figured out the hierarchy. Some of my cousins were trying hard to figure out where being Konkani stopped and being desperate began.

On Eid, they would exchange salams as the Arabs would, making the *Qaaf* sound resonate deep enough to reach their gut. They would wear Arabian attire—the long, white *kanzu* (Arab dress) and the *agal*, or ring, around their heads to hold the red, chequered headscarf, which we now associate with Yasser Arafat. They reeked of trying too hard.

Watching their peculiar behaviour, I was strongly tempted to ask them whether they couldn't see how awkward and silly they looked—like a chicken emulating a ballerina—in their need to be Arabs.

Utterly undignified. *Nako-nako.*

Subdued parents maintain a thin veil between the world and their family. The veil between me and the world was like gossamer. Ami failed to protect herself and she failed to protect me as well. What Ami couldn't thwart, I ended up absorbing.

When I was a toddler, she smelled like jasmine. She looked like a princess, magnificent in her quiet power. She was as white as snow, clad in the nylon kameez she tailored for herself, magically caring for everyone, keeping the house clean and the clothes washed. Most nights were comfortable and snug. Abu was there.

Then Abu was gone.

Everything that Ami's people represented was overshadowed by Abu's absence.

Labels take a life of their own. I was a misfit all right but that was only because Abu had died. No matter how hard they prayed, they would all die. Even the woman with the special-needs, forty-year-old son would die, leaving her son behind. Or he would die first, leaving her purposeless.

You, the person who is forcing me to do my Ramazan prayers at 3 a.m., will also die. You with your lust for submission, will definitely die. Your unflagging zeal to organize the community centre, the

magazine and the potlucks won't save you. You with your impeccable
cooking will die for sure. Faithful uncles, devoted aunts, sacrificing
caregivers to in-laws, all you good people—very much headed towards
the dark abyss. You with your droplets of holy ZamZam water and
you twat of a human being who invented the slur kuku-paka, *will*
also die. But first you will lose so many you love.

Since Abu wasn't going to come back, I had to learn to
navigate this family's politics so that I could go back home and
create Abu again.

Somehow, I just had to make it out alive. I had to find the
light before they extinguished the memory of who I was when
Abu was alive.

KHALAJAN IS NEW AMI

All roads lead to sex when you are a teenager.

After flirting briefly with common sense and staying away from older Khalajan, my path crossed again with Khalajan's a year or so later. My hormones were running riot by this time, and I had learned to play games with my body that culminated in mind-blowing pleasure. If I knew one thing from studying anything sacred, it was that all pleasure came at a cost. You could experience boundless joy but if you were a girl, the joy was accidental, and you had to invariably return it to the universe from where it had been misplaced. It was nice to know incidental joy. It was great to feel loved naturally, easily and almost automatically, like it came from another place, other than my will.

Hey glad tidings, go back to whence you came; you don't belong with me.

Khalajan didn't just knit and do the *New York Times* Sunday crossword puzzles during her downtime after breakfast, she also read trash novels like *Mills and Boon*. Everyone knew of her penchant for these romance novels and no one made a big deal of it. These novellas were available by the thousands, each possibly 50,000 words or less, woven by the raunchy imagination of women of leisure. The settings were either in the cities or in the countryside, essentially containing lots of make-out sessions and rapey sex.

Although I was even more dyslexic in Arabic than Urdu, my English reading skills were respectable. But thanks to my obsession with her titillating collection, I would find ways to hover endlessly around Khalajan's private library which was housed in an imposing display case made entirely of mahogany wood and went all the way up to the ceiling. The top half had a sliding glass cabinet and the bottom half was an opaque wooden cupboard which effectively concealed its torrid contents. She had neatly arranged her best china and her children's sports trophies in the top half and the lair of her dark imagination reposed in the bottom half.

At the time, this did not strike me as odd at all. So what if older Khalajan was our moral compass? She was addicted to novels where sexual excitement included biting into the nipples of eighteen-year-olds until they bled. No, not odd at all. To me, just because she had the books did nothing to diminish her status in the family. She was not endorsing the content. Far from it. She was only polishing her English. It was a test of loyalty to read these books and still be dedicated to the holy path where one submitted to the will of the divine.

One day, Ami was clearing out the clutter in the house and discovered some *Mills and Boon*. The covers of the erotica ended up getting an impromptu facelift with newspapers. Ami asked Khalajan whether she wanted her books back, as Ami was done with them. Khalajan asked her to keep them.

As I was the only one there, Ami said, 'Aisha is too young to read this now.'

Khalajan looked at me and said, 'Of course, she is too young, I didn't mean those books, I meant the Urdu storybooks beneath them.'

Ami said, 'Okay, that makes sense. I was wondering why you thought she was eligible to read these books.'

The awkward moment reconfirmed to me that I was not to ever know of the existence of the books, let alone sneak them into my pyjamas and read them in the bathroom whenever we visited Khalajan.

One day, when I ripped the newspaper, I saw the cover depicting a woman of questionable character, leaning into a man. The title was *Lucifer's Angel.* I had a lot of fun with that book. The book eventually got re-read and when I returned it, I feared that I'd get caught because it was so dog-eared.

I credit Khalajan for my ability to make some sense of the English language, for making me believe that all white women were desirable because you could take them, because no meant yes and also because most men went out and then came back to the women. The women waited for them. To make yourself desirable, I felt, you had to be White. Or you had to have the best of both worlds (like Khalajan) and reconciled to the simple, godly life and its concomitant rituals, but then also dabble in Lucifer's world. Maybe I envied her.

Books are books and reverence or no reverence, there was a time and place for each kind on the spectrum of knowledge.

Khalajan caught me returning one of the books on a lazy afternoon. My cheeks were particularly flushed because I had just read a delicious scene.

'What are you doing?' she asked in the ever-so-big voice she had, her dupatta perfectly in place.

'I was just—'

'Just what? Tell me,' she demanded, her eyes as big as saucers. 'I have eyes, you know. I want to hear it from you.'

'I was returning your book to its rightful place.'

'Why were you touching my books in the first place? You have a dirty mind, don't you?'

'No, I didn't know what these books were, this one especially,' I held up the newspaper covered one and stared at her innocently.

With one long-legged step she was beside me and had grabbed the scruff of my neck. In the next second, she yanked the book out of my hand, 'Give me that!'

She stuffed the book back in the cupboard, slamming the door so hard that I thought the delicate hinges would come apart.

I cringed, half-expecting a slap. '*Astagfurullah*. Stay your age.'
'Sorry.'

'Sorry!' she mimicked to humiliate me further.

I knew I was in big trouble. However, it is a fact that any child would be curious to look at a book, mysteriously covered with a newspaper, without meaning any mischief.

'I am sorry. I didn't know.'

'If you had shown the same enthusiasm in reading the Quran, you would've learnt Arabic by now.'

Two steps and she withdrew into the kitchen where she belonged—the place where everything made sense, from where she controlled everything because she made the most perfect *gulab jamun*, the most delicious biryani and the most disgusting cabbage.

In Khalajan's world, if the good person does one bad thing, should the good person be labelled as bad forever?

And if the bad person does one good thing, should the bad person be labelled as good forever?

In which case, it's fairly easy to change Khalajan's opinion of a person.

Khalajan and grown-ups like her always had the strength of mind to unravel their knitting if something went wrong and start over from scratch. I learnt to knit and purl, but always had the fear of making that one slip and seeing the entire project coming undone.

Every good girl knows things cannot be undone. You get one shot at everything. At life. At being a good girl and at knitting together the perfect life.

Older Khalajan was the self-appointed moral police. Grown men blanched at the thought of being interrogated by Khalajan.

Khalajan had thick black curly hair, like a horse's mane. Her tresses, anointed with coconut oil and woven into a tight braid, threatened mutiny like the bound feet of nineteenth-century Chinese girls. I was petrified of Khalajan. She was aristocracy, buoyed by the propriety of *New York Times* crossword puzzles in the mornings and a vast collection of all the right things—a rocking chair, a much-beloved daughter, hot water and an honourable and good-looking man for a husband.

She was also pretty if you could consider old women pretty. From where I was standing, I could see more nose than I would've desired, and the flared nostrils didn't make for a fuzzy feeling. I would see her nostrils even when I shut my eyes, like the afterglow of a too-bright, light-bulb filament. I did, however, admire the curls she would cut short, nestling by her plush ears. There was a certain amount of daring to all her moves.

When she had hot flushes, everyone knew. I thought that, for a woman who demanded demureness from me, she was so much like a man—unabashed in taking up space in a room and demanding she be noticed.

Khalajan taught me how to be angry and she also taught me to read the Holy Quran. It was frowned upon that I was soon to get my period and still hadn't recited the sacred book thrice, as was expected in order to be admitted into the league of practising Muslims. I also did not know the four *kuls* by heart and well, that was just shameful. Ami told Khalajan that it was sad indeed, but that Khalajan could redeem me by taking me under her wing. Khalajan both hated and loved this. She hated teaching me because I was daft, perhaps because of my dyslexia, and she loved it because nothing gives a menopausal woman more joy than 'fixing' bad girls. She was harsher than she needed to be, but I was told that it came from a place of love. Even when I was a little girl, she would braid my hair too tightly and when I'd wail, she'd smack me with the comb and say I was way too whiny for a girl.

Aisha is always crying. *Jabb dekho rona!*

There are a few things that were considered as criminal as crying.

There is a term for it now, toxic positivity, but then, I was considered thankless and ungrateful for all the trouble I caused. My sadness inflicted daggers across everyone. The least I could do was not do it publicly. Crying into a pillow is the only way it seemed I was to manage emotions—save them for later.

Happiness was supposed to be fetched like an orange from a tree. Failing to fetch it was pathetic—like fat people and beggars. I discovered that Khalajan was not as smart as everyone assumed. Bullying and authoritarianism only went so far. She would seethe, muttering under her breath, when I messed up while studying Arabic. *Allah meri tauba. Tsk. Tsk. Tsk.*

She would feel very ashamed of me and ask for God's forgiveness on my behalf. Her embarrassment was clearly mine, but it was radioactive. I felt awful and humiliated. I was no longer five years old, getting my hair braided taut like a punishingly tight corset. I was twelve or thirteen. All I was being asked to do was read Arabic. How hard was that?

I was equally, if not more, afraid of Arabic as I was of older Khalajan. When I saw the script—*Aliph, Laam, Meem*—my heart would immediately be inundated by its unworthiness and puke into itself. Reading it was nigh impossible. Arabic represented the impossible heights of moral perfection. What was I even doing attempting it?

It didn't recognize me either and looked back at me like I was a total stranger. For the life of me I couldn't figure out which letter had three dots above it and which one had two dots under it. It's not like I didn't want to, because my terror far outweighed my recalcitrance. I couldn't get my head around the idea that I was a student of a new language. To Khalajan, it was a foregone conclusion that I was not one of the blessed; nonetheless, she and I stumbled around the edges of trying. It was traumatic.

And then, one fine day, the fear gave way to cleverness. I figured out that Khalajan didn't understand the words either; she had zero cognition of someone's incoherent babbling of Arabic words,, words which were nowhere in the Holy Book. However, I had a basic idea of the general sounds and I learned to patch them together with confidence.

I would not touch the book, though. No way. That would be the day when hell froze over.

One day, Khalajan had disappeared into the nether regions of her home to cook like the good homemaker she was, having commanded me to read on, now that I had mastered some fluency. Khalajan suddenly erupted into the room with the ladle, alarm writ large on her face. I stopped reading and looked up, half-expecting a thwack across my head with the spatula as she had caught on to my scam. Instead, she walked over to me, giving me a heady whiff of garlic, onions and Yardley perfume.

'Re-read what you just read. That was way too fluent to believe.'

I gulped.

'Khalajan,' my voice throbbed with righteous indignation as I gathered the remnants of my dignity and self-respect, 'I think I've started my period. My panties feel bloody therefore I cannot touch the holy book.'

'Okay. Read it without touching the book.'

I read it, from memory, exactly the way I had done earlier. I didn't blink once and swayed as I intoned the Arabic words. Devotion got you points.

At the end of the paragraph, I looked her in the eye. No gulping this time.

'Very good. If you're this good, maybe you can read the next two recitals of the Quran on your own?'

'If you have faith in me, I can do that,' I replied, continuing to hold her gaze.

'*Hai mere* Allah!' Suddenly galvanized by the smell of charring onions, she made a beeline back into the kitchen. And that was that.

No hell for me because I had lied through my teeth and refrained from touching the Quran while fake reading it.

Khalajan 0. Aisha 1.

And with that, Khalajan's status in my eyes plummeted to that of a lowly pawn. Her magic no longer worked on me. If she could not detect my con-artistry with the holy book, what was the point of all her holier-than-thou? I was just as holy, bloody hell!

The guilt came later. Much later.

I did my pardon prayers, twenty *rakats* as penance, even eighty sometimes, to beg Allah for forgiveness. Sometimes I would talk myself into thinking that my crime was moral in nature hence forgivable; at other times, I would be convinced that lying to older Khalajan was akin to defrauding the state, and it was only a matter of time before the Federal Bureau of Investigation (FBI) agents frogmarched me off to be stoned in the football field.

Lying to Khalajan had amazing nectar, but very fleeting. The enormous guilt felt like it was emanating from a divine source—the omniscient. There were times when older Khalajan would sermonize me about being truthful and respectful of one's elders and the perils of the grave, and I would almost want to make a clean breast of the fact that I still didn't know how to read the Quran, and my fluency with the holy language was 100 per cent faked. Instead, whenever she asked me how my daily Quran reading was going, I'd say beam and say, 'Brilliantly.'

KHALAJAN FAILED IN
WAYS ABU DIDN'T

Some man must have broken Khalajan, but she never ever mentioned him. Sitting amidst a gaggle of women, Khalajan held forth instead, with tears in her eyes, about her brother's wife who was so mean-spirited that she had refused to buy Khalajan some tangy oranges when her tonsils had hurt.

In the Quran, which Khalajan taught me to deeply revere, there is a verse that decrees kindness towards all orphans. Like all scriptures, it vows hellfire and brimstone upon those who are cruel to orphans. Khalajan's brother's wife was not mean to Khalajan. She just didn't give in to a child's whims. My Khalajan, however, was mean to me. Therefore I was an orphan.

If someone is mean to a child while their parent is alive, then are they really alive? Was Ami really alive?

I was Khalajan's hand-picked whipping boy. Khalajan derived pure sadistic pleasure from spewing her poison over me, almost salivating in her exhilaration at tormenting me. She used labels to tell a story about who I would become.

Khalajan humiliated and chastised me in public so often and so loudly, that I became synonymous with shame. Khalajan chose me because Abu opted to leave and departed this world. That is the only thing that made sense.

Khalajan considered me a nuisance—just as the protagonists in those stories like *Anne of Green Gables*, where the scrawny teenage girl was always bad news? Her rancour was almost a smell with a colour: barbecue who and the stench of period blood, of a greyish-maroon hue like a corpse in twilight.

Khalajan was in the kitchen. The gulab jamuns were cooking slowly in a large stew pot on a large, coal stove. The fire would crackle sometimes, the coal coughing up a gout of conflagration, threatening to engulf me even when I was all the way by the kitchen door. As she stirred the gulab jamuns with a circular spatula she looked like a witch hunched over a bubbling cauldron. Both the khalajans were discussing me when I walked into the kitchen and the moment I stepped in, I realized I was going to get an earful because I had been caught doing something wrong—I hadn't a clue what. In any case, all my instincts screamed to me to bolt in the opposite direction.

'Why ask your cousin to drive you all the way to Nairobi West? Is it all that crucial to fetch your clothes?' Older Khalajan had two deep, vertical grooves between her eyebrows, just like I had and just like Abu had. Now her frown looked like a pair of pillars holding up her forehead.

'I beg your pardon?' I said, playing for time.

I *had* asked my cousin to drive me home for a fresh pair of clothes because I had come to my khalajan's straight from school. Now that there was a plan to go to mini-golfing with the cousins, naturally I couldn't just go in my school uniform. Heaven forbid I be seen by someone from school—it would be deeply embarrassing. Even after that episode of being slapped by my uncle in full public view and being marked a pariah at school and in our community, I still had some remnants of ego left and didn't want to add insult to injury. So, when my cousin kindly offered to drive me home for a change of clothes, I thought that was really sweet of her and readily accepted.

Now, fast forward to her mom, my aunt, being annoyed with me.

'Who do you think you are, bossing my daughter around, huh? Why does everything have to revolve around you?' She was yelling now and younger Khalajan, trying to keep the peace, told her sister to lower her voice, simultaneously admonishing me at a lower decibel level.

'You have to make sure it's convenient for people to run your errands. Your cousin is pregnant and we don't want her taking needless risks,' said younger Khalajan.

The fire crackled and almost conflagrated older Khalajan's turquoise dupatta with human-sized tulips on it. That dupatta design did not make sense—the petals were too large.

I froze despite the heat in the kitchen. There was so much food being prepared. There must have been a reason for it, although I can't remember what the occasion was. I generally dissociated and only caught bits of sentences because with all the barbed and hurtful remarks directed my way, my ears were the most unsafe place to live in, so I learned to block sounds.

You are very self-centred.

You should wear your own clothes. Why do you assume it's okay to borrow our daughters' clothes?

Why are you pushing my daughter around . . . all for your two-penny clothes?

Why aren't you ever prepared in advance?

I think I burst into tears.

Why, Khalajan? Why do you hate me so much? Why am I being humiliated and belittled by two grown women? What did I do to deserve such treatment? Is it such a crime to accept a cousin's offer of a ride and make a quick trip to pick up my clothes for the evening? Aren't I entitled to any fun at all? Why me?

There are a lot of other people in the house. There's Shabana, Fahim, Salman, Sarfaraz and Farida and then there is Baji, Bhai and Bhaijan. Granted my siblings are paragons of virtue, but it wouldn't hurt to pick on them sometimes. Then there are my second cousins hanging about in South C—you could fry them and eat them too if you so wished.

The eighties were a time when sticks and stones could break one's bones but mere words could never hurt anyone. If you bellyached about sensitive feelings being hurt, you were a likely candidate for getting a broken bone or two. You were scornfully reminded that you were born in a far more civilized era because had you been born a generation ago, the uncles wouldn't hesitate to use their belts to discipline children.

So, although I was routinely humiliated, I wasn't sure whether I was better off or whether there were others who were also victims of such targeted prejudice.

Why, Khalajan? Why do you always pick on me? I'm not particularly obstinate or obnoxious; I am just slightly odd. Perhaps that is because I don't belong to your uterus like your own offspring, nor do I belong in your yard like your other sister's children.

I wanted to be loved by Khalajan. She was everyone's gold standard. Any chance of my metamorphosis would begin with her forgiving me.

I think I made my way to younger Khalajan's house, which was next door; in fact, attached like a dirty nappy held together by a safety pin. Older Khalajan was the dirty nappy and younger Khalajan was the safety pin keeping things together. I remember sobbing uncontrollably. Later, I would come to recognize the existential sobbing to be associated with period blues but this was the first time. I was down in the doldrums.

Think of a well.

Then think of someone pushing you into it and you watching as they cover the well with a large circular stone.

Listening to their receding footsteps. Wait.

Know that they have left for good and will never come back.

As a child, I didn't have all the answers. But I didn't wonder for a second where my ami was when I negotiated this abusive teenage phase. Not for a moment did I think, Ami will come and save me.

Never.

I only knew Ami wasn't hovering over me like a guardian angel because she didn't want to be there. She was elsewhere and she wanted to be elsewhere. First, she was taking care of Abu for two years; then, she was grieving; and soon afterwards, she would be trying to make her mark in the social echelons by claiming to be a good grandmother.

I didn't expect anyone to come to my rescue, neither Ami nor any of my siblings who were 'settled' in their own married lives, not even my dead father. There was just me.

But I wasn't enough.

My tongue, cleaved to the roof of my mouth, would not retaliate. There was no flight-or-fight response, but neither would I freeze. I would attempt a confused combination of all three— making squealing sounds inside myself, a sorry creature with an axe in its spleen.

Everything felt like a jolt.

There was a chasm between the child world and the adult world, and I didn't belong in either. I belonged to no community. The Konkanis only liked themselves, issuing themselves non-transferable tickets to the club and throwing tomatoes at people who were half-castes like myself—imposters.

Why, Khalajan? I hate having to contend with all this pain without a valid reason. Give me a reason for the rejection. I can take it. What I can't take is ambiguous grief. Fabricate an answer, if need be, but tell me.

I never understood why and I really do want to know why I was never good enough.

ABU IS DYING, ABU IS DYING, ABU IS DYING

At some point, Abu decided that he had very little time left. He wrote in one of his letters 'my blood aches'. To this day, I wince at that line. I see Abu's eye sockets crying out for help, and his jaw overshadowing his flaccid cheeks. Age is not kind to anyone, to the sick and the old especially.

This was Abu and very much my nine-year-old self's abu, but I only knew that he was no longer nice to look at. Where was the wide, square forehead, off which he would comb back his jet-black hair, with a neat right-side parting, so neat that each tooth of the comb left a row of indentations on his scalp in a straight line?

Abu decided that there was no time left and, therefore, his children must marry. People thought marriage was a rite of passage into adulthood. A ritual would define it and then you could cross one more item off the checklist of familial duties. Marriages required weddings and weddings required money. They also required people moderately willing to be terrorized into marrying the offspring of Abu and Ami. Bhaijan, Baji, Bhai. I was too young to marry, at least under Ugandan law.

Abu was a bit obsessive about his bucket list. *Marry off Bhaijan, marry off Baji, marry off Bhai, hand me over to Bhai, providing him with enough wherewithal for my future marriage.*

Bhaijan, Baji and Bhai married their cousins.

After Abu was buried in 1992, almost a decade after the start of the civil war in Uganda and almost thirty-five years since he had made Uganda his home, everyone who was making decisions on my behalf decided, in a stroke of evil genius, that it would be a wonderful idea to take me as far away as possible from the only home I knew. I would move in with the dwarfs (as I thought of Ami's side of the family). Like Snow White, I would cook and clean along with my ami in exchange for a sense of community and belonging.

I was livid. I wanted to be around people who were grieving Abu. Not only did no one·know Abu, but they made it a point to erase what I had of his—the Pakistani identity.

So soon after Abu died, I really didn't need my supercilious cousins mocking me for being a Pakistani, but they invariably rubbed it in.

'Why did you need Pakistan?' my cousin, an ace cricket player, asked.

'We wanted to create a peaceful country where we could practise our own religion,' I replied. I was using the words and sentences from speeches Abu made to me on self-determination and religious disharmony. However, I was so out of my depth here that I floundered amidst my jeering kinsmen.

'Shut up, Aashi. There is no need for the two-nation theory if there are more Muslims in India than they are in Pakistan,' he said.

'Well, you guys missed the bus when everybody was migrating,' I retorted.

'It was a bad idea,' he argued. 'Mr Jinnah was too selfish to think things through. We didn't get left behind. We didn't believe in the so-called dream.'

(Laughter)

They always travelled in packs. There was always an audience when someone took me down.

After a few civil wars, water shortages and high-school exams, it was now 1995, and I was mostly alone in my new house in Nairobi.

I think I missed my old life but I didn't know it at the time because there was zero-tolerance on cribbing. Even if someone died, you didn't complain because you got fresh milk and lentils. Where's your sense of gratitude, girl?

I was a very Pakistani child but, by now, I had started calling myself an Indian. I was deeply unhappy to be living a lie but pretended to be happy. I was also very poorly dressed. I didn't like God, but Allah was my only go-to so I was praying a lot, reciting my *surahs* and kuls, cleaning myself ritually after my periods and beseeching Allah to grant me purity.

I had to give thanks for everything, including farts, I kid you not! I was only twelve but something about me disgusted Ami's family. During this existential crisis and figuring out high-school biology and Kiswahili, the language I could never speak, Ami decided to give up on me forever and move to the US.

At least that is what short spaces of time away from Ami felt like at the time. Yes, she had only gone there for the birth of my first niece, but she may as well have written me off.

Ami was ace at domesticity and most of her kids lived rather than died, so it made sense for her to jump ship to oversee the birth of her grandchild. I stayed back with the Konkanis who were kind enough to let me sleep in their beds, share their porridge and clean their house for them.

Until they didn't want me in their house.

Whenever they saw me, they would humiliate me either physically or verbally. Did I have a special power and not know it or was I just the gunk under the shoe that everyone tried to rid themselves of?

I would skulk off to sulk in a corner. When I asked Ami why her family was bullying me over politics, she would merely say that they didn't know better and that Jinnah was a political colossus in the eyes of South Asian Muslims, whether they loved or loathed him. She also told me that Nanajan had always had a Jinnah portrait in his room. The two-nation theory was real because Nanajan had experienced prejudice first-hand. There were always two classes in India, Ami explained as best as she could, but she didn't divide them based on religion, she divided them based on the ones who had to leave versus those who had to stay. By this time Abu was long gone and, although I was miles away from his stormy grave, he haunted me with nightmare after nightmare—*Abu alone, Abu in pain, Abu mocked, Abu drowning, Abu shot, Abu unwell . . .*

Things shifted abruptly like a deflated balloon. One minute, we were merrily airborne and in the next, life had sandbagged me. My mother stopped fading into Abu's background and started fading into other people's backgrounds—everyone's but mine. I couldn't stand her because everything about her reminded me of death and sulphur.

Ami drew gardens from the earth. The moment Abu faded into it, she was back at it, drawing gardens for others. I watched my ami replace my abu, one garden at a time, one scent for another. It was unforgivable. I knew of no bigger betrayal than forgetting the dead.

I promised to carry Abu inside me forever. I promised to avenge his forgetting. I would bring him back to life from the earth. I would grow my own kind of garden. No one would forget him ever again.

ABU TOOK AMI WITH HIM

Abu's death segued seamlessly into Ami's existence. She would walk into the room, and it was like Abu's corpse had walked into the room with her. She was the only thing standing between my future and the dark memory of my human guardian angel's perfidy. If not for her, Abu would be a good memory—with the smell of books and ink in fountain pens. With her sad eyes, her downturned lips and her youthful skin, she enraged me enough to want to run away from home or punch a hole through a wall. She was death itself—a beautiful, fifty-something year old woman, slouching around in dull clothes, pretending to breathe.

Ami seemed to say: I'm here for you.

But existence to ensure my care was cloying.

In a world that only men mattered, why would God care about a woman's loathing for her mother? But, of course, I could not even think that out loud. Perhaps this was why she even smelled of death now.

Hello Ami, please knock before you walk into my room next time. Also, I would rather you be dead. I would rather it was Abu walking into my room. Yes, you. Be dead.

It may have been teenage angst. It may have been a case of adults being pathetic in their personal grief. Either way, Ami needed to do as she was told by someone else other than her dead husband. I had never seen her be spontaneous; always, always, under instruction.

That was the currency she could trade in—subservience in exchange for pity. There was always this sense of our walking around, mother and daughter, under this black cloud of bad luck. If we scrubbed away the pink mildew in their bathrooms, maybe we would be able to eliminate that cloud. God and being a useful domestic help were her only currency. I detested both with equal vehemence. Why negotiate with the bottom-dwellers? God was for the forsaken, the unfortunate and the detested.

I got all the culture I needed from my own home without being frightened for my soul or Ami's. My own home, where Abu donned his lungi and Ami read to him and they both took moonlit walks, where Baji made meticulous notes about the human skeletal system, where Bhaijan got to be mentioned in the news for topping finals and Bhai was always hunched over some mechanical contraption. These familiar sights and sounds were my refuge and although there were other nice things there in Kenya, it was merely a holiday destination, whereas Uganda was home.

Uganda was where one felt secure enough to be intrepid, insular, rude and obnoxious.

Kenya was where you had to be polished and outwardly put-together; and sophisticated even if you were just a child.

Uganda was the backstage with the raw and ugly human conditions, but Kenya was where you had to give the performance of a lifetime.

I left Uganda. It was a ride on the rural, public transport which sometimes had people carrying chickens and goats, like the White people do on airplanes nowadays, as emotional-support animals. I remember looking out of the window, feeling the numbness of a person swallowed by a whale.

Before we left, everyone visited Abu's grave. I didn't because I hadn't the courage to bid a final farewell. I think I now put it down to moral ineptitude. It was the proper thing to do. If Uganda were Kenya, I would've been coerced to go along and say a prayer for him and maybe it would've been the electric-shock equivalent of closure.

But I was filled with an inexplicable rage without quite knowing that I was angry or why. They didn't let me go to see him buried. I was shunned and excluded. And now, it was too little too late. When you're a child, you think everything is done *to* you. Even objects do things to you. Homes abandon you. People abandon you. Trees ask you to get lost. Even dead bodies become animate, especially if you once embraced them as your own.

I desperately needed the sense of security I had felt in Uganda. One cannot be acting a part for a lifetime—I needed to be somewhere where I could just be me.

I wanted Kenya to be over there. To remain over there. Kenya was exhausting—too much sea and sun. I wanted Uganda to be my every day. Before Abu died, I had only short sojourns in Kenya, where I felt like a fish out of water. However, my acute discomfort was transient and effectively offset by the marvels of modern life.

Things changed.

That Kenyan, fleabag-state-of-mind came home to roost. Home that was Uganda became lost. It evaporated, while I was distracted for only a second, never to be claimed again.

Abu chose to remain in Uganda, a place that I once called home, 6 feet underground, in a 6 x 3 foot grave under a mango tree in a university campus near a football field.

ABU BETRAYED AMI

At some point in my middle-school years, while I was studying the mating of animals, human anatomy, iron ore and the Mesopotamian rivers of the Euphrates and the Tigris, Abu decided that his illness would define the way he looked for seven days after he was dead. With Abu's cancer diagnosis came loss. Not of the person, or the father, or the protection of patriarchy. I lost time. Time stole from me mundane mornings like lathering Abu's shaving foam, using shaving cream and shaving patches of him, his smooth skin underneath the blade revealing a brown I have so come to love: his submission as an offering while I shaved under his chin; his asking me to not be afraid, but being afraid himself as I shaved him, cutting him eventually here and there; and his casually sticking toilet paper on the assortment of nicks and cuts. My hands unsteady on the Gillette blade, which slid from my slippery and nervous hands, until I had to use both hands to steady it. His face would be a constellation of tiny, red tissues and he would pour, carefully, of course, three drops, four at best, of Old Spice on his hands and pat it on his cheeks. He wouldn't wince.

Why would he let me shave him, delay him for work in the mornings in that tiny, dingy Ugandan bathroom we all shared?

I assumed that I wouldn't allow it any other way. The fact that I had such ownership, as a little girl over a sixty-year-old man, was not just a good thing, it was a very good thing for Aisha, the girl, if not for anyone else.

Time stole from me my favourite moments where things were done with no potential gain—like sitting in his chair.

During his period of illness, we also took a gruelling trip to Karachi and Hyderabad in Pakistan. I didn't know this then, but it was a goodbye trip.

The first thing *Phupho*, his sister, said to him when she saw him was, 'Younger, what have you done to yourself? You look black!'

Returning to Uganda from the month-long sojourn in Pakistan was like returning with a prisoner of war. The summer heat in Pakistan had drained Abu. In Hyderabad, I'd had a terrible time with cousins who would take play too far and touch too much. Ami was wholly wrapped up with working tirelessly for Abu because his tummy could barely keep anything down.

At one point, when she saw me sleeping, entwined in a girl cousin's arms, she was aghast; she woke me up and told me to get away. I think if a girl cousin, much older and wiser, starts to rub herself against you during an afternoon siesta, all you can do is play dead and wait for your Ami to discover you. Credit to Ami and to the universe that she found me and rescued me.

It was a strange time for my body to decide that it had a sexual mind and a sexual outwardly expression. My body, still lanky and flat, was becoming a cupboard for others to raid on a whim and before I could react or even process it, they had taken what they wanted. It was like a mugging, but I was yet to figure out what they had gained and what I had lost.

Abu's colon cancer and his misdiagnosis and unnecessary goodbye travels coincided with my loss of control over my own body. I had learned to please myself without understanding that Allah's wrath would befall me however many repentance rakats I prayed in *namaz*. The only thing I could discern was that Abu was leaving me because I had been bad. I fancied Maroof, the son of the Bengali university rector. I fancied Jane Eyre's charcoal sketch of the kiss. I fancied Ami's bras and ranging alongside these dark desires was the stark reality of a very nauseous and diarrhoea-prone father.

Abu stopped reading. He tried, but reading didn't happen to him.

His books languished on the shelves in silent protest at their neglect.

Was he God-like in his omniscience? I had repeatedly been told that parents are the conduits of divine will. I had disobeyed them. I had stolen from Abu's wallet when I wanted to show off at school and I had dumped my milk into the soil in the flowerpots when Ami wasn't looking. I was also an involuntary victim to this emerging cult of strange power that lay within whatever was between my legs. Filled with remorse, I repented often and whole-heartedly; nevertheless, Abu only got sicker and eventually stopped calling out to me or talking to me.

Abu no longer taught me things. As a routine, since the day I was born, I had always been summoned by Abu every time he walked into the house but no longer. I felt an acute disappointment in his neglect of me.

He slurred when speaking to me, as if in a cryptic way he was signalling his deep displeasure. Did he even recognize me?

I was in a skirt and a white-and-light-blue striped top. My hair was in a half up-do, my smile, still untamed by tradition, and my skin, tanned brown with the excessive outdoor activities. I sat with Abu in the shade of a tree whose fallen flowers carpeted the ground around us—some bright spark decided it was an ideal setting for a photoshoot.

I posed for the camera.

Soon afterwards, Ami came to my room. 'Aashi, I don't think you should wear these clothes again.'

'Why?'

'You're developing breasts and it looks bad in this outfit,' she replied.

'Ami, what looks bad?' I was genuinely shocked that something was on me, something other than . . . what was already on me.

'Your breasts are perky and prominent now, so you should wear a dupatta.' The ground beneath my feet slipped a bit.

'Like older women do?'

'No, no. Not like that. A small one.' I gulped.

She turned to leave. Then, she turned back to me and said, 'And also, when you sleep with Abu, hugging him . . .'

'Yes?'

'As you're growing up now, that's no longer okay.' I said nothing. I felt nothing. 'You're a big girl now. Okay?'

'Okay.'

I wish tears had welled up. I wish I had just broken down and wept for my lost childhood. I didn't. Instead, I may have returned to homework, or my fascination with threads and the magic they could make with fingers. I may have turned to myself for a distraction. I ought to have cried because it was at that precise moment that I lost Abu.

Ami made me lose him. She was the culprit. He didn't want to go. She wanted to separate him and me.

ABU TAUGHT ME DARKNESS-BENDING

I loved Abu more than I could ever love Ami because Abu was important to me. He had important hands. He would use his hands to dip his fountain pen into ink and write in cursive text in important pages. He used his hands to mark transcripts. The finality of the tick marks he gave his students or even the crosses on the pages were not lost on me, even as a toddler in pigtails and a middle parting (exactly as he had wanted). Abu was important. His hands would never demean themselves in a kitchen sink or a cheap plastic pail. His hands pointed. His hands decided. Sometimes they condemned.

Most times, they were used for kindness. Like swooping me up into his arms. They were not frivolous hands. Abu had hands that mattered.

Abu had no hair on his back and chest, but his fingers were dark, thick and hairy. I would ask him why his fingernails didn't have hair because all the rest of his hand did. He would chuckle and say: *Mehra, look at what she just asked.*

Abu taught me to draw the map of East Africa, the outline first traced from the atlases, followed by a thicker outline with a pencil on the faint line—precisely on top of the first line, so no one could tell it was done twice. Then I coloured the outline of Lake Victoria in the middle of Uganda, Kenya and Tanzania. Abu would open a special tin containing his colour pencils and allow me to colour the drawing. Not in the normal way, but as topography artists did. He would use his half-moon nails to hold down a scrap of plain paper and colour that was a deep, dark blue. Then he would help me hold paper, the coloured part face down on Lake Victoria, as if to kiss it hard, and press down until my map's Lake Victoria reflected the colour of the real lake.

I had seen Lake Victoria a few times, with its algae-ridden banks and waters that were blue-black from pollution. I had seen the dam on the lake, a favourite picnic spot for the Ugandan-Pakistani community, and I had seen it abounding with pink flamingos wading in the waters so the lake resembled an expanse of cotton candy floss. It was Abu's hands that made Lake Victoria look regal in its careful caricature. He made everything my eyes saw disappear—scale matters, accuracy matters and it was the man with the pen who decided the final picture.

Abu was larger than life for me.

Abu taught me calligraphy. His *meem* would be a perfect meem. His *hamza*, a perfect hamza. The dots above *tay*, were perfect dots. He taught me how to hold the calligraphy pen without staining my hands with ink. He was patient when my calligraphy looked nothing like his.

My small, soft and fair hands were nothing like his. His were as large as the East Africa map we drew, softer than mine and as dark as the night.

Every few months or so, Abu would ask me to compare the size of my hand against his—palm to palm—to measure how much I had grown. My hand would still be tiny, but he would always appreciate my growing bones and say: *Mera bacha bara hogaya hai.*

Then he would proceed to read my palm. Yes, I would be very generous. My thumb would bend backwards all the way to my wrist. Yes, I would 'sail through' a successful marriage because my love line formed a perfect boat shape when both my palms were placed side by side, as if in prayer. Yes, I would have children. I wanted a hundred children, I declared to Abu. Abu laughingly complained to Ami: *Mehra, dekh yeh kya keh rahi hai.*

Ami would tell me to hold off on my eagerness to proliferate quite so abundantly because toddlers should not dream of such things.

Ami: *It is inappropriate.*

Me: *But being an ami is so nice.*

Ami: *But saying so isn't nice.*

Me: *But I only say it to Abu.*

Ami: *Saying it to your abu is especially not nice.*

I was determined to have a hundred babies, but Abu told me I would only have two girls and a little boy. I was disappointed, but I vowed to myself to rectify this dearth as soon as I got to be in charge.

Abu's hands would also alleviate my pain. He would massage my temples when I had a headache. Circular motions, just the right pressure for my soft head, and soon I'd be fast asleep.

Abu also had a way of getting me to do things I was terrified of. Darkness frightened me. In most of my childhood pictures, I have a haunted look, as if I was afraid that something would leap from the shadows and attack me.

Behind the corner where Abu parked his motorbike, the entire universe converged into a stygian darkness. It was my bogeyman. I couldn't see beyond a certain point after nightfall, and what lay beyond that point was the devil, in my lurid imagination, doing non-consensual things to me for all eternity. It was a portal to another world.

When the Ugandan army called at your home, it wasn't for a friendly visit, it was death knocking at the door. That is what these men did when they dropped by: they would emerge from dark corners, darker than the night, skin glistening with Vaseline, their guns heavier than their food, descending unexpectedly upon families that were going about their chores and daily routines, blithely unaware of the fate to befall them—then there was a knock.

There was a bathroom window, beyond the place where Abu parked his bike.

I would pee in the loo, but I would look outside through the window, expecting the knock. Dreading the arrival of marauding soldiers.

One evening, I was in the veranda, playing with a ball made of polythene bags and rubber bands. The ball rolled beyond Abu's bike and that was goodbye ball.

Abu was on to me. Abu: Go get it.

I ran away.

Abu: Come back!

Heart pounding, but return obediently. Abu: Go get the ball.

I opened my mouth to let out a noise between a gasp and big sob. Crying came easily.

Ami: What is it?

Abu pointed and Ami silently watched from the door that overlooked the veranda around which she had planted gardenias in tin pots that advertised oil and flour. Today, Abu's target was her littlest one.

Abu: Go get the ball. Me: Ami!

Silence.

Abu: If you are frightened of something, you have to go and touch it.

I was nearly peeing my pants by this time. Tearfully I faced Abu, unable to defy him.

Abu: I'm standing right here. Go and touch the bike. Me: NOOOO!

Abu grew all the more determined. He pointed again, walking towards me remorselessly.

Me: Ami!

I knew I needed her to save me. I knew Ami had turned on me.

Abu: Okay, fine. Go close to it at least. My legs were jelly. My tears wouldn't stop. Abu: Go. Touch. It. I. Am. Right. Here.

Me: Nooooo. Please. Ami.

Abu: You have to touch things that frighten you. You have to. By this time, I was hiccupping with great, big gulps of air. My world was crashing around me. No one was coming to rescue me and the darkness crept even closer. But enough time had passed for me to realize I had to somehow appease this monster that was once my father.

Abu turned me towards the darkness, towards the window, the shadows and the vast unknown.

Me: Okay, but please don't push me. Abu: I'm right here.

I looked at it, squinting to make out the least scary parts. I could see the outline of Abu's motorbike. I took a step forward. I could touch it if I simply reached out. I walked back to Abu.

I had to have won something. He was the one to grant me my trophy. I had stopped crying. Abu looked at me and held my gaze.

He repeated: You have to touch what you are afraid of. I ran into Ami's open arms.

She changed me out of my wet pants.

ABU AND AMI AND THEIR IN-BETWEEN

I straddled the border between Ami and Abu—sometimes loving Ami more than Abu, sometimes loving Abu more than Ami. They let me sleep between them on Sunday mornings when kindergarten was off, or when the war kept them indoors. I would choose one of them at a time. I'd sit up in their bed, wake them both up to announce that today I was Ami's and not Abu's. Then I would change my mind and throw Ami off the deep end in a child's whimsy.

Baji and Bhai and Bhaijan were so much older and entirely immersed in their studies for me to have to compete with them for our parents' attention.

Abu would take me to his office on his bike. One day, when Baji got to go in my place, my universe splintered. I opened my mouth wide and wailed.

Ami took a stand against this tantrum by insisting that Baji go with Abu. I saw them pull away—Baji holding Abu's waist just as I did.

Ami said that as Baji was also Abu's daughter, she was entitled to go with Abu sometimes. But the thought of her riding with Abu made me miserable. Ami ignored me. It only made me feel more numb with grief. I lay on the kitchen floor and wept until Abu returned home. I had lost my voice with all the wailing.

Most of my time after that horrid episode was focused on how not to be replaced.

Sometimes Abu was deliciously fatherly. He would let me climb on to his back while he was eating and not reprimand me even if he choked on a fishbone because I was climbing on him. I wouldn't have it any other way. Abu's shoulders were mine and he was mine at my time and on my terms. When Ami reached into Abu's throat to retrieve the fishbone, the shock of the near-death episode faded. I went back on to his back where I belonged.

Ami was also deliciously motherly. All that good food, and her magical palms would brush my hair away from my forehead to clear the universe of all harm; and the way she would pray and blow the prayer on every part of me; and the cute names like Aashi, Guria and *Beti*—all too safe and powerful. Nothing was unsolvable for Ami. She got rid of lizards with boric powder and rat poison, and she removed stains from my socks with ash soda. When Abu died, the border I straddled between my parents collapsed like a detonated wall. There was only a wasteland. It's not like Abu had died and Ami was all there was. Abu died and I became everyone's. I was everyone else's on their time and on their terms. They hurt me as sadists hurt the vulnerable, but to me their cruelty was inexorably linked to the man who no longer let me own the world.

When he died, I was ten years old. I didn't know that the world was going to knock me down with a sledgehammer and leave me to die, abandoned, along the rocky coastline of condemnation and judgment. When Abu died, there was so much confusion and turmoil that I was almost relieved he was gone. For a while, the voices in my head fell silent.

No one can fault me for being a bit excited that my father had died. Death has a fanfare. It has drama. It's almost a beginning. It's a forced migration into another land. Like an exile you didn't choose. It brings opportunity and for an in-between girl like me, rural and underexposed, I thought maybe I could get to be in cities with malls.

Weeks later I was still bewildered, but he had gone by then and his body must have started decomposing.

Abu's two-year illness made me hate my life in Uganda. Everything became unpalatable. Uganda wanted me to be Ugandan. A loyalty was asked of me as I got older. Our skins were different. But they didn't let me be different.

Diana, my best friend, was also my biggest bully. Stella was my second-best friend and she always made fun of me for not being African. I was dancing like an African in the school choir and she found that hilarious. That exclusion started feeling unfair. When other girls teased me my friends egged them on.

I was sick of not having the right kind of hair, the right kind of nose, the right kind of colour. Even my self-loathing didn't feel right. The teachers beat me too much, for too long and too hard. Whereas there was trauma-bonding between the classmates before, now it was just cruel and unusual and there was bonding, trauma or otherwise. I didn't feel like I was part of my African family any more. They wanted me to be them or get out.

But get out and go where?

The corporal punishment started breaking me down after Abu died. With some kind of twisted justice, my classmates and I were asked to fetch the sticks from the bush land behind the school. Then the teachers would flog us with the canes we ourselves had chosen. If we chose wide canes, we got more surface area of the cane on our skin and it would hurt like a bitch; on the other hand, if we picked a thin, flexible wand, it would cut through our skin like a whiplash, also a bitch. I never used to cry before, but after Abu's passing, school floggings would make me cry so hard that my hiccups would go on well into the night and steal my sleep. I felt supplanted. I felt Abu had betrayed me by allowing death to ride his motorbike. I knew Abu died of disease, but I couldn't shake off this inner conflict that Abu somehow chose someone else over me. That Abu left on his own accord, most certainly. That he may as well have ridden his bike into his own grave.

I started sleeping at the edge of the bed with one hand on the wall beside the bed, using the walls as a security blanket. I still do. It grounded me in a world that was spinning out of control.

I've heard people say that when someone dies, they take a piece of you with them, but Abu took me whole. He took the Ami I knew with him too. Life has happened to me since 1992, and all of the bad parts can be credited to being a dead man's daughter. All the good parts have felt alien and fleeting, guilt- ridden and unreal.

Uganda took my father and shoved him 6 feet under.

Although they didn't take him home, I could do so and take him to his rightful home in Pakistan.

AN ANGRY OLD MAN
LIVES IN MY HOME

When I think of a home, I think of a round mud hut with a thatched roof. I think Uganda when I think of home. When I think of play, I think of climbing the mountain with a 50 foot straight-line waterfall. If I sat on Abu's prized armchair and looked at that mountain from our front porch, I could almost see the waterfall moving, almost hear it thundering down.

No, we didn't live in a mud house with a thatched roof, but I really didn't know whether having a brick house with a tin roof was any better.

I was fascinated at the way Ami managed to grow and graft her gardenias into face-sized, multicoloured magic. Sometimes the colours merged to form a whole new colour in the flower. The red-and-white blossoms became light pink and at other times, they sprouted random red or white petals. When I sat in Abu's armchair, the garden, filled with Ami's flowers, filled me with wonder, waterfalls and gardenias singing in my ears.

Abu came home early that day. Maybe it was the nausea. He startled me with his harsh tone.

The music stopped. The gardenias peed their pants. '*Jee* Abu,' I said.

'I said, what's in your hand?' Abu said.

The two vertical lines between his eyebrows were distinct and deep. I've inherited them. I've also inherited this utterly painful moment that tipped me straight into hell. This was no armchair moment. Abu towered over me as I casually lounged in the chair. Our postures were from different universes.

I looked down at my school uniform guiltily. There were iron filings scattered all over my lap and around me. In my hand was a large cylindrical magnet. I had been playing with the iron filings and the magnet, the invisible, forcefield of the magnet almost ostentatious in its magic.

Abu repeated the question.

'Abu, I just found it lying around the sand pit at school,' I lied in a tiny voice, forgetting that, as a teacher, Abu instinctively sensed a lie.

After Diana, the prom queen, ended her friendship with me, some nameless, faceless loser from the backbench thought it opportune to climb the social ladder and gave me the magnet. Muindis like me had some appeal. I took it from her with some arrogance.

This was no story to tell Abu, so I thought I would just tell him I had found it. I squinted into Abu's narrowed eyes. His power was unmistakable. It almost felt like Abu was going to retract something that he had given me—something like life.

'Abu, it's just a magnet,' I said. My voice shook.

'So you just picked it up and brought it into my house?' 'I . . .'

'Did you steal it?'

My heart was racing. I needed Ami. I needed the waterfall. I needed to watch her grafting. I needed . . . something.

'No, Abu, it was just lying there in the sand pit near our school.'

'IS THERE A SAND PIT IN YOUR SCHOOL NOW?' he thundered, his decibel level rising with his ire.

'There's some construction going on in school and some parents complained to Mr De Suza that kids don't learn under the trees.' This part was all true.

'Do you think picking up something that doesn't belong to you is okay? If it doesn't belong to you, it is stealing.'

I was trembling now. Ami walked out into the porch to see what the ruckus was all about.

'*Kya hua?*' she asked gently, a tiny smile playing around the edges of her lips in an attempt to defuse the situation.

'She picked up a magnet that doesn't belong to her and brought it home.' His tone was accusatory and he was clearly directing his fury at Ami now. Ami had failed hopelessly as an arbiter. I felt bad that Ami was being told that she had produced thief.

'Apologize, *beta*. You know this is very bad,' said Ami sternly. 'You don't take something that doesn't belong to you. It doesn't matter that it didn't have an owner at the time when you found it.'

'Sorry.'

I always stood firm during an onslaught, but her kindness was my undoing. As I looked down at my lap, the tears brimmed over.

There I sat on Abu's armchair, unravelling.

Abu screamed at me some more. Something about honesty. Something about violating a code. Something about his child not demonstrating values that he had upheld all his life. Something about being disgraceful.

'You will return this thing that does not belong to you,' he said. 'Okay, Abu. I'm sorry,' I repeated, my words punctuated with pathetic sniffles and my nose running.

'She will return it tomorrow,' Ami said to Abu, gently taking him by the arm and leading him indoors.

Abu hesitated at first, glaring at me, and then relented to follow Ami's lead.

The forcefield had changed. The iron filings had fallen to the floor, somehow, the gardenias and the waterfall no longer a fascination now.

I sat on the armchair for hours before I had the courage to silently sneak into my room.

I avoided Abu all day that day. Everything that could possibly go bad had already happened to me; nevertheless, I lay low to ward off any further bad luck.

The next morning, I dressed for school silently.

Although Ami tried to make light of the situation at the breakfast table, I continued to sulk. 'Someone got sent to the cleaners for a silly magnet.'

Abu had made me feel like I was a criminal. How was this funny?

In a sullen and silent protest, I starved that day. I watched the new classrooms being built; the sand was sourced from the sand pit. We would also get better latrines. No more shitting in holes behind trees.

I hated Ami so much that I wished she would be a different Ami.

I returned the reprehensible magnet to the nameless, faceless Black girl. This time I was telling the truth. *Bambi*, she said in Luganda. What a pity.

Bambi, indeed.

ABU HAS HARNESSED THE POWER OF DEATH

Abu's illness came to me in intervals, like train stations you notice in a stupor on your way home, only to realize you were headed in the wrong direction all along.

I wasn't as alert as I ought to have been. I should have known Abu was dying.

At first, it was piles. Treatable. No big deal. We would go to Kenya and sort it out. We went to Kenya and came back but Abu was still crapping blood.

I was in the kitchen as inconspicuous as the vegetable rack when Ami and Baji were talking to each other. Baji had a serious expression on her face. Ami was diligently making the roundest rotis in the universe.

'It seems like it's the disease,' Ami said to the round roti. 'The disease?'

'It could be he has cancer,' Ami said, placing the roti on the *tawa* (pan) with her knobbly fingers. I must mention her rickety legs at this point because she suddenly seemed to have grown so much shorter.

There was a pause and then Baji said, 'We'll just have to wait and see.'

Ami made a new *payra* (doughball) for a new, perfectly round roti. I continued to eavesdrop on their conversations, while they didn't acknowledge my presence.

The second thing I remember overhearing was that it was better for Abu not to get chemo treatment. The colon cancer was too advanced.

Then, one day, Abu himself told me that he was dying and that it was far better that he died than Ami.

Abu and I were on a banana palm-leaf mat under my favourite tree which had scattered its flowers, which smelled like Ami, on the grass. Abu chose this sylvan setting to deliver this terrible news.

'You're a girl and girls need mothers. You'll know why when you're older.'

'Abu, I wish it were Ami who would die and not you,' I said.

He must have been horrified by my words but on some level he may have felt pleased to be the favoured parent.

I overheard Bhaijan, Bhai and Baji discussing who would break the bad news to me. Bhaijan, being the oldest and the wisest and a doctor to boot, won this lottery.

Our home was suddenly filled with more cousins than were necessary. So, the lot of us went for a walk. We wore closed shoes because otherwise the maggots in that dusty path tended to infest your toes.

So, Bhaijan held my hand on the maggot-ridden path and told me that Abu had cancer and I was going to die.

I am fairly sure he said Abu was the one dying, but sometimes one's ears can play tricks. He told me I should be brave because I was a big girl now. The kindest part of the entire maggot-path walk was the way he held my hand with his thumb gently massaging the back of my hand. It felt like he was transferring all of his courage and confidence to me. A dozen or so cousins followed behind us in a sombre procession.

It was mission accomplished.

Eventually, someone in the group announced that it was lunchtime.

We had to cut short my take on Abu-has-cancer and head back.

On top of everything, Ami had the less than pleasant task of warming sewing needles and sticking them into my yelping cousins from Kenya, to extract the yellow and gooey maggots from their toes. With the composure of a true stalwart, Ami refrained from slapping them for not keeping still.

I started avoiding Abu just as he began avoiding me. When I was eventually asked to sit by his sickbed, he was in a deep coma. The rest of my relatives played cricket and carried on with normal life. That is how humans deal with an elder on their death bed. They play ball like idiots outside a dying man's window and leave a little kid to sit with the dying man.

The unmistakable duty of the person sitting at the bedside of the dying man was not lost on me. I was to report to the cricket players when the sick, old man kicked the bucket.

After an hour of sitting with Abu, I mustered up the courage to look at him.

The bedsheet he lay on was green. Behind his headboard was a window with a net covering to keep out the disease-spreading mosquitoes. The window had a lever to control the glass louvres of the window. The louvres were open at the time, perhaps for ventilation and to help circulate the air to dispel the smell of impending death.

The mosquito net dangled from the ceiling above his bed. Unlike the netting over the rest of our cots, this one was knotted closed over Abu's head like a hangman's noose that was taking a break. Who cared if Abu was bitten by an anopheles mosquito; in all likelihood the blood of a dying man would kill the blood-sucking insect.

Die, mosquito.

My gaze rested on Abu's beautifully wide forehead and his full head of hair without a single strand of grey. The hair that grew thick and springy away from his forehead, was as yet unaware that he was sick.

As I sat beside him, I whispered to his hand which I was holding. He had large hands like a farm labourer. No one would have guessed that these hands only held fountain pens, calligraphy pens and chalk. These hands had held books and had held me as he carried me aloft on his shoulders.

I vowed to myself that day to never forget his hands, to take my memory of them everywhere with me. His wide and square, blue-black nails were thick with the promise of calcium.

How long would the calcium in his nails last? Would it outlast his heart?

I stole out like a thief who had committed identity theft of her father's mighty paws.

Eventually, they allowed me to field in their cricket match. The ball was hard and could've hurt me if I had batted or bowled. I didn't really care, anyway, that I wasn't playing a more pivotal role in their ballgame because I had already taken Abu.

WITHOUT ABU, THE TEEN YEARS ARE HELL

'Tell me what happened?' Ami said, gently stroking my hair.

Ami always smelled of Nivea cream—a mix of jasmine and the milk of human kindness. There was nothing unkind about Ami, except her deliberate ineptitude with my toast part.

'I don't want to talk about it,' I wept.

'You can tell your ami,' she coaxed, stroking my hair. I felt tender and loved and I wanted to love her back so much. However, the rebellious side of me wanted her to forestall her kind and gentle assault on me when I was at my most vulnerable, as I lay with my head on her lap. I wanted her to keep stroking my hair until I fell into a deep coma. I felt I ought to be stoned to death for what I had done.

The fear of disappointing Ami and the rage I felt towards her for neglecting my needs battled for supremacy.

I had done a very bad thing. 'I cannot tell you because you won't understand. You never do,' I said.

'I think I already know what happened.' Now she was also crying.

I sat up, horrified that the news had reached her before I could tell her in person.

'Did they tell you?' I asked.

'They're not your enemy, Aashi,' she replied.

'They didn't even give me a chance to tell you what really happened,' I said.

Ami always insisted I must second-guess myself when I felt someone was hurting me. She always said they had my best interests at heart. It was like the cry-it-out method for young babies. Babies cannot self-soothe. Stop their bawling without giving them reassurance or breaking down their psyche. When people hurt me, they hurt me. How is there an alternative to what had been experienced so viscerally?

I was devastated that it was going to be worse than I imagined. 'I won't say anything to you. I will not chastise or reprimand you. I will only listen. I promise. Please tell me,' she said.

I dissolved into more tears. 'They hurt me,' I said.

'Who hurt you?' Ami asked.

'Mamujan, Khalajan and my cousins,' I replied. More hair stroking.

I blew my nose into my nylon dupatta. It wasn't really absorbent. 'I did something bad and they found out,' I said.

'It's okay,' she said.

Slightly encouraged, I said, 'I shouldn't have left school in the middle of a schoolday to go to Selena's home to have lunch with her grandmother,' I said.

'Was that all you did?' Ami asked, a hint of sarcasm and mistrust in her voice.

'Yes! Why? What did they say I did?' I demanded.

'Hush. Speak softly. Mamujan is downstairs and will hear you. You know he doesn't tolerate your yelling at me,' she said.

It was already over. The verdict had already been passed. They had taken my mother from me as well as everything she stood for.

'Younger Mamujan told me,' she sighed finally.

'I didn't do anything!' I protested. 'Why don't you believe me? Why don't you trust me?'

Ami paused, and then she went for the kill, 'How come younger Mamujan found you with boys?' she said.

I fell silent. *I was with boys.*

'I was with one boy. He's Selena's cousin and he drove Selena, me and her older female cousin to have ice cream. That was when Mamujan saw me. No, I was not with boys.'

If there is one boy, does that technically mean I was with plural boys? Ami went on, 'He saw you, out in the city, in the middle of a schoolday.'

Although she was not being accusatory, I felt the chill of being at a grand inquisition. She was no longer my mother. She was theirs.

I fled. That was the last time I ever wore a dupatta.

I locked myself in my room and wept for days. I didn't go back to school and Selena was no longer my friend.

It was weird to have your uncle storm into the principal's office for no real offence, threatening to take the school administration to the police for gross negligence. There was so much ado about my truancy.

Trauma bonds. Trauma separates.

I thought friendship endures phases but the truth is, friendship is only for a phase.

Mamujan had told Ami a vastly embellished story: apparently, I routinely played truant from school along with Selena; Selena's family ran a prostitution ring serving up naïve schoolgirls like me to paedophiles.

I wondered whether Manujan believed his own hyperactive imagination. The truth was miles away from what Mamujan saw. It made me wonder whether Mamujan himself was guilty of something bad. Yes, I went to Selena's home. I had planned this months ahead. I was her best friend and she wanted to show me off to her dado.

We had lunch. We talked at the table with her family. They were told we had an early release day from school. They were happy to have me over. Selena's dado loved me to bits.

'I must take you to Lahore with me,' said Dado. '*Mashallah.*'

Selena's family was Kashmiri and Shia and a bit too beautiful for Konkani standards.

Dado called for her grandson. She opened her tiny purse and gave him some money to buy us girls some ice cream. She insisted that her older granddaughter go with Selena and me for ice cream. She kissed me goodbye. She wanted me to be dropped back at school safely. Her grandson grudgingly drove us around.

Tall and voluptuous, Selena's baji looked a bit overripe and over made-up for Nairobi, although maybe not for Lahore.

Selena was a bronzed beauty with blue-green eyes and luxuriant hair that flowed in waves, looking a bit like Venus rising from a stormy ocean, and she was enchanting. Nothing about the bunch of us at the ice-cream parlour, called Snow Cream, blended into the background. We were happy. We were joyous.

Maybe Mamujan thought he saw a post-orgy celebration.

Nothing about living with the Konkanis was happy. There was a whole lot of prayer, devotion and instruction. Everything was grey and boring. There was also very little ice cream sanctioned by older women who loved being older and being women. Selena's family was incredibly happy that day; I was treated like royalty.

Selena's father was an even bigger delight than the mom or the dado. He just ate quietly and asked interesting questions. He was exactly what I felt a dad should be—tossing one-liners at lunch, mostly munching his food, being a very tiny part of a largely women-centric family while his mother visited. Most men I knew were deathly patriarchal and they were served food first. But Selena's dad was the last to serve himself and even asked his wife whether she needed water. The kids ate first.

At the Konkanis', this was sacrilege. The children came last, and the adolescents were the worst of the lot. Adolescent girls were considered a hazardous landfill. The men ate first. Food was served, and there was always a person doing the serving.

I was thinking of all these things while I was at Snow Cream ice-cream parlour. The ice cream was creamy, cold and sweet and had sprinkles on it; that moment was so beautiful. The ice cream was melting sweetly in my mouth and no one I knew was around to spoil the fun.

When Selena and I were done with the ice cream, we headed back to the car. I was wearing Selena's clothes because wearing my school uniform would be a dead giveaway that I was playing hooky. Nairobi, for all its commercialism, was a small town in the early 1990s. Almost all the brown kids were identifiable by the brown adults in town—the local Blacks didn't give a damn. To them, all brown people were landfill.

On our way back to the car, laughing high-spiritedly perhaps from the sugar high or the exuberance of just hanging out with a friend like Selena, I was confronted by my cousin Salman.

'Hi,' he said as he strolled towards me. I was flabbergasted. I almost threw away the sprinkles.

This was the moment of truth.

You know how you have a split second to drop to your knees and confess all your wrongdoing but a devil of mischief prompts you to stand your ground. You may have broken some rules, but the rules didn't make sense anyway. In any case, I was with Selena's family and they would vouch for me.

'*Assalamalaikum*, Salman Bhaijan,' I replied.

'I'm with Dad. We were just wondering why you're not in school at this time,' he said.

I looked towards the car he indicated. Mamujan was at the wheel. 'Who are these people?' he asked.

He was parroting a script he had been asked to say to me. I realized he was watering down the intensity of the rage which his father felt.

'I am with my friend Selena and her family; we had an early release from school, so we decided to have ice cream,' I said.

'Are you okay, and do you need help, are you safe?' he asked. He was reluctant to go back without me.

When I bid a swift goodbye to Salman and climbed into Selena's vehicle, I knew everyone in the car was tense. The mood had gone from light-hearted and carefree to bleak and ominous. I asked Selena's cousin to drive us away.

The moments that followed were strange. Suddenly, I couldn't recall being all that close to Selena. She was happy to entertain a friend who was a loser but loyal. Where she came from, her parents probably knew she skipped school and were okay with it as long as her grades were okay.

I was living with my aunt and her family now. In this house, grades mattered, but purity mattered even more. Truancy was tantamount to promiscuity. I had only gone to an ice-cream shop but the adults, who were in charge of me in Ami's absence, had no idea that I had gone there.

Even if I had asked the Konkanis for their permission to go for a safe and family-supervised outing within the confines of the city in which we all lived, they wouldn't have granted it to me.

'No!' was their default. That is how the Konkanis survived in Nairobi.

Selena was not particularly clever but she had an air about her, an everything-will-be-all-right air. Something I found fascinating. She was rich, confident, light-skinned and conventionally beautiful enough to pass off as a White. She knew something that others didn't—that eventually everything would be a-okay.

Selena's was the epitome of bad-girl behaviour. There was very little talk about what happened after I was caught having ice cream but mostly everyone, both at home and at school, thought I was a prostitute and Selena's male cousin had paid for sex with me.

Konkanis hated blue-eyed Whites; to the Konkanis, they were synonymous with deceit.

Meanwhile, life as I knew it was ending for me and the splintering sky was falling on my head as it always did. There would soon be another funeral for sure.

I was a tramp. I was a slut. My virtue was being saved for my husband, but now I was sullied.

I was a village girl and clueless about sex. These insinuations were levelled at me at a very young age. I discovered that there were lurid rumours about me.

I found out about sex in its full depth only after my marriage. I figured out how my cycle worked when I was pregnant. This is the right way, the acceptable way but despite this path, my reputation after this ice-cream incident made me less valuable.

I exchanged my purity for a dowry but somehow marriage was far less dishonourable than talking to boys without permission for an ice-cream cone with adult supervision.

I digress.

It is painful to talk about that day when I lay in Ami's lap, even if quarter of a century has passed between then and now. It is painful because I was sexualized when I was not even aware of what a period was; when I was unaware about what potential sexual chemistry could hold; when I was more interested in ice cream and father figures and actual fatherliness than I was in young men who could seduce me in cars. What I did with Selena was far from a high-risk situation. Breaking a rule of two is a rite of passage during puberty.

If my daughter were to do this, I would be cross with her for not letting me know first. However, I would first ask myself why I had left a teenaged daughter at the mercy of a bunch of conservative and narrow-minded relatives who could potentially damage my little girl's sense of self.

When I finally re-entered school, after D-day, Selena was nowhere to be found. She was around, of course, doing Selena things—sneaking off behind the water tanks in the cricket ground next to school, picking fights with teachers and skipping chemistry class. Unless she was ignoring me, we would've interacted at some point during the long schoolday, lunch, cooking class or the reading room. Selena was keen to have me in her home before the ice-cream incident, but my embarrassing family was so off-putting that she stopped talking to me. This was another ending I didn't ask for.

ABU IS YOUNGER MAMUJAN BECAUSE TEENS MUST HAVE DADS

Most of high school was spent shuttling between buses that would take three hours a day between school and home. Then there were the mandatory prayers and the mandatory onion-slicing and garlic-crushing that were soul-destroying for the teen in me.

Struggle was supposed to build character, but they turned me into a bratty little devil. I was an unhappy young woman. Of all the unfortunate things that had to happen to me, being flat-chested really was the worst. I was sufficiently domesticated but hated it. And there was far more waiting at bus stops than I would have preferred.

The unthankful person I was accused of being, I became.

Instead of being a cry baby, I sucked it up and became vengeful and disagreeable.

There were times when I was late, or the bus was early, and I would have to outrun the bus and find it at the next stop. Missing the school bus was a nightmare because there was no possibility of my staying home; some relative or the other would drop me off at school, making it abundantly clear that they hated me more than they hated the Nairobi traffic.

I was called lazy and sneered at. All this made me show up on time for the bus most of the time. The bus itself was hell. If I ever found a seat, it was usually on someone's lap, because the bus was often over capacity.

Nairobi felt like my brain was shrink-wrapped.

I knew from the moment that I walked into school the day after that cursed ice-cream fiasco that I no longer controlled my narrative.

There was a huge brouhaha at school. One of my Konkani friends told me that younger Mamujan had stormed into the headmistress's office, demanding to meet me.

When the person sent to fetch me from class reappeared without me, Mamujan was livid, as was the headmistress.

I went to Muslim Girl's School and wore a hijab. Mrs Marge was a fierce headmistress. She wore beautiful saris with bodysuit tops, often black, covering her long, slim arms and reaching all the way down her sides. She made heads turn, but she had a nasty wildfire inside her, just waiting to blame the world for every pain she had ever felt. She cut a terrifying picture to the students, her jaw placed as if she were muttering the scripture backwards, like in a cult.

I was told there was a lot of yelling in her office on the first floor of the admin building about the failure to protect Mamujan's precious niece from thugs and pimps. When Mamujan told her off and accused her of misplacing me, I bet she wanted to unzip his mouth, pull out his guts and sew him up again, just for daring to speak to her in that tone but instead she decided that revenge was best served cold and directly to his niece. Although she did not appreciate such inconvenience on a Thursday afternoon, she merely chewed the back of her Bic pen and let him vent his spleen. She sent him off with a promise to get the matter sorted.

He either heeded her or had to be escorted out by security. An angry man can only be mollified by a woman or cowed down by her fierceness, but neither makes him feel solid.

I returned to school, quivering on the inside but tight-lipped on the outside, and wholly oblivious to the severity of the turn of events. Although I quietly resumed my classes and headed back home in the tardy school bus, I expected to be ambushed at any time.

I wanted Ami who was not there. She was in America all through my first year of high school, doing American things—like helping raise my niece.

I dared not miss Abu. What would Abu do anyway?

I sorely needed some of Ami's nagging, her cooing and her mollycoddling now. I was, after all, a child who had just lost her father. The world was bewildering and friendships had limits.

When I hopped off at the bus stop, I was in my green skirt and white shirt, which was emblazoned with the Muslim Girls School emblem, a mandatory white salwar underneath the skirt for post-puberty girls, black, buckled shoes and a white hijab that was supposed to keep me on the straight and narrow.

After being spotted at the ice-cream joint, the fifteen-minute walk from the bus stop to Khalajan's South C home was as arduous as a trek up Mount Kilimanjaro. I walked into the house trying to appear as normal as possible, although my colon's contents felt frozen. I greeted older Khalajan, who opened the door for me, and asked her for a glass of milk. Good girls drank milk. Then, realizing that she had no clue about what had transpired, I walked to younger Khalajan's house next door where I was living. I strolled in deliberately and greeted her as well. She was in the kitchen washing some pears. I still remember how vividly they gleamed. I casually chatted with her about my day at school in a vain attempt to wing it past the looming catastrophe. With the eternal optimism of an inveterate gambler, every passing second felt like things were looking up for me—until they were not.

I casually slid off the kitchen counter and ambled out to my temporary room upstairs. That was when younger Mamujan came down. I could hear his breathing before I saw his face, mere inches from mine. He ground out through clenched teeth that he had just heard my fabricated story to younger Khalajan about being let off school early. He accused me of being a liar and a cheat, even though I had only lied. His hands moved close to my face and then what I was dreading happened. Younger Mamujan, a grown man of fifty-something, hairy as a wolf, slapped my left cheek like he was a lumberjack.

Although I was expecting it, nothing prepared me for the impact of the back slap. His knuckles hurt me with their brutal velocity and his anger maimed whatever was left of Aisha that day. I held my hot cheek and stood there, gazing down at my white sock. Somehow my shoe had come off. There must have been a scuffle between my black shoe and the fourth step on that stairwell. I must have blanked out. Forgetting pieces of what took place. I was hurt, someone hurt me.

There was yelling. My cousin and my khalajan—and there could have been more people—restrained Mamujan, the women screamed. Also, there were long silences, just heaving chests. Older Khalajan had mysteriously arrived at that moment. This was not how I thought it would end. I could not have imagined that I would be physically assaulted. I felt dull, like someone who had been mugged and left with only the one thought, *This is my fault.* The Khalajans were tsk-tsking. Mamujan was raging on, telling and retelling the story of what he had seen with his own eyes. I was a disgraceful woman. The audacity to lie blatantly to my elders—I was a special kind of evil or something to that effect. Maybe shame and remorse would've been the appropriate response to get me redemption; instead, I resorted to more lies. I had been badly raised.

He kept saying: Stop telling lies. You liar. You bitch.

The repetition made his mouth foamy, like well-whipped cappuccino froth.

I wasn't even crying at this point. The tears came much later.

The slap had been very hard. My neck hurt from it. My face felt swollen. Think of a bullet train breaking the sound barrier. I had held my face so it wouldn't run away from me. It was pulsating with a life of its own. I drifted in and out of that moment, but I do remember the relief and the shock. Ever since Salman Bhaijan discovered me, I had known things would end badly. I had half been expecting the truth to set me free.

The truth was that no crime—moral or legal—had been committed. I had only responded to an invitation for lunch from an older woman visiting from Lahore. They had cooked me home-made daal and curry, and then there was harmless ice cream. How in the world did I end up as the target in a witch hunt?

Still holding my face, I was dragged to the bathroom downstairs by younger Khalajan to wash up like I was a rape victim or something. She made me scrub my face and say the cleansing prayer I was taught to say after my menstrual period. The prayer was called the prayer for cleanliness. It asked God for permission to no longer be dirty.

Now sobbing, the tears hot against my red cheek, I tried to tell younger Khalajan that Selena's father had been there too and that I had felt safe, that this was all a huge misunderstanding; but she was harsh with me, taking over and scrubbing me herself. She said that I ought to be ashamed of myself.

'How can you use your dead father to get pity for a heinous act? You've abused our hospitality and brought shame upon the family.'

I sobbed.

'You were entrusted to my care by *Behainjan*; what will we tell her now? How will we ever face her?'

I hiccupped, sadly.

'Your father's body is not even fully cold in his grave and look at what you did? *Besharam.*'

Now all I felt was anger and rage at the way I was being soaped. I was silent.

'Have you no shame hanging out with boys like that?' More tsk-tsking. 'That too in the middle of the city.'

I wept.

'Look at what you've done to our *izzat.*' I was silent.

'Look at how much trouble you have caused our family. I've never seen my brother this angry in my life. And all for what? For some hanky-panky with some boys?'

She was right about that. There was no gain. In retrospect, what a high price to pay for a bit of freedom from the prison of my aunt's house. I was mortified.

I was forcibly bathed in a tiny bathroom, but the unclean feeling wouldn't leave me. I kept apologizing but, by this point, but no one would have it. I was eventually alone in the room allocated to me. Alone to mull things over. There was silence in the house and in my soul.

I think I just wanted to give up that day, but my stubborn heart wouldn't stop beating.

My cousin, who eventually returned from physics class after school, didn't speak to me that day. We shared the room. She changed into her nightdress. I did not. I was facing the wall, crying.

Sometimes the sobs would escape me, but she didn't console me or offer me a glass of water. She just turned away and slept. I had been unanimously consigned to Coventry.

How does one come back from this? I was thirteen. I felt like a common criminal.

No boy had touched me.

That day the ground beneath me cracked wide open. Both Ami and Abu fell into it. No dahlias for anybody.

Go home. The party is over.

ABU COMES BACK TO ME IN FLOWERS

I cannot bear to look at a hibiscus flower. It is too heartbreakingly pretty.

Perhaps I cannot look at it because it reminds me of my shadow self. A shadow self is something that implores you to be agitated, perturbed and upset without fully understanding why you are upset. The hibiscus has an outpouring of its maroon-red petals, velvety, rose-like with a long, shameless stalk reaching out from underneath, way past the petals into the sky. A hibiscus is unabashedly a hibiscus. I look at it and it reminds me of how it was to be a child.

I remember how it was to be short and tiny. To wake up and wonder what Ami–Abu would tell me to do. What dress would they make me wear? How many times would they remind me to pee or drink up my fruit juice? Would they forget to bathe me? Would they remember that I didn't like skin on my milk or would they insist that I have it because it was good for me? What kind of day would Ami–Abu make me have?

The hibiscus reminds me of blood clots and dried-up hearts, sore from bleeding without anyone caring that I bled.

Before, they were merely hibiscus flowers to me too. They were to me as they were to themselves. I was in the garden. Abu was with me. It was that kind of Ami–Abu day. Abu broke the hibiscus from its branch with a careless snap. He peeled each petal with even fewer moves. One. Two. Three. Four. Five. There.

Ami had bathed me, made me pancakes and dressed me in a lacy dress. Abu was fifty-something.

'What's inside?' I asked. 'Everything,' Abu said. 'Everything?' 'Everything.'

He peeled open the flower's tube where everything was and held me by the chin as he always did.

'Open your mouth.' I opened my mouth.

He dumped the contents on to my tongue. I smiled.

He nodded.

I cannot see his face. I can't remember it. But I remember the strength of his hands as they held my chin and the springy black hair on his brown knuckles.

The *everything* tasted like a secret—under our noses, simple and satisfying.

If I could, I would have emptied all the nectar from that bush that very day. But Abu told me that we must leave some for the bees.

I have left the hibiscuses alone for a long, long time now. There are no more Ami–Abu days. I bathe and dress myself.

I choose my own nectar, depending on what addiction I need to serve. My own two feet, often with nail polish on the toes, take me everywhere I think I want to go.

Abu was soon sixty-something. For a boy who was fourteen at the time of the India–Pakistan Partition, it was soon going to be time for him to go. But I wasn't ready. I wasn't ready to leave the bold flower behind. I wasn't ready to leave the *everything* behind. No one cared that I wasn't ready. The thing that especially didn't care was the hibiscus. They witnessed my dependence and still betrayed me. After Abu died, even the flowers were animated, capable of staying connected to me yet choosing not to.

THERE IS NO MANUAL TO HELP YOU FORGET HOME

I did feel a bit like Ami's forcibly grafted dahlias—artificial with a lot of pressure to become a flower. Flowers carry an unnatural burden to be flowers. And, when grafted, it adds to their pressure to be beautiful.

When Abu died, the universe told me to just suck it up. I wasn't permitted to let the universe crush me because there was so much to be grateful for.

I felt like the things that had once been gentle were no longer gentle. I felt my inner world was parched but I had to appear waterlogged.

There was a lot of packing going on and there was talk of making me come back to Uganda to sit my exams after a year. Swift replacements were happening when I hadn't even had my fill of Abu's life.

Uganda was home. A swing had been mounted just for me, the lastborn in a household of four children. The swing had a wooden plank hoisted on a brown nylon rope on the most perfect branch. I would put my bottom on the plank spontaneously. There was hard earth beneath the swing, where my feet had discouraged the grass from growing, as the balls of my feet propelled the swing higher and higher, my pigtails flying. There was a sense of being unaware of the environment around me.

Isn't that what home is? A place to let one's hair down without fear of reprisal. A place where it was okay to forget.

On some lovely days, which were most days in tropical Africa, the tree would scatter its flowers on the grass around me as swung back and forth like a pendulum.

Abu would come home at 3.30 or thereabouts in the afternoon. He would walk along the path that was at first a dirt road and then tarmacked and flanked by flowerbeds. I remember the fanfare around home improvement—Ami planting the flowers, Bhai rolling the tarmac truck with the workers and me watching because I got to watch without being punished. Ami grafted the dahlias for no reason. Blue and white, pink and white, red and white.

She would slice a branch diagonally and patch it up with another diagonally cut stalk. Then, she would glue the two together with Vaseline and bind them tightly together with banana leaf and some ribbon. Two weeks later, the no-reason dahlias would flower, with some petals white and others blue, pink or red. Bhai worked so hard to make sure the gravel was levelled by driving the heavy, road roller over it more times than was necessary. He supervised the pouring of the tar. He asked me to sit further away from the tar.

'If you touch it, it takes your skin away, maybe some flesh too,' he warned.

I obediently sat faraway, but close enough to watch.

Abu stopped wearing his safari suits and replaced them with salwar-kameez.

There was Abu's folding chair, with enough crisscrossed, wooden contraptions to fascinate me and a tarpaulin that hung from one end to the other like a hammock, but not quite. Ami replaced the tarpaulin often enough because it would fray, having been sat in so much. I was allowed to sit in Abu's folding chair on the tiny porch. Back then, this porch seemed to go on forever. Although I do not remember Abu's face anymore, I would smile whenever I saw his face when he came home from work and find me under his study table. We would say hello and I would presumably emerge from my secret hiding place and tell him all about my day—my knee scrape, my adventures at school and how mean my best friend Diana was.

Home was where things happened, but those things were okay to happen because people went out of their way to make things better—that 3.30 p.m. was nice and nicer were my naps with Abu, because naps were necessary and they were how you restored yourself to do things.

A dead Abu meant two things: I was abruptly without a home and I was going to be punished every step of the way.

A dead Abu meant no more carefree thoughtlessness, no more being eagerly waited for, no more shoes where I once kept my shoes, no more waiting for someone at 3.30 p.m., no more Abu and all the possibilities that came with Abu—the gene game that Ami played with dahlias, for instance. Things ended. Things were no longer okay. The things that happened to me were not okay and no one gave a damn. Along with the bad things came the realization that no one asked me who had annoyed me. So many people made me cross but there was no one to complain to.

A dead Abu meant a dead me and meant that the man who peered under the table to look for me almost every day took away with him my past and my present and my future—a third-degree burn that leads to multiple organ failure. That was how it felt. One by one, everything in my tiny empire collapsed. I realized something was precious only after I had lost it, which led me to conclude that I had lost it all because of my lackadaisical attitude and negligence. I had to move fast and change with the times like the rest of the adults and genetically mutate the dahlias, build roads and whatnot, to progress like the rest of the adults.

But no matter how hard I ran, I still couldn't see Abu's face peering at me under his desk.

The same entity that took everything away must bring it all back. For now, I was being punished. Did Abu go because he couldn't bear to stick around and watch all the bad things that would happen to me in his absence? Was it his good karma that spared him the pain of seeing his little girl hurl herself against the world, knowing that his feeble old bones would be ill-equipped to handle it? Was death the anaesthesia from the grief that I would go through?

If so, then good.

If his staying could've protected me, he ought to have stayed. It's unforgivable to leave a vulnerable child unprotected and unloved in this world. Abu was the one who did the wrong thing. He left when he knew people are unkind to children in the dead- Abu club.

If I were still that little girl and Abu looked under the table for me, I would look back at him and memorize everything before cancer ate it.

I would say to him: *Don't leave. Don't leave . . . ever. Bad things happen when you leave. Abu, take out your notebook—I have a list of names of people who disturbed me plenty. Abu, I want you to tell me what to do to the people who hurt your* pyari beti. *I don't know what to do with the long list of people who hurt me.*

The pact I made with the ticking clock was to allow me breathing space—but the hour hand moved too fast. There was no time to waste and I had to be a responsible dahlia.

Immediately after they buried Abu, we moved from our home in Uganda.

A grafted and repotted plants. I really was the favourite plaything of the gods, wasn't I?

That was when I had the idea, a kind of a prison-break plan, if you will. I was going to get away from this lunacy. I had vowed this to my fist, my elbows and even my knees. I swore that I would never knuckle down to permissions or wait for someone else to allow me the tiny privileges of choice of what to be, who to talk to, what to wear and what to think.

I would only kneel to one man instead of ten. Things would go back to the simplicity of being a father's daughter if only I could be my husband's wife. I would transfer the reins of authority over me to one man—my husband.

My husband would give me the universe in my right hand. It's true that Abu granted me freedom in exchange for nothing.

It's also true that my husband would give me freedom in exchange for marriage, but it was the next best option available to me.

PART 3

BRAND LOVE: BE MORE LIKEABLE 2.0

Dear Benevolent Boss,

Yes, I am distracted. I am distracted because I'm heartbroken. My husband is dying at an undefined rate. I want to have some control over the matter, so I've arranged my life as it would be if he weren't around.

You can't pay me enough to fix this need to stop him from dying and simultaneously toss him into the abyss.

I cut people off, like at the dinner last night, because I am on a drug called Effexor, 75 mg, for my depression. This is a potent stimulant, so it reacts with my complex post-traumatic stress disorder and makes me demonstrate attention-deficit behaviour.

When I told my psychiatrist this is not the right drug for me, he said it's the best drug for the high-stress environment in which I operate, and therefore I must shut up and continue taking it.

You are not the first person who has told me I am distracted. You are the fifth. Seven people say it's uncharacteristic. That my core is calm.

I've taken matters into my own hands and have tried to wean myself off the drug by micro-dosing the morning Effexor. I am almost down to 25 mg now, but the withdrawal symptoms are terrible. My brain doesn't know how to stop, how to pause or how to focus.

Yes, the CFO didn't like me—he didn't like me because my filters are low with people in authority. I may have talked to him.

People in authority have routinely been awe-inspiring for me, but because I almost died from the admiration, I now hate all people who have compelling life stories and power to boot. I feel a hostility rising within when I see them. If I don't hate them, I fear I may love them. Those are the only two poles I know.

My brain is broken. My heart is broken.

I don't have a bed to sleep in because both my girls finally moved in with me.

They don't get along with their grandmom any more.

My daughters are upset the adults in their lives don't have boundaries. They say I am 80 per cent child and 20 per cent adult. I immediately threw a tantrum and cried myself to sleep when I heard that. I felt it was unfair because I stayed in an abusive marriage, because girls need dads. Bhai said so.

My life is so warped, dearest Benevolent Boss, that even Bhai couldn't fix it. He went back. He said it makes sense for me to live separately, given the chaos Yasser and his ami have added to my life.

Imagine that. My hero says whatever his kid sister is doing to mess up her life is the best thing she can do, given the circumstances.

You asked if you are doing something wrong with me to have me fail like this, although not in these exact words. Well, if Bhai can't fix this, you can't either.

I can only thank you for your feedback, say I'd like to make you proud and shake your hand at the door.

I can only say I am the furthest thing from a boss woman, but I'll be damned if you ever find out from me how empty I am of courage, spirit and will.

I'll be damned, Benevolent Boss.
Benevolent Boss, I'll be damned.

Regards,
Aisha Fayyazi Sarwari

I got a range of comments at work:

You look like you've had no fun in your life. I can show you fun. You look so stuck up, open up.

You need to not be too exuberant. Let people speak and only speak when spoken to.

Why aren't you liked? You need to fix yourself and be liked. Smile more.

You take up too much space in a conversation and need to let others feel more important.

Be more likeable. Be more likeable. Be more likeable. You can't persuade if you aren't liked.

You gotta work on this area of your performance evaluation. I'm giving you this feedback because I'm on your side; someone else would have just let you go. Just take a demotion if you are struggling with interpersonal skills.

Just go offline if you can't handle work. But if you show up, you have to show up with some executive presence.

Your overwhelming state at work is hard to watch and makes me very nervous as your supervisor.

This is directly out of *The Feminine Mystique*. It hurts, nonetheless, because I can't feminist my way out of a sexist workplace because I am already marked down for it.

Trouble comes in threes.

In the spring of 2021, I checked into the Dinshaw Avari Hotel in Karachi for work, but the front-desk officer, a young, underqualified man, ticked me off with his rudeness, telling me to self-pay when the policy was bill-to-company. He made me wait far too long for a midnight check-in, telling me not to interrupt as I tried to explain. I went to the room he gave me; there was mould on the walls, the loo flush was broken, and I fell asleep without changing on the world's lumpiest mattress. Not before I wrote a nasty Google review.

When I write nasty reviews, I generally feel guilty. I carried that feeling with me into the climate conference, where I made notes on environment, sustainability and governance—the new buzz on legitimizing big business.

In manel after manel, men had gone over how great they were for standing for the environment and inclusion. Talking points were repeated as often as they were forgotten.

The Benevolent Boss had asked to meet me somewhere between his panel and lunch. I had misread his invitation—he wanted a private talk, but I had called the whole team to present updates to him.

Benevolent Boss endured it for ten minutes and then kicked everyone out so it was just me and him.

I stood up to get tea and cake to battle my migraine.

This was my first meal in the last two days. If I didn't eat now, I would get that nasty serial migraine that feels demonic and personal.

'Can we have a moment, Aisha?' asked Benevolent Boss right before I started to eat. I pushed the tea aside and faced him.

There was something about Benevolent Boss's tone that made me freeze.

The tea was darker than usual, even by Karachi standards, and looking at it out of the corner of my eye made me nauseous.

Some of it had spilt in the saucer, soaked up by the uneaten cake. 'Sure, Benevolent Boss,' I said.

'I've been wanting to have this conversation with you for a while,' said Benevolent Boss.

I gulped.

He had my attention.

'I thought it best to have it in person,' he said.

I looked at him, earnestly intrigued, but effectively too hypoglycaemic to wrack my brain.

'Things are not working out,' he said.

The tea-dipped cake had gone cold, soggy-cold. I felt a bit like cake.

Knowing that this was another of those moments where I was smaller than the world around me, the best thing to do was wait for the largeness of things to engulf me like an amoeba.

He continued from the *Harvard Business Review* CliffsNotes: I am not sure if I'm not providing the right support. If I am doing something wrong. But you've not been landing well lately.

He was a pro. There was more. Lots more.

Meanwhile, I was so unprepared for this ambush. I really thought the awards I got over the year for good performance gave me space. Also, just that week, *Dawn* had published my name and picture, calling me one of 'The Bosswomen of Pakistan'. There were five other people. There was a boss-girl picture of me with the copy. Sadly, for them, I was the most striking. That cover photo. That viral news story. The social media buzz. My family WhatsApp uproars. Hundreds of LinkedIn congratulations. I was thinking, I am unlikely to get told off, let alone have a conversation where I could be fired.

I gulped. I needed tea. I needed soggy cake. Anything to escape the thumping of my heart and the rising effervescence in my gut, almost like the wall mould.

He continued: 'We all feel you are a mess, unless, of course, you arrest this downward spiral now.'

I nodded only because at this point just looking at him would make me weep.

The tears made my eyeballs glisten like the emoji that has tears that haven't flown yet. Soon he would see it, and then this conversation would become about my capacity to handle air, water, earth and fire.

I talked to myself in my yoga-teacher voice: Diaphragmatic breathing. Diaphragmatic breathing. Activate the prefrontal cortex. Deactivate the reptilian brain, your body isn't in danger.

I nodded, making boss-woman eye contact and calling forth my two decades of workplace experience.

Getting no response from me, he asked, 'What's going on? I know you have a lot on your plate. I know Yasser's sick. I know you only have so many hours in the day. I know this is the third year of the pandemic, there is fatigue. I know all that . . .'

He had me at Yasser. I was already disassociating. His lips were moving gently, as if he were a college essay. Maybe at another time, I would admire him.

Yasser. Yasser. Yasser.

There were two ways this could go.

I could sip my now-poisoned tea, gently dip my soaked cake in it, munch-munch and say, 'Thank you for your feedback. Can you give me some examples that can help bring this to life?' So I can make him sound stupid to himself.

Or I could just be his favourite person and cry into his supportive corporate kindness and say it's so hard to get through the workday with the life I have. Help me figure it out?

I said, 'I am going to agree to the fact that I am overwhelmed. Maybe it was because I powered through two Covid bouts and one dengue attack without taking time off. I should have taken your advice.'

Benevolent Boss let go of the onslaught. Maybe my voice shook and he saw that I was after all an uneaten soggy cake in need of a hug.

'I do really honestly want to make the best public affairs director out of you that this company has seen,' he said.

Nice try with the rapport, Benevolent Boss, I thought.

I also thought, I need to see him out the conference room door and end this before I break.

So I stood and reiterated that I was supremely lucky to have a mentor looking out for me. I shook his hand and walked him out the door, where he paused.

He held my hand like a brother who had punched little sis too hard and now didn't want mom to know. Looked me in the eye and said, 'I'm sorry to pounce on you when you have two days of a tough strategy session here in Karachi.'

'I'm paid to figure it all out,' I said, looking back in the eye at him.

Standing, I felt stronger. More space in my lungs to breathe.

I walked back into the room. The team jumped back in. I wiped the doom off my face because it would be wrong to pass it on to them. I chit-chatted and sent them off.

After they left, I put my head into my elbows and cried, the hair bun dipping in and out of the cold tea as I wept as though not a soul in the world was there for me.

I called Yasser.

I cried into the phone with him as the staff cleared up the conference room. They cleaned around me and around my tears.

'You should have told him,' said Yasser. 'I can't,' I said.

'It would get you pity points at least,' he said. 'Precisely why,' I said.

Yasser and I had separated a year ago. I had moved to an apartment nearby.

Since then, I slept alone every night on a floor mattress. I wanted that impermanence because I kept waiting for things to be all right so I could go back home.

Bhai came to patch me up with Yasser.

When the patching-up failed, I finally bought a bed to sleep in.

The permanence of the bed without Yasser was the new normal.

There was no soul in the world who loved me.

A month later, when Benevolent Boss unleashed his aggressive version of tough love on me, choking on tears, I asked him what I had done wrong.

On the other side of the phone call, I heard him pause.

'You have to send a town hall agenda weeks before the town hall. You can't do it at the last minute.'

'Benevolent Boss,' I said his name purposefully, 'I've done a lifetime of town halls. Town halls usually have leadership updates and then some featured updates. No one reads agendas until a day before. Our employee pulse survey shows 41 per cent of us feel burnout. I'm not going to be over-efficient in an era of bare survival.' Having pushed him back, he said, 'Fine, I have been hard on you because I feel you're slipping constantly, on the big and small things.'

'Let's discuss this in tomorrow's one-on-one meeting,' I said. I could have used more corporate jargon like 'meet bilaterally' but that would sound too militaristic.

In our one-on-one, I closed the door behind me.

I had wept all night over his insulting phone call, and now all I had left was to fight.

'What do you have mental space for?' I asked.

Benevolent Boss sat across me on his buttoned leather sofa, one leg tucked under the other, his stance friendly. His eyes narrowed questioningly.

'I mean, do you want to talk work or do you want to talk us?'

'I'm okay,' he said, nodding.

'When you hired me, exactly a year ago, I told you I am nursing a dying husband with a fatal, long-term, high-care-intensity disease.'

He nodded, 'You had said full disclosure, and I know you had said there would be bad days.'

'Now I am telling you, I am not fit to be outside a mental asylum, and in a more humane society, I'd have checked myself in.'

'I knew things were bad. I wasn't aware they were this bad.'

'I don't like being the perfect victim and my nightmare is gathering pity points that somehow converge into unfair advantage at the workplace. I don't want Yasser's tumour to be the bane of your workplace challenges. I'm aware you've signed up for a full person, not a quarter person.'

'When Ismail and I hired you, we knew this. We are in,' he said.

'So, not ever wanting those pity points, you should know that I'm a dysregulated person. My body cannot do anything on its own, even sleep on its own. I need a chemical aid. So, I am on a very strong anti-psychotic and anti-depressant regimen that my body doesn't agree with, but which my psychiatrist, Dr Faisal, insists I must learn to live with.'

Benevolent Boss is the calmest person I know, a Zen master's exterior. Inside, I knew he was a Zen master's soul. But I'm also aware that corporate life takes the Buddha out of men and replaces it with Judas. He will come down hard on me if he needs to.

I said, 'Since your last feedback about me talking over others, I tried to taper my meds off because they gave me a very ADHD vibe. But, naturally, I ended up with a mental breakdown of a mild version, called Dr Faisal weeping and begged him to get me off Effexor 150 mg. I explained to him that I need a relaxant, not a stimulant. So, what you see in me is a mess.'

He nodded.

I said, slowly, 'I'm not rude to you when you give me feedback. I over-explain only because I feel my anchor is gone. What grounds me becomes the surfboard upon which I have to ride storms. I work for people, not brands. You are whom I work for and whom I want to give power to. You, for several reasons, and to some extent, Ismail in Turkey, who is my actual supervisor, are people I give power to consciously. That power is not subtle. It's large.'

'Okay. I get it,' he said.

'Therefore, may I suggest that your leadership style with me reflect that dynamic? You need not bring me to a point of shame and humiliation for being a no-good minion. You need only to say, I'd prefer you prioritize sending the agenda weeks before because it makes me nervous and doesn't bode well for your own credibility.'

He nodded.

'You get what I mean? Behind your interpretation of my misconduct is my own chaos masquerading as the promise to never disappoint you.'

'I do,' he said.

He added with a thoughtful hand on his head and his elbow on the sofa arm, 'I have a similar trigger. I've struggled being a somebody. So, when I see someone not treating me as a somebody, I get into either a detached mode or a come-down-hard mode.'

'I hear you,' I said.

But you need not. All I have for you is gargantuan respect, and all you need to do with that information is tuck away your sledgehammer and take out your fossil-excavation chisel.

'Just say you want something, and it will be done,' I said. 'But, you see, it won't be done,' he said. 'The part you struggle with is the doing.'

'Benevolent Boss, interpersonal skills is the only issue I'm facing here. My work is on track. I'm triple-hatting and you haven't had a call from global saying that your Pakistan team needs to deliver. I may not be the favourite candy-striper of two of my seven stakeholders, but I'm very busy keeping work that matters most on track so you never get that call for your team to speed up. You have only got calls for us to slow down. Can I get credit for that?'

He smirk-sighed. 'I do give you that credit!'

'Where else am I expending my energy if it's not to make the good better?'

He said in his presidential voice, 'I just want you to understand a few things. You can delegate up; give me your work. You can delegate down. You can delegate laterally. You can take time off. You can slow down. You can identify people in the franchise team to temp for you on a project or function. You can—and don't misconstrue this—leave and start afresh. You can take a demotion to a junior position, because I know you are the kind of person who can swallow your pride and not let it define you. But what I don't want is a breakdown.' I smiled from the indignation I felt. I hated the idea of a demotion and hated it more because he suggested it. It was time for me to build him a scenario and make him feel shame.

I said in the voice of someone who likes glory, 'Think about it. Twenty years of management experience, and I am very aware I can choose one or two or more. I can't and won't slow down because I didn't get here because I slowed down. What brought me here is likely to keep me here—the momentum.'

'Yes, I see,' he said. 'Otherwise, you go down.'

I said, encouraged by his understanding of how dead people live, 'Also, I've lived a few lifetimes to know life happens in cycles and in spurts. In a few weeks, my meds will settle, the new position below me will be hired, my other associates will be better trained, and it'll all be okay.'

'Okay,' he said. 'Okay,' I said.

We shook hands, shoulders squared. Two people with daddy issues, two people resolved beyond their dad wounds.

'Thank you.' 'Thank you.'

THE MAIDS CAME AND WENT

I've chopped my share of onions for the communal pot, washed dishes that piled up even before I was done drying them on the rack, scrubbed toilets, folded laundry and ironed Yasser's shirts in the Lahore heat in June and felt not an iota of the pride I was told I would feel. I hated all of it and wanted someone to rescue me from it.

Maids were offered to working women like me who wanted to use their heads and not their hands. They were offered as an alternative to the ubiquitous housework no one complains about, but should. Maids came and went. There was Meero who Ami, as I also called Yasser's ami, loved to punish by pulling her pigtails. When I protested, Ami said that Meero had got knocked up once and that she had had to take care of it, so she's aware of Meero's moral disorder. So Meero from the village would disappear one fine day when I had to leave for the office and there was no one to hand the babies to. Then I would have to either cancel work or ask Ami to please go it alone. It was thankless, and if I found it thankless—the diaper changes, the baths, the meals and the grubby hands in sockets and fridges—then she, of course, found it thankless. Which sort of explains why Meero would get herself spun around by her pigtails. Or so I thought, conveniently.

When you are in a state of fear, the hours in the day go to things that make you forget that things are fundamentally wrong, with the idea of other women taking care of your children, like work and Gantt charts and Post-it notes all over your computer monitor and schedules with tack pins on a soft board.

After Meero came Annie, the family maid. You know those faraway cousins looking for adventure by living in the house of a city-aunt who was the first to become a doctor in a family where women still are second wives of ugly men. Annie was nice to have around, to fetch Ami stuff like Advent bottles or bibs or just stand there and listen to Ami's account of having had a bad day, while they both juggled with the daughters I'd birthed. Annie had really bad teeth and her hygiene was a big issue, but again I fell back on the workplace that gave me technological challenges to solve. Like explaining to people why they should buy my recruiting tools for two thousand rupees when they didn't even know there was this thing called the Internet. If I had a banner day and sold three recruitment tools, I didn't need to think about whether my kids liked Annie or if Annie liked babysitting my kids, rent-free.

After Annie, I think I convinced my mother-in-law that we needed to stop depending on village help and recruit a proper nanny. The office boy had recently married a young girl from Abbottabad, and she was the perfect person to manage the house for a handsome fee. The girl turned the house into filth and chaos, and after Ami spied on what the couple did in the servants' quarters, they left.

Then came Meero, back with her accented Saraiki, making us get off the sofas she had to deep-clean just when we had settled in front of the TV to brush off a long day. She would kick up a fuss if something fell on the floor she had just cleaned. She was always singing devotional hymns called *noaas* with Ami, mostly about young children being martyred and blood and betrayal and the romance of victimhood, of being wronged and just utter torture. The Shias have been wronged, but I couldn't sleep during workweeks because Meero and Ami would buddy up to remind me of this all night, all day long and all night long. This was till Meero messed up or demanded too much from us and then it was pigtails-yanking that ensued. She packed up and left in the wee hours of the morning. There was a lull in the house the day Meero left. The house would be sparkling, the newspapers in their hundreds dusted and then returned to the piles and piles they would make up to the ceiling. The Tupperware washed and sparkling, returned to ornament the kitchen. Plastic shopping bags were cleaned and returned to their rightful place as shoe covers around the room's walls. Frames were dusted with a wet cloth, the walls around them discoloured in the exact shape of the frames—cheap painting prints Raza Rumi once gave me so I could feel bougie in the house in Faisal Town. Meero was so much more valuable when she left us. She was cacophony. I was told she played catch with Yasser when he was lonely and therefore almost all her sins were forgiven, except that someone in the family knocked her up when she was a teen and that she is too much sometimes.

Eventually, I put my foot down. If there was Meero, I couldn't remain employable because she disappeared sporadically. My kids needed childcare because I was clearly inadequate and unavailable. Tasneem was sweet and entirely submissive and polite. Early marriage and the husband tagged along everywhere. I'd tried to move away from my in-laws when Yasser moved to Islamabad, thinking the nuclear unit needs to be strong before the extended family is strong. Tasneem allowed me to head the business unit for the company in Islamabad, and she allowed me to tell Ami, you're not the boss of my kids any more. The girls, slightly older than toddlers, one acing her class two and the other in the cutest pigtails, were just fine with Tasneem. I almost felt as if I had a good marriage; we were a unit, mommy-daddy-and-children. No in-laws telling you when to wake up, no telling me how many ounces of milk my little ones should drink and certainly no bloodshed sleep stories by Meero, in her piercingly haunting and beautiful voice, crying out for the anguish of Hazrat Fatima, Hazrat Zainub, Bibi Sakina and all womenfolk who were dealing with the wars men waged where arrows fell on the men they most loved.

No more of that. Wake up in the morning, have breakfast in bed, get the kids ready for school and kick off work in the home office before a home office was a thing. Life was good. Yes, sometimes we would wake up in the basement house and step into six inches of sewer water overflowing from the loos because the drainage was terrible, but it was the cost of freedom.

'Give me liberty or give me death,' American revolutionary Patrick Henry had once said. Someone came up with that knowing disaster is headed your way when everyone around you hates your guts.

Eventually, Tasneem got pregnant, and I'd taken her to enough hospitals for check-ups to realize that I was her maid. She went to the village for the harvest and never came back. She pulled a Meero on me. Work was disastrous for months. I was doing kids' meals and school runs and trying to prove to my boss that this move to Islamabad was for the best when my sales commissions were as dry as Meero's menopause.

When Bushra came into our lives, I had already lost the gold chain Bhaijan had got me from his first pay and the pendant my cousin had given me. The temp maids would swipe things instantly and I wouldn't have the bandwidth to surveil or reprimand them.

I wasn't grasping for pigtails, but I was desperate enough. The sleep was gone, and my relationship with Yasser was strained.

We would put the kids to bed and then head to the home office to fight. The entire basement portion was tiled like one giant bathroom. We learnt it was to cover the flooding situation.

I was crying and Yasser was angry.

'Why are you even here in Islamabad?' he yelled. 'I came for you,' I yelled back, crying.

'I don't want you,' he said.

'Why don't you want me here? Don't you miss me when we are apart?' I said.

'I don't want you,' he said slowly, letting the words land.

I knew there was an office romance. I asked if it was Irum Ahmed he was into.

'You're messing it up for me here,' he said. 'You've upset the apple cart,' he said.

'Mama and Baba are alone, there is no one to make sure Mama is okay and the kids are a mess,' he said.

'But I came for you,' I pleaded.

I was certain that if I continued to live in Lahore and Yasser in Islamabad, we wouldn't be able to remain married. I had come back to claim what was mine. Yasser was mine. Even if he didn't want me, my youth allowed me enough open-heartedness to look past his angst and be with him. I hated sleeping without him; the girls sprawled on either side of me in Lahore, and god knows he was up to no good in Islamabad. He was my man, and even Ami's mom told me to go live with my husband.

'You are a selfish woman,' Bari Nano told Ami when we visited for the holy month of Muharrum.

'Send your *bahu* to your son. You are ruining their marriage.'

I used that wizened old soul's words to catapult me into Tasneem's firm childcare.

Until Tasneem had her own childcare needs.

But Bushra, the colour of charcoal with a smile of gold, walked into my life and saved me from the humiliation that all the men in my life were hurling at me. No-good wife. No-good mom. No-good employee. Bushra reversed all that. She took care of Zainy. Zoe was mine mostly. Zoe was a picky eater and a picky human picker. Zoe would tell me that Bushra would smack Zainy, but I didn't believe her. Zoe was the most brutally honest child; she had inherited her father's autism and had no filters. But I chose not to believe her because if Bushra went, I felt my marriage, motherhood and money would all vanish.

Bushra continued to beat the spirits out of baby Zainy, and it just didn't register to me as abuse. It was cloaked as 'it takes a village to raise a kid' and the village is large and has a self-protective mechanism. I was insane.

For years, this happened under my nose, and I chose instead to focus on how attached Zainy was to Bushra and how that wouldn't be possible if Bushra was abusive. As for Zoe's fibs, maybe she just didn't like anyone else being a mother figure.

I was also insane because, in my hyper-aversion to classism, I felt the staff, like me, were like a third gender. We were neither men glorious for doing big things, nor were we women relegated to the drudgery of cleaning pans and pots. We were formidable women who worked. They worked and I worked. They were my family. They literally kept me and my family alive so I could also dabble in a semi-big thing like expanding market share in north Pakistan.

I had no idea that Bushra had it right. I was not like her. She hated my kids because they represented what her kids would never have. She had it right because she said here is one delusional *Amreeka-returned* getting off on helping the poor by having them eat the same food and letting them watch TV with us in the drawing room. Until one day Bushra's husband was watching a cricket match and wouldn't let Yasser flip to prime-time news. I snapped and ask her and her family to leave and respect our privacy.

It took Zoe seven years to tell me she had memories of Bushra hitting Zainy so hard and so fiercely that Zainy would stop breathing while crying. Slap after slap across her tiny face, shocking her over and over again, until Zoe would scream for mercy and bring the house down and threaten to tell Dado.

While I was scaling the heights of an unknown start-up, my child was being scared by a woman whom I had paid to protect her.

Bushra was let go because her father once yelled at me for being late in making him dinner. I thought, *Wait a minute, why do I have a father-in-law in Bushra's dad who lounged in the servants' quarters?*

When I decide to let someone go, the decision is swift.

I had no regrets. If I saw Bushra, I would do much more to her than what Ami had done to Meero.

Nisha was with us for over seven years. The kids would brawl with her, but sometimes she brawled back and made them bleed.

I looked the other way.

Letting Nisha go meant that Ami and I did not have a buffer. Maids were always under Ami's supervision. Ami, by this time, was frightening and control-freaky. Initially, it was her germ-phobia that ruled everyone in the house, with the maids under her tight control, but soon it expanded to other areas of life, like individual freedom and religious freedom. Both Yasser and I didn't agree with Ami's iron-handed grip on the staff but we would lose every fight. Ami came down hard on us. Post-retirement domesticity added multitudes of wrath to Ami's mean streak.

Ami would tell Nisha to wear a dupatta and would try to convince her that her version of Christianity was wrong—Jesus was neither crucified nor resurrected. Nisha stood her ground and said that is not what god believes. After all those hymns with Meero, Ami should have known better than to make people feel bad because of the alliances they had. Ami also told Nisha that her father's recent death was no reason to keep going back home for her leave; instead, she should use the fact that there was nothing to go home to, to allow her more days at work. I felt that pain, but I was selfish enough to think, better Nisha than me.

I had to keep bringing home the pay cheque. Work was my freedom from the loss of control I had at home.

Everything has a price, I would believe in those days. And for this service of enduring my mother-in-law's senile phase, I paid Nisha a premium and apologized. Nisha, as you can imagine, suffered, but she also knew how to get compensated for it. In my eyes, she could do no wrong, she endured a lot and she was like my daughter, entitled to everything we were. I gave her a brand-new Lenovo laptop, so she could learn and entertain herself. But she took it to her village during the Christmas holidays and never brought it back. When I confronted her, she denied it.

Ami's meanness was like alcoholism. It was always accommodated by the people around her, and she was always let off the hook because her capacity to expand chaos was bigger than her capacity to contain it.

Enough maids have come and gone, from Najma to Margaret. Najma touched Yasser's ass while he lay asleep after his chemo and he confessed to me, swearing that he didn't reciprocate. Margaret went to check on her ailing mom in Karachi and never returned. To keep up with Ami's senility after Yasser's abu's death, I paid them double, up to fifty thousand rupees. But they served and stole, took and betrayed, and stayed back to never come back again.

I get it. They must do what they must do. I'd become transactional. I didn't violate boundaries any more. And I continued to take their sick kids to hospitals. They remained my people.

It took so many therapy sessions for me to realize that they could take care of themselves and that sometimes they have deplorable conduct.

It took so many years to become Yasser's mom, but I am firmly there.

On one such mundane day, between earning a living, raising kids and being exasperated by how hot the country was, Yasser was leaving for Sweden to attend an Internet rights conference.

Airport drops were never simple when it came to our family. There was fanfare, planning and control-freakery. No one just called airport cabs.

The family, all of them, had to see the person off. Especially if that person was Yasser.

The anxieties about who drives which car would dominate everything right till the time Yasser boarded the plane. Then everything would repeat on his return and his airport pick-up. Everyone fussed over Yasser. Especially Ami.

This time around, we decided to take the substitute driver. As it were, drivers were routinely fired or they quit or they went to the village for Eid and never returned. On this occasion, the driver had been dismissed with Yasser's carefully crafted SMS: 'Your services will no longer be required.' The driver showed up for work nonetheless because he obviously couldn't read or write, not just English but neither Urdu nor Punjabi. Yasser was unable to understand that his world wasn't everyone else's world.

Meanwhile, I was enmeshed with the people who helped us. I felt so much more kinship towards them than I felt towards my family. That was perhaps part of my psychosis or maybe it was because the grind culture came as naturally to me as it did to them—we all survived by trying not to get killed by the system. We—the help and I—split the universe into the oppressors and the oppressed.

We had the usual help: A driver for school drops while Yasser and I worked; a maid to scrub the house clean; and a *mali* to tend to the garden and also wash the car porch. Nothing any middle-class family could not afford.

I thought I was the help. My years of delusion mounted. When they got yelled at, I cried. Frankly, it is easy to think that way when you remind yourself of the tasks I was responsible for when they went off to the village for deaths in the family or Eid or weddings, sometimes for months and other times not to return. If they weren't around, I was responsible for their tasks; neither Ami nor Yasser helped.

Someone had to clean the loos and the driveway. Earlier in my marriage, the backyard had seven dogs and you really couldn't *not* clean up twice a day. The staff were the reason I could escape not just the drudgery of housework but the utter dysfunctionality of it. Ami believed cleaning only required water and soap, and the occasional washcloth. Otherwise, you made do with your hands. She was a doctor, but she was a hoarder first. I say this because a doctor would know not to ever leave oil jerrycans underneath the sink cabinet or roaches would show up and with them a whole ecosystem of zoo animals, if you kept it up long enough. Sometimes those cans stayed there for over six months, until I had enough firepower to get rid of them. They were to be given at the right price to the peddler but if he acted too suave, Ami would say, 'You aren't getting our half year's worth of oil cans.' His loss. At least, that is what she thought. I had to pay the staff to throw them into the nearest city dumpster. Ami would also have to go to weddings and funerals. Those would be the days I would be armed with gloves, Windex, Harpic, Pledge and drain openers, and sometimes if the gunk was too bad, acid. I would scrub and scrub, yet when Ami came and re-colonized my home, she said I was a bad homemaker. 'Look,' she would show Yasser the mugs, 'she doesn't clean the edges of the mug handles.' Yasser would bring it up like a serious matter in the evening, 'Listen, just wash the handles too when you wash the mugs. I saw them and they actually had not been washed properly.'

The help shielded me from all of this. The disrespect. The disorder. The hierarchy which I felt was blatantly unfair. How old or how good of a maid did I need to be in order to reign over my own mugs and my own mug rack?

I have made it a point to not raise my voice with mentor-in-law, but there were times my voice would go grainy from the screams, proving to her that the plate rack should be next to the sink so it could drain the wet plates. She would insist on using it like a showcase. Everything would rest on the vanity boards—juicers in white shopping bags, state-of-the-art non-stick pans in white shopping bags (because the help are so stupid they scrape off the non-stick material) and, of course, the large rack with all the plastic plates one could ever need or want, and all in different colours. Ami said it was best to use the bad plates and leave the good china (in white, dusty shopping bags) for when the important guests came.

Here's the thing with dysfunctional families: there are never any guests over, unless there is nationwide flooding or someone's death and funeral, when free lodging wins over insane kitchens and insane people.

I was always seething when I got home.

Ami would scrub Zoe and Zainy's toys, but she would not hold the same standard for other things, like seven-year-old boxes for collecting ketchup sachets from ordering out, which we did a lot. Since I was terrible at scrubbing the handles of mugs, I retreated into not being a kitchen person. Still, I tried to cook, and when I did, Ami would yell from the loo that I'd given her an ulcer and diarrhoea because the food was not clean enough or too spicy or something mysterious.

That was the thing with Ami and Yasser's personalities—someone had to be blamed for their discomfort.

No one, however, had the right to ask them to change so that *they* generated less discomfort.

I married them and inherited all their losses. The one that came before me, the one that came after me and the one that was yet to come because of me.

I noticed this blame-Aisha phenomenon the day Yasser had an accident while he was on his way to the airport to catch a flight to the Netherlands.

The new driver was a novice. He rammed Yasser's abu's car into another one.

Naturally, when the initial shock subsided, I asked the driver to move the car to the side of the Rawalpindi highway. The other car also moved to the side. This event happened before Yasser's tumour and was a time defined by his bad behaviour, always jumping to conclusions, always rash and brazen.

He got out of the car to hit the driver in the other car. I pulled him back. A crowd had gathered.

In the crowd were some transgender people, long, yellow *parandas* in their braids, flowers, and tiny mirrors in their hair extensions, their skin grey from trying to conceal the dark skin they wanted to un-skin.

The obvious debate ensued over whose fault it was. Some people in the crowd deduced from the tyre marks that our driver had been driving way too fast.

It's a highway, Yasser protested to the crowd, lawyering up and insisting that the other guy had cut across the road out of line.

The transgender folk felt rather badly for the man whose collar Yasser would grab now and again and, with finality, said it was our driver's fault. And with one how-dare-you look Yasser dashed towards them, perhaps to strike them—it wasn't clear because they outran him on the highway for miles. But as I stood there in a resigned-to-kismet state, I saw the fervour in Yasser to blame the other man so bad that he was now chasing a bunch of transgender people because they stole his argument from him. Now and then, one would turn around and curse Yasser with their words—*twanu kiray pavay*, may your corpse be eaten by worms, *laanat*, *laanat*, curses upon you.

I blended into the crowd and watched with disappointment. As if understanding that Yasser's biggest punishment was himself, the other driver straightened his collar and drove away.

Soon enough, the crowd dispersed.

I sat back in the car and waited for Yasser to return. Eventually, he did, his shirt soaked to his skin, panting.

We silently drove to the airport. He was crying.

I knew why. This was his abu's car, and Yasser couldn't differentiate between Abu's car and Abu.

'It was his fault,' he muttered.

'Say it,' he turned to me in anger. He was asking me to understand that he was in existential pain.

I handed him water silently. He refused to drink, adamant. 'Say it!'

I didn't because deep down I knew I was safe; he wouldn't miss his flight to teach me a lesson. If I didn't admit we were not to blame, then I was to blame and then he would be vindictive, but I didn't care because he would be on a plane soon.

When he boarded and I could finally leave the airport, I said sorry to the driver who I felt would have been miserable throughout this episode. If I'm his wife and I feel so insecure, imagine what he feels.

I was selfish and in my own way perpetuating some strange sort of undignified slavery—making it just comfortable for them not to leave even when they wanted to. The staff were the reason I could go to work. There have been so many days, cumulatively even years, that I couldn't work because there was no babysitter or maid or driver. In the hierarchy of things, I was next in line after the help. At times, Ami gave mouldy, leftover food to the staff only when I said no to it.

Not that I had all the control I craved at work, but no one made me clean the toilets. Judge me all you want, a big reason I came to Pakistan was that there were maids to do that.

Yasser's ami is right: maids are masters.

THE LAW OF AVERAGES

The most fun I had, those sticky, happy moments that refuse to leave your head, was during non-bad days. If those days coincided with Sunday, life was bliss. Sometimes I would unwrap myself from Yasser's arms to have the breakfast the girls served in bed, and it always amazed me how I was once their breakfast. The little things gave me joy. The way the light fell into the room during sunrise. The chirping of the birds. Early morning weekend hikes on the Margalla hills that fascinated me with their rock formations, flora and fauna. I was deliriously happy enough to think I saw some birds more than once and I made them mine. I prayed, in the order of priority, for the girls, for their dad, for their dad's mom, then my mom, then their mamus and mumanis and khala and *khalu* and cousins and whoever they love and has loved them, and then in the end, I prayed for their mom. It was hard to pray for myself. I self-loathe, but it was easier when I remembered that I gave two children life and they like their life sometimes.

The most fun I had was knowing that I was in my country.

My friend Sadia bought chickpeas from a hawker outside a bank, and the newspaper they were wrapped in had my picture and a newspaper column taking down a male parliamentarian for insulting women parliamentarians. I thought I had arrived in Pakistan that day. When I was called into work and asked to tone down my politics on TV shows, I felt that I was worth more than the pay cheque.

And yet the pay cheque was so worth living for.

Despite all the hype about going into self-owned businesses, which I tried and was fairly successful at, the pay cheque gave me the anchor I needed to feel some things never change. I always had money in the bank in the month's first week. How glorious was that?

My own money, until online banking came along and I would part with it by the second week.

My own money for a few days, nonetheless.

I chose my charities. I chose my thoughts. I chose what to publish. I chose whom to take on.

This was life on my terms, end-to-end; even the entrapments were mine.

If I cribbed, I cribbed because I was disappointed, not because I was regretful.

Between performance reviews, office dinners and awards and recognitions, something about work-life made me go back to it even with black eyes and fibromyalgia.

The maids worked enough for me to keep showing up. Yasser's ami was always there, and this provided so much life force that it was overwhelming. But it was there, and there is incredible value in being overwhelmed—it doesn't let you forget there is a pillar in your life. My daughters have a grandmother, who, after her husband's death, merged a few elders into herself and came down with the force of Thor's hammer on everyone. Yasser shuddered before her, I shuddered before her and her granddaughters love her like one loves an elder.

A banner day is when I'm eating mangoes. That alone makes Pakistani summers worth it. Sometimes, when there is load-shedding and the electricity is back and the fans and ACs hum, that's also me arriving into the bougie parts of Pakistan. No shanty town for me. I have travelled in enough rickshaws to love my occasional business class.

I am the only person who can make myself laugh until I grunt. I deliver punchlines before they are ready and muck up the timing of jokes, but I'm witty. I have joked about my misfortunes. I know to some extent, this story right here is funny because it is predictable. Girls like me recreate their dads because they haven't resolved death, get into tight corners, and sometimes they even get beat up and run down. Yasser laughs at all my jokes, no matter what. When we gym together, we compete on time and calories, and that makes me want to get ahead of him. When he publishes, I want to publish. When he is revered, I want to be revered. Yasser may have got resentful of my apparent success, especially in his brain cancer days, but he has shown up to every event I have hosted, liked each of my Insta pictures and googled me enough to almost stalk me. I like his attention, his obsession with me, and I like to keep it there. My beef with life is that he didn't obsess over me enough, for long enough, consistently enough. I unravel when he wants other things than me, including Jinnah.

The going joke is that Yasser, Jinnah and I are in a relationship and we both choose Jinnah.

Yasser kisses my daughters with a ferocious sense of belonging that I only wish my abu gave me.

When things worked, they were clockwork.

Thankfully, Yasser and I were together to brave the forces of summers and hate and apathy. Thankfully, we never wanted to leave each other at the same time.

I think, although I'm not entirely sure, that I got my feet, my voice and my spunk from all the love Yasser gave me and could have given me.

I think Yasser permitted me revenge.

I WANT HIM PUNISHED

One cannot avenge family, though.

Desi families normalize disrespect.

After Yasser's first surgery, his ami, whom I called by the same name I called my ami, began a new and vile campaign to make me a scapegoat.

Who do you think you are?

Where the hell have you come from to ruin us?

What have you ever done for me, fed me lavish meals? Why did you have to collide with our world?

Why do we have to bear with you? You are not a doctor, I am.

Everything is not about money.

All you think of is your status; that won't work here.

I have to spend all day covering up for your inadequacies.

In Punjabi and with some serious hand actions, this was just too much for me.

I also felt entitled to a bit of queening since I had saved her son's life. *Where is your sense of gratitude, woman?*

Work was getting tougher. Everyone wanted me to be likeable, when the fact was that I wanted them to be punched in the nose, bloody.

I was designing a coffee-table book with a technology interface for the tech giant I worked for. This required a lot of coordination and focus. The vision was to never make the twenty-five years of the technology company coffee-table book feel like a book. There were seventy-two videos that would play on each explainer of a page—advertisements, interviews and archives from the nineties, when women had puffy hair and GSM was the hottest news in town. I was good at telling stories and I told a good story.

Ibrar was unhappy.

He was unhappy with me.

It was 8 a.m. and Mackenzie was teaching us how to be better leaders.

I was steadying my heart rate by reading the *New York Times* and sitting in a corner of the room, away from people who thought networking was not a waste of time.

When I noticed Ibrar was over my head, I took a deep breath and looked up at him. His pelvic bone touched the edge of the *Times*, almost polluting the text.

'Why don't you like me?' he asked.

Like every insecure man, he had brought another man with him to take a woman down. I looked both men in the eye, conscious that I was sitting and they were towering over me.

'*Walaikum Salam*, Ibrar *saab*. Hello to you too,' I said. 'What is your problem exactly?' he asked.

I turned the page of the newspaper, trying to buy time.

He continued, 'You have every Tom, Dick and Harry featured in the coffee-table book, except me.'

I looked at him, genuinely confused.

'It's too early in the day, Ibrar saab. Can we do this another time?' The guidebook on PTSD says that when you are triggered, create space, define your request in clear terms and identify that you are unwilling to engage in combat.

I did all three.

'Ibrar saab, I am truly unaware of why you aren't featured in the book. I agree you should be, but not now,' I said slowly, delivering the punch.

The man next to him was smarter and left.

It was when Ibrar's posse left that I understood what Ibrar meant by mentioning the men who were featured. This wasn't the first time someone had accused me of sleeping my way up the C-suite, but it was the first time someone had implied that the C-suite had to sleep with me to get featured in a stupid book that would be shelved in people's attics for years to come, irrelevant, like how we now consider floppy discs.

I recalled that only three months ago, Ibrar had given me feedback on my performance on a 360-degree tool called Elevate, saying I didn't do his work. I only did what my boss and my boss's boss told me to. He may have had a point that I should build more networks at peer level, but it was delivered crassly. And conversely, since we were peers, I could complain that he didn't do my work. To Ibrar, women like me were only secretarial, and therefore, refusing to ask him to give me work validation meant I thought he was unattractive.

I emailed a screenshot of that to myself to mull over later, because the language he used was reminiscent of the performance feedback I got from my boss and my boss's boss—your peers are unhappy with you. My peers, it seemed, was only Ibrar.

Here he was, standing over my head, throwing a tantrum because his picture wasn't in a book project I was supervising. *Why don't women get away with such self-aggrandizing behaviour?*

Drunk on his own anger, Ibrar went on, 'What do I need to do to be one of your favourite men? Tell me so I can do that. I mean, I don't get it.'

I inhaled.

'Can you wait till I respond to you on email about this issue you've raised? I'll ask my team and get back to you,' I said, calmly. At lunch break, after five hours of learning how to be better corporate leaders, I composed an email. I quoted Ibrar verbatim, asked my team why he wasn't featured in the damn book, and also that if I hadn't deliberately left him out, I wanted a full-fledged apology from Ibrar for the way I was treated that morning. The accusation, I wrote in the email, was that I had chosen to keep certain men in the book and vetoed other men based on my personal preference. I said I needed an apology for an attack on my professionalism and my personal integrity.

My boss called seventeen times during the rest of the day. I didn't pick up. Partly because I felt very guilty. I felt dirty. Yes, I liked Adil, Ali and Asif much more than I liked Ibrar, but that bias could not have got in because I wanted it to. There were 3000 people in the company, many of them worthy of being featured based on some criteria—hierarchy, diversity, business interest, etc.—and Ibrar just didn't make the cut.

It felt as though it was my fault that he didn't make the cut.

I felt that I had to make this man feel better about his ego bruise.

It was reminiscent of the abuse I was facing at home.

Ibrar and Ami's attack meshed into one, and because I couldn't take Ami to the cleaners, I reported Ibrar to the sexual harassment committee.

I eventually left the organization. Professionally, it was downhill from there; things got hostile.

Ibrar didn't get his picture in the floppy drive either. Win-Win.

HOW DOES YOUR GARDEN GROW?

I did not understand compound interest, nor did I get mark-up. As such, I failed to have my money make money, and I succeeded in having my banks take money from me. Credit-card debt would mount without my fathoming how I could spend three hundred thousand rupees in a month.

There was a time when I used to try and manifest money by visualizing a million rupees in my bank account. The dream number would never go beyond a million. It hovered there like a caged bird. I spent money lavishly. My language of love was gift-giving, and I would love to get Yasser, Ami and the girls gifts when I felt inadequate. I threw social parties on my rooftop and in my garden so people who needed connections got connections and those who needed jobs or gigs got them. Even before organizational behaviour gurus such as Adam Grant, Guy Raz and Brené Brown said that real value came from connecting people with each other, I was doing it intuitively.

This is why the hustle was no stranger to me and I would get money if I wanted money. I would sell my time and my smarts, and in a month, or maybe two, my account would be credited, and I'd get back to feeling adequate and capable.

The marriages that I knew merged women with the men that bought them, and the fact that I could earn made me feel estranged from my earnings. The moment I would get my pay, my gig money or bonus, I would part with it like it was lava in my throat—I'd have to vomit it out before it consumed me from the inside.

The guilt was visceral and if I kept it, it would grow mould. It had to be in circulation, away from my being, for it to be pure. At first, I thought this was all the economics I'd learnt in my college years: grow the country by spending in the country and all those post-9/11 calls by Bush junior to go out and spend during Christmas. But no, this had to do with growing up Ugandan, the fact that if the volume of our TV was high enough, we were likely to be robbed and killed, in that precise order, and we had the same associated with wealth.

Hustle and work the nights, write up reports for the World Bank on tourism in the Punjab, a closing report for the dengue outbreak and the crisis team's response for the World Health Organization, redefine the EU's policy on rural uplift, restructure the board of investment's investor engagement process, write up communication strategies and plans for the rule of law reform in Pakistan, redo CEO résumés on LinkedIn, anything, anything— short of writing term papers for students, anything.

And the money would need to be chased, because sometimes, even the EU made me do work and then said the funding had shifted. And all those annoying meetings at coffee shops where I paid for the endless carrot cakes. If a new inflow didn't come, I'd naturally be down and mouldy, but not for long.

All this extension of my time and energy in exchange for money ended when I got a better job. The paradox was that I fell back in my disposable income when prestige followed and people said I had finally arrived, professionally speaking. My tax payments were appalling because my income was higher. My take-home was shameful. A better job made me worse off. I was making what I had made in my early thirties.

This decline in my income constricted what I would consider freedom, because earlier I could throw money at any problem before it became a problem.

The thing was that Yasser's recovery was not going well at all and his seizure activity had intensified. His focal seizures, or what lay people call emotional seizures, where the brain's electric activity would turn him into a Tasmanian devil, swirling about and taking everything down with his tantrums, got worse, day by day. Yasser was no-filter Yasser, and Yasser was just one blob of harmful acid. He burnt me the day I was packing for Amsterdam.

Unlike earlier times, my visa was last minute, and I didn't know I'd go until a night before the flight. I was frantically lining up things at home, and also prepping for a big conference day at the headquarters, with big corporate folk who had to like me in order to keep funding my projects, such as digital tech in girls' schools and 4G-enabled smartphones that were at the price of a feature phone and also incubators that supported rural women. People like me delude themselves into thinking these things make a real difference. Only governments make a difference. I wasn't aware, and I thought a lot rested on my shoulders and a lot rested on my ability to be liked by the white folk.

It would be my first time there, and although this was a work meeting, there was excitement. I also felt I needed a break from Yasser's endless obsession of being a barrister like Jinnah, that too from Lincoln's Inn.

He had messed up his last online exam and had to retake it, and the whole thing was a huge blow to him and his sense of identity. If he wasn't a barrister, what was he doing masquerading as a Jinnahist, or even a lawyer for that matter? A case law called Denton kept him awake at night. Since he had answered incorrectly, everything became about the case, and round and round he would go talking about it, sitting, sleeping, at parties we would hardly be invited to.

At one point I almost screamed: no more Denton. Months and months, on and on he went, *Denton, Denton, Denton.*

So yes, there was a sense of release when it came to escaping Yasser because I didn't know his mood swings were so passionate because of the clinical distress his seizure activity created in his brain. I thought he was just Yasser, but on steroids. Of course, eventually Dr Moughise, from South City Hospital in Karachi, was contacted and all was well, but there were these eight months of hell. One minute Yasser was saying horrendous things to me, and the next he was calling me names. Our fights became increasingly about my money. His complaint: I no longer supported him.

'Can you please let me pack?' I said. I was folding the only pantsuit I had and kicking myself for not dry-cleaning it in time. What was I supposed to wear in freezing Amsterdam, jeans and Uggs?

I made a mental note to take my glasses. Sometimes all I'd have were my contacts.

I tried to focus on what I was doing, but his mood was not something I could handle with my word hacks any more. And frankly I didn't like him and he didn't like me. We sneered when the other walked into the room.

'All you care about is your Amsterdam visit; you don't give a damn about me,' he said.

'Please don't. I have a flight in a couple of hours. I'm anxious before I get on a plane, you know that,' I said.

All because Yasser's anxiety about redoing his bar exams made him feel inadequate, he now had to make me feel inadequate.

'Why wouldn't you give me your buy-in?' he said.

'Yas, I'm totally cash-strapped. This job doesn't let me have a side gig because it's a company spokesperson position, and I feel like I'm trapped with more prestige and less money,' I said.

'You think I don't know that money appears when you want it?' he said.

'Yas, that's unfair. You know we share our tax returns. What can I possibly hide from you? I spend everything I earn,' I said.

I closed my bag, put a combination lock on it that Bhai had given me, with the same password code on it that he had set. Tiny reminders of who I was before I was me.

I don't think Yasser appreciated my pushing back and refusing to send him off after his educational pursuits. That Harvard incident where I bankrolled him and he had an affair on my tab, tumour recovery or no tumour recovery, was too much of a personal blow. I wasn't going to fund more of his self-actualization projects. Saying no to him now came naturally, after almost two decades of saying yes cheerfully; yet it was the hardest time in our marriage.

Yasser did not like it at all. He accused me of being self-serving, of stifling money, of wasting it, of not making enough—his ramblings were so hurtful that as he dropped me off at the airport, I begged for him to turn around because there was no way I could actually do conference work in this defeated state of mind.

'Take me back home. I want to go back to sleep,' I said. 'Now look at you, being a full drama queen. Who's throwing tantrums now? And when did my distress ever stop you from boarding a flight?' he said.

He then added, '*Mein bhaar mai jaoo*. You said that you'd stand by me but all you are doing is serving yourself. You don't understand my dreams.'

I forgot my contact-lenses solution and case, glasses and my computer charger on that trip. I was so depressed, I stayed in for all group sightseeing visits to the Dam Square. Instead, I stared at the ceiling and only ventured out in the middle of the night because I had made the walls of my hotel room weep. The trip was just a big fail.

The only reason I boarded that flight, crying and sobbing, by now second nature, was because he wouldn't take me back home. I've always used work to distract me or even anchor me, but by this time in my career, it fell short of even having a tiny bit of entertainment value.

Work began to fail me as an alternative path to the disrespect at home. A chorus of do-more-do-more.

I felt the toxicity of what I called my 'here'. I felt the here and now turning on me. I felt a loss at the question—where are you from? I am from here—no longer adequate. I was no longer fit for here.

The streets of Dam late that first night felt strangely familiar. The canals were lit up in melancholic yellow streetlight because of sativa and the plain realization that I was not loved. Yasser was routinely combative towards me, but sooner rather than later, he would be both apologetic and deserving of redemption, because he intellectually and emotionally abhorred the person he was when he hurt my feelings.

That remorse was replaced with more belligerence: You ruined my career by dragging me to Islamabad. What you earn is mine because I supported your career when I could have supported mine. I gave up my life for your ambitions and fame.

I believed him. He was the only one who knew me well enough, long enough, intimately enough to see me for who I am. I think I did get fixated on having a pay cheque, that maybe he did give up things for me that I may not have actively asked for, but he had made room for me to run and now he was resentful. I hated that he still didn't trust me. The only remedy I had for this was to pray to Allah that he went back to not seeing me as his dream-destroyer.

He was no longer any of those redemptive things, and if I had Stockholm syndrome, the man who was the source of it stopped validating me even in his lucid moments.

I had no man who loved me, and worse, his wrath was rational, not emotional. He gave me dates, facts and details to confirm that I was the one who had ruined him.

I was told that I parted with money too soon because I felt it had brought my family hard luck, that homes were made by women who spent time in the house, and still I lost on every count. I chose the poison of working to stay away from a home that was inhospitable and quick-sanded the money because of that guilt.

Either I'm a good wife or I'm a money whore.

I wanted both lives: I wanted validation from the people whose identity I was willing to merge into because I chose them and they chose me, and I also wanted to have my money merge into the unit. An influential English juridical document from 1765 defined married women as having no legal status independent of their husbands. A man 'cannot grant anything to his wife,' it stated, for that 'would be to suppose her separate existence.'

Yasser gave the family everything he earned. He even sent me money when I needed it, despite being sick and finding the job market hard to stay in. But it is also true that Yasser didn't grant me any land or car or gift beyond the amount he refused to give Tehreem at the wedding night. That's because he was challenged mentally to part with what he owned, that he loved me nonetheless, and also that I—a brown, feminist, independent woman—never really needed anything from him.

Perhaps it was the lack of needs that made us struggle.

It is sadly also true that modern marriages in Pakistan are stuck in the 1760s, where the man granted the woman protection, and in exchange, she 'performed everything' for him. Generation after generation of women have been performance monkeys.

I was, after all, my mother.

I was, after all, my mother-in-law.

WHAT DO YOU WANT TO SOLVE FOR?

Both Yasser's abu and my abu were absent—so we saw love as transactional, and both fathers left us hungering for some recognition that we too are people. We were left with the idea that we had to be good to be loved, we had to be good to be guaranteed rights, and if misfortune came, it was only because we are bad. Daddy issues united Yasser and me.

Jinnah helped culminate that obsession into all the guarantees we ever needed.

Hence, my Jinnah obsession. Hence, Yasser's Jinnah obsession. Hence, my coming to Pakistan.

Hence, Yasser's Lincoln's Inn dream, wig and all.

Yet, we both ended up being even more transactional than our parents.

I wanted him to never give me anything, no rescuing in exchange for performance of any sort. All I wanted was to be wanted without being needed, so I could be sure it was me he wanted.

He wanted me to buy into his dreams because his dreams were the endless sea and he wanted me to be his dad.

He accusing me of hiding money from him and not believing I was broke.

Me wanting complete financial independence from my husband, but then feeling inadequate when no one came to save me when the piggy bank was dry.

His dad accused his mom of hiding money from him. My ami had always looked to Abu to bankroll her dreams.

He feeling that it was a bad deal he'd got for choosing self-serving me.

Me feeling that I worked so hard at distributing my wealth instantly into rentals, groceries and staff salaries so as not to be accused of being self-serving, and yet, here we were.

No one told me the economics of marriage are inescapable even when you don't depend on your spouse.

I imagine it sometimes, a life of domesticity. And when I'm drunk on self-pity, I wonder how bad could a small footprint really be. I would wake up, cook and clean, and maybe even have time for naps. My kids would go to local metric system schools and grow up to be normal Pakistani girls wearing dupattas on their heads in public transport on their way to college. And how bad would that really be? At least I'd never get to hear that I was never home. At least my girls would always know where to find me. Maybe I'd be feared. I'd have time to pray, to rest and relax, and hold my own. No bottled water, more hepatitis, more public hospitals and more unruly neighbours. Yes, it would be a life full of limitations and irritants and the insidious cycle of scarcity that poverty brings to hearts and minds, and I hate that to my core. But like every other suffering I've worked around, I'd find a way to be resilient to this too.

I'd certainly not be sitting in this new here called Amsterdam— on a school playground jungle gym, twelve feet above the ground, smoking up, thinking how the big fat moon betrayed me.

But then, I think of what Bhai always told me about the big life.

One, he said, you've chosen a big life and yes, big lives can be big messes.

Two, he said, there is no guarantee that small lives do not have big messes. One can hermit away in tiny caves, away from people and misfortune, and still not escape the mess. If nothing else, a wild bear will come and maul you.

He didn't say, may as well live the big life. He didn't have to.

I promised myself I wouldn't try dumb recreational drugs again because they make me sob so bad.

I got off the jungle gym with the help of some friendly people walking their dog at 3 a.m., who could see I was in distress and couldn't figure out how I had got so high.

Apparently, it's common there for people who smoke pot to find themselves in places they are unfamiliar with. I descended from my big life into a tiny taxi. I showed the driver my hotel key card. The bell boy at the reception, seeing how incredibly puffy this brown Muslim girl from Pakistan trying to live a big life was, charged the taxi to my room and sent me off to bed with a fresh glass of lemon water.

At the conference the next day, when I finally showed up in jeans and wet Uggs, my boss Ali looked me up and down, coffee in one hand and a bagel in the other. Networking time was almost ending and if the company pays for you to show up, you show up. Kieren was our global corporate communications head and I had one job—to impress him. He too, like Ali, stared at my wet Uggs for an uncomfortable length of time, wrinkling his nose at the foot of his round glasses with a polite smile so I would not think it rude.

'Fashionably late,' Ali said.

'It is hard to be me, Ali,' I said.

'A great first impression,' said Kieren.

'It doesn't get any better. And Kieren, I promise to make it worse from here,' I said.

A chuckle from both men in top suites.

If they chuckle, they let you keep performing.

WHAT YOU CANNOT AFFORD,
YOU MUST RETURN

Yasser and I sat across the doctor's desk in a posh Lahore hospital. Although Yasser had joined me late, we both kept looking at the wall clock because we needed to get back to work. Elsewhere is where we wanted to be.

My breasts were hard and full, pressing against the maternity bra so fiercely that the harness up top kept popping. I had added two more breast pads so the milk wouldn't leak on to my clothes. It was time to breastfeed Zainy. Medically I should have still been feeding Zoe.

I needed to get back to work to express my milk with the high-end Advent breast pumping technology my *bhabhis* had sent from the US. A working mom was fully equipped to be a working mom but not equipped to be a mom. I kicked myself.

Yasser kept walking to the doctor's office window to see if his car had been snatched—a fear he has never been able to outgrow. I knew he had an obsessive-compulsive disorder by this time, but naming it made it just as hard to endure. His constant checking and re-checking of the car and his belongings made me nervous. I knew if something happened to the car, I would be blamed.

I was praying that nothing would derail this session, because there was a life force growing inside me that I needed to force away.

Newton's law—a body in motion will remain in motion unless a force greater than it is applied to stop it.

I was getting a steady pay cheque, but my family was fitfully disgusted at me for it.

I was a working mother but being a mother and working at the same time was fraught with barbed wires and loyalty tests, many of which I had failed.

I had entered the workforce to escape domesticity, but it had found me and killed me.

I had realized early on that I would have to ration domesticity and motherhood, otherwise I wouldn't survive both.

Working versus mothering. A poor trade.

A bad reputation in exchange for monthly paychecks.

I did twenty years in exchange for nasty commentary— slut, money whore, bad mom, bad wife, bad employee and bad daughter-in-law. Naturally, I played down my work life.

I didn't know I would find myself hostage to so many things as I sought independence from the man. By the time I found out, it was too late.

I learnt soon enough that my time, my money and my motherhood were not my property. As a result, all of these were scarce. As a result, I had to steal all three back from the men that owned them.

If I stepped on a permission mine, I had to seek permission, and if I chose to do what I wanted, the consequences would be grave, often career-limiting or even life-limiting.

Even my oblong-tilted uterus was not mine; it belonged to the state by way of legislation, and then the men in my family.

But these rights also belonged to my work because you had to step away from work to have kids.

Men were frightening and powerful. Men could hurt you. They could hurt you by blocking you. Which was why you needed to have secrets.

I needed three men's permission to do what I wanted with my reproductive rights—my boss's for time away from work; my father-in-law's for time away from the sacred joint family unit; and my husband's permission for doing away with what the law said was rightfully his unborn child.

This twenty-five-year-old me was not short on determination— my body still robust, despite enduring two childbirths back to back, my hair still in the high pony Yasser once adored. I was still all there. This was why I was certain that I was in the midst of a crisis, which needed resolutions not ad hocism. It was time to admit failure and remedy it. Surely there must be some remedy for not using protection.

I needed great force. I had finally found a doctor who was willing to put in that force.

The four lady doctors whom I had contacted earlier had reacted with utter horror.

'Who gave you our contact? Are you spying on our clinic? Who told you to come to us?' one of them yelled from inside my palm-sized black BlackBerry.

I'd got her phone number from the Yahoo.com directory. 'I'm going to report your name to the police. Just you wait. I give couples the gift of fertility, the gift of life. You are a shameless woman,' she yelled. 'You are not even worthy of being called a woman.' She would spit at me if she could.

I was shaking. I thanked her for her time and hung up.

I was afraid she would go to the length of tracing my phone number and have me reported or imprisoned. She was so angry at me, and her words menacingly clear that she considered me a murderer.

On the Internet, all the information I found was just as moralist as the Vatican and absolutist as the Sharia—accompanied with pictures of tiny pink feet the size of fingers, held gently by grown-up hands.

I would not dare confide in anyone. No family could know.

No friends could be trusted.

I knew everyone would talk me into keeping it. More time passed as I searched for someone to help me deal with Newton's law. More days meant more growing; my belly was popping already.

Yasser and I sat in the fifth doctor's waiting room. Dr Saeed had talked to me on the phone before meeting me.

He had a condition before he would operate—my husband had to give him permission.

I didn't want to tell Yasser, but I had to. This could go either way. Yasser had bent down on his knees and kissed the force. Just like he had the first two times I was expecting.

Yet, he came to Dr Saeed's. Yet, he was sworn to secrecy.

There was mercy somewhere in him.

Dr Saeed walked in finally, an hour over his expected time. He moved purposefully to his chair. He nodded. His white coat had a fountain pen in it, like Abu used to have. I noticed the pen achingly. I was caught between the need to cry and the resolve to remain dry-eyed.

Crying would signal confusion; I was not confused.

Dr Saeed knew I needed more force to cancel out what was growing.

'Yasser?' he said.

'Yes,' Yasser nodded. 'I know Aisha is sure about ending the pregnancy,' he said and tightened the grip of his fingers around my shaky hands. Yasser held my hand awkwardly. I didn't hold it against him. I was so grateful he was giving me permission. I was also very afraid he would withdraw it.

Dr Saeed addressed only Yasser. It was like I was almost not there.

'The reason I've called you here is because I don't want any trouble,' he said in his doctor voice.

Yasser was only twenty-six, and he had never thought he would find himself here.

It was his lunch break too. He was working for *Daily Times* and an elite high school, and in these businesses, people are afraid of being late; they are afraid of other people above them and they are afraid of not being taken seriously.

He didn't want to be here.

He got up abruptly and checked on his car again as Jail Road buzzed with chaos and traffic, angry and hungry men—it was Ramzan, and it was half boiling point. He came and sat down again.

Yasser loved babies more than I did. He considered them little animals only in need of food, air, water and sunlight. He loved petting animals. He thought things grew on their own and one shouldn't make a fuss. All you had to do was not hurt them deliberately.

I vehemently disagreed that things just grew on their own after two years of being broken down by sleepless nights, the ringing in my ears, mastitis that made me crack open like an egg, and gastro hospitalizations for Zoe and jaundice hospitalizations for Zainy.

Yasser's world was all delusion. Yet, there was serenity in his delusion. His love for little creatures was firm. Unshakeable.

To Yasser, I too was loved like he would love an animal—a very simple form of love, and perhaps deeper.

I knew this because he would pet me like he would pet cats and dogs. Pulling my hair back from my forehead with the cup of both his hands, tapping my nose like I were a pup and sometimes even blowing air into my face until I blinked away from the impact. He was playful and even enjoyed a little bit of torture.

With Zoe and Zainy, Yasser had burping duty and rocking-them-to-sleep duty. When he saw them sitting merrily among their playthings, he banged their heads together and laughed when they sobbed. Then he rushed to console them. To Yasser, babies were playthings. He wound them up and down for pure joy.

The social awkwardness vanished when he was near kids and pets; he transformed into this pure form of being. He felt no threat from them, he became lighter. Animals and babies gravitated towards him like they had heard some secret call.

Yasser's abu wasn't really there. And Yasser's ami was a single working mom, when all those three roles were very difficult to play alone.

His only family was his mom, and when she realized he couldn't have another brother or sister, she got him his first Russian pup called Bushy. Bushy helped Yasser make sense of the world. Yasser was an undiagnosed autistic child, and Bushy didn't judge him for that. With Bushy, Yasser needed no friends. He had his history books, his obsessions with Sher Shah Suri, Caesar, Ataturk and Jinnah.

Bushy's kids and kids' kids passed, but even after two of our own human pets, Yasser wanted more—more human and animal cubs around him, nestled in a farmhouse in Lahore's Bedian district, a place where mustard seeds rustled in the wind. His love for pets cost me a lot of sanity. In addition to the extra workload of managing eleven pets and keeping the home clean, there was the constant barking and noisemaking I could do without.

Yasser never had friends, except me, but our home was always a zoo. Like every zoo, there was a zoo caretaker, a nurse and a patron—none of those roles were Yasser's. His mom made sure that her son remained unburdened.

That was her language of love for him.

If he had any duty towards me or the kids, she would step in to ease him.

This was why I disagreed with him on parenting workload. He didn't know what he was talking about when he said kids were like pets. Pets, I believed, were like kids.

When Yasser was a toddler, he travelled to a village in Khushab for Eid with a herd of animals because he couldn't bear to part with them—bird cages, pups in the cars everywhere and sometimes turtles in fish tanks on someone's lap.

Everyone in the village thought Yasser was an *anokha ladla*— an overindulged boy who was more concerned about the animals than the humans. Traditions of slaughtering and eating them on Bakra Eid were utterly detestable to Yasser.

The Abrahamic practice was positively banned in our home. Yasser's mom would protest to keep up with the Joneses, but then he was her anokha ladla, her prized creation.

'If we ever have a son,' Yasser said to me during one of our youth-infested pillow talks about having a son, 'you know he will be your spoilt brat.'

I would turn to him, my palms under my face, and smile.

The talk about having a boy made me uncomfortable because everyone had prayed hard for me to have a boy the first two times. I detested it on account of my daughters, who deserved a fighting chance, and the fact that their being girls was seen as a disadvantage.

I knew Yasser's mom was disappointed in me, especially the second time.

I knew she had been making *mannats* for me to give her a grandson.

'You will make him a spoiled brat exactly like my mom made me one,' he said.

'If I'd make him a spoiled brat, what would you make him?' I said, humouring the moment's softness.

'I would slap the shit out of him for kicks. Lots of *chapere*,' he said.

We laughed because that would be very true. Yasser liked most creatures except little boys.

'Zoe and Zainy are so amazing,' he said. 'They are,' I said.

The levity was gone. No pillow talk.

This was real life. It smelt of antiseptics. There was a chart about the pill and the importance of birth spacing. Yasser didn't want to be sitting across from the doctor. He wanted to leave right away. He was crying like he had when Bushy's kid, Nono the Anonymous, had to be put down at the vet.

Dr Saeed, unfazed by the crying, went on.

'See, Yasser, you are a young, educated boy, but you'll have to appreciate that people make these choices with certainty, and then instantly go back to regretting it.'

Yasser looked up at Dr Saeed as if to say, 'I already regret it.' 'So, I would say, this is part of the complexities of life and death. I don't mind that, but I prefer things to stay clear here in this office. Sometimes, that regret becomes a nightmare for me. The hospital gets ransacked by men who say we killed their heirs. You know sons are of great value in our society,' he said.

Yasser nodded.

Dr Saeed wanted us to commit that we wouldn't have any regrets in the vicinity of his office.

'But other things are important too, besides male heirs, such as the socio-economic context of the mother, her health, confidence in being a mother. We cannot ignore this either,' he said.

Yasser nodded, but got up once again to check on the car.

When he came back and sat again, Dr Saeed poured him a glass of water. Yasser took it but didn't drink.

'You are both young. I wanted to talk the decision through with you. I also need you to sign a consent form.'

Yasser nodded again.

So did I. I nodded anyway, even when I knew my nod really didn't count.

We took the tissues that Dr Saeed offered to us like a good shrink. The tissues ended up sticking to Yasser's nose, and I plucked the white fluff from his mouth and nose. I did so instinctively. Lovingly. I was always fixing him. He let me fix him.

This old couple's rhythm started from day one. Today, however, I desperately needed something he had.

'Can I understand why you are making this choice, Yasser?' said Dr Saeed.

An awkward, long silence ensued.

I went first. I always went first—the neurotypical in me was always activating, starting, drawing up the tiniest blueprints of who would say what and when. I always started things, and that made it easier for Yasser.

I cleared my throat.

'I have had two daughters in the span of about two years right after my marriage. I haven't been able to cope. I had to call my mom from California to help me. I have both of Yasser's parents to help. But it's still too much. We all haven't been able to cope,' I said.

'Unfortunately, a mother's distress is not a good enough reason. Can you give me something more medical?' said Dr Saeed.

I took a deep breath and tried again.

'I have post-partum depression. I have memory loss and haven't been able to focus on the kids because of the insomnia and chronic migraines. I'm still breastfeeding my younger daughter, when I should be still breastfeeding the first. They are both under two and a half years. The third will take more than my body can give,' I said. 'I see,' Dr Saeed scribbled. 'That's better,' he added in his good-doc voice.

'Yasser? What do you say to that?' he asked again. 'Yes,' Yasser said.

Yasser refused to make eye contact. He looked down at the tiny pieces of shredded tissue paper strewn all around his khaki pants. I made a note to clean up before leaving.

I had ironed those pants in the morning. It was very hot, I was sweating. There was no fan where the iron stand was and that was a life-design flaw, not just a design flaw.

'As I explained to Aisha, there may be clarity on her part, but I'll need it from you too.'

Yasser tried to maintain eye contact this time. 'Yes,' he said again, slightly angry.

'Yes what?' Dr Saeed put his pen closer to his notepad.

'I believe that the right to conceive, the right to have a child or to birth a child should be the mother's and the mother's alone. A mother understands what is best for the child. Therefore, Aisha will be the one to choose to go ahead with the full term or to abort,' he said.

He said the word.

'That's very . . .' Dr Saeed paused.

'Would you not want to convince her otherwise? People change their mind a lot when it comes to this . . . this situation.' Dr Saeed wouldn't let it go.

Yasser kept looking down, but there was a firmness in his voice that I recognized from our San Jose years.

'No, I won't try to convince her. She has convinced me. This is Aisha's body. And what is in her body is also hers. We have come to you with that, together. Please help her so we can be better parents to our daughters. Now is not the right time for her,' Yasser said.

Dr Saeed nodded. 'Okay,' he said. 'Okay then,' he said again, almost as if this were the first such conversation he had had. 'I want you to know that the procedure will be lengthy because the pregnancy is advanced. Aisha will need post-op care, and we will have to make this look like a natural miscarriage. This is illegal in Pakistan. Our laws and society function in disharmony, and I feel this is a right that rests with parents. I request your full cooperation for this to be quiet.'

Dr Saeed let Yasser cry some more. More tissues. More water. 'You must be careful next time, Yasser. A woman is most fertile when she has just given birth,' Dr Saeed said to Yasser, pausing for emphasis.

Yasser nodded.

He also told Yasser that if he used the pull-out method again, he may as well pray to Jesus. It doesn't work.

The contraception talk could really wait. As could sex. I became veraciously desirable to Yasser when I bore him kids. My athletic body contoured, and I think, he preferred me thicker. Look at where that got us.

This childish wantonness had to end. The world grew up very quickly. Only a few years ago, I was in college, taking frivolous one-unit classes like line dance and recreation 101. I had work. I had taxes to pay. I had lots of bills that I was terrified of missing due dates of. I had lots of fear. Lots of people to answer to.

I also had to get back to work so I could get paid and thereafter pay Dr Saeed.

This made me shift in my seat with restlessness.

This was a lunch break consultation. Lunch break was forty-five minutes. This had taken two hours.

My boss had noticed that I was always shifty at work and his hyper-surveillance had increased. He had installed a biometric machine at the door where I needed to thumb-scan in and out, like in a prison. If I did less than forty hours a week, I got a pay cut.

There was a direct link between time at the desk and responsiveness at work. He said this to me when I had walked in dishevelled after one of my many failed clinic visits. Boss was not happy I was spending so much time in the loo pumping milk for my little pup, and he was also upset about my clinic visit. He wanted me to make money for his dot-com company, and he didn't want me to pump on his time. He had bought my time from nine to five. I had consented to it. He had a paper that said so.

This was why he was upset with me. He felt I was stealing from him.

My milk was leaking at Dr Saeed's office just thinking about walking into the office and pumping the milk out. The breast pads were soaked.

My Gulberg office wasn't far but Lahore's traffic had got insanely choked at the Nehr.

After I'd pumped out my milk sitting on the toilet with the top down, I would have to immediately freeze it in the office kitchen for the next day. Then I had to remember to take it home with me. In the middle of all this, I'd have work of some sort—making sales calls, explaining the new product idea to the developers, planning the next event and dealing with internal reporting. I also was an editor of some sort. My job was also to review message boards for a Muslim matrimonial website.

I had to be meticulous at work over the next few days and months because someone had to fund this callous disregard of my fertility. And it would have to be my boss. Of course, I'd take an advance. Of course, it would not come easy to beg him to give me a pay advance.

Dr Saeed may be gentle with his medicine, but he conducted abortions and liked his money, in cash, up front, and that too lots of it.

I'd have to persuade Boss by putting in time at the specific location of a work desk or it won't count. Preferably I'd be going home very late in the evening. Last one out, first one in, was a winning formula for the biometric machine.

Yasser didn't have it easy either. He had to make sure both jobs stayed because this procedure was costing us four times more than the birth of either of our two other babies. We signed the forms we were asked to.

Yes, we won't sue. Yes, an act of God cannot be blamed on anyone.

We were out of our depth.

I was the one who had never lived in Pakistan, but it was only when I needed to fix this situation did I realize that Yasser too had no network of friends or family. Just like me.

He had his school friends who were incredibly warm but useless or they were very resourceful and considered him and, by extension, me, upstarts and losers.

There was no one to turn to. No one to trust or even confide in. No one who would cover up a murder for you. People do bad things, but those bad people have friends and alibis. Yasser and I were the only two friends we had.

The next day Yasser and I conspired to lie to all three grandparents. Yasser's mom and her hyper vigilance knew that something was off with me.

'Why do I keep throwing up?'

We had to lie to Yasser's dad, who had more control over me than my own husband.

We also had to lie to my ami, whom I had called for support with raising the girls, but she had ended up witnessing such utter insanity that she was worried sick for me. I couldn't add more conflict on top of what these three old people were experiencing.

Lying didn't come easy to Yasser. He tried. We rehearsed what he would say to my mom, his mom, his dad and our two babies.

We made up an excuse that a Karachi work trip had come up for me all of a sudden. We took permission from all three grandparents for me to stay overnight at a hotel alone in Karachi, and that sounded very undignified to them.

Nonetheless they let me, with a warning that we were not that 'type' of family that sent off their women to do something hard in the name of a job. This should never happen again, they decreed.

I agreed because I had to.

That fake overnight stay allowed us enough time to check into surgery and return the next day, back to work and home, without anyone finding out.

If someone found out, I'd lose much more—the marriage, maybe.

The surgery procedure is not without complications, but it is finally done. I am back in the recovery room drifting back to life. I see a fan. I see a lady doctor with a stethoscope around her neck. She is egregiously beautiful. Her hair, I notice, is waving in the wind from the air conditioner. I can almost be her hair, which is slowly fluttering around her pink cheeks. They are naturally glowing from all the lifesaving she is doing.

Yasser is here too.

I see him and find him looking lost.

I call out to him with a hunger to run into his arms, but my throat is so dry from the anaesthesia. He can't hear me. It's like I'm not there.

Yasser is looking out at Jail Road traffic like a defeated Mughal king.

I feel responsible—for defeating him. No more Bedian farmhouse dreams of many children and Bushy lookalikes running about. I am poorer somehow.

I failed to give him what he so desperately wanted—little me and him just scattered like gold dust all over the mustard fields. Like my freckles. Everywhere. Thriving in the sun.

I see him crying. He didn't stop this for days. I turn over to my side. Moving with all the tubes and connections coming out of my urethra, my veins and my heart, I throw up into the bin conveniently located under my bed.

My happy ending is now in a bin chunky from breakdowns of all kinds.

The unnecessarily gorgeous lady doctor called a nurse underling is helping me clean up my mouth and reinserting tubes that came off.

'It happens,' she said making notes into her clipboard.

She is perfectly detached from this situation that Dr Saeed warned us people change their minds about.

Yasser comes to me and holds my hand. He touches my forehead. I feel faint.

I look at the doctor closer as she pokes at me, checking my eyes and throat and vitals. She is the most beautiful woman I've ever seen. Perfect skin. Bet she is also very fertile.

'Do you want to know what the baby was?' she asks gently, hanging on to her clipboard, like I hang on to my laptop.

I nod. I am deliriously smiling at her. 'It was a boy,' she says.

I nod. My smile is gone. She doesn't seem that beautiful any more. Okay, I say again and again.

Yasser is gently pushing the hair away from my face. The tears make them stick to my face. It's done now, so I can let go.

Our boy travels with us at every age. Every year he grows a year older.

Every airport terminal, every birthday, every song, every pet, every celebration and every funeral.

We couldn't afford to travel life with the real him.

MOTHER-IN-LAW GOOD GIRL CERTIFICATIONS

It's impossible to not write about Yasser's mom. I didn't do this thoughtlessly. It was a scheme. If I were large-hearted enough to call her by my ami's name and mean it, it would be a life of love. If my mom birthed me then she also half-birthed my life partner, and by that twisted logic, my mother-in-law was my half mom, and together we would raise each other like the super chicken we were—all individually gifted in our own way.

Calling Yasser's mom Ami, I thought, would create a declaration of loyalty that would never be suspect. My sense of adventure would make room for all of us to work out any future problems. Besides, I would apply my smarts to the whole thing. And thrive.

In my understanding this whole thing was just the typical insecurity that typical Punjabi mothers-in-law have when their only sons go off and find a woman far-far away and abandon them. How bad could it be? As long as I was breathing, I would be generally okay.

Generally okay was a very honourable aspiration; it wasn't the moon, and therefore, achievable.

In April 2022, Pakistan's leading newspaper *Dawn* profiled me as one of the six 'boss women of Pakistan'.

Bhai called me right away. He told me that Yasser's mother was truly deserving of that accolade. His tone was definitive and factual. He presented verdicts with the finality of an old, wizened soul who prioritized peace at all costs. He was a cultist when it came to protecting the collective family system.

I married Yasser under the pretext of bringing love, not assets to this new family.

Yet, I quickly learnt that I needed to get out of the house to save my life, and because I couldn't just run out on the streets of Lahore's GOR 5 sector, I had to find shelter in something more legitimate. Something that permitted me to stay within the system yet allowed me to seek belonging elsewhere. Work was supposed to be a modern version of domesticity; whatever I gained at work, I promised to give back to the home.

So when I married and recognized my struggle to be accepted rested on so much more than being nice and congenial, I jumped at the first job offer that came my way.

If anyone deserves my title of boss woman, it is Bhai. The brother who made me climb trees for the sake of it also introduced me to the formal job sector in Pakistan.

If there was someone who doesn't deserve it, it is my mother-in-law, who made the home so hostile sometimes, from general lack of agency and undermining me as a mother and a homemaker, that I went to work even when sick.

Bhai introduced me to his Valley tech geek Hassan.

In the third week of my marriage, Hassan called and said he is starting a Silicon Valley-based firm. He said he was looking for someone with the Bay Area work ethic to take it from zero to one. Would I be interested?

I think I was saved by those words.

I think my marriage was saved by those words.

Although the hierarchy of mortal men I hero-worshipped went something like this—Jinnah, Abu, Bhai, Yasser—I was willing to fit Hassan anywhere between Bhai and Yasser because he had given me a pay cheque.

A month after my wedding in Karachi, I returned to Lahore and walked into the only skyscraper in the city. One that had only eleven stories. This three-by-three cubicle was solid ground from which I navigated a new and exciting life, one that sometimes felt like a category-three storm and at other times a sunny morning.

I sat in my cubicle and smiled often into space. It had been four months since I left San Jose to prepare the wedding in Karachi. This was the first non-nomadic existence I had ever had. This was mine and mine alone.

Sitting here gave my heart respite. My new home with Yasser sometimes felt like a state of disrepair with its over-fluctuating, bad florescent lighting. I was thrust into someone else's home— Yasser's ami, Yasser's abu and the dozen farm animals cramped into a condo.

Ami, Yasser's ami that is, was so spent with me. It upset her that I was in her territory. This came as a shock to me because she was very happy to have me marry her son before. She was lovely in her emails to me and on the phone. I was trying hard to understand what I had done wrong to anger her so, but it was my work cubicle that allowed me the opportunity to not overthink it.

We started with two wrong feet, Ami and I, yet work let me garner the mental strength to deal with the grief of being rejected by yet another mother figure.

At the wedding, the breakdown of my dreams kicked off during the *juta-chupai* tradition. This is when the bride's sisters take the groom's shoe and extort money playfully.

Tehreem, my Pakistani American bestie, made a point of creating a ruckus at the wedding. She was doing what was expected of her by the very Punjabi tradition I was becoming part of. She felt these traditions served an important purpose, that the groom's family ought to feel that the bride is worth some trouble.

She wanted to create enough friction for Yasser to realize that sending me off to live with a new family would require some loyalty tests. These traditions were invented to disrupt patriarchal entitlement, but at my wedding, the events unfolded in a way that only strengthened chaos.

You make a mess of things, take the groom's shoes and ask for a sum of money in exchange for it. Pretty straightforward. Tehreem took on this role like a pro. Not only did she disapprove of love and early marriages, but she also really didn't think Yasser had much to offer. Maybe it was because she was a Memon, and Memons are known to be calculating, that she said her maths didn't add up. Why would I be compelled to marry Yasser?

I told her it was love. Love for the shared values we held dear, specifically for Pakistan. It was the big stuff like Pakistan's narrative we must contribute to, and of course identity and paying taxes in a country we belonged to. I explained Yasser was a son of the soil, and I could use that to stabilize my constant immigrant life. Tehreem reluctantly let me have my say. She did tell me I had essentially described daddy issues.

Four of my friends, who had travelled from Nairobi, Karachi and the US to be there on this special day, joined her cause—to wish me luck. They all sang Bollywood songs and wished I thrived and was loved dearly.

The newly wedded groom, Yasser, perhaps felt everything was happening too fast too soon. We had registered our wedding with the local Karachi mosque and the registrar only a day before this shoe-hiding moment. He felt that the 20,000-rupees ask for his *khussa* (shoe) was too much and told Tehreem he would pay only at best 5000 rupees. Ami, his mom, now mine, also said no way in hell were these American kids going to spend her hard-earned money on fun and games. She also said to my friends: 'Who do you think you are?' Yasser concurred with her: 'Tehreem is not even Aisha's sister.'

'If Aisha's Baji asks, that's a different matter,' Yasser said. 'Even if Aisha's Baji asks, no,' said Yasser's ami to a bunch of giddy young boys and girls.

My real Ami was somewhere in the crowd, rather unwell, disappearing like the setting sun because she knew I was headed into something unhospitable.

'Aunty, give some money to Tehreem so we can move on to the other rituals,' said Baji, reading the room and realizing this was headed towards a shit-show.

'No, it's a matter of principle,' said Ami and Yasser, like in an orchestra, booming over the gathering crowd.

Yasser's ami clutched her black bag with a fake logo tighter and her mouth turned downwards.

Tehreem clutched on to everything she had learnt in negotiation class at Harvard Kennedy School. Later she explained that giving in to a bully was never a good idea. It was best to escalate when a violation happened the first time, and not giving the bride's side money for a shoe only because it was expensive was pathetic.

So Tehreem escalated and went off to find a car jack. I don't ever remember being loved this fiercely since that day, and so publicly too.

She removed her high heels, tucked her *lehenga* between her legs and took off the rims of Yasser's car—not the tyres, the rims, and not just one, but all four.

When the *baraat* came towards the car, Yasser found this act of defiance rather generally-not-okay. But he had an ace up his sleeve—he walked with the baraat towards the road without one shoe. This bully was not part of the coursework at Harvard.

Eventually, the ruckus grew, and Ami was mad, as was Yasser. Bhaijan was summoned. The car rims were returned and re-fitted, and we made our way home.

By day four of my wedding, a period we call the honeymoon, I had had four upsetting incidents related to Yasser's ami.

My own ami and family were long gone. Baji had stayed on but I wish she hadn't because she got to witness something that she hasn't been able to un-witness.

Day four: Ami had been in our bedroom in Faisal Town, fixing Yasser's cupboard. Baji felt that was a breach of my privacy, especially from an Australian sensitivity; now that we were married, things had changed.

Ami said Yasser was her son and she'd raised him with love. Day three: On the day of the *valeema*, the groom's reception, Yasser's ami took me to a beauty parlour in a ghetto. As with all ghettoes, people who have means stand out like a sore thumb. The moment I stepped out of the taxi with my very expensive lavender designer *jora* that was a gift from the groom's side, the transwomen laughed out loud.

I stepped over open manholes in my glass-like high heels and went into a narrow street where women were standing with unusually low-cut blouses, and perhaps temped as beauticians, mothers and sex workers. Yasser and some of his cousins were with me. He yelled at Ami. The tiny street echoed with venom.

This was a shock to me. I'd never seen a son yell at his mom before, in public.

Yasser said, 'How could you bring her here when the valeema dress cost four lakh rupees? The make-up from this place will make it look worthless.'

Ami explained equally loudly that the parlour was right next to our house, hence convenient because it cut the commute. Besides, the woman here was a renowned threading expert.

'We are here for make-up!' Yasser protested.

Ami had incredibly hard and thick chin hair, the colour of licorice (which I later had the honour of threading till my fingers bled). If she could do that, I could get my make-up here, but I think that by marrying into this family I absorbed a lot of the shame they already had for being un-rich.

A crowd had gathered around to watch the dramatic turn of events.

This 'scene stealing' behaviour of Ami and Yasser had family witnesses. Two of Yasser's female cousins were with me in the salon watching the yelling outside from the glass door. They were rather bewildered, but not because of Yasser and Ami bringing the house down, but because I was reading the book I had brought with me—*Scheherazade Goes West*. Rashid Mamujan had given it to me as a wedding gift, and it was my first Islamic feminist text. I think that I was reading a book as a trauma response. A lot had happened that I had no control over.

Eventually it was decided that I was to get my make-up here. Right here at this apparently godforsaken place of vice, a place known to cake women up in percaline white foundation.

Alma, the make-up artist, seemed decent enough but very worried for her business prospects after accusations were made about her outfit being cheap and down-market. She asked me to intervene. It only occurred to her that the bride could have a say.

I bookmarked the page where Fatima Mernessi talks about the male gaze. I walked to Ami and Yasser, charged like two bulls with a testosterone overdrive in equal measure, and politely asked them to let Alma do my make-up because there was hardly any time left for the valeema, and I had never owned any make-up, so I would need her to work on me.

Ami responded to me with sarcasm and repeated what I said: '*Lo*! Time *nahi hai*, there's no time.'

I was crying during my make-up, having thawed somewhat from the exhaustion of the flight between Karachi and Lahore, and the general change of universes. Alma was upset at me. 'If you keep crying, this will get worse,' she said.

I stopped crying but the tears were relentless. Alia and Amna watched in silence.

Later that evening, after the reception was over, the photo-ops were over, the guests had gone, and the family I knew had flown away with worry in their hearts. I sat at the dressing table in our hotel room—after all this was the honeymoon—and I wept a bit more unabashedly. There was no more energy to disguise the fact that I was offended to the soul.

There was no more spirit to pretend that things would be generally okay.

There was a force here—now we know it is called generational trauma—that was bigger than me. Maybe not because it was overwhelmingly evil of passed down pain, but because I was so incredibly timorous. I was so cursed. I was also convinced that I was cursed because I had done something wrong. I was like a bad low-budget movie where the hero just can't catch a break.

Ever since Khalajan, no maternal figure had been so hateful towards me for being bad.

I had survived it by running away to another continent, because I thought Konkanis were not my people. These people, for whom I had given up life as I knew it, people who had chosen me back, were not my people either. It had to be me.

Alia was unforgettably kind; she gently plucked out the bobby pins from my hair hive like they were chrysanthemums. She let me cry, she let me be sad while she undid the parts of me that were meant for the world, one sob after another. She was the kindest witness to my future pain. She permitted me silence by taking forever to slide off my pins from my hair, so I could shed tears in peace. We never talked about it again, but we didn't need to. She understood that when I was reading the book, I was delaying this moment of defeat.

Day two: I overheard Ami talking to Zee and Enn aunty about my body.

She said I was flat. Her words felt like a dagger because I was deeply insecure about my body developing late; my body had almost grudgingly inched towards becoming curvy, almost as if it knew it was a bad thing. And there was Ami in the room next to me with other women, strangers, talking about how my facial features weren't that great either. Enn aunty said I wasn't that bad-looking and that these days men liked girls that were flat and plain.

Zee and Enn aunty were like Cinderella's stepsisters, colluding and making personal commentary like sisters do, but with a slightly sinister twist.

'As long as Yasser likes it,' one of the sisters said. 'I don't know how he can,' Ami said.

'To each his own,' Aunty Zee said.

'Yes, to each his own,' Ami said with a sigh.

After this, I was to go to Ami like a dutiful bahu and have her dress me in gold bracelets that Abu, Yasser's abu, had bought me. Without flinching, Ami gave me a kiss and said I was the most beautiful woman that her son could have ever chosen. I looked at her icy-cold eyes, I felt the ice in her veins, leaving her hands and entering mine. I took my hands out of hers. I took off the gold bangles, trying not to be hateful, and I asked her politely, in a controlled voice, to safe-keep them for me, which she dutifully did by wearing them herself and calling me a good girl. There is a photo of me looking down at the bangles, and I feel so removed from that young girl, because feeling what she felt that day would shatter me into a billion pieces. I stayed shackled into that moment, waiting for my time to come to this day.

Day four: I saw Yasser was in Ami's arms, crying. I had never seen anything like it.

She was cradling him in her lap and he was crying. He said to her, 'What has gotten into you?'

'Don't be sad,' she said to him. As if the pain she caused him came from elsewhere.

'Why was she hell-bent on ruining my life?' he asked his ami.

Hours before she had had a frank conversation with me at the breakfast table. She began by saying that she was not my maid and I should wake up early and make my own tea. Yasser was still sleeping at this point, and I didn't know that then, but I was already pregnant. I apologized, but I felt that her stepmom, whom I called *Apajee*, had put her to it. That didn't feel so bad. I put it to banter and said I was happy to make breakfast the next day and that it wouldn't happen again. She was already on the next topic. I was also told by my in-laws that I had come empty-handed, dowry-wise. None of this agreed with the image I had of them, of modern, educated and progressive people.

My mother-in-law's modernity was exemplary in the era before my marriage. She was self-made. She had broken feudalism's balls. She had studied medicine when it was not okay for girls to step outside the home. She had rejected a suitor whom she was bound to from childhood, thereby kicking off a family feud that had also broke her brother's marriage. And so on and so forth.

I should have got my scoresheet out—like, the ace branded furniture her son was sleeping on was from Bhai, and was uncomfortably expensive; the gold was passed on by my bua; the three million rupees my father had left me by going to work in the last six months of his cancer before he went into a coma. I wanted to also mention that my value lay in my education, which frankly was not Bhai's responsibility, yet he still paid for my international student tuition.

Bhai did this despite the fact that his first duty was to his own children. Although no one said it to me, I always felt like I was a burden to my family, because of being a half-orphan. My mere existence made people conscious that I was a leech of some sort. Someone had to take money from somewhere legitimate to feed and house me.

'I am a very expensive asset,' I wanted to tell Ami.

But by this time, to Ami, I was too powerful and had to be put in my place because I'd already seen her being disrespected by her son, followed by some insult-hurling moments between Abu and her. I had also learnt that she was left on her own every alternate day because Abu went to live with his first wife.

It was like my entry into the new family made me absorb all their existing issues and perhaps if I wasn't witnessing their disorder, it didn't really exist in the first place.

Trained in the language of truth and fairness, and a bit of Islamic feminism, I fought back for my rights. I said, 'Ami, you are a disappointment.'

Ami made me instantly regret saying that.

What happened afterwards was so terribly unfortunate because I was merely a guest in a new house, just missing my family. A cacophony of thick Punjabi accents arose, directed squarely towards me.

Finally, Yasser came downstairs, demanding an end to the nonsense. But he too was upset at me. He asked me to shut up because I had disturbed his slumber and his mom, in that order of priority.

'So, shut up. Don't create chaos in our house. We don't believe in yelling.'

I refuted that claim by saying, 'I'm literally the most silent person at this moment,' to which Ami lifted her hundred-tonne black bag with the fake logo and walked out in disproportionately high heels.

People leaving me alone and walking away frightened the hell out of me.

I broke into a whiny apology. 'Please don't leave, I'll go. Or better yet, I'll do things, anything you want.'

'Too little too late,' she said. Then there was crying. As I sat on the stairs, I saw Yasser trying to convince his mom to not ruin it for him, but he was doing so in her lap. I found that to be a breach of privacy. It was like my mother-in-law was getting access to me naked. This was my husband, also my future baby's dad. Why in Allah's name was he in his mom's lap? She cooed and then calmed him down, promising to tolerate my bad behaviour just for him. Just because she had raised him with a lot of sacrifice.

* * *

The office was home. I was there first thing in the morning, before everyone.

That Saddiq Trade Centre had a ridiculous-looking clown effigy that climbed down as the glass escalator went up. Leaning against the lift with my pouch now visible to others, I looked sadly at the clown. It was a metaphor for my life. If I went down, Ami and Yasser went up. We were related by diametric forces. I had to be very careful not to go up or inform them that I was going up, because when they were down, there was hell to pay in the form of dysregulation and chaos.

'Credit where credit is due, Bhai,' I said on the phone when he called to congratulate me for being all over social media for the boss woman piece almost twenty years since my first cubicle in Lahore.

'Yes,' he said as if to make sure.

'Don't forget the people who shape us, Aisha,' he said.

'Ami is the reason I am called the boss woman of Pakistan,' I said.

Maybe he heard the ice in my tone.

'I'm not saying you didn't show up to work all these years,' he said.

Yes, he had sensed my mild resignation. 'It is true that she is the reason I worked,'

'It is also true that she is the reason I continue to work,' I said.

'Okay then, take care,' Bhai said and we hung up.

Just like I'm deathly afraid of people walking out the door, I am so afraid of people hanging up.

GREEN BACK BOOGIE

My first pay cheque in Pakistan was a big deal. I gave it all to my mother-in-law. I told her I really didn't want it for myself and, more importantly, giving it to an elder would make it grow. It was enough to buy three plane tickets from Lahore to Karachi and back. Now I could buy maybe forty of those tickets.

Between then and now, my money may have grown, but I've shrunk.

After almost two decades in the workplace, I called a driver who worked with me to bail me out of a maxed credit card at a restaurant. I was at the Mocca restaurant at Beverly Centre in Islamabad. I'd taken my team out for a lunch and the corporate credit card I was over-relying on had rejected the transaction pin. Shabir bhai was our family driver on whom I leaned when Ami needed to go to the village for funerals, weddings or when the family needed hospital visits. Anything that was marginally a crisis was his domain. He was a true Pindi boy, calm and collected, with a devotion to kids and a great sense of human capacity to generate irony and humor. In front of him, my family life, largely a secret, could be exposed without judgement. 'Assalamulaikum, Shabir bhai.'

'*Allah ka shuker*, all is well.'

'Yes, Yasser is well. I'm in a bit of trouble. So, I'm in need of money. I'll need about thirteen thousand. No, actually in a month won't do, I need it now. I am sending you the location pin. Thank you.'

I turned to the manager standing on my head disrespectfully. 'Help is on the way. Just a few minutes.'

'What if this man doesn't show up?' he said. 'Shabir bhai always shows up,' I said.

I was humiliated for being hounded like a common criminal by this overzealous restaurant manager who should know the customer is always right.

He truly believed I was going to walk away without paying for a lunch of seven people, just because none of the credit cards I had worked.

'Try the card again,' I insisted to the manager. 'Ma'am, it says right here: Insufficient balance.'

People were looking. They were giggling. I looked dignified but was very shattered.

The people on my speed dial were gone. Yasser had a brain tumour. Tehreem was gone. Another best friend, Dee and I had had a fight.

My family had already sent me a lot of money for Yasser's surgery.

Anyone else would use this situation against me.

After almost an hour, the manager asked me—*Kya position hai* (What's the status)?

He may as well have asked me to do the dishes. Maybe my Mac, my Bose earphones around my neck, and my Michael Kors handbag made him hesitate.

I said, 'Shabir bhai will be here in a few minutes.' I glared at the manager.

He walked away shaking his head.

It wasn't just a few minutes. Shabir had to come from Rawalpindi. He was driving an Uber and hardly sleeping. I'm sure he was asking friends for money. He was more reliable than anyone I knew. More importantly, Shabir knew it all. There was no shame when it came to him.

When he came, he handed me thirteen thousand rupees in an envelope respectfully and said, 'I'm waiting outside.'

He knew that if I had no cash, my cards wouldn't work and hence I wouldn't be able to call an Uber as well.

Yasser was using my car.

I was angry at my mum-in-law and had refused to use Yasser's abu's car.

'Thank you,' I said to him after I paid the manager, making a mental note to never come to the restaurant again. Shabir drove me to work silently.

'I'll pay you back soon.'

He was my person for matters like this. For saving face, and for respectability. He knew keeping someone's debt was never okay.

Shabir did all the insane secret errands for me. He refused to sell my last piece of jewellery.

'Shabir bhai, I need money, don't drag your feet, just do it.'

'Baji, that is all well and good. I understand hard times, but not this piece.'

'That is what jewellery is for, Shabir bhai. Just get the highest quote and bring me cash.'

'Baji, *nahi*,' he said almost refusing. I shook my head defiantly. We must.

We stood outside the blue glass telecom tower where I worked. Yasser's surgeries and the trips to Karachi had left me dry. My friends were angry at my choices. Most people had disappeared because I was sad and pathetic, and both these things are infectious. There was no one or nothing else to turn to except Bua's jewellery from 1913. The family heirlooms, the intricate carvings on the beautiful bangles, necklaces and rings—these minerals, the stardust were all the friends I had. I had never felt more alone in my life, but there was no time for sentimentality. I had outborrowed from the banks, their markups were killing me. I was so bad with money and rolling my credit that this stardust I was selling would go directly into my utility bills—gas, electricity and maybe even the Internet.

I didn't mind borrowing from evil banks on exorbitant interest rates, but there was something very revolting about owing my country money. My taxes were always paid and my utilities never went beyond their due dates. I wore that fact like a badge of honour. The currency of hard work in a grind culture served only the utility companies. Whatever I earned was spent on living.

Shabir came back to my workplace three times that day. He interrupted my meetings and annoyed me with his calls and his fixation with this one piece of Bua's jewellery because he couldn't fetch the price it was worth.

'What is it, Shabir bhai?' I said.

'It's not my place, baji,' he said, his head down, looking at his feet.

I nodded.

'Please don't. I think you are making a mistake,' he said.

'I have three loans from three banks and a balance transfer facility, and all of them are gone. My provident fund at work is maxed out. My work advances are all drawn. I literally have no other asset,' I said.

I felt I owed him an explanation because he was hurting for me. 'But they are from India. They are heirlooms,' he said.

I was tired. I wanted my ami. I wanted Bua.

I was tired of not getting the whole money thing. I felt incredibly stupid. I knew I was not cut out for domestic life like these women were, but I didn't know I would fail so miserably at being a working mom.

'I'll sell my plot. You can pay me back when you have the money,' he said.

A few work colleagues passed by as they entered the office gates. I smiled at them weakly. My phone started ringing.

I took my phone out. There was a team meeting overdue.

I sucked all the compassion for this kind man into my gut. 'You are right,' I said.

He smiled.

'You are right, it's not your place. Please don't come back without the money,' I said.

I tipped him well. He didn't say anything. He would usually protest.

I deposited the money into my account. It was a tiny amount compared to what I thought it would be.

Shabir later told me that the man behind the counter at the gold market in posh Islamabad downtown had crushed it with his hands and thrown it in the gold filings pile to be smelted.

I paid all my utility bills that day. I owed the government no money. I felt light.

START-UP GRIND: SAVIOUR COMPLEX
WITH THE DAVOS MAN

Hassan Rahman was the ultimate Davos Man. He was the Silicon Valley whiz-kid who had returned to the native land in 2002 to serve his ailing parents. He was fond of saying, 'I'm the only son.' He was also fond of saying, 'I made my first million at Intel.' He discussed his success in a sort of third-person form, his tongue thick from trying to contain the stammer that would sometimes give way to awkward pauses and clicks of the tongue. His favourite words were scale, well before it became popular to say so, and productivity. He thought in dollars and often drew the sign on a glass board with a whiteboard marker, explaining like a professor. He did not graduate from Stanford but his bio initially said he did coursework from there, and eventually the coursework part fell off like an autumn leaf. I was a college student at San Jose State University, where I studied business initially and then radio, TV, film, theatre and new media. Hassan was a name hard to miss in the tiny Muslim community. People revered him by way of envy— who does he think he is. They would call him a namedropper or a one-track money mind. He came home once or twice to meet Bhai. I remember his car being rather sporty and red.

He was Bhai's friend at the University of Wisconsin, but their how-we-met story is one of mutual admiration, albeit grudging. Hassan had hacked into Bhai's university student email. At the Muslim Students' Association lunch, they exchanged notes on how it was done and how it could have been done better.

Their friendship was often defined by a life of pranks. Pranks that were sometimes based on their hacking genius.

At one point, Hassan even faxed an FBI-most-wanted memo to Bhai. It scared the daylights out of him because it had details about things that only Bhai knew. Bhai and the government. FBI could have investigated him and found out. He followed the fax up with a phone call. Hassan had a thick American accent, one he couldn't shed even after living in Pakistan for decades. Bhai and Hassan were both immigrants but only one of them had more at stake.

Over time, Hassan would become my connection to both California and my family. I started off as an editor for the social media website's blog and soon transitioned to being the marketing lead, and then transitioned into sales, where I made some bucks. This was followed by some big-impact projects as a director. It was a six-year journey in knowing and working with Hassan. We sold people Internet tools at a time when my customers didn't even know what the Internet was. My first pay was 20,000 Pakistani rupees which was roughly 350 dollars. I earned four times that much as an intern in the US. Hassan was a master persuader, so I was convinced any US college grad could never make more than 350 dollars in Pakistan. I think co-dependence defined our terms. Hassan-this, Hassan-that. He became the all-knower.

My father-in-law used to say, 'Don't do it so much that when Hassan says move to Karachi, you move to Karachi.' Abu used to say, 'We don't need you to work, you are only working because you want to.' When Hassan said, 'I need you in Karachi for Pakistan's first job fair,' I asked Abu for permission, him being the man of the house and all, and he gave a familiar grunt—'I told you to be careful.'

In my father-in-law's world, no man other than him should have the ability to get me to travel to another city.

I looked up to Hassan because I had seen him build an empire from an idea that existed only in his head and it gave me immense hope.

Hassan taught me everything about work process engineering, the commitment to weekly bullet point updates of what I had done and what I needed to do. It was always a three-way: me–money–Hassan. He first gave me about twenty dollars when I was a student, fundraising for the screening of the movie *Jinnah* in the San Jose State University auditorium. He said I was doing a good job and that he would bring the cash to the screening or something thereabouts. It was a proud moment for me. Life made sense. I was doing Allah, Abu and Jinnah's work.

As people flocked to the auditorium, the only building reminiscent of a university in that institution that was known for its tech beat, I smiled and waited for Hassan to show. I don't think he did. I ran a terrible Pakistan Television Corporation (PTV) print on the theatre reel. People complained. I sat in the front row as the Pakistan Students Association president, unmoved, glued to the story of Pakistan's founding father in the tech hub of America. People liked the gesture, thanked me for the community service I did and went back home. I was overdressed that day. I had worn the deepest sea-green frock gown, made a nineties puffy blow dry and allowed myself to put on make-up. Yasser saw a picture of me from that day in *Pakistan Link*, a local paper.

Yasser and I were instant-messaging on America Online (AOL) or Internet Relay Chat client (mIRC) after arduous hours of dial-up connections and disconnections.

'I disconnected,' was our go-to phrase when the call dropped, and we wanted to explain we didn't just disconnect.

Hassan wasn't at my wedding in Karachi or at the valeema in Lahore, but he and Yasser enjoyed a somewhat cordial exchange when he came to pick me up from work. However, before this point, there was a slight tension because my ami suggested that if I liked Hassan, perhaps Bhai could let his friend know and we could be arranged in a marriage. I thought nothing of it. Ami didn't say whose idea it was, but I supposed she didn't think of it independently.

After this information was conveyed to Yasser, he made an HTML website of his own on his Rutgers.edu domain that clearly had Yasser's initials YLH in the URL—which stood for Yasser Latif Hamdani. On this website, a piece of art really, there was an oversized picture of Hassan, smiling and toothy, with text in a large font that read: I am a *chootiya*. I am Hassan Rahman. I made my first million dollars in my ass. Yasser showed it to me gleefully. I gave it the same attention I had given Ami's suggestion. I didn't, at the time, understand that websites were cached. Yahoo was the only search engine and search engines were really more about porn than they were about life. Until one day Hassan stood behind my workstation and asked me to search his name, which I dutifully did and there it was.

I told Hassan I knew nothing of this, my shock at being found out had perfectly disguised itself as the shock of seeing it for the first time. Hassan walked away shaking his head. He left me to drink gallons and gallons of Tang at my desk. I was bulgingly pregnant with Zoe, and I desperately wanted her to be an astronaut and therefore I was drinking Tang; that's what I had heard they drink in space.

I think Hassan cared about me. He also cared about the family of his workers, often taking a few hours off work to celebrate birthdays and company wins, but soon enough, he would return to being a boss, asking us to do more. His desk was stacked up against the glass windows of the Saddiq Trade Center overseeing Fawara Chowk square—on the one hand Jail Road and the Gora Kabraastan cemetery, and on the other Main Boulevard and the new nerve centre where soon brands like Crocs, Tim Hortons, Hardeez and McDonald's would open.

Mostly, when I wasn't drinking Tang, I was sleeping on my keyboard. Hassan would wake me up, his face crinkled like a littered cigarette pack and rather irritated. He would say I was making others sleep. I'd fall back to sleep soon after he was done waking me up. Afternoons were hard to stay up and work. To my right sat a woman who was a graphic designer. She had made the company logos and mascots. Sometimes she would get mad when I ate her lunch. Fayyaz, the designer, on the other hand, would be happy when I ate his lunch. He understood mommy and baby needed good nutrition. He designed search bars and web pages, but not like the ones Yasser made. His had forms and logos.

Faraz was all the way over to the other end of our cubicles. He was the intellectual one. He, Yasser and I were very good friends; we often had lunch together in the food court upstairs. Sometimes we would force them to turn off Bollywood songs—we didn't come back to our country to listen to this shit. The three of us felt we should do that because we had chosen Pakistan as Pakistan was. Our self-righteousness made sense back then.

I'm not sure why Faraz had been hired but he was always writing his novels at work. I asked him to tell me how, because all I'd ever wanted was to write, and he smiled politely and said, 'It's about the journey of writing, you see.' He stared at me with eyes that said: not you, not today, not ever. Faraz now has a large agriculture farm and lovely kids. He is not a published novelist.

There was a developer from Faisalabad who slept at his desk because he was sick, and Hassan almost fired him for it. This developer got arrested for stealing source code. In this first-of-its-kind cybercrime reported to police, policemen with batons tried to get him to give back the code, hoping it was like jewellery they could reclaim or a computer they could return. Hassan explained to them that he had stolen a secret formula. I bet it wasn't easy to be him.

Hassan worked hard. In fact, he worked all the time.

He saw things others didn't—when to launch, how to test before launching and how to never let a developer tell you this could not be created. I reverse-engineered and designed things I never thought the Internet was ever capable of. Hassan would listen very carefully to the notes I made during client meetings, and then asked me to put it into buckets of features that we would then offer all companies. He said, 'If you make it a website for jobseekers, the companies will follow.' He was a bitch of a taskmaster—you had to be always on the road. He would not be happy if I had less than seven meetings a day with potential clients. He believed in resales, upsales and repeat sales. All three were important. It was design thinking before design thinking was a fad. My commission cheques became fatter and fatter.

The cheques helped pay the fatter and fatter credit card debt, made fatter and fatter by the growing baby formula and diaper bills. I got to do things I wanted. A spa day. Or taking a cab instead of a rickshaw to work when the car was unavailable. I contributed to the home by covering for the kids' needs, like maids, and mine and Yasser's. I gave my first pay to my mother-in-law, and I told her to pray for my earnings to be prosperous.

When Zoe was born, I got a Naseeb.com jumper. When Zainy was born there were gifts too. When Yasser's abu died, Hassan and his wife, Saadia, came over for condolences. Hassan was family. He was a slave-driver and my father-in-law's forebodings did come true, yes, but I felt enriched in his presence. I also knew that without work, I would be embroiled in the day-to-day violence and chaos of my new home reality. Hassan was adequately familiar, and just as adequately distant. His money philosophy was hard not to adopt. When clients would talk, I would do quick mental maths to see if their faces were worth my time. People soon became worth the return-on-investment. I started sizing up humans based on my commission cheque.

Mere chit-chat was an unacceptable waste of time.

Despite my ruthless attitude, Hassan accused me of being too lenient with clients.

He would tell me to walk away.

He said, 'If there is value in your pitch, they will call you. Don't devalue products by chasing too much.'

His confidence about things that did not even exist baffled me. He was rich because he behaved rich. He made for a good origin story. He started up with only 35,000 dollars and some advice from a LinkedIn CEO, and set up Pakistan's best and most renowned tech company, paving the way where there were none.

For six years my job was to make sure every recruiting manager would post an open job on the Internet, instead of print. I was taught to sell the Internet industry before the job portal, and if I did it right, they would always choose the brand. We got rounds and rounds of funding. The long and short of it was that Hassan was the Davos Man—talking the talk.

Hassan also had the ability to flatten my confidence, and his success made it all the more real. I'd be sweating in my car, making sales calls on my way to sales meetings, and he would ask me to do more to reach my targets.

He asked: What was I *really* doing? Was I working *for sure*? Well, the numbers say otherwise. What about the promised cheque from the client? How many times did I follow up?

He said, 'This is looking bad. My overheads in the Islamabad office are high and the sales are not growing exponentially. You either grow exponentially or not at all. I'm giving you till Friday to bring home all the cheques from clients. A promised cheque is not a real cheque.'

I had several bizarre conversations with him, but the one about maternity leave was the most depressing. He plotted my absence on a glass board, X and Y axes. Two large crossed-out lines stood in the middle of the graph. 'So, let me understand this correctly. You are saying that I keep paying you for work that you will *not* be doing. Yes?'

'No,' I protested, 'I will be back soon after Zoe is born,' my hand on my very large belly.

'How do I know that?' he said and added, 'I can only motivate you to make money when and if you work. Does this proposal make sense to you—me rewarding you, using my very limited start-up money, for work that has not happened?'

'No,' I said in a weak voice.

'Good. I knew you'd see the sense. You go take your time. Come back to work when you are ready. I can't pay for something I didn't have anything to do with. Just do the maths.'

I came back to work ten days after Zoe was born. She would not latch at my breast. I had several stitches from the rips of birth, the bleeding wouldn't stop and the child would not stop crying even after colic drops and warm-oil tummy rubs every night. I wanted to go back to who I was. Yasser's ami was a doctor and frankly, a much better mom than me. She said my milk wouldn't let because I didn't eat, although now I know she had no clue about the tiny-but-potent quantities of colostrum. She also said I gave Zoe a boil on her neck because I was keeping her dirty. Hassan was the mother I needed when Zoe was born, so I drifted towards the only good mom I had. There was no shortage of that at Rozee.pk. I would express my milk and put it in the freezer and take it with me, to be fed to Zoe the next day. This was unheard of but I didn't give a damn. My baby needed my milk, and I was determined to give it to her, especially because I was a bad mom. I would cry in the bathroom a lot because the mastitis was getting worse and worse by the day. Sometimes Hassan wouldn't let me leave when it was time to express my milk. At one point, the milk leaked from my breast pads and made its way into my shoes.

I don't remember asking for a day care. I think it would have been futile.

The day I'd had enough was when Javed, the rotund accountant, drank Zoe's frozen milk.

It is true, Javed had propositioned me once before, but I never could believe it would transcend to my postpartum days. Javed had called me to work on the false pretext of learning MBA economics from me because his English was weak. And when I showed up to work on a Sunday to teach him only out of the goodness of my heart, he came on to me. He said he liked me and he wanted to show me 'a good time' because it looked like I needed a good time. I was genuinely shocked. He didn't seem like the kind to take such liberties. Also, he didn't fear that Hassan and I were family friends—something that should have been enough of a deterrent. Javed could lose his job.

When Javed told me it was he who had drunk my milk, I just couldn't hold back my tears any more. I sat in the tiny kitchen on a tiny kitchen stool and wept. Fayyaz brought me his lunch and kept it next to me quietly and left with a pat on my shoulder. It took me one hour to express one ounce of breast milk and it hurt so bad. The toilet stank but there was no other place to do it. This man didn't understand what that one ounce meant to me.

Yes, it was the office fridge I had placed the Advent bottle in, and yes, it was a communal fridge, but everyone knew it was for baby Zoe. There was a silicone nipple on the bottle. How could anyone drink from it?

I don't think I told Hassan.

Asif was the office boy. One day Asif took 40,000 from my bank account. I was saving that money for Zainy's birth. Asif knew my ATM PIN and I would always send him to take out cash. I paid Asif a good tip for things he would do for me outside work. When I realized my bank account had been wiped clean, I went to Hassan, fat and pregnant the second time. He was upset for me, but he was also upset at all the commotion at the office. Hassan helped me file for the CCTV footage. When we found out after weeks that it was Asif who took my money, Yasser took him outside the office and slapped him a few times. He had fast deteriorated in the parenting years into someone unrecognizably fast to grow angry, quick to resort to punches to people other than me. I was embarrassed of his behaviour but it was a lot of money for the family, and we were all counting on it.

Hassan allowed me to take a loan from the breast milk drinker, Javed. I signed the loan contract and slowly paid it off. I think maybe 5000 at a time. Hassan was a lifeline, but he often became my noose. I had so much money anxiety at this time of my life that I spent it almost the instant I got it in my bank account. My first bank account was at Habib Bank AG Zurich because Abu banked at Habib Bank, and also the bank happened to be on the other side of Main Boulevard, Lahore. It was easy for me to cross and get cash when I wanted it, if the ATM worked. Men catcalled at me as I crossed the street but besides that there was no real inconvenience.

When I was on maternity leave with Zainy, Hassan allowed me one-month paid leave. By this time there was an HR department, and although local law said three-month paid leave, I think both Hassan and I needed each other. I was now one of the most senior resources and certainly the most senior woman in the company. My work spoke results, and I had synced to Hassan's language. It was an exciting time in Pakistan. Musharraf was in power, the Basant festival made the kites of all colours glisten in a blue canvas and, as far as the eye could see, Pakistan was going to be a modern state that would have made Jinnah proud and right, and both Yasser and I could tick off that dream. I did well at persuasion. I did well to be loyal to Hassan. I did well to be loyal to Hassan in his language. It was, after all, just like the arranged marriage my ami had in mind for me. After all, all security is financial security.

Sometimes I was a bad office-wife.

One day, when I was working, no longer sleeping, but typing away, I realized everyone was away from their desks.

They had congregated in the conference area and were complaining. They knew very well Hassan was out and did not like people touching office property or not discussing how to make the office money. Some of the louder men said that Hassan was selfish and would not allow for local holidays, that it was unfair because everyone else got time off. I did try and deflect it by parroting Hassan—get back to work, no time to waste, it's a start-up phase, productivity matters, man hours matter, efficiency and whatnot. Two days later there was a full uprising. In the absence of HR, I took the troop of employees to Hassan with a sense of self-prescribed authority. I also let him know that unless he did something, he would be considered a jerk who only cared about his fast cars; besides, time off was a labour right. I looked at him for his response. By now I was a boss-lady, I had dealt with all personality types between home and work, and no one could frighten me. I was only in my early twenties and the fierceness was still gleaming.

Hassan looked at us with a face that could have spewed yellow bile on us like in the film *Exorcist*, but he instead yelled, half stammering: 'Is this . . . this a . . . a union?!'

Hearing the word union, as if a slur, half the revolutionaries ran back to their seats at the speed of light. I turned back and no one was there, which is fine, courage is not for everyone. They left me alone to face his wrath. That was fine too. What wasn't okay was how Hassan had chosen to say all his hateful words to me, right to my face. He didn't as much as look at anyone else.

I found his choice to turn his wrath at me unbearably mean. It was misdirected rage. It was a veiled threat, but it was also an unveiled threat. Control the masses or off with your head. I realized that my familiarity with Hassan was a huge liability, he went overboard to remind everyone he wasn't happy with me and that he was especially upset with me. He could toss me around to create the circus he wanted. I was dispensable. The hierarchy of things was determined.

I walked out of that situation worse off.

I may have been Hassan's blue-eyed girl because I brought in the sales, designed the web interface, had an acute sense of where the business was headed and was agile enough to pivot, but just like marriages, office marriages depend on the man liking you back. My likability had plummeted. Hassan had changed his mind about me.

Somewhere about this time, Yasser got a job in Ufone, the government telecom company. I convinced Hassan that I was ready to be the head of sales and marketing for the entire north region, that I could relocate to leafy Islamabad and covertly take all the business back from this competitor mom-and-pop online job site. I did what I promised. In three years, I had taken them to the cleaners, while I worked from my basement. I had a home office.

Zoe and Zainy were toddlers and the maid would watch them while I worked within earshot, supervising this modern version of an integrated life. Sometimes the door between the home and the office would be open and the women I had employed would catch a glimpse of Yasser in a towel coming out of the shower—it was work-life chaos. Sometimes my mother-in-law would visit, and she would be loud enough for my clients to hear the dressing-down she would give to the maid for not changing the kids' diaper properly. Sometimes Zainy would sing Punjabi songs while we had strategy meetings—*Mai suaajora paya tadi-farmaash-tey*, I wore red on your special request.

It seemed inappropriate for a toddler to sing a seductive song like that while we looked to win over the government, banks, telecom and development sector.

I hired five women. Dee was a brigadier's daughter. Soon she went on to become one of the richest women tech CEOs in Pakistan and was often on panels with Hassan and the World

Bank Country CEO. She came in as an intern and taught Pakistan
how an engineer could turn dust to gold by selling mobile content
to millions.

Dee and I became friends, although I'd employed her as a
junior in the office. She became someone I relied on in so many
more ways than one. She was younger, so I felt perhaps we would
outgrow each other.

Yasser sometimes referred to Uncle as a Christian Taliban for
always chasing Dee's love interests away. Dee and I would sit in
my broken red Alto, or her tiny white car that was basically a
box with wheels, and trapeze through the twin cities of Islamabad
and Rawalpindi making sales calls. She had the 'seatbelt refusal'
syndrome, and when we would go on food calls or sales calls, I'd
strap her seatbelt in when the cops were nearby. We took our
clients by storm. We talked sense. We won by persisting. We
brought home fat cheques and fatter chocolate balls from this
obscure bakery next to the office. Sometimes we brought home
more paratha rolls than cheques and we would be under heat from
Hassan, who abhorred anything that didn't look like exponential
growth.

I taught Dee how to cheat the patriarchy. She credits me with
telling her that oppressive forces must be stolen from without
shame. That shame is a tool that only helps those already in
power. She was the little sis that I never had and who did a zero
to hundred all on her own accord. Somehow Uncle thought she
was always safe with me. I double-agented Uncle and let her fly.

Hassan led me to Dee. All his sins are forgiven for that.

That friend who I've always wondered would cover for my
murder—Dee is that friend.

YES, MINISTER

My relationship with Pakistan transformed. Once a mere conscientious citizen, I was now a part of its broken system, employed by it and somewhat enslaved by it. I was the government. Finally, there was power. I wasn't just a government employee, but I was the director general of the investment board, often reporting directly to the chief minister of Punjab, Shahbaz Sharif, who became prime minister of Pakistan in 2022 after ousting Imran Khan.

Despite the glory, power and prestige of being part of this lost Mughal dynasty's capital, Lahore, I inherited a recurring dream about shit.

In this dream, there was shit. There was a toilet. They both disagreed with each other.

That had been my nightmare since forever. Not metaphorically, a real nightmare that leaves your sheets wet in shameful sweat and disgusting public defeat.

I would wake up flummoxed.

The shit in my nightmares would whirlpool in the loo but never disappear under the spell of modern plumbing. It would resurface like a monster that always has something on your smallness. Often, right after this dream, I'd dress up for work and head to my parallel universe of pay cheques, order, free market economics and the golden rule that there was no such thing as a free lunch.

I was never afraid of working hard. It was the ultimate currency I'd never run out of.

The nightmare was birthed right after I started this job. In the prestigious loins of 23 Aikman Road, GOR 1, Lahore, specifically. Leafy, gated, elite to the core, guarded by the forces that guard any head of state. I'd flash my employee card, and they'd double check the car sticker and licence plate, and my trunk and engine, before letting me in. You came in via the gate next to Punjab Club and you left from the exit near the zoo. GOR 1 was GOR 1. Banyans protected it and colonial-style residential plots in red brick and lovely vines decorated it. The cars had green number plates and most homes had low walls.

If I wanted, I could run there in slacks with a cocker spaniel at my heels and it would be okay. If you were in, you were in. The Punjab Police, known for its brute force, would protect my honour because they would know some big man would kick their ass if they dared not to.

Aikman Road was the office where I held my third steady job at twenty-six.

It was where I spent the most time at work. I was a big girl now and I had got here through the rare miracle of merit. Purely hired through a job advertisement in the paper that I applied to by licking an envelope shut after stuffing my résumé in it. A committee of four, including the chief minister of the province, hired me. I was confident and impressive in the interview. Buoyed by my business acumen and my negotiation skills from years in sales, I got an offer immediately, even before I returned home to Islamabad in a public bus.

Three years into the job and I was promoted from director to director general. The British system had left this part of Pakistan deeply hierarchical, and this job grade felt like holding the world in your palm. Some Punjabi men in the bureaucracy had spent a good three decades to be director general, so this was a bit of a problem. As far as my youthful and slightly arrogant self was concerned, this sounded like a 'them-problem'.

My interactions with these men were far from pleasant. One of them, the bald-headed Director General 1, who had the voice of a three-year-old girl, would ask me to get under his desk and switch on his computer for him. Another, Director General 2, with a topless beard, called me to his office to reprimand me sternly for emailing him late at night because it was inappropriate to disturb the peace of a family man like him.

Perhaps my job grade was a 'me-problem'.

The red-brick architecture of 23 Aikman would speak Punjabi if it could. Eco-architecture before it was a fad. It was built by Nayyer Ali Dada, a man whose name is taken mostly to create a mic-drop effect. The lighting, the arches and angles and its spiral staircase were made for grandness.

The modern plumbing, however, didn't care who Nayyer Ali Dada was, what the Punjab government was and what GOR 1's colonial ass-licking was.

I had chosen an obscure toilet to cry in. I did a lot of crying at the workplace and most of it was in washrooms. I was crying because this forgettable research associate girl, with a forgettable name and an unforgettable nose, said to me: 'You don't strike me as the sort who cares about children. It surprises me that you have decorated your workplace with crayon sketches of toddlers.'

I had said something forgettable to defend myself and excused myself to get a glass of water.

Instead, I had gone up the marble staircase to the executive office where the CEO was supposed to sit but had been unceremoniously fired by the chief minister. I knew it would be safe to go there. Lately, it felt like I finally had protection from the patriarchy because I was the patriarchy. But things changed.

The CEO seat at Aikman Road was a revolving door, but this CEO's exit had come to bear heavy on me because I was always considered to be close to the one who was removed.

I didn't know this at the time, but people talked behind my back that I had slept my way up. It didn't help that I was seen crying after he left.

Unaware, I had gone to Director General 2's office weeping that I felt harassed and targeted at work. Someone had moved all of Zoe's and Zainy's drawings from my soft board and put them in the bin. I was so distraught that I had gone to the man I had no expectation from.

But he was also the new acting CEO.

The man continued to nod while I wept and kept asking office boys to come in for signing this paper or the other. He could have offered me privacy, but this was his moment to rejoice and spread office gossip.

He sipped his tea, which he had too many cups of. He said: 'I have an observation about this. I think that you need to talk facts. Why don't you tell me what code of conduct was violated? If you cannot, go back to your desk and finish your work. It's a very busy day.'

I cried some more, but thankfully he gave me something to do.

I thanked him. I called all men 'Sir' in that fancy building with secretly flawed internal plumbing.

Now, in the safety of the non-existent CEO's white-tiled, well-lit bathroom, I let a rush of nausea rise like a tide, subside and rise again just in time for me to make it.

It was the longest road—first to the CEO's room, then his exclusive washroom and to the intimate vanity where I rested my elbows and waited for the emptiness in my gut to leave my body. It's okay, I said to my pale shadow in the wall-sized mirror.

Then I breathed and said it to myself again.

It's okay.

I nudged myself to let go because it was safe. I had bolted both the CEO's office door and the washroom door. Double protection.

It's okay.

I did let go.

I shat it all out. Whatever my gut held, it didn't any more. I emptied what was inside me into the loo.

All done. Muslim shower. Flush. I washed my hands with the Dove liquid soap and wiped them with the Kimberly Clark hand towels from the Kimberly Clark hand towel dispenser.

I breathed out. 'Humans have guts. Gods don't.' It's okay.

Except it was not. I looked at the pot and it was overflowing with shit.

The nausea was back because I realized I had used a really dirty loo. It was clogged and I had to find a way to unclog it before it overflowed into the bathroom, into the CEO's office and down the spiral white marble stairs. The speed was uncanny. Pure horror.

I took care of it eventually. I always took care of shit eventually. I always landed on my feet. I wiped everything off. No evidence. No trace of chaos.

But the nightmare wouldn't leave me. It came to me at random times every year, twice in bad years, maybe even thrice.

That evening, I took sick leave and boarded a Daewoo bus to Islamabad from Lahore where my family was, where my toddlers were and where their tiny hands and tiny crayons were. I was going away from the politics of the Punjab government's swift firing squads that made me feel like I was their next victim; away from old banyan trees and ivies and oaks that masked the putrid stink of bureaucracy's snail-paced intellectual corruption; away from the jackass who clogged the CEO's bathroom plumbing; away from the last safe space that was left for me in the world.

I never cried in bathrooms after that. I never went into public loos. In private ones, I tested the plumbing many times before going.

When someone said terrible things to me, I braced myself, instead of getting sick to my stomach. I turned all the condemnation and anger inwards. This job changed me. Fundamentally, it altered how I saw the world. It traumatized me by making me feel like I was in control and held power, then it stripped me of it, made me subservient and paranoid of what the next moment held. It gave me time anxiety.

Getting this job was so important to me, I had to change cities, commute for hours on weekends and for hours on weekdays. I lived in such a makeshift situation. All for that title on my résumé.

Even the daily commute to Aikman Road was hard. I had a car all right. It was a tiny maroon Suzuki Alto that I was so proud of. Yasser's abu got it for me on lease and I sent a picture to Bhai and Bhaijan in the US with a subject that read: check out my new wheels.

The ignition didn't work without a man or two pushing it manually while I revved it up.

Someone, out of spite, had scratched its bonnet, its petrol gauge cover had fallen off and its lights never worked because I had rammed into so many trucks on Multan Road on my way to work. None of this mattered on a one-way street in daylight. The problems started when I had to take two-way streets at night. Lahore's fog is merciless in the winter. Dense and almost like a serial killer, lurking, scheming, plotting. The Alto was *my Alto*. I parked it on Aikman Road and had the audacity to cover it for safety with a slightly more dignified material than polythene.

I lived with Yasser's cousin on the wrong side of the tracks, an hour away from Aikman Road. Lahori elite often joked about eating dust in Thoker to define the depths of poverty. I lived in a rented place half an hour beyond Thoker Niaz Baig—a famous chowk that Lahore converged into Grand Trunk Road–Multan Road–Motorway–Raiwind. Places that meant the dark and dingy working-class side of town. People who lived on Aikman Road only came here to pass through and probably never read the signs.

Raiwind was known for two things—the Tableegi-Jamat party congregation that happened there and that the Pakistan Muslim League Nawaz party headquarters and personal farmhouses were there. So, depending on what time of the year it was, I'd be stuck in my Alto to let pickup trucks with men and colourful *lotas* pass or to let the luxury cars pass by. The traffic police would be alert and on edge like the queen of England was going to personally waltz across Thoker.

I would be very warm in my Alto. Its heater never worked because of a manufacturing flaw. Neither did its air conditioner. Sitting in my car, windows down, uncomfortable and rather alone against the elements, I felt annoyed at these antics of powerful men blocking roads that were meant for the common people. But

I literally turned all my rage inwards by not feeling it at all. I was in some sort of perpetual shock at the state of my life.

My desperation to work for the government came right after I became the de facto man of the house. Yasser's father had died due to a sudden heart attack while I was working in Islamabad. Yasser had taken it so badly that he was out of commission mentally, and I knew we were no longer kids. While Yasser was mourning, I grew up. Even though he was working at a telco and earning well, the financial loss from his dad's passing felt insurmountable to me. I decided to quit my job with the start-up I had worked with for almost six years and look for a job that paid better.

Yasser became a new person after his father died—just callous and angry and ready for a fight anywhere and everywhere. I was worried he would soon lose his job because of his interpersonal challenges. I knew he was grieving, so I overcompensated by stepping up my professional game. I felt Yasser's father's loss. For all practical purposes, my email to Bhai and Bhaijan was to show off my new dad, not my new wheels. In Yasser's abu's passing, I felt the same aftershocks I had felt when my abu died. Everything was scattered. I coped by stepping into Yasser's abu's big shoes, even though no one asked me to do that.

My grief was tiny, and I didn't permit it before Yasser. After his dad's funeral, Yasser slept for two weeks straight. He was inconsolable and only a comatose sleep would permit him some peace. He eventually went to work, but before that he tried to strangle a guard at a wholesale store for a tiff, he told his boss off on an open floor for being historically inaccurate about Jinnah, and he upped his Internet game, devoting hours and hours to discussion boards and comments. Yasser's abu also took with him the childhood that Yasser and I had basked in.

His mom and dad would drive in the front of the car and we would be in the back, holding hands and being silly, clueless kids. They would notice but pretend not to notice. They had perhaps the most dysfunctional relationship I'd seen but Yasser's love unified them, and by extension, my warmth illuminated us as a unit. Yasser's dad told him early on that the one greatest thing Yasser had done was marry me. That was all the validation I've ever needed.

Yasser and I may have had two baby girls of our own, but in those early years, it was Dado and Aba, as our girls called them, who were the primary parents, and we just played with them, threw them in the air. I breastfed them and Yasser burped them, but we returned them to their people who doted over them so much that our parenting skills lay dormant.

Now, on the Daewoo bus, almost on the verge of being fired from a job I felt I shouldn't have taken, all because I worked closely with a CEO I shouldn't have associated with, I realized I was in deep shit. I was also heading to a home where I was the de facto Aba. I got the groceries like he did. I parented Yasser like he did, giving him room to act out and be difficult, reassuring him not to worry about finances, and I also took up the role of appeasing Dado, who had become clingy towards Yasser, reverting to a very early mother-child bond that reeked of co-dependence. She wanted to fix his closet; she wanted to cook him a specific meal; she wanted to decide where to put the plate rack. She knew what her son wanted. Who was I to come in between a mother and her son? The unit had really disintegrated and with it my status in the home.

I was Aba only for the groceries, not as the authority figure.

Dado was also Aba.

Recently retired, Yasser's mom felt that her purpose in life was to remind everyone that she was the Punjab government's first highest-ranking female officer in the health department and that she had saved hundreds of lives as a doctor. With this reminder came the need to place the plate rack where she wanted to and determine all the items of clothing in Yasser's closet, and the order of his shoes.

She also wanted to keep opening my mail, just because. I had to smash enough cell phones into the ground in rage to convey to her that I took my privacy very seriously, and no, she could not spill over her trauma to my mail, to which she responded, 'Which lover's letters do you need to hide from me? I'm just opening banking paperwork.'

The day I left Aikman Road to go to a home that didn't feel like mine, I sat on a cramped bus with no legroom and my back was literally in a forward-leaning position even if I pushed the seat all the way back. It was kicked by the person behind me. It was a five-hour bus ride, a forty-minute shuttle ride from Rawalpindi to Islamabad and then a thirty-minute shuttle wait, and if I caught a late Daewoo, I would end up missing the connections and the gaps would make the travel extend to seven hours.

My life at this moment felt like there was no room for me. The shit dream would just not leave my pre-frontal cortex.

Spinning and spinning and overflowing—like the power of exponentials—doubling every twenty seconds. A conflagration of my fears for the world to see and my helplessness in keeping it all contained.

I was not landing on my feet.

I was diving into an empty swimming pool skull first from higher than a hundred feet.

When I reached home eventually, around midnight, I realized Zainy had a high fever.

I cuddled Zainy and Zoe in my arms and finally knew where the nightmare came from—I feared for these two younglings so much.

I feared that they were half-orphaned like I was after losing their granddad, Aba. I feared that their Dado had lost her bearings, and that their dad was bereft in pain and that as their mom I had no capacity to stop working so incredibly hard at keeping my job. Just like Uganda after my abu, their lives were going to change for the worse, through no fault of their own.

I gave Zainy Calpol and then Ibuprofen. I kissed her and Zoe tenderly. I told them stories about Uganda. They listened with their big eyes and their thick eyelashes, heavy and tired from the day and from absorbing my fears.

Yasser was at his computer. Dado was yelling at me for resorting to medication first thing a child got sick.

Zoe, Zainy and I cuddled in each other's arms. This was fracture. I missed having a dad so much.

I had only tonight, tomorrow night and the following day before I headed back to 23 Aikman Road. The countdown started. I had to make every moment of motherhood count. Zainy put her burning tiny palm on my face and Zoe listened intently to my chirpy make-believe world.

I decided to stay in Islamabad till the last minute. I would take the midnight Daewoo from Islamabad to Lahore instead of a daytime one, so I could stay with the girls longer. I would arrive at Aikman Road directly on Monday morning.

Showers are not as important as babies. Even for mothers who are not the good type.

I wish I could punch that research assistant's unforgettable nose so hard for calling me a bad mom.

I ate my anger instead.

Now all the feelings go into my nightmares.

GOVERNMENT LINGO: THE WOLF IN SHEEP'S SUIT

Saleem was like a scrooge. Pale, bald, three folds behind his neck, hook-nosed, slightly humble in gait and if it was sunny in Lahore, he was pink. His jaw seemed like an afterthought on God's part. Yet, back when he was my boss, he may as well have been Jonny Bravo. The jaw and EQ both seemed adequate and majestic. You only see what you want to.

In my younger self's defence, men were my gateway to surviving in the pay-cheque world. Someone had to sign the pay cheque. Men were it. They had to do important things or tell other important men to do it for them—the signing, the not signing, the delaying of the signing, the promptness of the signing, adding less tax to the signed amount, adding a bonus to it for good performance. In my entire work life, twenty-odd years, I never got an unexpected bonus for good performance, but I expected it every month, and every month closed my payslip email with a disappointing sigh. You are somehow made to believe that there is a gold pot at the end of the rainbow that you'll get if you do the grind like a good salt miner.

Either way, if I wanted money in my bank, I had to kiss up to The Man. One way or another, I had to work for a labour market that was not made to benefit the labourer.

My mistake was to think that there was a way to crack the system through hard work. I thought that I was, in fact, quite principled. I tried to never have an extra meal on another's dime or ride with men in authority. For the pay cheque, I would stay up three days in a row, not even go home during deadlines, not shower, because, well, that's the honourable way to *halal* your *kamai*—to make it kosher and legitimate with hard work. Otherwise it was tainted.

If you are from this part of the world you'll hear this a lot—the idea that you are given salt by your master, so you cannot be a *namak haram* or dishonest. There is an Amitabh Bachchan Bollywood film about this very value system that is inescapable if your parents aren't smugglers or monied. That you have to be grateful to the salt and cannot be disrespectful to the employer, master, father figure and borderline divinity which has provided you with this daily bread, this damn pay cheque that buys the bread.

I was frightened of the accusation. It was the worst thing anyone could have said to me—that here was a worker bee, buzzing around, looking busy but doing nothing. Shame propelled me in a nuclear way. It turbo-charged me to madness, and I was obsessed with being a diligent, spotless employee of the month every month.

There I was, typing, at God-speed, my feasibility reports or my press releases or event briefs and so forth, thinking the sun rose from where Saleem, the CEO, walked humbly upon the earth. There was something wrong with this man, but I was the last to know.

Someone advised me to drop him like a sack of potatoes. I was appalled at the suggestion. Drop him where? How was he being carried by me? But people can see things clearer than you can when you are busy living your life by the code that Amitabh Bachchan was only portraying, not living by. 'You brown-nose Saleem too much,' someone else said to me. I thought that was terribly accusatory and suggestive when in fact I was only doing my job.

My duty was to go to him when he called me; agree with him and give him my wise counsel when he asked for it.

Sometimes the advice Saleem asked for was a colossal waste of my and the government's time.

'What do you think of this picture?' Saleem said.

I looked at a passport-size picture of a young man looking back at me from the corner of my thumb.

'What about him?' I asked.

He smiled and took the photo back from me.

'You asked for me?' I said looking at him, my eye contact communicating professional but polite posture. I would always be very rushed to get to the point.

'Who is he?' he persisted.

'Who is who?' I persisted, genuinely not sure what he meant. He again gave me the passport-size picture.

I held it dutifully and shook my head. My irritation would often present itself in the form of two deep-set lines between my eyebrows. Some hated it. Some found it endearing, I suppose.

'I have no idea,' I said to him.

My voice was harsher. I almost tossed the picture back on the desk. I tapped my pen on my notebook which was full of scribbles that I thought would one day take me to that mysterious unexpected bonus, that pot of gold, that good salt.

I wanted to get to the meaty part. Had he summoned me to discuss a business trip, where I would save the day? Or a visit to the chief minister's house to get in a memo in time? To get a summary moved? To fetch a PC1, a document that activated large government infrastructure projects? To think of a media plan? Which was it? I asked him again.

'This is me,' he said, smiling his teeny-tiny smile with his pointy teeth.

'Who?' I asked. But now I knew better, so I added, 'Oh, okay. You look nothing like that now. This must be many, many years ago,' I said.

This is who I was. I was brazen. I was unaware of the politics of the workplace. Having just birthed two daughters who were very young, I was very much a newly-wed in my own head, just juggling the dynamics of marriage in a joint-family system. I was unaware that this very old fatherly gentleman was trying to get something out of me by showing me his head-full-of-hair passport picture.

I was just tired. I wanted something. Some prize. I was very clear that the only way that could come to me was via the validation of other people, most often those who signed my cheque. They loved my work. So more work, more cheques. Simple maths.

I stood up after a few minutes of sitting there like a Barbie and watching this man type into the keypad of his huge computer with one pink finger, the man I found semi-inspiring because he was supposed to be smart. He was an ex-banker. He had left his plush job at Credit Suisse to be here serving us mortals, instead of being in the investment capital of Dubai. Lucky us.

'Let me know when you want to discuss work,' I said and walked out. There was a whole lot of America still in me.

I didn't like time being used for anything but making money, meaning or good content for both.

This was a polite way of reminding the man when he was distracted, that work was what paid his bills too.

Men were stupid, sometimes you had to remind them. They forgot, often. But that was okay. They took well to reminders.

It was when he reminded me of his picture again that I felt a bit queasy.

'You didn't even think it was me in the picture,' he said.

We were in the car, going to a work meeting. This time I knew what picture he meant.

'No, I didn't.' Polite smile. 'You look nothing like that.' He smiled and looked out of the window.

'My mother was still alive then. I was a different man.'

I stayed silent. I knew when a man brought up his mom, you had to shut up and listen.

The politics of the job were strange. The old guard had left, and the new era was upon us. It was Orwellian. There were fascists but the new leaders were still not defined as the good people because frankly the definition of fascism was at large.

There was Director General 2, who walked around the office in his wet and squishy prayer slippers and his trousers above his ankles before he prayed.

The day he called me to his office to complain about my behaviour, I was particularly stunned.

'Do not send me late-night messages,' he said. 'When did I do that?' I asked, confused.

My notebook that I had got from the World Bank visit in DC and my Piano pen both lay open and unused, except, of course, for the entry of the date. It was too early in the morning. I hadn't even had my morning tea when he had summoned me. I knew he was only in an acting role in his position. I didn't, therefore, take him seriously. Still, this month, and a few months in, he oversaw signing my pay cheque.

'Am I lying?' he asked. Expanding his self even further.

I responded with a stare. I learnt to do that to men. Feed them no drama, so they had to explain themselves.

'You have done something very improper,' he said.

I looked at him, the frown between my eyebrows deepening. 'You sent me late-night messages when it was time for family,' he said.

I looked straight into his soul.

He continued: 'It is improper. My wife was very upset with you.'

'Can I see them?' I asked.

He pushed his Blackberry to me.

I picked it up. Encouraged by his silence, I scrolled through his apps, went to his messages and put the screen in his face.

'No messages. I sent you no messages.'

'You sent me these messages,' he said, taking the phone from me from across the desk which would soon not be his. Perhaps he was mad about that.

'What is this?' He showed me my email. 'Look at the time at midnight,' he said, waving the phone.

'These are work emails!' I protested, half in astonishment, half embarrassment, because I felt like I had been caught.

'Yes. Email messages,' he said.

'You were literally on CC in this email because the deadline to submit the data to the Industries Department was yesterday, and I had been working all day to complete it on time.'

'It is not okay. You can complete your work on time, but don't send me these late-night messages. It is not respectable behaviour. I am not one of those men you usually email. I have a family,' he said.

I wanted to protest further. My tea had arrived via an office boy here in this room instead of my desk.

We were peers technically, this man and I. Thanks to the public–private experiment of the Punjab government, this grade-22 officer—which is apparently a big deal since the British Raj—and I, a mere dimwit twenty-something college grad, were on the same pay grade. He had put in forty years. I had not. In fact, I was so dismissive of people like him, his fake propriety, his *jee-sir-jee-sir-sir-sir-sir* on the phone to anyone who could hurt him.

I just laughed at his face and walked out of his room, sipping my tea.

I couldn't believe this archaic man was calling me a homewrecker for doing my job.

This was an episode from *The Office* starring Steve Carell. Pathetic.

They say the last laugh matters. His was the last laugh. It is always the old guard that comes back again and again and again. The experiments with the private sector, with all their tech whizz and new-age kids, were puny compared to what the colonial legacy, bureaucracy and the inertia of ad hocism left us. They were many and we a few. They were old and we were not. They were not smarter than us but they were relentless and they tire as easily as us. They waited for their turn patiently, and they watched like vultures. They descended because they could smell death before death came to visit us. They understood the inevitable. They studied pendulums for a living. They caught waves. They lay low. They always fetched the best jewels from the sea because the tide brought in all sorts of strange ideas, but the storms always left for other places.

His 'yes-sirs' got him many CEO seats for many years.

I continued to do my work as I knew it, cc'ing him when and as work dictated. Deadlines were deadlines. I report to the system. I worked for the country, not for a man who could not tell that 10.30 p.m. was not late night.

Worse than Director General 2 was Director General 1.

Director General 1 had the voice of a cheerleader. His crown was bald but, for some reason, his hair on the sides was as loyal as a British hedge maze, trimmed and very dark and healthy. He was a big man horizontally. Not to fat-shame him, but I feel this is important information. I would request him to move aside so I could perform the task he had instructed me, but he would move in a walrus-like fashion, inch by inch and just a bit and in a jerky way.

Director General 1 would make me get under his table and switch on his computer for him.

Every evening someone would turn off his computer. Plug out the wires. Every morning, I'd be asked in his cheerleader voice to get down on my knees, crawl into the space under his desk, right where the grey carpet was folded and crumpled, unwashed and neglected by the cleaners, who would vacuum around it but never where most of the dirt was. I would get on my fours, no harm, work is work, all work is honourable, and plug the wires back, switch on the CPU machine and ask him if he could see the red light on his monitor. Sometimes I'd make the mistake of getting back up before checking and the wires would be loose. I'd have to again jimmy the plug back in the socket.

So he would insist on sitting, so he could do the important job of telling me if his computer monitor light was on or not. In hindsight, it was really weird that he continued sitting. I was the general manager for International Marketing. If anything, just the tiles would make this ask unbecoming. I didn't understand what score his sick mind was settling with this power move, but, to his credit, he was not sleazy. He was polite and sometimes added 'beta' for clarification.

What a fool I was.

Director General 1 came to my desk one day. Seeing all my Zoe and Zainy artwork of '*Mama I love you, Mama when will you come home, Mama you are the best,*' he said in his rubber-ducky voice: 'Where are your Gantt charts, where are your targets, where are your calendars? This is not right. This is an office; you cannot put private things like this here.'

I laughed supportively at his joke while I typed away at my computer that didn't need another person to switch it on. Then, I realized he was dead serious. He actually sent an office boy to remove the tag pins from the softboard. Thankfully I caught him in the act and told him politely but sternly that I would put him in a wood chipper if I saw him touch my daughters' things ever again. Word was out that I took my private things very personally, that my personal was professional. It made me so self-conscious that I would refuse to let Yasser come to pick me up or have anyone even know who he was.

However, the pictures in the office remained. For a few years at least. I am proud to say that I was the one who removed them on my last day of work. I went on a Saturday when I felt I'd be fired and put everything in an A1 paper carton box and took them home. I was right. I was fired the next day.

Fazal saab was one of the nice ones.

The day I went to collect my severance pay, an okay sum, he was very sad to see me go.

He kept shaking his head. He was the first person I met at this job. The first person who coordinated the hiring. The first person who asked me to sit in the waiting room before the interview board for this position. I remember writing his name and number down after the interview to ask him if I got in. He called me, and said, cordially and in a welcoming tone: '*Bohot Mubarak.* You are now the Punjab government's director for communications.' I remember smiling. I felt a familiarity with him. He kept me informed when the politics was brewing against; when Saleem was fired. He was the one who tipped me off that I might be fired too. 'But Fazal saab, why would they fire me? I have a ninety-eight per cent rating?' I cried. By this time, in the department of the benevolent master, I was worn out and had cried in front of almost everyone, including Director General 2.

'You have to see who the rating is from,' said Fazal saab. I cried some more. Fazal saab passed me the tissues.

The office boys were instructed to give me some of my favourite sweetened tea.

'The thing is, these people think in camps. Saleem and you are thought to be in one camp,' he explained. He urged me to take a sip of the tea. I held the cup in my hands, sobbing.

'It's unfair. I've got a ninety-nine per cent rating from the other bosses too. You know this Fazal saab,' I protested.

'What matters is what they think,' he said. 'I am in no camp,' I said.

'I know, I know. I didn't believe it myself until I read your diary,' he said.

'Sorry? What diary did you read of mine?' I asked as I wiped my reindeer nose.

Fazal was young and savvier than the old bureaucrats. He had a sort of Dev Anand-look about him; his side parting etched in stone. He ought to know the difference between a diary and whatever it was he thought he had read.

'I read your letter to your friend where you talk about your father and all your feelings,' he said.

I wanted to stare him down with my intimidating look. I wanted to give him the same wood-chipper warning, but it was too late. This was one of my own people who had gone into my files in my computer and accessed my private notes. My letters to my close friends. Letters that talked about private things, private matters, matters of the heart, matters pertaining to my life, my marriage, my people . . .

'I know it was not morally right to read them, but something in me told me that you were not the type of person they were making you out to be,' he said.

His eyes were all-knowing. 'I know what you know. I know what you have felt. Whom you loved. I have reviewed, read, maybe even saved what you wanted hidden.' His eyes continued to be kind. 'I know you were not in the camp of any of these men,' he said.

'Thank you,' I said.

I signed for my severance cheque and left. I was glad that I had taken a few dozen paracetamols, the only drug I had access to that I could abuse. I was glad I was too numb to think about the devastating ramifications of having my private life exposed to a person in the government. The fact that he knew all my daddy issues. The fact that he knew things that I rambled into my computer for catharsis. God knows what all I wrote over the last four years, in what state of mind, and whom they were intended for.

I was glad I didn't fight with Fazal saab. There has to be one person whom you think is not bad.

Fazal saab messaged me later on the severance pay cheque day: 'You looked like a fairy princess in your white dress. White is beautiful on you. I felt like hugging you.'

I owed him one for helping me prepare for Director General 1's ultimate power move. I refused to let him be in the bad-guy category for breaking into my hard drive and reading my private content, obviously through the IT department's help.

I blamed myself for being stupid enough to use the work network to do private stuff. It didn't matter I was doing it on my personal computer. I was saving it on the network drive. I am an idiot, and I deserved what happened to me. I refused to make him the bad one. No. If bad men were a spectrum, Fazal saab was on the other side.

Director General 1 called me to his office. By this time, he had inherited a better desk. As things go in the salt mines, he also got a minion awarded to him for his position. Just to sit at his computer and draft things that Director General 1 wrote in shorthand and then type them into the computer on his behalf. This clerk, and that is what he was called, Clerk, also then got the honour of switching on the computer by plugging in the power socket.

'I have good news for you,' he said. This threw me off. I smiled. 'Thank you,' I said.

I thought I had struck that gold pot, that bonus . . .

'You're fired,' he said, trying to sound like Donald Trump from the *The Apprentice*.

My smile froze. I continued to smile like an idiot. Confused, but also finding it unreal.

This was home. I had no home. This was home. I was the Punjab government.

'We no longer require your services,' he said.

My smile lingered. My head spun. I would have been prepared for this moment had it not been for his good-news comment, his girly reassuring chirpy voice and his non-alpha stature.

He gave me a termination letter. 'Read it to me,' he said.

It was like in the movies. That high-pitched deafening dog whistle. That slow motion movement, as if one were under water. That out-of-body experience. Somewhere something was happening, somewhere else. Slowly, I came back to life, but weeks later. I snapped back into reality behind my tiny car's wheel. On the bus back home. While cooking. When peeing. And then I'd go back into that silent movie that my life was.

I was fired.

I was a *namak haram.*

Saleem made people believe I was part of his camp.

He knew he was going to get fired. He knew I was an ally, for whatever reason a fifty-something man feels a young college grad is his ally. But he did, and yes I was guilty of that having flattered me. The sun rose from him, remember. The boss represented the holy bread.

Saleem knew he was going down. He had read between the lines. He had fallen out of favour with the chief minister. He claimed that he had stopped a frivolous investment, something-something, and that he was an honest man and would not do dirty work and all that jazz.

He asked me to intervene. I was twenty-something. I intuitively knew this was above my pay grade, but stress kills brain cells.

I asked Saleem, 'Where do I come in all this?' He said, 'Oh you are in the eye of the storm.'

He continued when he saw how bewildered I was.

He said, 'The CM only trusts you. Did he not ask you to email him the presentation on his private account last month?'

I said, 'Yes but that was on his request. I cannot really send him anything unsolicited, right? I really don't know what else we can do to help you.'

He said, 'You must do what's right. Be honest and email the CM and tell him my termination is wrong.'

I was back in Islamabad. I was telling Yasser how Saleem had been fired and how my days were numbered and how this was very stressful. Yasser fell asleep. He often fell asleep. I think I was triggered about his absence more than I was about the job—Yasser checking out like that. I didn't know at the time that it could be tumour-related. Around 2013 it was about half the final size, about two centimetres in his right temporal lobe. Unaware of the medical iceberg ahead, I always felt he abandoned me at my most critical moments. I knew I had to chart my course and save my job alone.

So I made a decision. It came to me clear as day. I could save the situation, just as Saleem had said.

I emailed my half-assed honest evaluation of Saleem's performance report card to the chief minister of all people. Unsolicited, childish, stupid, dumb and utterly self-inflicted. Nothing is private, remember.

I emailed him at some ungodly hour. Nothing worked in my favour.

I was swiftly terminated by Director General 1 a week later.

I asked on what grounds I was let go. I protested I was a top performer. I begged and said I had done nothing wrong. I was told I was insubordinate. I did get my severance, which was kind considering that crossing the establishment can leave you without what's due to you.

All I did was school the CM on why he should not fire Saleem and why it was bad for the organization. I may not have been the harlot, the fallen women of the Victorian era, but with that email, I had tied the noose around my neck, inadvertently, mostly because I was PMSing and my husband had fallen asleep while I had narrated how I could lose my job.

Had Saleem manipulated me into it? To what end? Why would he taint my early career in Pakistan with a scandal? Or did he like the fact that there were others who went down with him? Did he enjoy my SOS visits to him, asking him for guidance and mentorship? He found a job as a CEO. He could get me a new job if he tried?

On one such visit, I took Yasser along.

I was questioning everything about my work ethic after getting fired. I tried to switch to a new version of me, of a person who was well integrated in society.

During one such visit, Yasser looked to me to answer a question he had been asked. He often did that. We were young, cute and unabashed about co-dependence.

When I visited Saleem again, literally begging him to get me a job somewhere because my savings were ending, he commented on our marriage.

'Yasser lacks confidence,' he said.

'I think he is very confident. Sometimes a bit too much,' I defended. I often had a knee-jerk response to anyone criticizing Yasser. I was then very unresolved about our relationship. Perhaps even had a version of Stockholm syndrome.

'He looks at you for everything,' he said. He watched my response very closely.

'Okay,' I said. I reminded myself to do the opposite of everything I had done before. It is better to agree with men.

He came around to my side of the desk. He put his hands on my shoulders and said something about the weight of the universe on them. Something about wanting to take it off my shoulders.

I stiffened underneath his touch. I abruptly shifted away. I stood up and faced him with my chair between us.

I think I was bewildered. I must have been.

He walked to me as if there was nothing about me that he could read. He hugged me. I stiffened. He said something about being there for me.

I stiffened further. I tried not to freeze, but I did try and wrack my brain to spin this another way. He was one of the good ones. Like Fazal saab. He was in my camp, remember. He couldn't be doing this.

Then he touched my lips. His hands were trembling. If there was ever a damp-squib moment in my life, this was it. I had got all the evidence I needed. I gathered my bag and swung it before my chest to block him. I walked past him, past his office, past everyone's empty work desks, past the night guard's curious watch, and got into my car. The keys wouldn't work because my hands were trembling so much. I reached into my purse for my phone and called my friend Naira, asking her who I was and what had just happened.

'This is sexual harassment, and you are a victim of workplace harassment,' she said. She had a master's degree from Curtin University in human rights. She couldn't be clearer.

I needed my ami. I wanted to hide in her sweet arms, her soft tenderness and her acceptance.

But what if she too blamed me? What if she said you shouldn't have been with a man alone.

All the rumours were true.

DEVELOPMENT GIMMICKS: #AIDTOO

I knew everything US-related would be fantastic for my career. I knew I'd thrive in anything that had an international component to it. It came naturally to me. My education fit. My ethos fit. I had determined early that if things were fair, and I was fair, and the system was remotely a meritocracy, I would rise and succeed. There were things about me that were honest and loyal.

What I didn't know was how to be loyal to a company.

There were the #AidToo scandals that poured in right after the #MeToo movement, in the US and globally. Pakistan was too anaemic to declare how aid organizations and men in them thrived by building programmes to neglect the communities they were asked to serve.

My first job in an aid agency was by the recommendation of my first boss at the government organization. I'd worked with Ahsan for a year but he had said I'd made a lasting impression on him with my precise use of words for a precise situation. He did take me under his wing. He also said I had the determination to run after projects until they were done. It was he who assigned me the biggest work responsibilities often in other countries with three-day deadlines, and I'd stay back day after day in the office till it was done. I respected him and of course admired him too, but most of all I wanted to impress him with my work. Ahsan was among the few men for whom I wasn't too much. He managed my exuberance by keeping me busy at work, upping my challenges. I grew as a professional at breakneck speed with him.

I loved authority. And his was easy to appreciate—Brown and Harvard University were perhaps the reason my American work ethic didn't intimidate him, but worked for him. He spoke in his affected British accent from Aitchison and often quoted the Black Swan phenomenon. For all his entitled life, the Lahori elite, the connections and the business inheritances, he did not shy away from seeing me as a person to look out for now and again.

He rescued me thrice, once by hiring me in my first government job and then when I was fired from it. In between, there was a frivolous accusation that I had defamed the country. Even then, it was he who made calls to get me off the hook on a sedition charge.

I spiritualized the development sector's horrendous record on people, planet and profit.

But Ahsan got me the aid job despite the fact that I didn't take his work advice and messed up. He told me repeatedly to stay out of the politics, but when I was asked for an opinion I was lavish in my 'observations'.

When I was accused of sedition by the mighty corrupt Sindh minister, Ahsan was the one who got me out of the thick mess. He told me not to, but after everything was resolved, I still sent a letter detailing the episode to the Sindh government about their minister's terrible professional conduct. Ahsan kept telling me to stay out of it, but I was compelled by the power of being an honest house slave. The government deserved to know.

I was under the assumption that when anyone was told of misconduct, they would thank me and rectify the problem.

It was laughable, and I was, for this reason alone, laughed at. I was working in Pakistan like work mattered and honesty mattered, and without both, systems would crumble. The only thing I was doing was looking ridiculous—carrying the load on my back and depositing it where I was told to and rushing back to carry a new sack of stones. I thought the more stones I carried, the more infrastructure I could build of something important—like bridges and technology and ethics. My talking points said so.

I believed that ethics and compliance mattered. If you saw something wrong, you reported it. If you were doubtful about conflict of interest, you asked. If you considered someone corrupt, you identified them to the authorities. And if there was intellectual corruption, people just not being true to their work, then that was the most unforgiveable of all decays and had to be reported.

I was the star of a sitcom—being important and thinking authority was godlike.

Ahsan still found me worthy, despite my naivety.

Could he and I hear the same music, so when I danced, I didn't look crazy?

He didn't dance to any 'crazymaking'. He played golf with the same people I felt were despicable. He admitted to me they were. He worked with those who I felt had no mantle but he'd converse with them like friends.

But for some reason, Ahsan refused to toss me off to the junkyard of honest workers who had it coming. In fact, he went out of his way to ask a minster to get me through to the aid organization.

He said to the then federal minster and senator of the Pakistan People's Party: 'Aisha is one of the most professional people I know. She will do all your strategic work without ignoring the admin around it—the trees and the forest, sir.'

Three months later the same minister, a senator from Karachi, had me working for him, via the aid organization's Competitive Support Fund. I had, therefore, two bosses, the one at the aid organization's project, which was tasked to improve fair play in business in Pakistan, and the chairman of the apex body that created investment opportunities. I may have been asked to leave by the Punjab government, and yes, I was the laughing stock of anyone who saw me there, working like a blind mouse, but I trumped them by working in the federal body that I knew they all looked up to.

I thanked Ahsan. He said to make nothing of it, that what he had said was true, and that his recommendation would not count if what I was did not make the company look good.

'Companies want good resources,' he said. 'I have such a crisis of confidence,' I said. 'That's a first, madam,' he said with a smirk. 'How so?' I asked.

'You don't fear a fight. You don't fear confrontation. You're too wedded to what you think is the truth even at the cost of your job,' he said.

'And look where it got me,' I said.

'Well, you certainly don't lack confidence,' he said. 'True,' I said, now smiling.

'You get a do over, in terms of understanding the culture of this place, which frankly is not great. Even I struggle with its polarities,' he said.

'Thank you,' I said.

'Welcome, madam. Just don't blow it up this time,' he said.

So, this was the first man who had helped me without wanting anything in return.

It felt strangely paternalistic. Paternalistic because Ahsan immediately fit into the saviour hierarchy like a jigsaw. Strange because I experienced it only in sporadic spurts. Therefore, it was all a jumble. Who was right, who was wrong, would I be okay, or would I not, would I mess it up or would I not?

I walked into the aid organization job with the objective of not being fired. This was a sure-shot way of being a sitting duck. Everyone could smell the fear on your skin.

The office was located on Ataturk Avenue in Islamabad's G6 area.

I had to move all alone from Lahore to Islamabad for this job. There was no point in moving the family yet. What if I continued my streak of getting fired? So, it would be just me for now. I would, however, need help getting settled in a new city I had never worked in before, except the home office when I was employed by Hassan's company.

Yasser helped me get familiar with the city. He drove me to the office to show me the way from the one-room outhouse that my mother-in-law had handpicked for me. At the time, Yasser's ami was de facto Yasser's abu. His abu had just died and his ami was looking for projects and people to own, and I needed to be owned. I had been fired from the government, which was unheard of in her world. She had served the Punjab government for thirty-five years. I couldn't even survive five. Sure, she had her share of stay orders after being asked to vacate her position. She also had court cases against her for trumped-up charges of harassing staff. She said that was all they got on her because she ran a tight ship and refused to pass the chain of money from pharma and health equipment procurements to the men in remote provinces. She was such a force that the places she was posted to would become polio-free, have improved health indicators and men would shit their pants at the rate of a horse stampede.

Both Yasser and I shat our pants with her in our lives. When she said eat, you ate. When she picked out this ugly room for me on Margalla Road, facing the Margalla Hills in F7 sector, I said okay. The exterior of the room was exquisite. Margallas were like a Monet painting. They were resting and inviting against the blue-blue sky. There were pedestrian walkways when in Lahore there were none. I stood on them, waiting for a taxi to take me to work. If I woke up at 6 a.m., I would find one by 7 a.m. and be at my work desk by 8 a.m. Islamabad was tiny. I figured that out.

Everything inside was a nightmare.

The room was literally the same outhouse that Uncle Jerome from my childhood had. It was like the return of the native. I was the native. I felt rather fallen. Like I had worked so hard at university just so I could be like Uncle Jerome in a three-by-three cubicle. At least he had his family. I missed Zoe and Zainy a lot. I had lived without them before, but being away from them right after getting fired and moving to a new city felt like banishment. The room really didn't help.

The mattress was torn. Its foam was epically mouldy. The tea-pink wallpaper was peeling off the walls from everywhere, vertically and horizontally both. The floor carpet was dusty and faded. The bathroom was so disgusting that I had to use three Harpic bottles to scrub it, and then follow that up with three shampoo bottles just so I could get the smell of disease away. It felt like I was living inside plant soil. I was the foreign object and the fungus around me was thriving. I cried in the room a lot, my heart racing.

I was so desperate in that place all alone that the only thing that gave me solace was praying. I often thought praying had to be done with a certain amount of everyday dignity. You showed up for duty to God, you found somewhere to put your forehead on the ground and you gave thanks to your maker.

This Margalla-facing outhouse only found me whimpering.

Ya Allah Madad. Deliver me from this hell. Forgive me my sins. Please give me my children back.

An old man, who lived in the main house, owned this place. He watched me in the morning with his teacup. I think he saw me cry once as I waited for the taxi outside the gate and didn't even bother. Until one day, when I was walking to the outhouse, he stopped me on the porch.

'Hey girl,' he said. 'Salam, uncle,' I said.

'Your mother is crazy,' he said. His teeth were not his own.

His voice thundered like he was going to kick me out.

'She's not my mother. She's my mother-in-law,' I said. I felt distancing myself from her was necessary for me to not get evicted.

'Why don't you like your house? What's wrong with it?' he asked.

I did complain to Yasser's ami, but she should have conveyed it back to him with some tact. She really did not have tact. None at all.

'Why? What did she say? I love this room. It's so close to work and I've already given you a three-month security deposit and a three-month advance as you had asked,' I said. I reminded him we had terms. This was Pakistan. Things could change.

'I don't care what you think or even if you like the place or not. If you don't like it, leave. But if I get one more phone call from your mother-in-law that you feel unsafe because the blinds are torn, or the lock is jammed or the carpets stink of piss, then I'll ask you to leave,' he said.

He was standing on the veranda of his big white house. I was standing on the downward-sloping driveway of his property, acutely aware of the difference in our heights.

I nodded.

He mocked my nod.

'Who is she anyway, this woman, this mother-in-law of yours?' he said. Disdain in every word.

'She's a doctor and she worked with the Punjab government,' I said.

'She sounds like an administrator.' He said the word like it was a slur.

'Administrator,' he said again.

'Tell her to do her administration elsewhere,' he said.

'Okay, uncle,' I said. Before he could say more, I walked to the room but it took several tries to get in because the key got stuck in the lock again. When I finally did, I wanted to jump into the cold, mouldy mattress and weep but it was so disgusting that I had to complete my meltdown standing at the door.

Much of my life has gone into overexplaining things that happen to me because the people in authority deny they happened.

I was working for the godforsaken federal government when I got a call from a recruiter offering me an interview at a local company called Abacus. I was going to be the vice president for e-Learning, which was housed under the outsourcing and new business wing.

It had been almost six months at the federal government but admin had not yet given me a room to work in. There were a few hundred rooms and offices, more desks than teacups, but no room for me. A young woman was kind enough to let me share her room—a shelter from roaming the halls and being evicted from conference rooms with my laptop bags and notebooks. Even she told me to never let anyone know that I worked from her room. It seemed as though the person who was putting these hurdles in my way hated my guts because my pay was the same as hers, and she had put in a lifetime in the government. It was Director General 2 all over again.

Bilal, the admin head, once in a room full of people waiting for tea to be served, said, 'I told her, it's Aisha's luck if she is getting paid 170,000 rupees after tax. It really is her luck. No need to fight luck.'

More tea, more waiting and more absolute exposure of what was to be a confidential part of my life.

So that call from the recruiter was a lifeline. 'Yes, I'll be there for an interview tomorrow. Yes, I'm in Lahore. Sure, will be there on time first thing in the morning.'

Taking a cue from the frequency of my evictions, I caught that night's last flight to Lahore and was home with my babies at midnight. I thought I was pretty smart. I didn't mind splurging on the air ticket, although I could only afford the bus—nothing churned my spending like the hope of an increase in income.

The next morning I interviewed in Lahore with the HR officer, a young girl called Hareem who refused to thread her bushy eyebrows and looked all the prettier for it. I was put through to the chief of outsourcing, Johnson, the same evening. I called in sick another day at the federal government. I had to get this job. My boss at the federal government would sometimes ask me how I was, in between work assignments and requests for talking points, but I always said everything was fine. Having landed here after a bloody nose at the Punjab government, I had to make sure I wasn't fired again.

'Thank you, everything is fine. I'll have your speech for the World Bank ready on your desk by tomorrow morning.'

They loved paper at the federal government office.

Back in Lahore, where I was planning my jailbreak, Johnson walked into the room for an interview.

He was not white like I thought he would be. He was brown, a Pakistani Christian. He was clearly addicted to Lays chips, packets of which he had by the truckload on his desk, which he would chew and crunch thoughtfully between bites. He spoke softly, almost purred. His favourite words were methodology and Oracle. Many years after my Abacus stint, I finally understood what I was meant to sell.

It was my fault that I signed up to sell 'enterprise resource planning software' without understanding what those three words meant individually or together. It was also the organization's fault for harbouring an imposter. I didn't have imposter syndrome; I was actually an imposter and the anxiety was off the charts—I suppose what a fish would feel in a tank full of monkeys. I didn't belong. They hired me thinking, 'She's done sales at a Silicon Valley-based start-up and is a Valley grad, how bad can it get.' I joined because I thought, 'Johnson is a chips-muncher, looks chill and half-way decent, how bad can it be.'

It was the worst. Job. Of. My. Life.

I had a corner office. It was all glass too. The title was super fancy—vice president of something. I wore high heels. I got a car from them, a white City. Yasser drove me in it from our home in Mohlanwal, Lahore—it took us an hour one way. We played good music. *Coke Studio* Season 5 was out. Life couldn't be better. I was with my kids and we all lived in a home we owned or would soon own.

I was getting 200,000 rupees, and because that was almost as much as Ahsan's wife got for her pocket money, I knew I had arrived.

* * *

I called Bhai, one of my top five SOS calls to Bhai.

I was sitting in the garden I had planted. Rose bushes, the purple jacaranda tree, and the dogs Nono and Tommy were at my feet. Zoe and Zainy were playing with the bunny rabbits Yasser had got them. There was sun in the garden, but not too much. Just right.

Everything outside was the opposite of the dungeon inside me.

'I'm getting panic attacks, Bhai.' 'What's the problem?'

'I can't figure it out? Maybe I feel like I don't know numbers, top line, bottom line, tail winds, ERP sales and frontline, whatnot. It's all Greek to me. I'm severely under-educated, Bhai. I'm out of my depth.'

'Hmm. Employers value authenticity, go tell them what you've told me.'

'Four gold medallists from the Lahore University of Management Sciences report to me. It's too early and I will lose my authority.'

'What about accountability?'

'Yes, but, it seems like I am just somehow supposed to have disclosed this before they hired me. I feel like a thief.'

'Just do some online courses from Stanford Executive Education on finance for non-finance managers. You should just know ballpark figures, not specifics, to get approximates right.'

'I can't afford to be fired again. Do you think I should tell them I should resign?'

'Why would you resign? They have just invested in you by confirming your job after probation. Tell them the truth about your confidence in managing things and ask them for a better orientation and training.'

Bhai was so practical. He thought I could just sign up for courses.

It had only been about nine months since Hassan said I had the morals of a bank robber. It had only been twenty- five months since Director General 1 had told me he had good news for me and fired me. It had only been three months since my neglect had almost killed my baby girl Zainy.

Dado took my toddler panda, pig-tailed, poutiest pout baby to Urdu Bazar of all places. God knows for what. Then, I relied a lot on Dado for all things maternal. In fact, if I wanted to take my kids anywhere I had to ask her for permission. At Urdu Bazar, the sawdust triggered an asthmatic attack in Zainy. I knew nothing about asthma, just as I knew nothing about ERP software.

I woke up the next day and found Zainy sleeping, but she was breathing in a strange way, just from her belly. I responded to that by going to work against my better judgement. Dado said she had it under control. She was the doctor. No one better to leave your baby with than her loving grandmom who knew everything about asthma because she ran the asthma and allergy clinic at Mayo Hospital before she headed Lahore's largest public hospital, Jinnah Hospital. Zainy was safe. I had never seen a child breathe from the diaphragm before, but I still sat in the car and went to make an impression on my new work colleagues at the consulting firm.

Ami called in between a meeting. I picked up. 'Zainy is in the hospital emergency room. Come home now.'

I apologized to the four young boys I was supremely intimidated by and proceeded to continue the meeting.

'You should go home,' said Ali, the one who was the smartest and made the most stunning new-age PowerPoints.

I listened to him just because I was intimidated. I took a taxi to the Bahria town hospital.

At the hospital, Zainy was on a nose concoction, being nebulized.

The nose tubes frightened me. Zainy's stubby fingers reached out for me. Mama.

I carried her in my lap and rocked her gently as she continued to be nebulized. She breathed laboriously into the device on her nose.

My heart sank 1000 floors down into the earth. Not only was I stupid, I was also a murderess.

I *almost* was; looked like Zainy may live.

'*Shh mama aa gai-hain*, mama is here.' I cuddled into her, tears streaming down both our faces. Me, a colossal failure. She, a child at the mercy of a no-good mom.

Her breathing became better. My crying wouldn't stop. I kept dialling Yasser. I needed Yasser like breath. Like my nebulizer. He picked up the phone finally.

'Please come.' He came.

He held me. He held Zainy.

Eventually everyone breathed better. There was even sleep. But somehow my mornings would begin with utter panic—a largeness, a street mural, a melting wax statue, something insane, something with more power than my lives combined would just come sit on my chest. The heart would lose its rhythm. I'd break into a sweat. The more I tried to calm down, the more the fangs dug in. If I fought back, I would choke. There was no escaping the panic attacks. They would last for half an hour, but felt like an eternity. I'd be late for work, and I'd also make Yasser late sometimes. Any noise outside my room would frighten me like I was three and the army was going to come get me. I would fear the kids were dead or dying, or worse, alive but in need of me and I wasn't capable.

At night, I'd be afraid to sleep. In the morning, afraid to wake up. Between sleep and wakefulness, there was a genocide of the planes of my mind, the floorboard of sanity cracking and I'd fall, floor after floor.

I'd kiss the kids goodbye, sit in the car with Yasser and head to work. At work I would wing it. Wait for payday and repeat. I wanted to take my fingers down my throat and purge. Not one for binge-and-purge, I did, however, want to remove whatever was eating at me from inside.

It wasn't Johnson. It wasn't my peers or the VPs, many resentful that I got to be the token woman in leadership without knowing shit. They saw right through me. It wasn't the past and its horror being so close to my jugular. It was something the body knew was wrong but the mind wasn't acknowledging.

If I were to guess, I think around this time, the knocks I got from capitalism and job servitude taught me that something was wrong with my marriage, something was wrong with Yasser, something was wrong with my life design and something was wrong with my parenting. I thought I was in danger. I was. I thought Yasser was in danger. He was. I thought my kids were in danger. They were.

I didn't just want to go to Johnson and resign. I wanted to go to Bhai and resign. If employers value authenticity, 'Bhai, could you too? Here goes, I made a mistake. Please come help me. Please save me. Do it for the children.' That would have been a more authentic SOS call.

I loved to over-explain myself because plain-as-day facts would be denied.

Yasser would tell me nothing was wrong. Dado would tell me the kids were breathing and all was well. Johnson would tell me that he was happy with my progress, whereas all I did was write on my glass walls with Sharpies to look cool and do nothing. When I looked at the kids and I saw how they breathed, I knew

I was living an insane life and I needed to escape it or build an alternative one very fast.

Everyone said everything was okay, because when I was in chaos, I was serving their version of stability.

I turned to meditation at this time in my life. I forgot how to breathe. I forgot the link between breath and voice. I regained both by using my diaphragm.

'Yasser, I'm having a panic attack.' 'Don't make me late for work again.' 'Ami, I'm having a panic attack.'

'How much more do you want me to do for you? I keep your kids for you all day long.'

I knew something. I know what that something is now, but then, it was just a stomach with legs—very hungry.

THIS PART OF MY LIFE IS CALLED RAUNCHY FARMING EXPERTS

Naira and I met on a farming project which required us both to travel across Pakistan for environmental scoping exercises and hold consultations. Value chain, farm to market, backward and forward linkages, GAP certifications—these are some of the terms we said all day long.

Naira was petite, brown and had a literature and human rights degree from Australia. She had won enough scholarships to earn her the book snob title she deserved. She read Borjes and took cryptic pictures of crows, and I felt smarter around her. The family was in Islamabad and this job was in Lahore, so I was back to being a desperate commuter. Unlike in the US where this is normal, I was an anomaly in Pakistan. No one ever does that, certainly not married women.

So when Naira offered me a drag of her Waziristan weed and a listen to Nusrat Fateh Ali Khan's *qawalis* on the twenty-two-hour road trip to Gilgit, at the foot of the Himalayas, there was only one thing to say to her: yes.

When we finally reached our hotel room, which we had to share, I noticed her looking at me strangely.

'What is it?' I asked.

'The girls in the office were talking to me about you,' she said. 'And?' I said.

'They wanted me to explain you,' she said. 'Explain me?'

'They wanted to know why you don't wear the dupatta,' she said.

She illuminated when she smiled, her brown eyes browner. I laughed.

What else could one say to being reduced to one's dress? 'And what did you say to them?' I asked.

'I said some people don't need to hide behind dupattas,' she said.

We walked into the room together.

With Nafee, as I call her now, I could walk together. She had a melancholic darkness about her that allowed me the safety I needed.

'Why are you hiding behind dental floss?' I asked. 'Huh?' she said.

I lifted her tiny, crinkled dupatta from her shoulder playfully. We laughed.

'I'm a Pathan. What these people expect of me is different from what they expect of you,' she said.

This stint at work taught me everything about ethnic politics.

Punjab is Punjabi hegemony. Khyber Pukhtunkhwa is tribal to the core, Pathans rule. Sindh is just Karachi, metropolitan, vast, arid in its thoughts and unpredictable. Gilgit Baltistan has Sir Aga Khan's civility and mellowness.

Naturally, I was sad when Naira was asked by my supervisor, Farooq, to go back to Lahore and complete the project reporting. She left dutifully.

Soon after, I found myself in a hotel room with my boss at 3 a.m. in Gilgit. There were mountains everywhere.

If those girls who wondered why I didn't wear a dupatta knew this they would say whatever happened next, I had it coming.

Farooq was our supervisor and like Naira, about five feet tall. Colourism is the norm among Pathans, the so-called warrior tribe of Pakistan, but Farooq was a dark Pathan.

Perhaps this played a part in what he did to me. He had tiny eyes. He talked a lot about the property he owned and walked with his chest out, as if it were leading the way. He liked me to sit across from him and would often throw in details about his personal life—married but now divorced and remarried. He owned enough property to keep his families rich but his first wife had turned out to be a pain and wanted more property.

'Fine, she can have what she deserves but not more,' he said.

Back in the Lahore office, I had to be a captive audience to his domestic banter.

The office, like most project offices, was in some rich man's house. So every room was makeshift and a bedroom once with large closets and a golden curtain rod. My chair was perpendicular to the desk so when I had to look at him, I'd have to turn my head right, obediently.

I was facing the door and looking at it rather invitingly. I wanted to leave. Such banter was necessary as some sort of customary loyalty test, but this was getting annoying.

Farooq only spoke in English because his native language was not Urdu but Pushto. It made me feel strange that I was listening to his family woes in the official business language.

'It's okay that you were late to our meeting because of the lawyer,' I said.

'It's okay?' he said. A tiny smile on his tiny mouth.

'I mean, you are here now and that's what matters. Can we plan the agenda?' I said.

'Agenda?' he asked.

'For the environmental scoping study launch in Gilgit?' I said, my voice slightly presidential.

'Okay, plan it,' he said. He sat back like he was watching me perform at a circus.

I suppose I amused him.

I ran over the main points of the six cities we were planning to go to: Karachi, Lahore, Islamabad, Peshawar, Quetta and Gilgit. He signed off on how I would conduct the events, plan the consultation with all stakeholders in all locations and align the consultants. This would mean I would need a whip to keep everyone on track. I asked him to officially delegate authority to me for these events on email, and that I would need weekly meetings to keep everyone on track.

I knew my work. I knew how projects needed to be lifted off; I knew how to keep them hovering in the air till it was time to land; I knew how to land them on the specific runway I was assigned to; and I knew how to rush home to my daughters after that.

This was still my probationary three-month period. I couldn't wait for my confirmation so the family could move permanently back to Lahore. Farooq was standing between me and that dream. So this banter-listening was important.

In my moments with Farooq, I looked at the door all the time. Doors were my friends. They always let me out of tight corners. But I never, for the life of me, could figure out how not to get into tight corners in the first place. It had to do with poverty of some kind, some idea of lack, of dependency. Pain is bad, but pain is hell when you are poor. Depression is bad, but depression is hell when you are poor. Separation is hell, but separation is an inferno when you are poor. Love is never there when you are poor. There is just fear everywhere. Fear. Fear.

Work was my door. Work led me to places other than where I was. Completing this scoping study for the project would get me to another door and then another until the final door led to freedom from poverty, freedom to be rich.

Of course, financial independence can be attained at any level of salary but my goal was to chase my own tail. To grow my pay by some percentage that I never figured out and then better the family's lifestyle and so on. Ultimately, I would die, and my kids won't have to do what I did.

It was pathetic if you think about it, but I didn't really have time to think.

That's the one thing the grind culture of nine to five does. It takes away your ability to be thoughtful. To-do list after to-do list. Commute after commute. Work travel after work travel.

I dreamt about shit in a toilet mushrooming like the H-bomb repeatedly. Sometimes it got more frequent, and the terror got worse than the disgust, sometimes the disgust won.

'You are very good at what you do,' Farooq said.

'I know,' I said. It was a matter of fact. As was my admittance. 'But you must listen more carefully next time,' he said. 'Listen to what?' I asked.

'When I talk. You should listen more carefully,' he said.

The small mouth small smile was not there any more. He had become menacing.

I wanted to say, improve your content, and I may listen better, but Farooq was my supervisor and a person who, I was sure, found me strange, and men don't like things they cannot understand.

If I were his boss, which I should have been, I'd do twice the work, better, faster and more cost-effectively. Instead, I had to sit across from him and be frightened of offending him as he insulted his wives. It was clear as day that Farooq had no leadership skills and he saw me as a threat. I could take him on, or I could just focus on the doors and get out.

'I'm sorry,' I said. 'I just want you to be happy with the work that you have assigned to me.' I said. No smile on my face either. 'Then it is fine,' he said. Pleased. The smile returning to his small mouth.

I walked out the door, but I returned.

'Can I please add Naira to the planning committee? It's important to have her input and ensure that our work is cross-cutting for gender and community involvement.'

'Good idea,' he said.

I think I wanted Naira there for safety. But the fact that she made it to Gilgit and was sent back made me wonder what was going on.

In the wee hours of that morning, the whole lot of us were in Farooq's room, going over the next plans for Quetta. After the meeting adjourned, he asked me to stay back and review the press conference.

I was already out the door, but I took out my laptop and grudgingly opened it up again.

'Can we sit on the sofas?'

We moved to the sofas instead of the lounge area in his hotel suite.

I sat next to him and started scrolling on my new MacBook. 'Any edits?' I asked.

'No. It's perfect,' he said.

There was sleaze in his voice which made me freeze. I looked at the door of his room. It was shut.

I closed my MacBook and stood up to leave.

'Where are you going?' he asked. 'Since there are no edits . . .' I said.

'I didn't say it was okay to leave,' he said. I sat back down.

Shit, I thought.

He smiled back, as if my thoughts were audible to him. 'I like you,' he said.

He went on for a good minute and a half in corporate language about how I impressed him. Then he said, if he could, he would marry me.

He was mixing sleaze and love.

A LITTLE PRINCE COMES TO PAKISTAN

'If I am attempting to describe him, it is in order not to forget him. It is sad to forget a friend. Not everyone has a friend,' Antoine de Saint-Exupéry wrote in *The Little Prince*.

I searched for a copy of the book in Urdu, *Nanha Shehzada*. The Pakistan Textbook Board had once published it, but it was out of print.

I too had a friend, Kevin. He was also my supervisor at the aid organization. He was superb at kicking off the project, flying in to repair the relationship between the Pakistanis and the people at the aid organization who were once immigrants but had become whiter than the puritans who wanted that American city-on-the-hill dream.

Kevin fixed everything. He was tall and it didn't hurt our eyes that he was handsome. He had a good jaw.

Along the course of my four years with the project in Islamabad, Kevin became at first a mentor, guiding me to steady my work—deliver only what was asked for. 'Don't make a meal out of it,' he was fond of saying to me. Even after I left the project to move to the Department for International Development, he let me stay on as a consultant to help me with money for Yasser's illness. He was fond of Yasser. They would smoke away on Beverly Centre's steps talking about military dictatorships. Kevin asked questions. Mostly he loved laughing at Yasser's humour, which involved making fun of others.

We once met in Monal where my friend Dee had just learnt that her visa application to the UK was rejected because they thought she would seek asylum. This was funny to Yasser because Dee could buy a few beach houses in the UK and more and though she was Christian, she needed no asylum. It didn't stop Yasser and Kevin from calling her a poor, rejected and deceptive asylum-seeker. Dee was a good sport about it but it upset me that they ganged up on her like that.

This was in 2013.

Since then Dee has been to the UK five times, Kevin died of cancer and Yasser is dying of cancer. In a somewhat evil moment, Dee and I had the last laugh over a high-five. Then we both touched our ears in a *tauba* for forgiveness.

I lost a friend when Kevin died.

We had an instant familiarity. We were connected at some energy node, as the Buddhists would say. When Kevin asked for something, I would go out of my way to make it happen. When Kevin offered help, I took it without protest.

'You seem like the person for this,' he said. 'Happy to help. Let me know?' I said.

We were on a work phone when work phones from Alcatel-Lucent were a thing. They took up a lot of space and interrupted your thoughts. I didn't mind his call. Not because he was tall and handsome and smart and a fixer, but because of that energy-node thing.

'You see I have a special friend,' he said. 'Okay,' I said encouragingly.

'She collects the book *The Little Prince*.'

I let him go on. I thought this white person was different. He was not like the other American rejects they dumped on the dark and dark brown continents of the world.

'But here's the catch. It's a famous book, I could get the English version anywhere.'

'Okay. You need the translation in Urdu?' I asked. 'Bingo,' he said.

'She collects them in every language?' I asked.

'She has it in almost all the languages, except Urdu and maybe a few more,' he said.

This news, this piece of heaven, that someone was so in love with a certain masterpiece of literature that they collected it in every language was like feeding a rat alfalfa. I had arrived because I was chosen by Kevin for this task.

I found Kevin the book after about half a year and presented it to him on one of his trips to Islamabad from Washington, and the joy on his face was worth every bit of trouble.

He paid me for it. I accepted the money. I didn't insist. I knew what it meant to him from his very private smile.

It took me many calls and follow-ups with the textbook board. I had to go all the way to the minister via journalists. I had to make personal trips to Urdu Bazar in Lahore and choke on sawdust.

It was on my to-do list almost every month—follow up with Ashfaq from Vanguard Books; follow up with the hawker in Karachi who I was told had a supply of the last print edition. I knew it was next to impossible to find it, but I also knew that in Pakistan, you had to keep at it. Along the chains of my phone calls and visits, I told everyone about Kevin and how his special friend had the book in every language and wanted it in Urdu to complete her collection. Almost everyone I shared this story with lit up just like I had, understood the magic it brought, and promised to let me know as soon as they found it. We had a network of eight to nine people, rich and poor, readers and non-readers, publishers and politicians, all equally invested in Kevin's personal passions.

We all found him the book.

The next task on my to-do list was: thank everyone who tried but couldn't find it.

I wonder what made me Kevin's person in Pakistan.

Maybe because he, Yasser and I got along. We showed him around. Maybe it was the book. Maybe it was my work.

Kevin was the first boss or supervisor with whom I had a comfort level that I'd never had before with a man in power.

He was Kevin before he was anything else.

In our fifth year of knowing each other, after I had moved on to another position, we went out to our favourite restaurant, Tiger Temple. Just us. Yasser was at Harvard doing his human rights fellowship and burning a hole in our collective savings and in our marriage.

'What's the agenda?' I asked.

'I want to pick your brain about something,' he said.

I had sent him a picture of his guard's house to let him know I'd arrived to pick him up. I had set the passenger car seat as far back as possible. What was he, six feet something? I still had the freshener he had bought when I had asked him and Yasser not to smoke in my car.

I thought I would remind him that I hadn't parted with it even after years of losing its intended purpose.

He sat in the car. He smelt good. I noticed myself noticing. Kevin was also the first man whose sexual prowess was unimportant. It just never factored in. He was not platonic, he very much had a sexual pulse, but there was a strange quality of friendship, undefined friendship, that trumped it all. 'I want to pick your brain too,' I said.

'Agenda?' he said, mimicking me and also trying to move the car seat further back and failing.

'How do you and Verdana keep close when you are so distant? She in Washington and you here in Bumblefuck Pakistan? How do you deal with the time difference and the indifference that creeps into long-term marriages?'

Unlike me, he was a thoughtful man, so he gave it a few moments before answering.

'We watch the same TV shows and then compare notes,' he said.

'It's not about the shows, yeah?' I asked glancing at him and also keeping my eye on the road.

'No, it's not about the shows, it's about finding it in you to cultivate something in common to talk about other than the kids. We don't miss our call. When we say we will call, we call,' he said.

'What else?' I asked.

Without telling Kevin I was sad, I told Kevin I was sad. I did this by asking him to tell me how he saves his marriage.

I was sad beyond the typical South Asian Bollywood sad. I missed Yasser from my spleen. The kids called me pathetic. They saw me, day after day, just lying on his side of the bed in a foetal position, hugging his pillow and crying into it with muffled hiccups. I knew it was a huge mistake to let him go to Harvard only two months after his surgery recovery. It was too much for a young family to endure without any help. But I was trying to give him a legacy, something to live for. And fellowships didn't come every day. Besides, I wanted the kids to know that one of their parents had something to do with Harvard. For all those reasons and more, I let him go. I found him a place, I dropped him off, I said goodbye. But I knew you can do the right thing and it can still be the wrong thing to do.

Kevin fixed everything. Maybe he could fix this too.

'Find something to talk about besides the kids, something that makes both of you show up for the other,' he said.

'Don't you need the other person to show up too?' I asked. 'What do you think?' he asked.

I nodded.

When I had called Yasser in the US, his morning and my evening, he had sounded exuberant—like my once San Jose boy. Back when he loved me, he had sounded like this.

It had unnerved me to hear that in his tone. I had felt out of control. I wanted him to be happy of course. But I wanted him to be happy on my terms and because of me. After all, I was happy on his terms, working hard for his family while he was away.

Why was he happy without me?

'He doesn't show up for me,' I said.

We had reached Tiger Temple.

Even Kevin couldn't solve that for me. That's not a time-zone problem. It was not something a TV show could fix. That was plain old loneliness.

We ordered green curry with prawns and Diet Cokes with ice.

Dumplings, of course. 'Your turn,' I said.

'Feminism. This thing of why men are like this towards women. I want to understand it,' he said.

'Ask away,' I said.

Between the food, the chopsticks, and my mouth and his, we discussed how men hate women. I told Kevin that the war against women was real, it came from socialization, from an inadequate distribution of wealth and status and, of course, from mommy-daddy issues. We talked about the role of women, and we talked about why women don't hold the abuser responsible. We talked about the fact that the hate was not imaginary, but real, because men had to give up power that protected them from accountability and bad behaviour. They wanted impunity and, now and again, there was a call for justice, even in the petty domestics of life, like who would take the trash out. Up till now it was an intellectual discussion. Then it got real.

'You know how you hate certain men?' he said.

'Ya,' I said instantly because I was not thoughtful like him. 'I used to be those men,' he said.

I looked at him, hiding my disbelief by chewing away, sipping to contain my gulp.

'I was terrible to the women in my life,' he said. 'And I see everything you are saying as an understanding of why I did what I did. Entitlement. Pride. Impunity,' he added.

I dismissed this information because Kevin was a friend. If he were a man I had to hate, I would have to forget him. 'It is sad to forget a friend. Not everyone has a friend.'

Kevin was the only person who was nice to me without wanting something in return.

When I last saw him for an assignment, he was coughing like he had lung cancer.

I said in my silly childish way: 'Why are you coughing like you have lung cancer?'

When I heard Kevin died, the first thing I remembered was that he never misbehaved with women in the workplace.

I stared at my phone shocked.

He knew all along. He was working crazy long hours to save for his son's tuition, he said.

He was apart from Verdana because Pakistan's hardship allowance helped pay the university fee off.

He had given me a look when I had joked his cough sounded like lung cancer.

He told me he had been shit to women all his life because he was contemplating his actions at the end of it all.

He knew.

I didn't know.

I saw Verdana put up Facebook pictures of his tired bony hands in the hospital. I sent her my condolences. I told her what she meant to him. What their son meant to him.

I didn't tell her what Kevin meant to me, lest she interprets our friendship a certain way.

I didn't mention *The Little Prince* book to her.

Yasser held me for hours as I cried for Kevin. He understood my pain. Few men liked me enough not to hurt me, even though he may have been mean to other women. Yasser knew that Kevin sharpened my sense of belonging to family without taking anything from me in return. Yasser held me gently and rocked me. He let me cry.

Yasser kissed the top of my forehead and said sorry to me over and over again.

CORRUPT CONSULTANT: FINALLY ON THE OTHER SIDE OF BROKE-TOWN

Work has taken me places.

I'd gone to Khyber Pakhtunkhwa, four hours outside Peshawar, to write up some stories about the UK government funding that helped community schools. This was a makeshift school in a remote area that served to bring literacy numbers up in a village where there wouldn't have been any education otherwise.

I arrived tired. I was told I didn't need a *burkah*, but that the area was conservative enough to need me to wrap myself up with a large white *chador*. I felt a bit white, an outsider looking in, a peeping Tom into the culture of my own people, but they were more foreign to me than swallowing plastic and expecting it to digest.

The name Sarwari comes from a tribe in Sarwar, Afghanistan. We are, if Papa is to be believed, Afghan Pathans originally, who then migrated to Ajmer and then to Karachi. These were maybe my people, but after several generations, they were stranger than white people.

I am an in-between myself—stuck between the worst of the Afghan Pathans and the white Americans.

When asked to veil, I had a visceral reaction, like a caged animal that finally comes face to face with the prey. I wanted to shred it.

I wanted hair and wind married to each other.

There was a new supervisor at work called Amal. She was younger than me, which I was naturally resentful about but she put performance pressure on me by always hanging out with the cool kids, which meant the white kids from the UK: Adam, Monty and David. Amal was the only brown girl who got to hang out with them at restaurants on lunch breaks. I was not invited, although I felt I was a better fit with them.

It irked me that she had a better name and a better attitude. She was closed off. She was stand-offish and would prefer to give me monosyllabic answers and speak only at me, instead of with me.

'Can you come here?' Amal said. Then she walked into the next room and sat at a table.

I followed her like a puppy. 'Sure,' I said.

It didn't matter if I grunted instead of saying that. She made me obey.

'What are you working on?' she asked.

I told her about the roadmap I was asked to deliver on. 'That won't do,' she said.

'Sorry?' I said.

'You need to be in the field,' she said.

'I'd love to but that wasn't part of the communications strategy we agreed on,' I said.

'The strategy is no longer valid,' she said.

'Has that been agreed upon?' I asked. I wanted to put up a challenge. She was taking me to be a clerk.

'Tomorrow, go to these locations after checking with the district education officers and get some beneficiary stories. I will need about seven when you return,' she said.

Muttering under my breath, I asked her follow-up questions to look interested in this very boring task. She answered in monotone monosyllables.

So here I was, in my white chador, stepping into the home of a schoolteacher at a community school. It was a dark and dingy hut and I stepped right into a pile of cow crap.

I still remember its crusty top and its gooey, soft, warm inside.

The cow was in the house, co-living with humans in their living room.

I stayed in the dung for a good minute or so before the hosts spoke in Hindi and laughed at me.

TECH GLITCH: CAN YOU TRY SWITCHING IT OFF AND ON AGAIN

If Hassan Rahman was the Davos Man, then Adil Sheikh was the Davos big tech, in the full glory of the role of lying to the world to sell goods that are necessary for humanity to succeed. Adil was fond of saying three things: I will give you a C minus for your performance. I think you need to understand how commercial works. You need to stop being an NGO aunty.

The last part he said to me when I pushed for more funding in education technology. 'You know you always come to me for things that will make the company drain money,' he would say.

When I wanted to confront Adil's bullying, I would walk to the third floor of the wonderfully corporate building, because I couldn't let anyone know how much he got under my skin. Instead of turning right towards his cubicle, I'd turn left towards the ladies' room and weep like a five-year-old against the unsanitized wall of the bathroom stall, just so I couldn't appear weak in front of a man whose main objective was to tear me down.

In my first interview with him, I thought things went well, we chatted casually, and I felt we hit it off, professionally speaking.

He didn't appear intimidating. His voice was like that of Director General 1, but he made up for the tenor by his modern CEO looks—always a white shirt and blue jeans with a very expensive-looking pair of shoes. I wasn't one to make up my mind about these powerful men in one interaction, so I withheld any judgement, except some phenotypic observations. But for Adil, the conclusions were made and the report card was delivered in detail to my boss. You see, Adil wasn't my boss but he liked to play boss. He told my line manager, Ali Naseer, that I had a long way to go to understand corporate and the way things were done there. He also told Ali that I would have to be 'handheld' throughout before I made any 'blunders'.

'Handheld?' I repeated to Ali. I felt like a 1980s camcorder. Handheld.

Still, I was adamant to not form an opinion about Adil. He was well respected and well liked, and modern CEOs like him had their work cut out for them. They were the lone brown people in a global board of white men who often second-guessed them. I would change his mind. If anyone knows one thing about me, it is the fact that I am self-motivated. If there is no work, I generate it. No one needs to hold my hand. Steering, yes. I would need steering. But that was what Ali was there for.

I was in tears during my first annual performance review. I had burnt myself out with thirteen-hour workdays. Five ministers had come to events I had arranged on behalf of the company. And in all five, they had praised the company before the press conference. That was a win in any context for one year.

But no. Ali told me I was too fast.

'Too fast?' I asked Ali. I was bewildered.

'Well, people have complained in the 360-degree evaluation that you come up with the idea and the next week when they expect you to work closely with their input, the job is done and dusted.'

'How is that a problem in an agile environment?' I persisted. 'And wouldn't I be downgraded if I waited for consensus and delivered things later than they needed to be?'

'Contrary,' said Ali. 'People will forget what you do, but they will remember how you made them feel,' he said, paraphrasing Maya Angelou.

'So, I'm supposed to slow down,' I said. 'Yes. Please slow down.'

So, after three such take-downs by Ali, I was beyond bewildered. I had failed. He gave me an ME evaluation, which meant that I had barely managed to meet expectations, never mind exceed them. If I was sized up to be handheld, and I worked so hard against that stereotype, how in the world was I being penalized for being fast?

And where was my feedback on the feedback? I thought it was 360 degrees.

Tears started falling out when his tone grew softer and he said, 'I know you are going through a lot on the personal front with Yasser.'

I felt that I had failed to keep my personal life from flowing into my professional life, whereas previously, these were two airtight compartments. He was right. Yasser had become terribly unmanageable that first year of jazz. There were way too many tantrums. I lost his earphones and he almost dumped me for that. He called at work and screamed into the phone while colleagues could hear. He would constantly hound me to talk to his mother when I was at an age where I wasn't going to hold polite conversation with anyone who had crossed me. The girls were teenagers—mornings were tough, they refused to go to school, or their PMS days led to communication breakdowns or they were generally distressed because they were growing up indoors in Pakistan. The house we lived in was too old and too porous, and I just didn't have a moment's peace to myself.

I guess I let that insanity cloud my judgement.

After I was done crying, he became less curt. Even though he seemed generally unfazed by the tears.

He said, everything I do has way too much effort in it. I work against the force and it destabilizes the ecosystem. That I should work effortlessly.

'There is a force within companies, work within it and work as if it comes naturally to you. Like if you don't do it, the world won't come crashing on your head. Your team of seven is scrambling about just like you, working hard and making everyone around feel like yours is the only department upon whose shoulders the reputation of the company rests. It has to be easy,' he said.

I nodded.

I wanted to say the department was literally in charge of all public and internal communications, crisis management, and yes, the reputation did rest upon its shoulders, and the team worked so hard because that was the only currency one should trade in— effort. All of this was supremely counterintuitive.

Adil was not as diplomatic as Ali.

Early on, I wrote him a long SMS from the bathroom stall. Something to the effect of my intellectual honesty and my need to only work for people who wanted me to work for them. I gave him full permission to ask me to leave.

He wrote back immediately saying that I had misunderstood him and that no 'overreaction was necessary'.

'Let's have coffee and talk it over,' he added.

Sometimes I would let him know what I thought about his misplaced questions. I explained to him that he was signing off on legacy programmes and I would remind him, 'I didn't sign up for them, you did.'

I also explained to him that the world had changed. In the new corporate universe, people and planet also mattered, not just profit. And no, I was not an NGO aunty, the new world order for corporates was all environmental, social and governance—focused, so sustainability was a critical leadership agenda that he must drive. Besides my title was communication and sustainability director. Directors were not C-suite, and if he wanted to change direction on the department he could do it, not me—it was above my pay grade.

But sometimes it was a magical showdown between the corporate powerhouse of Pakistan and me—a soon to be perimenopausal woman who cleaned up well enough to look as young as an intern.

Maybe it was simpler. I was on the wrong anti-depression medication.

I had just changed my selective serotonin reuptake inhibitor medication. This one made me have zero inhibitions.

Unaware of this new Aisha, Adil called me into a boardroom discussion to roll back the work we did in the Khyber Pakhtunkhwa province and de-fund the incubation centres. These centres were the only way women in remote areas could have access to start-up capital and education.

Naturally, I resisted it on three counts: One, why fix something that wasn't broken; two, the return on investment was high, it was a drop in the bucket for MY budget and we got to publish wonderful stories on how the firm was transforming lives; three, it achieved four of our Sustainable Development Goals targets that we reported back to global and they loved this stuff.

The board meeting ended with some back and forth which I paid no heed to, but then Adil called me for a one-to-one discussion the same afternoon, looking rather upset. He then said the unforgettable words of my career: Don't ever give me feedback again.

'Pardon?' I said.

He said it again slowly.

'I don't appreciate you giving me feedback. Especially in front of others.'

I tilted my head right.

'You mean to say the head of communications should not give the chief executive any feedback?' I said.

He considered the stupidity of his edict with an inward sucking motion.

'Yes. You will never give me any feedback,' he said.

His anger was, for the second time, now spilling on the small round table before us. The three glass doors around us were making our fight visible to the entire executive floor. One wall opened to a clear blue sky and the Faisal Mosque poked out of the greenest Islamabad.

'Let me get this straight,' I said, crossing my arms in front of me, unfazed by now, thanks to the new medication.

'So, you want me to be your personal blow-up doll,' I said. He opened his mouth and closed it several times and I let him. 'Sure. I don't mind,' I said as I stood up, leaned closer to his very now-crimson ear and whispered: 'But first, you'll have to contact HR and change my job description for that.'

'Thankfully we work in an organization, not a top-heavy company,' I mumbled on my way out.

I walked out, closing the glass door behind me, but it had a loose hinge that ended up making a colossally large bang. Loud enough for everyone to turn around and see my aggression, Adil's anger and my nonchalant walk back to my desk on the ground floor.

Adil had asked me several times to sit next to him on his floor. I didn't do that because he wasn't my boss, just my boss's boss. There was a structure to things, and it wasn't up to me to obey people's whims, regardless of how much power they had. In my head, I took instructions from my boss.

When I refused to sit on the same floor despite many reminders, I suppose Adil felt rejected. He thought I was one insubordinate low life who didn't understand corporate leadership at all.

I knew that he had an immature side to him and didn't understand that structures protected leaders more than they protected worker bees like me. I could obey him and sit next to him but three things would happen. People who were slotted to sit next to him would wonder what I had done to deserve the perk. My boss would wonder downstairs why I wasn't at work and my team would do whatever the heck they wanted. So, no thanks. I'd been slut-shamed at work before, and I wasn't going to let it happen again.

Adil hated me. My own boss felt I was ahead of myself. The people around me were obviously bitching about me working like a lead consultant instead of a team player. All my friends were gone.

TROUBLE COMES IN THREES

Adil's wrath was upon me at work. Ali stepped out of the supervisor role into a bigger one and left me hanging. Worse, I reported directly to Adil now.

It was at this time that my friend Tehreem and I had a falling out.

Yasser's tumour was recurring slowly and in a sinister way, like a quiet leech.

All my universes collided, Adil, Tehreem and Yasser. All three relegated me to being unworthy. I wasn't the person they wanted in the room.

Tehreem had had a fight with Yasser on Twitter about Nadim, another Amreeka-returned person. Yasser had pointed out that Nadim tended to change his views about democracy depending on who was funding him. Tehreem was Nadim's friend, and she found Yasser's tweets obnoxious, so she decided to tweet him directly, calling him a bully and a terrorist for getting people to stand back from their views.

I was often shamed on public forums for being Yasser's wife because his online conduct was embarrassing and rude.

So, her attack on Yasser, especially when she knew that he was mentally compromised, felt like an attack on me.

It felt like an attack because friends are aware of your context. I felt attacked because her jab was also on my loneliness of being in the life I was in—working full-time for money that hardly allowed me to be comfortable and not having any family in Pakistan. It was also an attack on Tehreem for being the only person who connected me to my life before Yasser, before Pakistan, before kids, before brain tumours, before heart tantrums.

Yasser, being a hot-blooded Punjabi, asked me to immediately unfriend Tehreem.

I remember putting my hands together for him to not do this. My pride didn't matter. All I knew was that I couldn't live without Tehreem in my life, in my life's inner circle. No matter how you looked at it, she knew exactly how to get me out of a bad situation. She felt all-powerful to me. I needed her to breathe. She knew who I was when I didn't.

Please don't. I begged.

It was very late at night. I was on my laptop doing what Ali Nasser had told me not to do. I was finishing off a report and responding to emails.

'Yasser, calm down please. This needs to be talked about,' I said.

'No,' he yelled. 'I've had enough of her.'

In fairness, Tehreem had always disliked Yasser. The tussle started at my wedding when Tehreem took off Yasser's car's rims because he wouldn't pay her 20,000 rupees. Yasser ended up walking the entire baraat on foot until Bhaijan and Bhai intervened. Her personality was so strong that it made up for a lot, but around him she was still combative. Despite cordial interactions and jokes at parties, Yasser and Tehreem had an underlying animosity. I would remind them both that I loved them and settle the broken pieces back together again.

When Yasser said he had had enough of her, he meant he had had enough of the ongoing feud that he thought he tolerated because of me when he really didn't need to, but now it had suddenly become a declaration of war after her public tweet.

Tehreem's tweet was all too painful for me. It got several likes and retweets. That broke my heart. Of course, people loved that she had, as a Yasser–Aisha ally, taken on Yasser's bad behaviour. I was socially ostracized; I felt it acutely at least in my own head. Everyone knew we were best friends; she didn't need to go at my husband so openly. It was drama for the tiny Twitterati community in Pakistan that thrived on the hero–villain–victim simplicity of the theatre before them. My life in full display like that was shameful and hurtful. The first stone had been struck by Tehreem.

Why would she do that to me? To a decade-old friendship that was integrated enough in each other's families? Everyone knew to hurt Tehreem was to hurt me. Her ex-boyfriends knew that. Her family knew that. My kids knew that. But it worked for Yasser too. Yasser sort of had the same importance for me as Tehreem did. He was the father of my kids, the man who unwaveringly stood by me when I didn't have anyone. I chose him. Just as I chose her. What was beautiful about both of my people was that they often chose me back.

It was beside the point that sometimes he was the cause of my anguish. But that was privileged information that only I had a right to act on. No one else with access to that information should define either him or me by it.

That information certainly had no place on a vile platform like Twitter.

I was mad at Tehreem too but unfriending her was never something I would dare do. She was the only lifeline I had. People had told me they found Tehreem awkward. They didn't know the

Tehreem I knew. They didn't know how she had rescued me in more ways than one. Tehreem was my mom, my sister, my friend and my co-criminal all at once. I was a mom to Tehreem, a sister, a friend and a co-criminal. She and I had debates on power, on quotas, on the equations of life and how to keep harm away. I was abstract and she was specific. Together there were many, many years of love and laughter. Until Tehreem had become my friend, there had been no numbers on my speed dial. Without Tehreem, there was no one to complain to. Asking to unfriend her meant that I would stand alone in a very hostile world.

We had our *halva puri* traditions where we spoke about wanting to settle down with men and simultaneously leave them. She and I were at different poles of our life stages, but we were seared at the ages we knew each other as roommates in Washington, DC—twenty-two and twenty.

Tehreem shaped me into the woman I was because she told me that it was possible to live by straddling two identities—Pakistani and American. She was doing that when the women I knew didn't even care about identity politics. Tehreem cared about Pakistan. Something gnawed at her like it did at me. You want something, you don't have to wait for you to want it back.

There was a confidence there, grounded in knowing.

She spoke of both countries with the intellectual prowess of a think-tank CEO, yet she was such a girl. Fond of her sleeveless Western–Eastern clothes and calling a dupatta a *duHphattHa* was adorable and statement enough.

They called her ABCD—an American-Born Confused Desi—I called her Taz, and she called me Aish. I didn't need anything else with her there.

Letting her go because my husband said so was a hard thing to do. I didn't like begging but I begged.

'Please don't, Yasser,' I said.

'Now! Take her off from everywhere now,' he yelled back at my artificially calm tone.

I knew that when Yasser was in his state, there was no winning. I had tried long enough for them to carry each other along, but now, without either of them putting me first, it was not going to work.

I messaged Tehreem on a WhatsApp group of the three of us, Dee, Tehreem and me.

I messaged on the group, 'You have no idea what relationships take.'

Then I left the group. I unfriended her on Facebook and Instagram.

I blocked her where I needed to and showed my dearest sick husband the screenshots of a Tehreem no more. It didn't give him solace. He went on and on about the betrayal he felt from me and from her. He was her friend too.

I went on working. I finished what I needed to. I went to sleep after giving Yasser his medication. I went to sleep after Yasser was snoring. I went to sleep but the new medication wouldn't let me. I stayed awake that night looking at the ceiling fan spinning.

After a few months of this impasse, after we tried to patch up, Tehreem had another fight with me about my decision to unfriend her on Facebook. We sat in her home in leafy Islamabad, on her cushy sofa, with her cute terrier, and her tray with nuts and crackers.

There was an air of hostility that I understood.

I explained that Yasser made me unfriend her because she took him on so publicly, despite everyone knowing she and I were best friends. It wasn't a Pakistani thing to do. You just didn't attack your brother-in-law, without the fear of alienating your sister-friend. It was just a cultural no-no.

'You chose a man over me,' she said. She was spiteful and angry. 'He's not just my boyfriend. He is my husband, there is a difference,' I said.

'Weren't individual rights everything you stood for?' she said.

'It is everything I stand for, Tehreem, but this man isn't well. That complicates things,' I said.

'You look at Yasser as if Yasser can do no harm. You are so blind when it comes to him,' she said.

'That's not true, Taz, and you know I've been as fair as I can,' I said.

'He is a bully,' she said.

I stood up. Her anger was very visceral. I was trying not to fight. It had taken many months to reconcile. Yasser had apologized to both me and her. She had said sorry to me but more for the mess than for the principle.

Tehreem's home was always a sanctuary for me but that was changing—the moment was hostile.

'I think I should go,' I said.

She stood up too, confirming the fact that I wasn't welcome in her home. I was welcome only if I was also looking at Yasser as a villain, just like she was sure he was.

But I had just nursed Yasser during his brain tumour, his pain, his needle trauma, the fear of his skull being sawed while he lay awake, calling my name. I had experienced his pain and he had pulled back into life because of that. I knew for a fact that my presence buoyed Yasser to health, and I wasn't ready to hate him. It was necessary, but it was too early.

It was going to be hard for me to see him as anything but a victim. He was battling his mortality, and every culture, modern or not, gave room for a woman to grapple with the gnawing everyday feeling of the death of a spouse. Literature makes room for it. Politics too. Even cold hard science.

It wasn't easy for me to have normal feelings towards a man who was going to die. It was all the more complex if that man happened to be *mera pyar*, my love, *mera katil*, my killer, *mera humsafar*, my companion, *meri vehshat*, my terror.

Tehreem demanded from me the clarity of a sage.

I was a hot mess. I gave Yasser the strength to wake up and take his meds and not yell too loudly for the neighbours to hear, and I gave him my shoulder to nuzzle into. Yes, that gave me power. His needing me gave me power. I am not ashamed to say that I wanted him to need me; I never wanted it to stop because I didn't know who I would be if it did.

Certainly Adil wasn't dependable. He was just a boss who occasionally crushed my spirit with acid. So blame me for wanting the only man in my life to need me, even if it was for fetching water for medicines.

I was teeny-tiny pieces of nothingness. Tehreem wanted me to be the illuminating sun.

We were both yelling as we walked out into her garden, where she had planted a bamboo forest to feel like she belonged in Pakistan. She was yelling at me to see things in Yasser that were rotten to the core—the terrorism, the hypocrisy and the dysfunction. I was yelling at her to see that it was not his fault. For all the talk of mental health stigma, no one sticks around when mental health presents itself in its non-sexy form—the terrorism, the hypocrisy and the dysfunction.

I screamed at her for the first time in our friendship: 'Yasser cannot even understand what he needs to survive day to day. That this man is just throwing punches to be relevant to a debate he is wedded to. Can't you see it as a cry for help instead?'

'I just don't like him,' she yelled back at my face and turned away from me.

I broke down.

I said from the goo in my throat: 'Then just wait.' 'I don't like him at all!' she said.

'Then wait for him to die so we can be perfectly happy again,' I yelled back.

I left the bamboo garden. I left her home, which she always opened to me lovingly. I left the third thing I loved so dearly, outside work and Yasser. I walked into nothingness.

People announce times and dates of death: I think mine was that day in the bamboo garden. I learnt that when people you love don't love you back, you die.

She had laid down terms—You, sad friend, you be a widow so I can love you again.

I had laid down mine—You, sad friend, will always be bound by what I feel for Yasser to accept me.

Right then, with Tehreem attacking Yasser like that, I felt like she was attacking me. That too, attacking me with a stick blender right into my navel, slicing through my tail bone, destroying both my sense of belonging and everything I ever felt towards friendship.

Over the years, Tehreem and I tried again and again like star-crossed lovers to make good after what happened that day. She gave me gifts that were so thoughtful and loving. She gave me the same house to live in to write this book, away from the stresses of work and home. She sent me lovely silky blindfolds, lacy underwear, earthquake alarms. I sent her words that told her how empty it was to move ahead in the world without her.

In our last fallout she accused me of being retrogressive because I sent her a red wedding dupatta for her wedding and my wedding head *tikka*. That piece of jewellery is a family heirloom. She had a western wedding with only close family in DC. I sent her what I sent her because I loved the idea of tradition and thought she may miss something desi.

She said it reeked of anti-feminist sentiment. 'You do know what red symbolizes?' she said. 'But that is not what I sent you that for,' I said.

'What could you possibly have sent me a red dupatta for?' she said.

'I honestly thought you'd frame it or something. It's only ethnic. It's only a colour in the colour wheel,' I said.

'I didn't even wear white on my wedding. And you sent me a red dupatta,' she said.

'I sent you that because I would send that to my sister,' I said.

But my words hit hollowness. Our friendship had outgrown us. We were different people. Perhaps we were both right. Perhaps she was totally justified in seeing me as a victim of a violent villain who turned poor old souls into oblivion. A victim who was so far gone, calling herself a feminist on the one hand and on the other celebrating the horror show that desi brides are.

The second-last fight we had was because she gave me her place for a week when I left Adil's job for a new one.

She had employed a young man called Sarfaraz as a house manager, who strode right into the house and I felt rather violated. When I complained to her that he had no boundaries, even if this was her home, she disagreed. She felt I wanted control. It was petty. I was petty. By then, we had both had enough.

We tried again at some future point.

At that time, Tahreem slut-shamed me. I said as I often did that I had the hots for a guy we both knew, and she sighed and said—why don't you just let him be happy.

I was playful. But even if I wasn't, I was appalled at the judgement from someone who walked me through my most intimate moments.

'What's that supposed to mean?' I said.

'I mean what I said, let him be happy,' she said.

I was in the mood for a fight so I said, 'Please break this conversation down. I am responsible for this man's happiness?'

'You know what I mean,' she said. 'No, tell me what you mean,' I said.

'I mean if you make moves, he will slip,' she said. 'Okay so, then that's on me and not the man,' I said. 'No man stands a chance with you, Aisha,' she said.

'Assuming that's true, his saying yes to me is also on me? That sounds like slut-shaming,' I said.

'People talk, Aish. These men say things about you,' she said. 'You've been in the US for two years now, Taz, how do you know how men slut-shame me,' I said.

'I'm just saying that these are sick men and they say things about you,' she said.

'Of course. I am said to sleep my way up, right. But when did my talking to my friend about a crush turn into my needing a nanny dressing-down on my conduct?' I said.

'I just don't want you hurt,' she said.

'I don't appreciate the stereotype,' I said. 'It's up to you,' she said.

'Let him be happy is a very loaded sentence. Could it be because you are newly married? I don't remember you having this stance before, or living by it for that matter,' I said.

'Well, I was wrong. I admit it,' she said. 'Well, that's super convenient,' I said.

'Fuck off out of my life. I don't have these beliefs just because I'm married. I have them because I don't want you hurt,' she said.

She continued, 'People talk about you being unhinged. These men are judgemental and old.'

'Your point is that I should live my life based on their standard,' I said. 'I'm tired of everything being about you. I don't need this in my life,' she said.

'Fine,' I said.

'This time let's not try again,' I said. 'Let's not,' she said.

I dove back into my last few days of work and everything felt like it was ending. I just couldn't restore trust with three primary relationships, my boss, my best friend and my San Jose Yasser.

We became ourselves more and more each passing day, further and further from a functional relationship, one with decency and kindness in it.

From these three relationships all I was left with was an employee certificate from the boss, a mulberry silk blindfold from my best friend and a wooden lioness figurine from my husband. They are like relics from a past life that I gave my all to.

OFFICES ARE NOT HOMES

I couldn't move. I couldn't even roll over to get out of bed. There was a problem with my bones. Or perhaps it was my nerves. I had decided to go to work but my body had decided to quit. Of all the obstacles standing between me holding a job steady, I didn't ever think my body would be one.

While I was bedridden for almost a month, Yasser was also having the worst time of his life; socially he was becoming a pariah.

People on Twitter called him a lower court's manhole—'*lower court ka dhakkan*'. They were taking the piss at his innate inability to walk away from a fight. To be fair, he called people personal names they would never forget. Often, he would insult people with an accurate description of their family's moral standing, and they would come back at him with all the power of Lahori elite classism, bigotry and ableism. They hurt him where it hurts—the pride of being good at his job.

Consequently, it hurt me too. Invalidating Yasser invalidated me, like we had this collective reputation. People tagged me in his insults, but, more importantly, you were only worth something if you were loyal. Yasser was a disrupter. He shook things up relentlessly with his rage, often rightfully so. Yet, I found myself wishing for some restorative time to live life mundanely.

No coincidence that Yasser's worse days often coincided with my worst days. He was like a big, grand old oak under whose shade I just couldn't grow. He was part brilliant, galvanizing, accurate and morally sound in his law, and part crippling in his ability to take me along in his cause. He was bitter like an old man when all I wanted was the boy from San Jose to like me truly, madly, deeply.

So when the world turned on him, I did too.

He had a terrible connection with others. In fact, almost all his interactions turned ugly at one point with little room for repair in relationships. Yasser had many admirers and a few friends; people were either enamoured by him or just apathetic. I also knew that Yasser struggled with something unnamable. Now we call it being autistic, having a tinge of Asperger's, having a low emotional quotient or being a bad people-person. Back then they called it 'lower court ka dhakkan'. This left him terribly insecure. It left me without a capacity to cure him.

Not knowing what led to public scandals and cyberbullying made it very hard for me to make sense of it all. My body was simply revolting because the external environment was larger than my internal skill set. I didn't know you could die from social condemnation, but I think that was what was happening when I turned stiff.

We both knew something was terribly off. Yet, we both remained wedded to the silence of never divulging the likelihood of a medical problem. While I was using crazy as a slur, I didn't think it could be as real as the sky over my head.

Many a time, instead of thinking there could be a tumour growing in Yasser's brain circa 1999, I'd yell at him to take his pills. That he needed a damn shrink. That he was messed up. Insane. Mad. I seethed and called him a *pagal kutta*, a mad dog.

He would come back at me with the same words—he would say I was just like the trolls on the Internet, taking him down instead of propping him up.

I was sick of moving cities, running like a *pagal kutti* myself with the mortal fear of losing jobs. There was always a distinct possibility that I'd be fired again because of my own state of upheaval. I was so afraid of going to work in the mornings, making myself tea, knowing that I'd be asked to leave that very day. Yet, every single day I showed up. Until my body turned into a cold, unmovable horizontal corpse.

My work fears took me back to my childhood nightmare about that unwell Ugandan woman who would parade the streets naked and very pregnant. Being laughed at and schemed against without having the power to fight it sent me spinning.

Not knowing what was wrong with Yasser was not limited to his underlying medical condition of a brain tumour. It was also not knowing if he believed that I was subservient to him and that it was okay to hurt me.

Over time, Yasser's salary and mine started becoming lopsided, like one smaller lazy eye.

I became a statistic. Most marriages don't survive the woman's higher pay.

Yasser started being angsty with me, asking me weird questions like—don't you think you've started behaving like a man when you come back home from work?

I often got dictates from my in-laws about not forgetting that home came first, to get back home in time to cook. Yasser would defend me fiercely against that kind of talk, but as we walked further and further away from being a two-income household and got closer and closer to being a woman-led household, those put-downs from the in-laws went unchecked.

Yasser would not just look the other way, he would expect me to keep peace by appeasing his upset parents.

Of course, it was unfair, and it felt unfair, but the joy of not knowing also absolves you from not having Stockholm syndrome. My time away from home became a ticking time bomb. It was less frightening if I was upsetting my boss than if I was upsetting my mother-in-law. Yasser's ami called my ami often to say:

'Aisha thinks money is everything. Tell your daughter to respect her elders. She doesn't listen to me. Just because she is an officer, she thinks she can take that tone with me. Why didn't you teach her any manners?'

One bad day, and she would call my ami and my bhai and crib to them, and my family would ask me to get back in line. The fact was that, after such an exchange between my ami and Yasser's ami, my ami would not leave the musalla prayer mat for half a year, praying that my life would get easier, that I would be loved by my mother-in-law and that my home would be happy and peaceful.

Listening to my ami worry about me wounded me. It reminded me of all the bruises she had experienced in her life and how the whole purpose of marrying far, far away was to spare her the pain. Ami got one call from Yasser's ami and Uganda's struggle reel would play on repeat in the nightmares right behind my eyelids.

Yasser also built this narrative somewhere after his tumour surgery that I had ruined his career. Had it not been for me dragging him across cities, he would be an established big-shot lawyer. While I defended against such hypotheticals, I knew there was an alternate world out there where I didn't take my job so seriously, and he took care of me.

Sometimes, when the girls were toddlers, I asked my boss to put in a good word for Yasser to a lawyer friend of his. I thought, given that this lawyer friend was from Yale Law School, running an American-esque firm, Yasser's hard work would shine through and soon enough he would make partner. I also did this at Yasser's request.

He had to give up a stable job in a leading telecom company to do so and shift cities—Islamabad to Lahore. He tends to forget this part; the fact that he was a willing party. After this lawyer and his equally privileged Ivy League friends chastised him for not knowing how to write, Yasser's confidence was so shattered that he came at me with the fury of a bull. I was the china store.

'You make me give everything up. You did it deliberately, didn't you? I could have been a leading lawyer in some corporate company. Now all I am is what they call me on Twitter—a lower court *ka dhakkan*. You wanted this—to see me destroyed?'

If someone would have told me that this boy, whom I had met in San Jose, would hurl such accusations at me, I'd have laughed like an evil villain. Yasser was the embodiment of liberal, secular, open, democratic values that always put individual freedom above all else. He was a rebel through and through.

I had his emails to me to back it up.

'*If I ever come between you and your freedom to live your life on your terms, show me this email.*'

Yasser's love was like a lot of zeros and ones in some bank vault for a defunct economy. This was Pakistan. What was relevant in the US, in the early stages of our courtship, was no longer relevant.

That part of my life was called blame.

I was unable to go to work for weeks. I would call in sick.

The mornings were a series of panic attacks. Panic attacks feel like your heart is a foreign body that must be expelled, while you try and convince your mind to help.

I stuck my head in the thin cotton blankets, never wanting to emerge.

I was on antidepressants, relaxants and a cocktail of painkillers, but the weight of shame drowned all of the modern antidotes to a rotting spirit. I was willing to try another day but the spleen and liver, pituitary and oesophagus were done.

If the people that I had come to Pakistan for didn't like me, accept me or nurture me, what was the point of trying to bring home a tax-eaten pay cheque?

Unknowingly, the diagnosis was made—I had a case of bad wife, bad daughter-in-law and bad mother.

I'd already been fired, so I was already a bad employee.

Nothing validated me as Yasser did. As the tumour progressed, I remained unaware that he was becoming more and more traditional, patriarchal, negligent and hateful. The domestic violence ended in year eight of the marriage, but the verbal abuse and gaslighting replaced it.

I used to ask Yasser in Punjabi, half joking, half desperate, '*Mai changi nai lagdi*, don't you like me?'

If I was lucky, he would pat me, tap-tap. If I wasn't, he would look into the distance, probably slaying his own demons, many of which grew out of his endless message board commentary addiction.

Many women cry themselves to sleep trying to be someone in a marriage where they have to reduce themselves to oblivion in order to fit into the largeness of a man's frail ego but not me. I had so much hope that the answer to the question I would often ask Yasser in Punjabi was, '*Aho*, yes.'

Until my body knew something my mind didn't—that he was no longer in love with me.

That abuse in marriage, any abuse, of any kind, of any degree, permanently removes love.

You may have care. You may even have compassion. But there will never be love in a place where you received violation after a promise of doing no harm.

My jobs may have gained from my abuse at the hands of a marriage that is designed to keep women in a constant state of chaos, because I worked harder, faster, wider, deeper and longer for years, decades even. I lost my wrists, my shoulder and my mind.

My body was constantly bracing. Peacetime was the worst.

I anticipated the next blow, the next manipulation, the next put-down, but when it didn't come, I went hunting for it, blood on my tongue.

I would pick fights with Yasser. I talked back at home. The biggest victims of my mistreatment were my children.

Desi marriages pretend to value family units but are terrible to the mothers that form them.

When you morally reject the values you stand for by showing up for the same people who oppress you at work and home, your body tells you to die off forever into the darkest pits of hellfire.

I've gone to the doctor for a black eye, broken jaw, frozen shoulder, locked jaw, migraines, depression, chronic depression, PTSD, anxiety, chronic anxiety, IBS, insomnia, fibromyalgia, night blindness, arthritis, ulcers, chronic ulcers and a vitamin-D deficiency.

I can't sleep without a pill, and I most certainly cannot go a day without the irrational fear of someone throwing a dagger of words at me and wounding me—thereby causing my children to starve.

Women cannot have a career unless their husbands permit it and live by it.

Desi women cannot have a career without emasculating their men.

An emasculated man is very dangerous.

An emasculated desi man will have impunity after he kills you.

I never really thought Yasser could kill me for going to office, but my body believed that if circumstances would make him kill me, I would get no justice.

My tombstone would read: she was a defiant, unloved woman.

When I asked Yasser the Punjabi of 'Don't you like me?', I was rooting for his pity, not his love.

I knew that I had lost the right to ask for his love when his sickness—both the tumour and his misogyny—was unknown but widely experienced.

Respect is another thing you may have. I never thought Yasser deserved to be trolled as he was after his job at that law firm, after his career became a downward trajectory of lower court appeals in his three-piece suits. I thought he was always more than his work, more than his circumstances. I always respected Yasser.

Even respect is not love.

It is only a small part of it. Zero plus zero is not one, no matter how many or how intensely the zeros present themselves. Love is defined by the absence of fear.

I was deathly afraid of Yasser.

That was the fear that propelled my career. It made me get out of the house for half the waking hours. It let me have a network. It permitted me to travel to gather myself into my body. Work allowed me to spend on the family, raise my girls and invest in my relationships.

In a way, Yasser's wrath, at the cost of my body and children's psychological safety, permitted me all-expenses-paid entry into the circus of the world where exiting was never an option—a lifetime membership to the market economy run by a bunch of rich white men.

All worthwhile things come out of fear. All futile things come out of fear.

TRUE, A HUSBAND IS A CAREER CHOICE

I was in Istanbul. Yasser had had his two surgeries and his chemo and radiotherapy, and much of his recovery was completed and mine too. Yet, the empty space that I once inhabited followed me, asking me to step in.

I was here for work. It was 2022. The pandemic wouldn't stop. It was a serial killer and the raised hand with a dagger was relentless—variant after variant.

The previous day had been dark for me. Amid the work meeting I was here for, my boss laid it out for our team of public affairs, communications and sustainability professionals from twelve countries—you've done nothing bold.

The impostor syndrome grew like a monster and because my boss Ismail sat beside me, every word felt as if it was a public performance evaluation and I had failed.

Yasser was calling, and over the years I had stopped taking his calls because they delivered either bad news or blame. So, I silence my notifications and only go to the phone if I am ready to face that part of my life. It's the deep breath I take before a walk on hot coals. Sometimes, Yasser just wants to say hi or I love you or you are poo, adoringly, and then I am unable to snap out of my coal-walk preparation.

I was expecting a 'hello, poo' when I called him back, but he was enraged. His tone, the same caustic entitlement. His sleeper chootiya awake and kicking again.

'Slow down.'

'I don't understand—why would you do that to me?' 'Dial it back. What did I do?'

'I told you to give me your bank statements for the UK visa application.'

'Yes, so?'

'You didn't do that. Why would you do that?'

'You asked me while I was on my way to the airport. Can you take responsibility for that?'

'Why would you not take it seriously?'

'Before I boarded the flight, I signed on a blank piece of paper for the accountant's authorization to get you what you wanted. That was very serious given the last-minute request.'

My tone was bureaucratic, his full of his tantrum voice. 'Well, congratulations, because he got me the statement from a bank that you use for petty cash.'

'Then you should have given him clear instructions to take the statement from the salary account.'

'I think you are just hiding your finances from me.'

I drew my breath in. I hated it when I answered his call to do the 'What's up, poo' talk and it turned out to be a coal walk. In twenty years I've been incapable of predicting which will be which and how I can save myself from the shock of deep sadness. My body intelligence fails me, my clairvoyance fails me, my love fails me. I should have known that Yasser gets very feral during visa application processes. I should have known he'd target me.

All of our fights concentrate around times he has to prepare and arrange things, anticipating some authority figure getting back to him so he can get access to what he wants. In this case, he wanted to go to London for his Lincoln's Inn dinner—just like Jinnah. It meant a lot to him.

And whatever setbacks came in the way, his obsessions, the voices in his head, told him that he was unworthy, that the world was conspiring and that those who claimed to love him would betray him.

My heart has a penchant to forgive, but only if the violations it faces are apologized for and not frequent. Yasser, perhaps because of his illness, fails on the second count. He may apologize but like a whack-a-mole, his words spray on me like venom often enough, then the apology, then the deliberate hurt and on and on.

I hover between anger and sadness.

I'm thinking: my people don't love me. He's thinking: my people don't love me.

One of us is deductive. The other has a metaverse in his head that makes things feel real.

'Listen, asshole, this is why I refused to come to London with you no matter how much you begged. You are wrapped around your own petty task lists without looking at the lifetimes behind you. Look at the scorecard.'

I thought my anger would stop him. He had learnt to apologize sooner rather than later and there was, of course, no beating. So, yes, my life had drastically improved, but in my own head, there were voices that spoke inside my bones. Yasser's willingness to hurt me was always enough to set off limbic pain and muscular pain as one big sort of stroke.

'But you went behind my back and sold your Bedian plot.'

'What? Do you know why? Because I was broke, you moron. I was broke.'

They were calling me back into the conference room. It was my turn to present.

'Why do you sabotage my work? Every time, every job, you've reached out and wrecked me. I can say that there is no evidence that I hide my funds; after all, you have vetted all my work contracts and seen my tax returns. But there is enough evidence that you always make it harder for me to focus on my job. A job that helps us all.'

'What am I supposed to do with this useless bank statement?'

'I'll send you an e-statement of the correct bank. But after that, I don't want to talk to you. I don't want to hear from you.

'I don't want anything more. Your finances are yours. Mine are mine. This is over.'

I switched off my phone.

I hated my phone because Yasser's anxiety always followed me wherever I went with it.

The conference room was silent. I realized that everyone had heard me from the washroom because it was a wooden room that echoed. I didn't care; so much had been lost from the beautifully constructed floorboards of Soho House, Istanbul. I was a new person. I was a broken person. Yet again, I would have to pick myself up. I knew how to do that. It was, however, going to be hard.

I presented.

I chugged a bottle of Blush and sat through the last day of the conference slurring my way through the corporate talk, then came up to my room and slept. I did talk to Zainy before I slept. She told me I looked adorable drunk. I told her not to ever worry about failing. No adult I knew figured anything out. All the scientists were wrong and stupid and couldn't figure Covid vaccines out. All the suppliers were stuck with all the port cargo.

'All the hearts are broken, baby Zainy, so don't worry if you can't figure out why your school kids are mean to you.'

I slept for sixteen hours. I woke up to take my medication in the middle of the night, and listened to the Calm app to put me to sleep.

In the morning, my boss asked for a briefing on Afghanistan, since it was my region. In my bureaucratic voice, I told him a million children probably died from famine and cold according to the foreign policy report and that our sales went down by 51 per cent as expected, but our local operations partners were okay to continue production. Thankfully, the Taliban liked our product. There was an empty me-shaped void. This was not treatable depression. I tried not to, but the me-void needed me to join her like that grounded cargo. When I can't run any more, I have no choice but to get inside her vacuum. There is a certain contentment to not outrunning your own manufactured hell.

Yasser's apology came. It always does.

I had a choice now to wait for his next insult or to not accept his apology until I had to play house-house with him. Or I could accept his apology and let him go.

WHAT DOESN'T KILL YOU

It was because I was often almost killed, frequently enough, sporadically enough, that I was in a constant state of grieving. I came with a set of beliefs. That people are good, that good things happen to good people, and that more good things than bad things happen if you are a bit more good than bad. The grieving had a shattering effect on that belief. For good reason too. It was an uninformed and unnecessary schema.

The transactional nature of work provided a container for all my losses—jaw-breaking, eye-ripping, heartbreaking losses—and the loss of loving Yasser dearly but not finding that love back. If I complained too much, I knew I had no way of winning, that there was no endgame.

Work had built-in structures for endgames. There were annual bonuses, there were monthly performance evaluations and there was the clocking in and out.

During the Covid-19 outbreak, somewhere at the end of March 2020, all of that structure fell apart. Grief atop grief, loss atop loss, coping mechanism failure after failure.

We had a board meeting, but before it started, we made a funeral *dua*. The first I heard of Covid-19 was when a colleague lost his eight-year-old niece to some mysterious, unnamed disease. The little girl went to school, came back from the nurse's room with a paracetamol and that evening she was in intensive care, then a ventilator and gone the following morning.

'Children should not die,' I said in the cold conference room. The walls were full of happy women selling cellphone talk and SMS packages.

'Children should not die, yes,' they all agreed. More nods.

'It's the end of times,' someone who had just come back from Umra said.

More nods.

Allah Khair.

We went back to working on how to package cellphones faster. Someone loaded a PowerPoint on to a regrettably large LED screen, and we continued to discuss headwinds and tailwinds. Someone brought coffee and doughnuts, and others made the usual commentary about being agile, saving man-hours, scaling up and sending out minutes responsibly.

That young girl's life stayed with me. It made no sense for someone to go that young and so suddenly. Something lingered heavy in my heart. That feeling didn't leave us even after the pandemic ended. The feeling that everything is not here at will. That they will disappear without saying goodbye.

After that day, at work we heard of some more colleagues' parents dying. More meetings starting with duas.

I was called into a crisis meeting.

The WHO had provided a directive to governments, the private sector and the public at large to brace themselves for what was a bat's fault. Wuhan. Virus. SARS. Covid-19.

I produced a page of well-researched memo fast as lightning, which was to go out from Adil to the 3000 people in the office asking them to pack up and go home immediately, as we figured out more details about a seemingly dangerous disease. By this time, there was no clarity that this was a pandemic.

We were finalizing the memo together on an open floor when some severely hyper-confident young woman started making fun of the Chinese and laughing like nails on a chalkboard.

Unable to ignore her grunting high-pitched laughter on this open-floor seating, Adil went towards the posse gathered around her.

'What's going on?' he asked.

'Nothing,' she said and broke into more laughter. 'You think this is funny?' he asked.

'If you think about it, a bat flew into a Chinese soup and now we are all going home,' she said.

The head of marketing, who had been given an exorbitant amount of money as bonuses during a merger, laughed at her joke. The two always travelled in packs.

'She has a point,' he, who now is a three-time homeowner thanks to Adil's generosity, said.

Adil said, 'I disagree. We have Chinese engineering consultants working with us. They neither appreciate your racism nor do I want a lawsuit on my hands, so please cut it out. Aisha and I are in the middle of serious work.'

'Sure. I understand. Sorry, Adil,' she said.

As Adil walked back towards me on the other side of the open-floor seating, she broke into a fake coughing spree, half laughing out loud, half flapping her arms like a bat, with the hyena chorus behind her joining in, including the legal team.

Adil walked up to me; we finalized the draft memo, sent it out and made a plan to start work-from-home, which included shipping chairs and desks to people's homes, thinking of subsidizing their mounting Internet costs and creating a somewhat predictable environment, because we led 80 per cent of the country's digital backbone. This was planning I'd never had the training to work on, but it was something that came as a natural consequence of feeling the world was ending.

Yet throughout that day, that woman kept laughing.

Women like her know nothing about how they destroy structures that provide lifelines for women like me. I hated her just as much as Adil in that moment hated the open-floor plan.

What doesn't kill you, eventually does.

Three years of work-from-home drove me to near insanity. The place I went to grieve sent me back home to grieve. So, home became where I got grief, where I stored it and where I simmered in it, never where I processed it.

Work-from-home, for me, meant working from nowhere.

People at home had no consideration for the work I did, nor the value. I was hated for my ambition and shamed for it. Bhai always advised me to make sure I come across as someone who happened to be working, uninterested in titles, and to be small. So that the challenges I faced at home could not be blamed on my ambition and if they were, no one should know about it.

Like the eight-year-old who passed in mysterious circumstances, Covid-19 was the beginning of the end of my facade of 'I work to contribute to the home', and the beginning of 'respect the source of sustenance'. I was no longer willing to pretend that my job had a very big contribution to affording access to the best health care. The pandemic, like a big reveal, brought down all the lies I had told in my life.

I became aware of the fact that my refusal to quit the job market led me to fortify the difference between good health care and bad health care. Work insurance always kept my family protected and I had nothing but gratitude for that. I was spared the pandemic, as were my loved ones because we had an endless supply of fully paid hospitalizations and drugs and outpatient visits. The pandemic wiped out the weak. I was not going to write off the power of the pay cheque. No matter how uncomfortable it made others.

Why would anyone laugh and make merry about viruses that could kill the poor and the unemployed? Nothing laughable about the eight-year-old girl and us who fear for our lives. Frequently enough. Sporadically enough.

All. The. Time.

DANCE LIKE EVERYONE IS LOOKING

I was trying out a sari in a five-star hotel in Antalya, Turkey.

This was the same purple sari I had worn a month before at my yoga certification ceremony. The ceremony took place at the 3000-year-old Katas Raj temples in Pakistan. I had managed to somehow keep my job and also complete an in-person, hands-on, 200-hour classical hatha yoga teacher training course.

Ami had seen enough pictures of me on Facebook in a sari to have warned me on the phone: 'Never wear a sari again. Pakistanis don't know how to wear a sari.'

I was defying her.

There was a plan. The plan was to wear a black top, black slacks underneath, then twist the sari into dignified enough pleats to tuck it all in and secure it with a safety pin. Then waltz into the final conference gala dinner looking like the queen I am.

I know I have no dress sense.

I know this because I got the worst-dressed certificate in high school.

But I know simple elegance.

I didn't have safety pins but I had a sewing kit, so I stitched it all up, into my underwear. There was no way this thing was going to fall off. I was all done and ready to walk out when I realized the *pallu* was too short.

I looked at the simple elegance I was and eventually stepped out of the sari. All of it that was stitched in. I looked at myself in the mirror. If I wasn't careful, I would look like the forty-year-old I was.

I sucked in my tears and arrived at the gala in a skirt and a shawl, my hair in a frizz. Looking like the disgrace I am.

My boss called me to come sit next to him. 'How are you?'

'I'm good, Ismail Bay.'

'You are late, all okay?'

'I wore a sari, but it didn't wear me back.' He smiled.

We watched some performers with flat abs do a belly dance.

I noticed there was a plate of half-eaten food in front of me so I moved it to the next seat, asking if someone was sitting where I sat.

Zarmene, my colleague from Dubai, came up behind me a few minutes later.

'You are in my seat.'

Buoyed by the belly dancing, I joked about Ismail asking me to.

She turned to Ismail and said, 'I find it upsetting that you gave Aisha my seat.'

Ismail said, 'The idea is to rotate around the team.' 'But no one asked,' she said.

I wasn't expecting her to be upset. 'I'm sorry,' I said.

'No. One. Asked,' she spelt out, her eyes bulging like she had Graves' disease.

I looked at the belly dancers to contain my sinking heart. I stood up and moved to the Pakistan table.

I tried not to cry. I was too grown up to cry.

I tried to remember what my therapist said—people have reasons to be upset, and not all those reasons have to be you.

It still felt like shit.

I left the seven-course Michelin dinner one-seventh of the way and got back to the room—the sari on the floor greeted me like a deflated purple balloon.

I sat next to it and cried.

No one knew this but it had been a hard week.

Yasser's ami had had her breast cancer mastectomy right before I left for Turkey. The night I had my flight, I was with her at the hospital. Although we are no longer on speaking terms, I wanted to go to be sure that my daughters knew I went.

Yasser's ami, as usual, said things that were weird. I didn't respond but I was triggered enough.

I was also very worried that something bad would happen. Yasser was a wreck. Hospitals are like death warrants for us. That night, Yasser slept on my lap in the tiny private room on a tiny sofa. 'I'm going to pull this curtain so your mom doesn't give us *nazar* and evil eye.'

Yasser smiled in his sleep as I compulsively cleaned his ear gunk.

From there, I went straight to the airport.

The girls were upset with me—that teen angst that is visceral and hateful towards the mom. I felt it and I felt sad about the fact that I may have been doing this, that or the other, but to my daughters, I was a plate-smashing, repeat-nervous-breakdown mom who was only good for some things like humour and credit cards—sometimes even those two things didn't work.

I was carrying all these failed selves with me to the work conference.

It was also summer in Pakistan, and it was not fun that there was no gas, no water, no electricity, no petrol and there was hyperinflation.

I let myself cry.

I let myself say and feel things that I felt.

At the feet of the sari, I said: 'I thought Zarmene was my friend. Why won't I be talked to with kindness? It wasn't my fault. I'm sorry. I want to go home to my ami.'

All the while I didn't know but I had a low-grade fever. This was the third time I got Covid.

The next morning, I decided to do what I do best—communicate.

I knelt next to Zarmene and said, 'I'm really sorry you were triggered about my sitting in your seat.'

'Don't worry about it,' she said. 'Are you sure?' I asked.

'My anger lasts a minute,' she said. 'A minute is too long for me,' I said. We hugged.

'Tonight, you and me on the dance floor, okay?' she said. 'I dunno, I feel a bit unwell,' I said.

'You have a whole year to slog away. Let yourself go one night,' she said.

'For the minutes that count?' I said. 'For the minutes that count,' she said.

This was me, frizz in my hair; some said it was terrible, I found it alluring. The sweat I had broken in the past three hours on the dance floor made my hair wavy and, dare I say, sexy. I was wearing red matte lipstick that didn't come off even after a good scrub. I didn't usually see myself in make-up, so this was me arriving into civilization like aid airdrops sanitary pads for poor women.

It gets better. They played 'Dancing Queen', 'Thriller'. And when they played 'Stayin' Alive', I went pro. My moves were in sync. My face moving with the attitude the lyrics needed. I rotated, sometimes with the girl from Karachi, from Azerbaijan, from Lebanon, India, Turkey and, of course, twenty-four cultures. I was unstoppable. 'Stayin' Alive' was our song—Yasser's and mine.

This was where it all started—the Scroll.in article that started the discussion about the memoir. It was where I wrote a piece for the publication to talk about Yasser's amazing resolve to write a book about Jinnah after his arduous surgery.

I was wearing truck art *khussas* because I was now formally at that age where heels didn't work.

My colleagues were impressed and proud—local stuck-up Pakistani woman resumes life.

I was speaking to all of them at the conference about Yasser's cancer and my fibromyalgia and my antidepressants and they would go get coffee. I know I travelled with death around me. People did not want that when they were on a mission to erase the memory of their prison sentence.

When they asked why I looked so tired, I said my mother-in-law had breast cancer.

They went to get their second cup of coffee. I have the ability to forget.

Music helps.

THE PANDEMIC GROWS INSIDE ME

I've got Covid thrice in a three-year-long pandemic. It's been one long brain fog, these last few years.

There was a dengue outbreak in Lahore, which I graciously caught also.

During the pandemic, I changed jobs from a telecom giant to a consumer goods giant. My pandemic interview involved being onboarded and not meeting my boss in person until after a year.

My job required reputation management, which meant that managing the company's pandemic face was part of my routine— back to work, hybrid work and flex work.

The good people at my giant company thought they were doing me a favour by asking me to work from home. They expected me to throw myself at their feet in gratitude. Instead, I threw myself at their feet, asking them to take the work-from-home condition back.

'I don't want to work from home,' I said.

'But aren't you a women's rights thing? More time with family?' asked my HR manager.

'Yes, but work-from-home doesn't work for me,' I said. 'Why not? It works for Maryam in Karachi. Why not you in Islamabad?'

'Maryam has a mansion. I have a studio apartment. Maryam has a whole floor as her office, I sometimes have no place to sleep in my own studio. Maryam's in-laws own half of a province,' I added.

'How come? I thought you rented a five-bedroom,' said the HR manager.

'I separated,' I said.

'I don't follow. Surely you can afford a room for quiet work?' she said.

'I separated and have to rent in two places rather than one— one for the husband and his mom, and one for me and the kids,' I explained.

She didn't listen to me and gave me the much-coveted benefit of working from anywhere, which meant that I couldn't work from anywhere.

Certainly not from home.

There was one meeting with the steering committee that I presented from the bathroom. In another town hall meeting I was hosting, my apartment lights went off, as did the backup power. I was in the dark, projected on a large mural-sized screen with only the whites of my eyes, appearing rather haunted. I went on. The show must go on. Several other meetings have had maids, kids and pets feature in them, but that is all considered cute and part of the new buzz of work–life integration.

No one, however, wants to see dysfunction and overwhelm—I was all dysfunction and overwhelm during the pandemic. Lots of bathroom crying. Lots of calling friends with SOS messages where they would ask me to breathe and repeat, it's okay. Lots of wanting to jump from a speeding car. Lots of anxiety that made me look for anchors in anything and anyone.

I would work from bed instead of working from home. Turn my Zoom camera off and bark my comments or instructions from my EarPods.

I gave all my work clothes away. What was the point?

Like every other predictable social being, I would be exhausted with the lockdown and go out and work or network. Inevitably, the virus was loving Covid fatigue.

When I would have had enough, the virus would have more of us. I must have lost over twenty of my friends and family, yet the idea of not having human connection would turn me wild with the hunger to connect. Then out I would go and go straight down from there.

The Sinovac vaccine did nothing for me, except let me pass through airport terminals.

The first time I got brave and emerged from the lockdown, I got the first Covid strain. Then got the Delta version that Bhai brought from Nairobi when he came to patch me up, and then the Omicron variant.

Delta was the worst. I lost my hair. I went bald so bad that the photos made me look like I had aged a decade. The bathroom crying now wasn't just depression, it was balding depression. I would look at my hand with chunks of hair on it and be appalled, aghast. The audacity with which they would clump out would break my heart.

I suppose that's what curses are like—everything falling apart all at once—as in those Bible stories with pockmarks on the Pharaoh.

There was always a dumb part of my cognition, unable to spell words, or write them, but now, with Covid brain fog, my brain was even blunter than my bones.

The guidebook says you got to repent, which I did. In addition to trying everything, including onion seed oil and zinc, I said to God, please forgive me. I figured the good Muslim girl in me felt that it was because I earned money that I had wrath on me.

But I also knew money during the pandemic was a huge lifesaver.

I could afford high-speed Internet, carrot peelers, car fuel, gym access, spa massages, retail therapy, and I could keep the kids in school. However, I couldn't afford to think I'd earned it. There was so much brown woman guilt.

It took me a long while to realize I didn't just fight for my right to earn, I fought for my right to earn for myself.

It was towards the end of the pandemic that I finally got a room of my own, something Virginia Woolf implored us feminists to do years ago.

My own bathroom mirror, my own car, my own closet and my own yoga mat beside my own empty bed.

All of this was well and good, but Yasser and I would video-call each other up on my business trips and look at our puffy faces and weep for being away.

I missed him. He missed me.

We thought things would be different, but this was what we had: a space between us, large and gnawing.

We talked on the phone as we used to in San Jose. I read out our old emails to him.

He laughed and said we were cute.

When I was down with Covid, he would still see me and kiss my feet because that didn't violate the six-feet rule.

I've always been petrified of Yasser being six feet under, but it is when the prospect of my dying comes up that life becomes laughably strange.

There is a pandemic growing inside me. Mutations and revolutions.

I want to isolate; I want to reach out and belong.

THERE ARE OTHER
MOTHERS OUT THERE

Nothing works in Pakistan. The ATM will eat your card. There will be a person in the elevator whose job will be to press the elevator buttons, but he won't press them right. The elevators won't work. There would be, for years, an energy crisis so the printing and photocopying wouldn't happen. Paperless economies may exist elsewhere in the world, but here, almost everything needed Yasser's national identity card copy. Sometimes, the clerks wanted it in colour. Even the barcode identity cards were always photocopied. Restaurants made you sick, even the good ones.

Political agitations led to blocked roads. There were so many diversions on my way to work that I almost always got lost going in circles. Sometimes, there were flight delays. There were no seat belts on the small city flights. The overhead bins were sealed with duct tape. Travel agents forgot to send you insurance or transit visas and you'd have to go back home and miss conference dates. Someone once almost threw a stone into my airport car but hesitated long enough for it to not hit the windscreen. Cellphone signals never worked. When they did, the government slowed

463

down the Internet. The conspiracy theories said the undersea cables didn't work.

The people were broken too. They would show up late. If you called them to ask why they were late, they would unapologetically say it was Ramzan and they chose to sleep in. All this time, however, I was obsessively living some sort of rulebook—showing up on time, working my designated hours, underselling my skills and passing on the credit. I was burning in an underdeveloped economy, refusing to bring my standards down just because others were lazy, ignorant or shameless in being freeloaders.

There was a tax to be able to live and that tax had to be paid by being charitable and giving your time and energy. Yet, with that attitude, I was always on the verge of getting fired. It was my intensity that jarred everyone. My performance-monkey attitude was reflective of some unresolved daddy issue that didn't have a place in a Pakistani workplace. Here, no matter what I did, I would be seen as transient. No one thought I was going to survive for longer than six months.

I refused to leave work. I was the last to leave. Office janitorial staff would empty bins around my feet to make a point that I had overstayed. They switched off the lights, the backup power and then they even locked the gates. I've had to call enough facilities managers asking them to open the door so I could leave. I did unbelievably work-obsessed things when even the men looked to leave for home, or golf, or drinking, or prayers, or women— everyone had a life.

I just felt that when I arrived at some successful destination, all this hard work would pay off. My mistake was that I had no idea what success looked like.

The cars got better. The rentals got better and the lamps and art got better. The kids got to go abroad to summer school finally.

I sold land to fund health crises but had enough to buy it back. As a family, Yasser and I didn't go bankrupt, didn't accumulate debt and didn't do big borrowing from relatives or banks. Hooray for middle-class dignity. But I was this horse running into an endless horizon. Galloping and becoming ultimately some sort of freak show for others to see.

I laughed at women who quit corporate to teach yoga. I wanted to become one.

It was humbling, that just stretching on a mat could give me more peace than the thrill of accolades, bonuses and business incentive trips abroad. I'd travelled to over twenty countries in the course of my career, but it was on the ground that I felt I belonged. It was when I walked on to the Margalla Hills of Islamabad that I felt a kinship with the yellow-tailed birds. Stepping into springs, climbing trees and taking Instagrammable moments of moss allowed me to get drunk on belonging. No one should dare say rock formations are not souls lingering in the space-time continuum. Or that when you are dehydrated enough on a mountain hike to see clouds mushroom before your eyes, that is more thirst-quenching than peach iced tea on a summer day.

It was through the mundanity of movement and stillness that the pay cheque became almost irrelevant.

Something would take me back to the pay cheque. Fear.

Something would take me back to that union of mind and body. Love.

Love was like this third power that existed between me and the external world. It became large enough to consume me. I heard it loud as a call to prayer. To wear my running shoes and get back home.

The last time I experienced the subtleties of love was in San Jose, when Yasser would call to me. It was a force. Perhaps there was youth, there was desire, but it was the same magic that mountains and mats have. Yasser stripped the needless, and what remained was purely life force. His and mine. The rocks and the floorboards have the same quality, of containing your wreckage.

When I moved out of Yasser's life, I got a tiny apartment next to our home. It was so tiny it barely could hold Zoe and me. To live, I had to get out. I would wake up and leave early in the morning so I could catch the sunrise in the middle of the hills. Wake up with the birds. Friends thought I was going crazy from the trauma when I talked to them about all animals waking one by one, waking the others up with their song. Now, I know it's eco-acoustics and it has a huge role to play in the interconnection of the forests and bushes. When Zainy moved into the tiny apartment too, there had to be someone to contain me other than Yasser.

People are flaky. Like stringy barks. They fall to the side as time passes like a mother.

They leave you.

Walking my feet, one after the other, climbing, contouring, moving, all this held me against this great void of an in-betweenness. Yasser was and wasn't there. I felt protective love but there was also intense anger towards him. Yasser decided to live with his mom and not with me. That broke my heart at first. It broke so hard and so bad that, for a year, I didn't sleep on a bed but on a floor mattress, hoping the transient state would somehow signal to him that home is with him.

When I finally gave up on trying to live together and got a bed, I was sadder than I have ever been. This is now my life, a single woman again on a single bed. The rulebook said never to leave your marital bed, but I had to move away so I could stay sane, stay employed and stay a mom to two girls who needed me now more than ever.

During those Covid years, work-from-home ruined me because it brought the disaster of my life into the Zoom screen. I was not even empowered enough to have one noise-free room of my own to work in. If I was home, I was expected to be domesticated. I was subjected to wrath and expectations, snores and general disregard for my professional boundaries.

I would have to beg Yasser's ami to not call the help names while I was working. She would shoot back with more yelling that she was sick and tired of me controlling her life.

This is who I am. I am old.

You can't change me. You change yourself. Money isn't everything. Make a home first, then talk.

Then Yasser too started echoing these hostile themes:

Haven't you started behaving like a man these days? Where am I supposed to sleep?

I need to watch Netflix. You go to the other room.

I knew why I left.

I left because there was a poverty of language when I lived in the same space with Yasser and his ami that seeped into my thoughts like cancer. It took my vitality away. It was because I loved them that their dismissal of me made me feel disconnected from the family of animals and life around me. I left because their condemnation of me was so direct and final and loud. Granted it was generational trauma and mental health presenting itself this way—scapegoating me. But I believed and perhaps still believe every word hurled at me.

To build myself I had to build a wall between the people I loved and the ones who claimed to love me back.

They don't teach you that at the South C finishing school. They didn't teach me that in college. It certainly didn't show up in any books I'd read. There was no how to rise above the love your loved ones give you. There was no how to say no to gracious love offerings by your in-laws or how to outgrow your husband's shadow of kindness. This was all sold to me as kindness, love and family. Sacred. Unquestioning. Good. How does one go out of their way, their budget and their brokenness to get away from what they have known all their life to give you sanctuary?

Moving out of that home, my rental home, leaving Yasser and Ami, felt like I was plotting a murder. I had to plan my funeral.

The most tragic part of Yasser's brain tumour has been in its cure. I didn't expect Yasser to live this long. I am still not over the grand mal seizure he had in my arms in September 2017.

He wasn't supposed to make it after that. He was supposed to not make it during the 18 October surgery in 2017. Or the radiotherapy in 2020. The chemo in 2021. The second surgery in 2021.

He was supposed to have caved in somewhere there. He's wanted to take his own life several times. During depression bouts. During fights. During his sleep.

Death doesn't ask us our preferred method of going missing into a pre-natal world. It's rather simple.

When Yasser didn't come back for me, I went out looking for something larger than Yasser that would anchor me.

Yasser and his ami's voices muted into a buzz of other lives while watching sunsets from the tops of the Margallas, the Mushkpuri range, the Miranjani ranges and the Thandiani peaks. Looking down on the Islamabad I left behind, it wasn't so bad that Yasser and Ami felt I left because I was a selfish, self-engrossed woman with too much power.

Gradually, even the love between Yasser and me came back, perhaps because of the distance. There was so much latent need between us at times that we cried while he said goodbye to me at the apartment and left me at the door. We wept in each other's arms, giving one final kiss but then returning for one more final kiss. He would stay on the phone with me till I fell asleep. We loved again but decided to never live together in one home.

He kept feeling I had moved on like the callous world regards him, me feeling he had shunned me like Abu. Goodbyes made us remember the other had wronged us. Yet, there was room still to find time to talk with better words. Kinder words.

I started calling him poo again. Eventually, we replaced love with poo.

I poo you.

I poo you too.

Our WhatsApp messages flooded with poo emoticons. We are poo people.

Decay has its place in ecology.

With time, the bitter words grew into rich soil, because that is what rot does.

It creates new life.

It didn't matter much that I ended up loving broken people. It didn't matter that I am and became broken people.

The glitch was the hack into a peace treaty between my brain and my heart, my adult self and my inner child.

When I scaled the Deosai plains, the same clover-leaf grounds that Ami used to hang clothes over when I was a little girl became all mine for miles before my eyes.

I found nurturing right here in malfunctioning Pakistan. Uganda was home. Pakistan is home.

Yasser's and my love gave birth to the exact same thing everything wants—more.

EPILOGUE

I fear that I have left so much out in this memoir.

I fear I have left the mundane out and the mundane is important. Those unglamorous yet joyful moments when the family is out on a drive and we sing along to the same song or invent our own family song where we all have one line to perform, in sync. Moments when there is a political disagreement over Sunday brunch, and Yasser and I tell our girls in a somewhat middle aged-like manner—You will understand when you are older. I look at him and I'm glad he is evidently breathing, alive and his glorious eyelashes still show up, enchanting the day.

I fear this memoir reads like I can't catch a break. I have caught breaks. Good things have also happened. I have benefited from the systems I have fought against. The duty-bound family structure has raised me and paid for my college tuition even though I had a dead dad. Having a husband has protected me from a lot more misogyny that I could have been subjected to and has given me the permission to have a voice without fighting society for it— just that one permission slip has eased my life considerably. My mother-in-law has practically raised my girls while I could barely drag myself out of bed each morning to ready them for school. Perhaps I should have elaborated on that.

This morning, Yasser was in bed. I sang *Time of My Life*— the final song from the film *Dirty Dancing*—to him, slowly and playfully. I jumped at him—like Jennifer Grey does with Patrick Swayze—expecting him to catch me like Swayze catches Grey in the movie's finale. Instead, Yasser put his bony knee out instinctively, knocking the wind out of my lungs. I'm not one for disappointment.

'We have to do a do-over,' I told him, 'In the name of romance.'

We tried again.

He couldn't lift me this time. I guess no real man's arms are that strong, but I did land on his chest, like a gentle seal. We lay there for a moment, his arms hugging me tight.

Then, I made breakfast for us.

It was a sunny morning. The sun in Islamabad is a bit too golden these days. It makes my eyes sting with the joy of it. The pigeons outside my apartment's kitchen window watched me as I made tea, with cinnamon and cardamom.

The thing is that when you have a story of a happily married woman—as far as the eye can see—with two almost-in-college kids, you want to believe in the fairytale. But in staying by Yasser's side loyally as he fought against a brain tumour, did I make a true feminist choice? When I began writing this memoir, I wanted to write something that exposes everything that is untrue about that question. Fairytales and good movies are nauseating when you compare them to real life and heart monitors and brain surgeries. There are more questions in real life than shinily packaged answers and perfect mid-air catches. Which parts of my life did I hide when I wrote my life's story so far? Which part did I protect from ridicule and blame and the inevitable gossip? How far do you hold a man with a malignant brain tumour responsible or accountable?

When you air dirty laundry, do you keep some parts hidden so that they stay moist and eventually get mildewed with time? I fear so much has stayed unanswered. I fear I didn't do a tell-all of my marriage. Perhaps I only did a tell-all of my traumatized, survival-ridden, frightened-child-in-civil-war-Uganda immigrant self.

I fear that I wrote the book chronologically—this bad thing happened first, and then later, I understood why the bad thing had happened. I fear that maybe I shouldn't have started telling you first about my confusion and later about my anguish.

When Yasser re-read this book, three years after I began writing it during the first wave of the pandemic, he was shocked. He wrote the foreword for this book, but he neither remembers being someone who could have ever hurt me like this, or someone who wants to be reminded of the fact that a hurtful Yasser exists. He wants to forget what I have reminded him.

In wanting to forget this story, Yasser believes his new upgraded good behaviour, that has lasted for a decade or more, should entitle him to a life where no one knows how sick he was and how beyond treatment his moods swings were. He feels, and perhaps rightly so, that this book will continue to haunt him in ways people always have—relegating him to being insane, incapable of kindness, incapable of the kind of intellectual brilliance that has produced so much of his life's work on Jinnah. It is a terribly prejudiced world, and that is a possible outcome of this book.

Yet in permitting me to write this memoir as truthfully as I have done, Yasser has done what a real misogynist would never do. He has given me a voice, at his own peril. Being a perpetrator on a page is far more damning than being one in memory alone. In standing by my life's story, he is making good on the promise he made me in 1999—on continuing to be my friend, on never impinging on my individual rights, and being, as our kids call him, a weekend lover.

When I talk of our girls, there is fear there too. They have, after all, experienced my own unacceptable behavior. They may hold me accountable in a similar way. Trauma or not, pain is experienced in the same way. Pain in adequate quantities is life, but pain in inadequate quantities is hell. But if Yasser doesn't remember, I can't forget. So I fear. His fear and mine are the same, even though we are coming at it in different ways. Community cannot be created without a telling. Yasser and I were very lonely in our treatment, trauma and recovery.

And so, in many ways, Yasser's do-over is a do-over for me too.

What twisted person accepts a situation where they are not wanted, and insists on belonging? I could have done this earlier. I could have expected Yasser to be unwell, without allowing the tumour to control my life as invasively as it has done.

In wanting to tell this story, I want to establish three things: you can never be sure you will figure life out through love alone; you cannot escape pain by dishing out more love, but you can fight through it with more teeth; and lastly, there is nothing more evil than a victim who feels they have been wronged and who seeks justice through some form of revenge. Victimhood should just be a passing phase, not a dwelling. So when you next hear of someone with an inoperable brain tumour—or mental health challenges like schizophrenia, epilepsy or autism—you will know that a diagnosis is always the beginning of an end. It is sometimes the beginning of a beginning.

For the last part, I feel that it is I who owes Yasser an apology. We don't say this enough, but our hate towards ourselves is what allows abuse to happen in the first place. I am not simplifying abuse, but I am saying, when possible, running is the best gift we can give our maimed self. Try running. There is nothing undignified about it. After all, I did the same. I didn't always stand loyally by my husband like a good wife should. When he wasn't well enough, I ran.

In the end, for me, I realized that all I could do was to ask someone to try again.

And again.

Life isn't as perfect as a movie, and you need multiple takes. Sometimes, you don't even get it right in the final take, but it's somehow poetic. That's where we all find home—in the midway.

When we ask someone to try again, we meet them halfway in this in-between that is life. This is my resolution—to have some good days in the golden sun of Islamabad, where nothing will die, and where we will all have the time of our lives.

ACKNOWLEDGEMENTS

During the pandemic, Yasser's book was published by Pan Macmillan, and is now considered to be the authority on Mohammad Ali Jinnah's life, on Partition and on identity politics. I was asked by Kanishka Gupta to do a piece that talked about how Yasser heroically wrote the book despite the odds of his sinister disease. The piece I wrote was published in Scroll and was called 'Stayin Alive', like the ABBA song. It hit a nerve. It was loved. It was widely shared, and it was revered. Thank you, Kan. For being both of our agent.

Then, Kan asked me to elaborate on that essay: Think of a book. I dragged my feet. Between a 9–5 job and a fast-dwindling sanity, I was barely holding myself together to embark on a creative pursuit. I wanted to write fiction; a memoir was far too real. How could I write about life and simultaneously live it? Kan came back to my radio silence by offering Narayani Basu, the author of V.P. Menon's biography, because she also wrote about a man in her family; she could help me through it. Narayani, I learnt later, was the one who edited the Scroll piece. She spoke to me from Delhi and her soft monk-like disposition, her literary brilliance and her lived experience all struck to me as a portal to get to the other side.

I confessed to her, 'Narayani, I'm sorry, but there is no story here.' She said, 'Just tell me what happened, don't tell the world.' It is Narayani who nudged me to talk about my mom as the ultimate hero of this three-generation journey. Thank you, Narayani. Elizabeth Kuruvilla, my editor at Penguin Random House India, for all the back and forth, the yes and the no, the false starts and the near ends, and the patience.

Shaista Aziz, the co-founder of our NGO, The Women's Empowerment Hub. She is a UK politician and councillor, an author at the *Guardian*, and the only Muslim woman I know who is potent with words and clear in identity politics, a firecracker in her spiritual strength, a fierce advocate for women not ending up as martyrs, and an astute observer of all oppressions. Thank you, Shaista, for the sisterhood and tribe. Nadia Naviwalla, for being my safety blanket between America and Pakistan, Danielle Sharaf, my lifelong bestie, who writes the meanest and most Mary-Oliver-esque poetry. Farah Shakir for being real in her friendship and enduring our collective losses. My cancer career's support WhatsApp group called Berne Brownies that powered me through a very lonely season after everyone I knew and love, left.

To Autumn for its music. To credit cards. To Margaret Atwood for *The Handmaid's Tale*. To Faiz Ahmed Faiz for his poetry. To the prayer mat. To yoga. The rosery. To the K2 basecamp Concordia for offering me the earth on my hike and the person who lent me all the gear, only to have it flow down a stream in a glacial river in a metaphor. To Serena Hotel Maisha Spa for its Zen sanctuary and responsive ambulance service. To Instagram aesthetics. To The Aga Khan Hospital's Dr Ather Enam and the power of his scalpel.

To all my paymasters and the perks they let me have, especially free petrol in a country near default. To all my humane therapists—

Daheem Din who first diagnosed me with complex PTSD, Anum Zakaria for walking me through not losing my sense of self during Yasser's treatments and extreme nursing, Fatima Hussain who allowed me to develop my own inner emotional radar which I once lost—I could never tell what happy feels like somatically until her. Therapists are our temples and mosques. Psychology dictates power and it is through this science that we can navigate the topography of our own charitable kindness and our own war scars. This is the science of choice. Of failure. Of shame. Of rebuilding. Thank you.

If I look back, my three *de facto* parents. It was Bhaijan who taught me how to write moderately well by sticking to one single theme, which I don't do well enough still. Thank you, Bhaijan. Bhai, for sending me a long letter when I was ten years old on how to be a writer: To log everything in a filing system of notes, organize ideas, read, write and keep journals, which permitted me to have a private corner of thoughts no one should have access to. Thank you, Bhai, for always telling me to start writing, and then never to stop writing. Baji, who thinks I am a rani for no apparent reason. That kind of love is the best survival oxygen mask I got when I was out of air. Being loved for existing, not performing. This story is for Ami and Abu, for Yasser and for Yasser's Ami and Abu. For our beautiful daughters Zoe and Zainy.